MODERN HAUSA–ENGLISH DICTIONARY

SABON ƘAMUS NA HAUSA ZUWA TURANCI

MODERN HAUSA–ENGLISH DICTIONARY

Compiled by

PAUL NEWMAN AND ROXANA MA NEWMAN

Assisted by

Ibrahim Yaro Yahaya and Linda Dresel

and

CENTRE FOR THE STUDY OF NIGERIAN LANGUAGES
Bayero University College
Kano

OXFORD UNIVERSITY PRESS

IBADAN—ZARIA

SABON ƘAMUS NA HAUSA ZUWA TURANCI

Masu Shiryawa

PAUL NEWMAN DA ROXANA MA NEWMAN

tare da

Ibrahim Yaro Yahaya da Linda Dresel

da

MASANAN CIBIYAR NAZARIN
HARSUNAN NIJERIYA
Kwalejin Jami'ar Bayero
Kano

OXFORD UNIVERSITY PRESS

IBADAN—ZARIA

Oxford University Press

OXFORD LONDON GLASGOW
NEW YORK TORONTO MELBOURNE WELLINGTON
KUALA LUMPUR SINGAPORE JAKARTA HONG KONG TOKYO
DELHI BOMBAY CALCUTTA MADRAS KARACHI
NAIROBI DAR ES SALAAM

ISBN 0 19 575303 8

First Published 1977
Reprinted with corrections 1979

Printed in Great Britain, at the University Press, Oxford
by Eric Buckley, Printer to the University

Published by Oxford University Press Nigeria
Oxford House, Iddo Gate, P.M.B. 5095, Ibadan, Nigeria

PREFACE

THE purpose in compiling this Hausa–English dictionary has been to meet the need for a modern, practical dictionary for use in Nigeria by Nigerians wishing to learn about one of the major languages of their country. It has been designed for native Hausa speakers who need guidance in matters of spelling, idiomatic usage, etc., as well as for speakers of other languages who are trying to improve their present knowledge of Hausa or who are just beginning to learn it.

The aim has been to provide a concise, compact, and readily usable dictionary. The selection of words has thus been limited to those words likely to occur in everyday conversation and in modern books, newspapers, and other mass media. The dictionary includes a large number of modern words recently adopted into Hausa, given in their approved form. For words not found in this dictionary—such as rare or archaic vocabulary, derived forms of basic words, or words limited to dialects other than the standard Hausa of the greater Kano area—one may consult either of the major reference dictionaries of Hausa: *A Hausa–English Dictionary* by G. P. Bargery (Oxford University Press, 1934), or *Dictionary of the Hausa Language*, second edition, by R. C. Abraham (University of London Press, 1962).

This dictionary was compiled by the Centre for the Study of Nigerian Languages, Bayero University College, Kano, under the general editorship of Paul Newman and Roxana Ma Newman. Its preparation involved the combined efforts, over a period of years, of a large number of staff and affiliated members of the Centre. Among these were, principally, Ibrahim Yaro Yahaya and Linda Dresel, as well as Dandatti Abdulkadir, Haladu Alhaji, D. W. Arnott, Dauda Bagari, Gidado Bello, M. K. M. Galadanci, S. A. S. Galadanci, Maikudi Karaye, Isa Kurawa, Murtala Mohammed, Hassan Moturba, Dalhatu Muhammad, Ibrahim Mukoshy, K. Rayan, Bello Sa'id, Bello Salim, Russell G. Schuh, and Ahmadu Bello Zaria

The Centre is grateful to the Hausa [Language] Board for their guidance and suggestions in the selection and standardization of loanwords and to the Department of Islamic Studies,

Bayero University College, for their advice on questions concerning religious terminology. Finally, the editors and staff wish to thank Professor Ishaya Audu, former Vice-Chancellor of Ahmadu Bello University, without whose encouragement and continual support this dictionary would not have been possible.

Centre for the Study of Nigerian Languages
Bayero University College
Kano

GABATARWA

BABBAN dalilin da ya sa aka tsara wannan ƙamus na Hausa zuwa Turanci shi ne, domin amfanin 'yan Nijeriya masu son su fahimci ɗaya daga cikin manyan harsunansu. Watau an tsara shi ne musamman domin ya taimaki Hausawa wajen gane ƙa'idojin rubuta kalmomin Hausa da sarrafa su. Har ila yau, zai taimaki duk 'yan Nijeriya masu son su koyi Hausa, ko masu son su ƙara zurfafa saninsu cikin harshen Hausa.

Hausa dai harshe ne mai wadatattun kalmomi, kuma yana cike da zantuka na fasaha. Saboda haka abin da aka yi wajen shirya wannan ƙamus shi ne, an zaɓi kalmomin da aka fi yin amfani da su yau da kullum cikin maganganu, da na cikin littattafai na zamani da waɗanda ake amfani da su cikin jaridu da gidajen rediyo. Kuma an tace hanyar rubutu da faɗar sababbin kalmomi baƙi, waɗanda suka shigo cikin harshen Hausa daga waɗansu harsuna, an shigar da su cikin ƙamusun. Amma duk mai yin bincike game da tsofaffin kalmomin Hausa, da kuma kalmomi masu nuna bambanci tsakanin hausar wurare dabam dabam na ƙasashen Hausa, sai ya duba su cikin ƙamusun nan *A Hausa-English Dictionary* na G. P. Bargery (Oxford University Press, 1934) ko kuma *Dictionary of the Hausa Language*, second edition, na R. C. Abraham (University of London Press, 1962).

Malamai masu bincike na Cibiyar Nazarin Harsunan Nijeriya ta Kwalejin Jami'ar Bayero, Kano, su ne suka tsara wannan ƙamusun tare da taimakon waɗansu masanan ilmin harshen Hausa. Mutane masu tarin yawa sun ba da taimako, kowa gwargwadon ikonsa, tun daga lokacin da aka fara tsara ƙamusun. Yana da wuya a ambaci sunayen duk waɗanda suka taimaka wajen tsara wannan ƙamusun, amma ya wajaba a ambaci waɗanda yake da taimakonsu ne aka sami nasarar kammala aikin, kamar su Prof. Paul Newman da Dr. Roxana Ma Newman (editoci), M. Ibrahim Yaro Yahaya da Mrs. Linda Dresel (mataimakan editoci), Dr. Ɗandatti Abdulƙadir, M. Haladu Alhaji, Prof. D. W. Arnott, M. Dauda Bagari, M. Giɗaɗo Bello, Dr. M. K. M. Galadanci, Dr. S. A. S. Galadanci, M. Maikuɗi Ƙaraye, M. Isa Kurawa, Alh. Murtala Mohammed, M. Hassan Moturba, M. Ɗalhatu Muhammad, M. Ibrahim Muƙoshy, Prof.

K. Rayan, M. Bello Sa'id, M. Bello Salim, Dr. Russell G. Schuh, da M. Ahmadu Bello Zaria.

Cibiya kuma tana miƙa godiya ga Hukumar Hausa domin shawarwari da taimakon da suka bayar wajen tsara rubutun kalmomin aro. Tana kuma miƙa godiyarta ga Sashen Ilmin Musulunci na Kwalejin Jami'ar Bayero saboda taimakawa da suka yi da shawarwari kan kalmomin da suka shafi addini. Daga ƙarshe, tana miƙa godiyarta ga Shehun Malami Ishaya Audu, Mataimakin Shugaban Jami'ar Ahmadu Bello na da, saboda ƙarfin gwiwa da taimakon da ya bayar wajen tsara wannan ƙamusun.

Cibiyar Nazarin Harsunan Nijeriya
Kwalejin Jami'ar Bayero
Kano

GUIDE TO THE USE OF THE DICTIONARY

I. MAIN ENTRY

Spelling and pronunciation

All main entries, single words as well as hyphenated and non-hyphenated compounds, are printed in bold face type. They are arranged in alphabetical order according to the standard Hausa alphabet: **', a, b, ɓ, c, d, ɗ, e, f, g, h, i, j, k, ƙ, l, m, n, o, r, s, t, u, w, y, 'y, z.** The "hooked" letters **ɓ, ɗ, ƙ,** and **'y** (known as "glottalized" consonants) are distinct letters from **b, d, k,** and **y,** respectively. In alphabetization, these hooked letters immediately follow their corresponding non-hooked letters. The symbol **'** represents the "glottal stop" found in words such as *sana'a* 'trade' and *jami'a* 'university'. In alphabetization, it is disregarded. All vowel-initial words are pronounced with a glottal stop although it is not written.

The main entries (as well as sub-head entries printed in bold face type) also indicate certain important features of pronunciation not shown in the standard orthography, these being vowel length, tone, and the difference in pronunciation between the two *r* sounds in Hausa. These pronunciation features are marked by the following diacritics:

(1) A cedilla **,** under a vowel indicates that it is short in contrast to an unmarked vowel, which is long, e.g. **gà̧ri** 'town', **gàri** 'flour'. This mark is only used in open syllables, i.e. those ending in a vowel. In syllables ending in a consonant, e.g. **bàmbam** 'different', vowels are not marked for length since they can only be pronounced short.

(2) A grave accent **\`** above a vowel indicates that it has low tone, e.g. **mà̧cȩ̀** 'woman', and a circumflex accent **^** above a vowel indicates that it has falling tone, e.g. **mâi** 'oil'. By contrast, an unmarked vowel has high tone, e.g. **rana** 'sun'.

(3) A tilde **˜** over the letter **r̃** indicates that it is pronounced as a roll or trill in contrast to the unmarked **r,** which is pronounced as a flap, e.g. **r̃ù̧bùtu** 'writing', **rų̧wa** 'water'. A capitalized **R** in proper names is always pronounced as a roll, e.g. **Rà̧mà̧lân** 'month of Ramadan'.

Distinct words which are spelled alike but differ in vowel length or tone are given as separate main entries and are alphabetized according to the following order: short vowel before long, falling tone before low, and low tone before high. For example, **gà̧ri** 'town' precedes **gàri** 'flour', and **ràina** 'care for child' precedes **rainà** 'despise'.

When a word has grammatically related forms which are spelled the same but differ in vowel length or tone, these related forms are entered in bold face type as sub-heads under the main entry, e.g. the adverbial form **į̧dǫ** 'in the eye' is found under **į̧dò** 'eye', and the intransitive form **cį̧ką̧** 'be full' is found under **cį̧kà** 'fill'.

Words which have the same spelling and pronunciation, but which are unrelated in meaning, are given as separate main entries marked by superscript numbers, e.g. ^{1}**gįyà** 'any alcoholic drink' and ^{2}**gįyà** 'gear'.

Variant spellings and cross-references

Some Hausa words have commonly used variants, contractions, or alternative spellings. If the variants are alphabetically close to one another, they are put in the same main entry separated by a comma, e.g. **ą̀bòta, ą̀bùta** 'friendship'. The order in which they are entered implies that the first is preferred although both are correct. If the variants are not alphabetically similar, the less common one is listed as a separate main entry and cross-referenced to the other, e.g. **gą̀bàrųwa** *see* **bą̀gàrųwa.** In the case of contractions, the contracted form is always cross-referenced to the full form regardless of which is the more common, e.g. **gûn** *see* **wųrin,** or **sai dą̀** . . . Alt. form of **sąyar̃ dą̀.**

Special notations for verbs

Some verb entries include items in parentheses immediately following the verb. These items, explained below, provide essential information about the form of the verb in specific contexts.

1. (**į/e**) following a verb, e.g. **hàr̃ba (į/e)** 'shoot', indicates that the final vowel of the verb changes to **į** before a noun direct object and to **e** before a pronoun direct object, e.g. *ya harba* 'he shot', *ya harbi zaki* 'he shot a lion', and *ya harbe shi* 'he shot it'. The notations (**cį/ce**), (**shį/she**), and (**jį/je**) indicate that the change in the vowel is accompanied by a change in the preceding consonant from **t**, **s**, and **d** or **z** to **c**, **sh**, and **j**, respectively. For example, **sàta (cį/ce)** 'steal' has the forms *ya sata* 'he stole', *ya saci hula* 'he stole a cap', and *ya sace ta* 'he stole it'. In other cases where verbs have somewhat irregular forms before noun and pronoun objects, these forms are similarly given in parentheses, e.g. **ɗibà** (**ɗèbį/ɗèbe**) 'dip out'.
2. (**dą̀**) following a verb ending in **-ar̃**, e.g. **sąyar̃ (dą̀)** 'sell', indicates that whenever the verb is followed by a direct object, **dą̀** is required, e.g. *ya sayar* 'he sold (it)', *ya sayar da doki* 'he sold a horse', *ya sayar da shi* 'he sold it'. In speech, the sequence *ar da* is usually pronounced *ad da* but the correct spelling is with *r*.

II. GRAMMATICAL CATEGORIES (PARTS OF SPEECH)

The grammatical classification of a head or sub-head entry appears next to the entry in italic type (see List of Abbreviations), e.g. **hùla** ***n.f.*** 'cap' indicates that the word is a noun with feminine gender, and **kįra** ***v.t.*** 'call' indicates that the word is a transitive verb. For some of the grammatical categories used in this dictionary, special explanations with respect to Hausa are needed; these are given below.

Verbs and verbal nouns

In the continuous tenses (see Appendix 1), verbs are normally replaced by verbal nouns (which correspond to present participles in English), e.g. *ya zo* 'he came', *yana zuwa* 'he is coming'. Regular verbal nouns which are derived from verbs in a systematic way (e.g. by adding *-wa* or by lengthening the final vowel) are not given in the dictionary. Irregular verbal nouns are indicated in the entries beside their corresponding verbs, e.g. **aunà** *v.t.* (*vn.* **ạwò**) 'weigh' and **ƙerà** *v.t.* (*vn.f.* **ƙirà**) 'forge'. Unless specifically labelled *vn.f.*, verbal nouns are understood to be masculine.

A word which functions as a simple noun as well as a verbal noun is treated as a separate main entry and is cross-referenced to the corresponding verb, e.g. **ɗinkì** *n.m.* 1. Embroidery. 2 *vn.* of **ɗinkà**.

Nouns

When a noun has feminine or plural forms, these are indicated in parentheses after the part of speech label, e.g. **bàƙo** *n.m.* (*f.* **bàƙụwa**, *pl.* **bàƙi**) 'guest'. When a noun has more than one possible way of forming the plural, as is the case for a number of nouns, only the most common or two most common forms are given, e.g. **ạjì** *n.m.* (*pl.* **ạzuzụwà, ạjujụwà**) 'class'. If a noun is entered without a plural, this means either that there is no plural form or that the plural is rarely used.

The genitive (*gen.*) of most nouns, i.e. the form indicating possession or linking, is formed simply by adding *n* or *r*, depending on the gender of the noun. When a noun has an irregular genitive form, this is included in the parentheses after the main entry, e.g. **ạ̀bụ̀** *n.m.* (. . . *gen.* **ạ̀bin**) 'thing'.

Pronouns

Hausa personal pronouns fall into a number of different sets depending on their grammatical function as subject, object, possessive, etc. For many pronouns the difference in grammatical function is often indicated only by a difference in vowel length or tone. The result is that a pronoun form may have one spelling but more than one pronunciation. For example, the pronoun *ni* 'I, me' is pronounced with a long vowel and high tone when it is an independent pronoun but with a short vowel and high or low tone when it is a direct object pronoun. For such pronouns the main entry is given without diacritics and full details on their form, function, and meaning are provided in Appendix 1.

Adjectives

Most adjectival words in Hausa are nouns as well as adjectives and are labelled *n. and adj.* These words usually have feminine and plural forms, e.g. **sabo** *n. and adj.* (*f.* **sabụwa**, *pl.* **sàbàbbi**) 'new'. In the dictionary, most of these words are defined adjectivally with the understanding that, in Hausa, these can also be used as nouns, e.g. **gurgù** is defined as 'lame' but it can also mean 'a person who is lame'.

Prepositions

Many prepositions in Hausa are derived from nouns indicating various parts of the body, such as **cịkin** 'inside' (from **cịkì** 'stomach'), **gèfen** 'just before' (from **gefè** 'side'), and **kân** 'on top of' (from **kâi** 'head'). In this dictionary, these prepositions are listed as separate main entries rather than being included under their related head nouns.

Ideophones

The label ideophone (*id.*) identifies a special class of expressive words used to describe sound, colour, shape, manner, etc. They are characterized not only by their expressiveness in meaning but also by their distinctiveness in form. Compared with other Hausa words, ideophones tend, for example, to be monosyllabic, end in a consonant, be reduplicated or have an unusual tone pattern. Some examples are : **fat** 'emphasizes whiteness', **r̃ą̀kwą̀càm** 'in disorderly state', **cųku-cų̀kù** 'being in tangled or ragged state'. Because of the highly expressive nature of these words, the dictionary definitions can only give a general indication of their meanings. Since ideophones are extremely numerous in Hausa, it has only been possible to include some of the more commonly used ones.

III. DEFINITIONS AND USAGE

When a word has more than one meaning, the different senses are numbered consecutively, starting with the most general sense. Examples illustrating the meaning or meanings of a word follow the definition and are printed in italic type. Phrases illustrating the idiomatic usage of a word are printed in bold face italic type, e.g. under the entry **gįzǫ̀** 'trickster' is found the idiom ***bakan*** **~** 'rainbow'.

Words which are never (or seldom) used except in fixed expressions are indicated by the phrase "Used in...", e.g. **ą̀hǫ̀** Used in *cittar* ~ 'ginger root' and **basasà** Usu. used in *yakin* ~ 'any destructive war'.

Grammatical restrictions or other requirements regarding the use of words are indicated by the phrase "with . . ." in parentheses before the definition. For example, the entry **gąyà** *v.t.* (with i.o.) 'tell' shows that this verb must have an indirect object; similarly, **dàddąrę** *adv.* (with **dą̀**) 'at night' shows that this word occurs with the preposition **dą̀**.

ABBREVIATIONS

acc.	according	m. or masc.	masculine
adj.	adjective	neg.	negative
adv.	adverb	n.	noun
alt.	alternative	n.f.	noun feminine
approx.	approximately	n.m.	noun masculine
conj.	conjunction	n.pl.	noun plural
contr.	contraction	obj.	object
dem.	demonstrative	pl.	plural
d.o.	direct object	poss.	possessive
e.g.	for example	prep.	preposition
esp.	especially	pro.	pronoun
etc.	etcetera	prt.	particle
excl.	exclamation	ref.	referring
f. or fem.	feminine	rel.	relative
fut.	future	s.o.	someone
gen.	genitive	sth.	something
hab.	habitual	subj.	subject
id.	ideophone	subjun.	subjunctive
i.e.	that is	usu.	usually
impers.	impersonal	v.i.	verb intransitive
ind.	independent	vl.	vowel length
indef.	indefinite	vn.	verbal noun
inter.	interrogative	vn.f.	verbal noun feminine
i.o.	indirect object	v.t.	verb transitive

SIGNS AND SYMBOLS

~ Used in entries to represent the main entry word in examples and idioms.

= Used between two words or phrases to show that they are equivalent in meaning.

* Signifies words formed with the agential prefix *ma-*, see Appendix 3.

† Signifies words formed with the locative prefix *ma-*, see Appendix 3.

‡ Signifies words formed with the instrumental prefix *ma-*, see Appendix 3.

A

ạ̀ *prep.* 1. At, in, on (ref. to place): ~ *Kano* at Kano; ~ *kasuwa* in the market; ~ *ƙasa* on the ground. 2. At, in (ref. to time): ~ *lokacin* at that time; ~ *shekara ta 1974* in 1974. 3. (Introduces adv. of state or manner): *na gan shi* ~ *zaune* I saw him seated; *tafi* ~ *hankali* go carefully.

a *impers. pro.* (vl. and tone vary acc. to tense, *see* Appendix 1) They, one, it.

ạ'a *excl.* What a surprise!

a'à *excl.* No! Not so!

ạ̀ba *f.* of **ạ̀bụ̀.**

ạ̀bạ̀dâ *adv.* 1. Usu. used in *har* ~ forever. 2. Always: *ga shi nan* ~ *sai barci* there he is, always sleeping.

ạ̀bạ̀dân abadìn *adv.* For ever and ever.

ạ̀bàrba *n.f.* Pineapple.

ạ̀bàsạyà *n.m.*(*pl.* **ạbasạyoyi**) Overseer.

ạ̀bàtạyà *n.f.* Overtime.

ạbàwa *n.f.* Loosely spun, coarse cotton thread used for weaving.

ạ̀bin 1. *gen.* of **ạ̀bụ̀**: ~ *ado* ornament, jewellery; ~ *dariya* sth. funny; ~ *nan* thingumajig, whats-its-name. 2. Used in *tafi* ~*ka* be on your way, be off! *ya tafi* ~*sa* he went on his way. **ạ̀bîn dạ̀** That which, what: ~ *ya ce ba zai yiwu ba* what he said cannot be done.

ạ̀bincị *n.m.* 1. Food, a meal. 2. Means of living: *ya tafi neman* ~ he went looking for work.

ạ̀boki *n.m.*(*f.* **ạ̀bokịya**, *pl.* **ạ̀bòkai, ạ̀bòkạ̀nai**) 1. Friend, companion. 2. Counterpart: ~*n aiki* fellow-worker; ~*n gaba* enemy.

ạ̀bòta, ạ̀bùta *n.f.* Friendship, comradeship. ***ƙulla*** ~, ***ɗaura*** ~ become friends. ***kwance*** ~ break a friendship.

ạ̀bụ̀ *n.m.* (*f.* **ạ̀ba**, *pl.* **ạbubụwà**, *gen.* **ạ̀bin**) 1. Thing, stuff: *ya sayi wani* ~ he bought sth. 2. Matter, affair: ~ *ya yi* things went well. 3. Property. ***mai abin hannu*** a prosperous person.

accà *n.f.* A grain common to the Jos plateau.

ạdạ̀bi *n.m.* Literature.

ạ̀dạ̀dạ̀ *n.m.* (*pl.* **ạ̀dạ̀dai**) Rectangular house or shed made of *zana* mats and thatch.

ạdạ̀di *n.m.* (*pl.* **ạ̀dạ̀dai**) Numeral, number, sum, total: ~*nsu ashirin ne* there are twenty of them.

ạ̀dạkà *n.f.*(*pl.* **ạ̀dạku, ạdạkoki**) 1 Wooden or metal case, trunk, box. 2. Dane gun.

adalcì *n.m.* Justice, fairness, righteousness.

adạ̀li *n.m.* (*f.* **adạ̀la**, *pl.* **àdạ̀lai**) Just, honest, upright person.

ạ̀dạ̀na *n.m.* 1. Inferior, low quality (of goods). 2. Inferior or backward person.

adạ̀na *v.t.* (*vn.* **adạ̀ni**) Look carefully after or preserve sth. (property or money).

ạ̀dàshị *n.m.* Contributing to a pool where each person takes the total amount in turn.

ạ̀dawà *n.f.* Enmity, hatred, opposition. ***abokin*** ~ member of opposition party.

àdda *n.f.*(*pl.* **addụnà**) Matchet.

àddinì *n.m.* (*pl.* **àddìnai**) Religion.

àddụ'à *n.f.*(*pl.* **addụ'o'i**) 1. Prayer. 2. In Islam, any prayer distinct from the five daily prayers.

ạ̀dịbâs *n.m.* Advance of money, down-payment.

ạ̀dikò *n.m.* Woman's kerchief, head-tie.

ạ̀dilà *n.f.* (*pl.* **ạ̀dilu, ạdiloli**) Bale of cloth, hides, etc.

ạ̀dịr̃ẹ *n.m.* Tie-dyed cloth.

ạ̀dịr̃eshì *n.m.* Address.

ạdo *n.m.* Adornment, ornamentation, decoration: *ta yi* ~ she is all dressed up.

ą̀dų̀dų̀ *n.m.* (*pl.* **ą̀dų̀dai**) Large lidded basket made of grass.

ądųwà *n.f.* (*pl.* **ądųwoyi**) Desert date tree or its fruit.

af *excl.* Indicates surprise or sudden recollection.

ąfà *v.t.* (*vn.* **ąfì**) Throw (grain, groundnuts, etc.) into mouth without touching it.

ąfì *n.m.* 1. Small handful of sth. (e.g. groundnuts or tobacco) thrown into the mouth. ***ɗan*** ~ a pinch of sth. 2. *vn.* of **ąfà**.

ą̀fîl *n.m.* Appeal (legal).

ą̀fįtątų *n.m.* Type of cheap cotton thread.

Ą̀fr̃ilų̀ *n.m.* April.

ą̀fų *v.i.* Be eager, anxious: *ya* ~ *ya sami kuɗi* he is eager to get some money.

ąga *n.f.* 1. Possessing a lot of sth.: *yana* ~*r ƙarfi* he is very strong. 2. Becoming well known.

ą̀gą̀dę̀ *n.m.* Plantain(s).

agą̀ji *n.m.* 1. Help, assistance, rescue, relief. 2. *vn.* of **àgązà.**

ągàna *n.f.* Smallpox.

ągą̀ra *n.f.* Tendon in back part of ankle.

àgązà (jį/je) *v.t.* (*vn.* **agą̀ji**) Help, assist, come to rescue of s.o.

ą̀gogǫ *n.m.* (*pl.* **ą̀gògai, ągogųnà**) Clock, watch.

ągòlą̀ *n.m.* (*f.* **ągolįya**, *pl.* **ą̀gòlai**) Step-child (child of man's wife by her former husband).

ą̀gųshi *n.m.* Melon seeds used for making soup.

Ą̀gustà *n.m.* August.

ą̀gwàgwą *n.f.* (*pl.* **ą̀gwàgi**) Duck.

ągwąja *n.f.* Type of large *riga* with round neck and slit-like embroidery design.

ą̀hâyye *excl.* Expression of pleasant joking between women, usu. followed by *ayyururui*.

ą̀hǫ̀ *n.m.* Used in *cittar* ~ ginger root.

ahų̀ *n.m.* One and a half pence in old Nigerian currency.

ąhųwà *n.f.* Leniency, pardon, mercy.

ą̀hųwo *excl.* Greeting used by women on entering s.o. else's house or coming upon a group of people.

âi *excl.* Oh yes! Aha! Of course! Oh, I see!

ai *excl.* Well yes, but . . ., mind you . . . (used during long discussions).

aibą̀ta *v.t.* Blame s.o.

aibų̀, aibį̀ *n.m.* (*pl.* **aibobi**) Fault, blemish: *ba ni da* ~ *a cikin wannan magana* I am not to blame regarding this matter.

àidîn *n.m.* Iodine.

àika (į/e) *v.t.* (*vn.* **aikì**) Send s.o. (on errand). **aikà** *v.t.* (usu. with **dą̀**) Send sth.: *na* ~ *da kuɗi* I sent the money.

aiką̀ce *v.t.* Work sth. out completely: *ya* ~ *gona* he completed the farm work; *ya* ~ *riga* he worked out the design on the gown.

aiką̀ta *v.t.* Do, perform, act: *na* ~ *aikin da aka ba ni* I performed the task that was given me.

àiką̀tau *n.m.* Small job given out to s.o. for wages (usu. farm work by men or grinding of corn by women).

àike *n.m.* (*pl.* **àikę-àikę**) Errand.

aikì *n.m.* (*pl.* **ayyųkà, àiką̀cę-àiką̀cę**) 1. Work, job, duty. 2. Activity, act.

ainįhi *n.m.* Essence, reality: *su ne* ~*n mutanen da na faɗa maka* those are the very people whom I was telling you about.

ainùn *adv.* Very, very much, truly.

ąją̀li *n.m.* 1. Fixed period of time, deadline, time limit. 2. Appointed end of one's life, fate, cause of death: *mota ce* ~*nsa* a car was the cause of his death.

ą̀ją̀mį *n.m.* Hausa written in Arabic script.

ą̀jandà *n.f.* (*pl.* **ą̀jàndu**) Agenda.

ąji *n.m.* (*pl.* **ązuzųwà, ąjujųwà**) 1. Class or form (in school). 2. Class, category, group.

ą̀jįyà *n.f.* (*pl.* **ą̀jįyę-ą̀jįyę**) Anything stored or deposited for safe-keeping. **ą̀jįyą̀** *n.m.* A traditional title.

ąjįye *v.t.* 1. Put down or away. 2. Store, save, put in safe-keeping, deposit.

ajįzi *n.m.* (*f.* **ajįza**, *pl.* **àjįzai**) Man with his human weakness: *duk mutum* ~ *ne* every man is imperfect.

ạkạ̀ *impers. pro.* (rel. past tense subj.) They, one, it.

ạ̀ kâi ạ̀ kâi *adv.* Continually, regularly, repeatedly.

ạkaifa *n.f.* (*pl.* **ạ̀kàifu**) Fingernail, claw, talon.

ạkàlạ̀ *n.f.*(*pl.* **ạ̀kàlai**) Lead-rope of camel.

ạkàn *impers. pro.* (hab. tense subj.) They, one, it.

ạ̀kantà *n.m.* (*pl.* **ạkantoci**) Accountant.

ạkạ̀si *n.m.* Opposite or reverse of sth.

ạkạwàl, ạkạwạ̀li *n.m.*(*f.* **ạkạwạ̀la,** *pl.* **ạ̀kạ̀wạ̀lai**) 1. Shiny black horse. 2. Smooth black-skinned person.

ạ̀kàwụ *n.m.*(*pl.* **ạkawụnà, ạ̀kàwụ-ạ̀kàwụ**) Clerk.

ạkè *impers. pro.* (rel. cont. tense subj.) They, one, it.

ạ̀kokọ *n.m.* Grey-coloured baft (cloth).

ạ̀kụ *n.m. or f.* Parrot.

ạ̀kul Here's a warning that if . . .: *~ na sake ganinka a nan, ka kuka da kanka* I'm warning you that if I see you here again, you'll have only yourself to blame.

ạkul *excl.* 1. Stop that! 2. (followed by rel. past) Don't . . .: *~ kika je* don't dare go!

ạkurki *n.m.* (*pl.* **ạ̀kùrkai**) Coop for keeping fowl.

ạkụ̀shi *n.m.* (*pl.* **ạkụsà**) Black wooden bowl for food.

ạ̀kụyà *n.f.* (*pl.* **ạwaki, ạ̀wàkai**) Goat.

ạ̀kwai There is, there are: *~ kuɗi?* is there any money? *i, ~* yes, there is.

ạ̀kwàtị *n.m.* (*pl.* **ạkwatụnà**) Box, crate, trunk.

ạ̀kwịyà *see* **ạ̀kụyà.**

ạ̀ƙallạ̀ *adv.* At least: *na ga mutane ~ sun kai dubu* I saw at least a thousand people.

ạ̀lạbè *n.m.* (*pl.* **ạ̀lạ̀bai**) Leather wallet or purse.

ạ̀lạ̀bo *n.m.* Yam or cassava flour.

àl'adà *n.f.* (*pl.* **àl'àdu**) 1. Custom, habit, tradition. 2. Menstruation.

ạ̀lạdè *n.m.*(*pl.* **ạ̀lạ̀dai, ạ̀lạ̀du**) Pig, boar.

ạ̀laikùm *see* **sạ̀lamụ̀.**

àl'ạjạ̀bi *n.m.* (*pl.* **al'ạjụbà**) Surprise, wonder, miracle: *zuwa kan duniyar wata abin ~ ne* going to the moon is an amazing thing.

ạ̀lạƙạƙài *n.m.* Continually pestering or bothering s.o.: *ya zame mini ~* he bothers me continually.

ạ̀lạ̀lạ̀ *n.m.* Food made of beans mashed with palm oil and spices and wrapped in leaves or tinned.

ạ̀lamà *n.f.* (*pl.* **ạlamomi, ạ̀làmu**) 1. Sign, symbol. *~r* ***carbi*** large dividing bead in a string of prayer beads. 2. Indication, trace, piece of evidence: *ga ~ za a yi ruwa* it looks as if it may rain. 3. Road sign.

àl'ạmạ̀ṙi *n.m.* (*pl.* **al'ạmụṙà**) Matter, business, affair: *wuyar ~ gare su* they are difficult to get along with.

ạlàmta *v.t.* Mark or indicate sth.

ạ̀lamtạ̀ *v.i.* Be marked or indicated.

Al'aṙshị *n.m.* The heavens (spiritual).

alatụ̀ *n.m.* Luxury item.

àl'auṙà *n.f.* Private parts of body, esp. male.

ạ̀lawà *n.f.* Any sweet made from sugar, honey, and/or fruit.

ạlạwayyò *n.m.* White calico cloth, shirting material.

ạ̀lawùs *n.m.* 1. Monetary allowance. 2. Allowance of space, room to move. 3. Allowance of time: *ka ba ni ~ ɗin kwana biyu kafin in gama aikin* give me two days' time to finish the work.

ạ̀layyạ̀di *n.m.* Oil from palm kernel.

ạ̀layyạ̀ho *n.m.* Spinach.

àlbạṙàs *n.f.* Leprosy: *~ ta ɓullo masa* he shows symptoms of leprosy.

àlbaṙkà *n.f.* Blessing, prosperity, grace, gift from God: *ƙasa mai ~* fertile, productive soil. *excl.* No! (in bargaining, used by seller to reject an offer).

àlbaṙkạ̀ci *n.m.* Good fortune or benefit enjoyed through s.o. else's grace or influence: *ya sami ~na* he benefited through my kindness.

àlbạ̀r̃ushì *n.m.* Gunpowder.
àlbạsà *n.f.* Onion(s).
àlbâshi *n.m.* Regular weekly or monthly salary, wages.
àlbịshìr̃ *n.m.* Good news: *na yi masa* ~ I gave him some good news. **~*inka*** I have brought you good news! (to which the answer is ***goro***).
ạ̀lewà *see* **ạ̀lawà.**
àlfạdạr̃i *n.m.* (*f.* **àlfạdạr̃a,** *pl.* **àlfạ̀dạ̀r̃ai**) Mule.
àlfạhạ̀r̃i *n.m.* Pride, boastfulness.
àlfar̃ma *n.f.* 1. Favour, generosity, kindness, leniency: *ya yi mini* ~ he showed me great kindness. **~*r Ubangiji*** the grace of God. 2. Nobility, high rank or birth: *mai* ~ His Excellency.
àlfàsha *n.f.* Obscene or abusive language.
àlfịjìr̃ *n.m.* Dawn, half-light at dawn.
àlgaità *n.f.* (*pl.* **àlgàitu**) High-pitched musical instrument, played by blowing on a double-reed mouthpiece.
àlgàr̃ar̃ạ̀ *n.f.* Sackcloth.
algạ̀shi *n. and adj.* (*f.* **algạ̀sa,** *pl.* **àlgạ̀sai**) Maroon (colour).
àlgûs *n.m.* Form of fraud in selling.
àlhạjì *n.m.* (*f.* **àlhạjịya,** *pl.* **àlhạ̀zai**) One who has made the pilgrimage to Mecca.
àlhạki *n.m.* Guilt, sin, offence: *ya dauki* **~*n*** *Audu* he sinned against Audu.
àlhali *conj.* Obviously, as a matter of fact, certainly. ~ ***kuwa*** whereas: *ana tuhumar Audu da sata ~ kuwa Garba ne ya yi* Audu is being blamed for the theft, whereas it was Garba who did it.
àlhamdụ̀ lìllahị̀ *excl.* Praise be to God! God be praised!
Àlhạ̀mîs *n.f.* Thursday.
àlher̃ì *n.m.* 1. Kindness, generosity, gift, good deed. 2. Material wealth: *ya sami ~ da kaka* he got a lot from the harvest.
àlhini *n.m.* Meditation about something sad.
àlhụdạ̀hụdạ̀ *n.m.* Senegal hoopoe (bird).
ạlìf *n.f.* One thousand (esp. used in dates): ~ *da dari tara da saba'in da hudu* 1974.
àljạbạr̃à *n.f.* Algebra.
àljan, àljạni *n.m.* (*f.* **àljạna,** *pl.* **àljạ̀nu**) Genie, jinn, good or bad spirit.
àljannà *n.f.* Paradise, Heavenly Kingdom. **~*r duniya*** delightful, luxurious place.
àljihu *n.m.* (*pl.* **aljihụnà**) Pocket.
àlkạdạ̀r̃i *n.m.* Value, worth, quality: **~*n*** *dola ya karye* the dollar has lost value.
àlkafụ̀r̃a *n.f.* Game of somersaulting in water.
àlkaki *n.m.* Sweet fried delicacy made from wheat flour.
àlkali *see* **àlƙali.**
alkạmà *n.f.* Wheat.
àlkar̃yà *n.f.* (*pl.* **àlkàr̃yu**) Unwalled town or urban area.
àlkạwạ̀r̃i *n.m.* (*pl.* **alkạwụr̃à**) 1. Promise. 2. Reliability: *yana da* ~? is he reliable?
àlkyabbà *n.f.* (*pl.* **àlkyàbbu**) Burnous, usu. worn by emirs, chiefs, and sometimes malams.
àlƙạlạ̀mi *n.m.* (*pl.* **alƙạlụmà**) 1. Pen. 2. Numerical figure.
àlƙali *n.m.* (*pl.* **àlƙàlai**) Muslim judge, judge. **~*n wasa*** referee.
Àlƙùr̃'ani *n.m.* The Koran.
allà *n.m.* (*pl.* **alloli**) Fetish, deity.
allạ̀-allạ̀ *n.f.* Eagerness: *ina ~ ka gama mu tafi* I'm eager for you to finish it so that we can go.
Allàh *n.m.* God. *excl.* ~? is that so? to which the answer is: ~ *kuwa* it is so.
àllambàr̃am, àllàmbûr̃ *excl.* Expression of denial, negation, complete refusal: *na yi na yi da shi ya hakura, sai ya ce shi ~ ba zai hakura ba* I tried and tried to convince him to be patient but he refused completely.
âlli *n.m.* 1. Chalk. 2. Fine powder ground from animal bone used by women in spinning thread.
àllo *n.m.* (*pl.* **allụnà**) 1. Wooden writing board used for practising Arabic script. 2. Blackboard, slate.
àllur̃à *n.f.* (*pl.* **àllùr̃ai**) 1. Needle. ***harbin*** ~ magical shooting of needles to harm s.o. 2. Injection,

innoculation. 3. Syringe used for injection.

àlmajįri *n.m.* (*f.* **àlmajįra,** *pl.* **àlmàjįrai**) 1. Pupil, student, learner, esp. of Koranic school. 2. Destitute or poor person.

àlmąkąshi *n.m.* (*pl.* **àlmąkąsai**) Scissors.

àlmàra *n.f.* 1. Fable, fantasy. 2. Fiction writing or narration.

Àlmąsihų *n.m.* The Messiah, Jesus Christ.

àlmųbazząri *n.m.* (*f.* **àlmųbazząra,** *pl.* **àlmųbàzząrai**) Extravagant person, spendthrift.

àlmurù *n.m.* Dusk.

àl'ummà *n.f.* (*pl.* **àl'ùmmai, al'ummomi**) Nation, community, the people, the public.

àlwąla *n.f.* Religious ablution.

àlwashi *n.m.* Rash promise.

ąmai *n.m.* Vomiting, vomit.

ąmąja *n.f.* Working lazily.

ąmalankę *n.m.* Push-cart with two wheels.

ąmalę̀ *n.m.* Big, strong male camel.

ąmanà *n.f.* 1. Trust, mutual trust, friendliness, peace: *akwai* ~ *a tsakaninsu* there is mutual trust between them. ***ba da*** ~ entrust. ***cin*** ~ breaking one's trust. ***riƙon*** ~ keeping trust. 2. Treaty, alliance. 3. Honesty, reliability.

ąmarya *n.f.* (*pl.* **ąmàre**) 1. Bride. 2. Anything new, esp. car or bicycle.

ambàlįyà *n.f.* 1. Flood, flooding, overflowing. 2. Congestion (of people).

àmbątà (cį/ce) *v.t.* (*vn.* **ambąto**) Mention sth.

[1]**ambųlàn** *n.m.* (*pl.* **ambųloli**) Envelope.

[2]**ambųlàn** *n.m.* (*pl.* **ambųloli**) Ambulance.

àmfanà (į/e) *v.t.* 1. Derive benefit from sth.: *mun amfani abin da aka yi mana* we benefited from what they did for us. 2. Be beneficial to s.o.: *abin da aka yi mana ya amfane mu* what they did for us benefited us. **amfàna** *v.t.* Used in *Allah ya* ~ may God bring good luck! **àmfaną** *v.i.* Benefit: *da na karanta littafin nan, na* ~ by reading that book, I benefited. ***na*** ~ thanks, but I've already eaten.

àmfàni *n.m.* 1. Usefulness, advantage, profit. 2. Produce, product: *~n gona* farm produce.

àmin *excl.* Amen, so be it.

ąmince *v.t.* (with i.o. or **dą**) 1. Trust: *na* ~ *masa* = *na* ~ *da shi* I trusted him. 2. Agree on sth.: *sun* ~ *da farashin* they agreed on the price.

ąminci *n.m.* 1. Trust, trustworthiness, reliability. 2. Friendship. ***ƙulla*** ~ form a friendship.

ąmini *n.m.* (*f.* **ąminįya,** *pl.* **ąminai**) Trusted or reliable friend.

ąminta *v.t.* Do or make sth. well: *an* ~ *kirar keken nan* this bicycle is well made and reliable. **ąmintą** *v.i.* (with **dą**) Trust: *na* ~ *da shi* I trust him. ***na*** ~ I consent, agree.

àmma *conj.* But, nevertheless.

ąmo *n.m.* 1. Sound (bell, drum, gun, etc.). 2. Echo.

ąmosąni *n.m.* Dandruff, scalp disease.

àmsa (shį/she) *v.t.* Receive, accept sth.

amsà *v.t.* 1. Answer or reply to (call, greeting, question, etc.). 2. Agree, consent to sth. *n.f.* (*pl.* **amsoshi**) Reply, response, answer.

àmsą-kuwwą *n.f.* 1. Echo. 2. Loudspeaker.

amshi *n.m.* Refrain (in song). ***'yan*** ~ chorus in musical group.

ąmųkų̀ *n.m.* Stretcher.

amyà *n.f.* (*pl.* **amyoyi**) Beehive.

an *impers. pro.* (past tense subj.) They, one, it.

ąnâ *excl.* Is that really possible!

ąnà *impers. pro.* (cont. tense subj.) They, one, it.

ąnąbi *see* **įnąbi.**

andira *n.f.* Shuttle of loom.

angà *n.f.* Anchor of ship.

àngąlalà *n.f.* Cotton fluff.

àngązà (jį/je) *v.t.* Push. **angąza** *v.t.* Push onto or into.

angò *n.m.* (*pl.* **angwàye**) Bridegroom. ***abokin*** ~ the best man.

angùrya *n.f.* 1. Cotton seed. 2. Piles, haemorrhoids.

àngųwa *see* **ùngųwa.**

ąnini *n.m.* (*pl.* **ąninai**) 1. Tenth of

a penny in old Nigerian currency. 2. Button. 3. Military officer's stars or ribbons indicating rank.

ạnịyà *n.f.* 1. Determination, zeal, fervour. 2. Goal. 3. Evil intention (usu. in curse): *~rka ta koma kanka* may your evil intentions fall back upon you!

ànkạr̃ạ *v.i.* Take notice, realize, pay attention.

ankwà *n.f.* Handcuffs.

ànnạbi *n.m.* (*pl.* **annạbawa**) Prophet. **Ànnạbị** The Prophet Muhammad.

ànnạmimi *n.m.* (*f.* **ànnạmimịya,** *pl.* **ànnạmimai**) Mischief-maker.

ànnạshụwa *n.f.* Joyous feeling, pleasure, merriment.

ànnòba *n.f.* Epidemic, plague.

ànnur̃i *n.m.* 1. Brightness, light. 2. Cheerfulness.

anyà Used to introduce questions of surprise or doubt: *~ haka ne?* is it really so?

ar̃ *excl.* Damn it!

ạra (ị/e) *v.t.* (*vn.* **ạro**) Borrow sth. which itself will be returned: *na ari littafi a wurinsa* I borrowed a book from him. **ạrà** *v.t.* (with i.o.) Lend sth. to s.o.: *na ~ masa littafi* I lent him a book.

ạr̃adụ *n.f.* Thunder, clap of thunder. ***na sha*** *~* I swear by thunder!

ạr̃ạfịyà *n.f.* Fine manufactured thread.

ạr̃ạha *n.f.* Cheapness, easiness: *yana da ~* it is cheap; *ina ganin ~rsa* I find it easy to do.

ạràngạmà *n.f.* 1. Meeting s.o. coincidentally. 2. Clashing together (e.g. of armies).

ạr̃as *id.* Used in *kayan ~* breakable goods (glass, porcelain).

ar̃ạshi *n.m.* 1. Verbal coincidence, saying what s.o. else has said. 2. Compensation for wounding s.o.

[1]**ar̃bà** *n.f. and adj.* Four thousand.

[2]**ar̃bà** *n.f.* Used in *yi ~* meet face to face unexpectedly.

àr̃bạ'in *n.f. and adj.* 1. Forty. 2. Forty day period after woman gives birth.

àr̃bạminyà *n.f. and adj.* Four hundred.

ạrèwạ *n.f.* North, northern: *ya yi ~* he headed north; *jihar ~* the northern region.

ạrewạcin *prep.* North of.

àr̃ịyà *n.f.* Arrears, back-payment.

ar̃mạshi *n.m.* Sth. very satisfying: *wasan jiya ya yi ~* yesterday's game was excellent.

ar̃nè *n.m.* (*f.* **ar̃nịya,** *pl.* **ar̃na**) Pagan, heathen.

ạro *n.m.* 1. Loan. ***~n baki*** saying sth. on behalf of s.o. 2. *vn.* of **ạra.**

ạr̃ụ-ạr̃ụ *adv.* Long, long ago: *tun shekara ~* many, many years ago.

ar̃zịki *n.m.* (*pl.* **ar̃zụkà**) Wealth, riches, prosperity. *~n kasa* natural resources.

ar̃zụta *v.t.* Make s.o. wealthy, rich.

àr̃zụtạ *v.i.* Be wealthy, rich.

Ạsạbàr̃ *n.f.* Saturday.

ạsạbạr̃i *n.m.* (*pl.* **ạsạbạr̃ai**) Mat made of reeds.

ạsạlatụ *see* **àssạlatụ.**

ạsạli *n.m.* (*pl.* **ạsạlai**) 1. Origins, stock, pedigree: *~nsa Fulani ne* he is a Fulani by tribe; *tun can ~* from the very beginning. 2. Cause, reasons: *~n maganar da aka yi yana da wuyar ganewa* the reasons behind his talk are hard to understand. 3. Principles, foundation: *~n gini* foundation of a building; *~n abin da aka gina Musulunci guda biyar ne* the principles upon which Islam is founded are five.

ạsar̃à *see* **hạsar̃à.**

ạsạwàki *n.m.* 1. Chewing stick. 2. Cleaning one's teeth.

as-as *id.* Sound used in driving away fowl: *yaro yana korar kaji ~* the boy is chasing the chickens away.

asfir̃in *n.m.* Aspirin.

ash *excl.* Expression of regret.

ạsham *n.m.* Special optional evening prayers after *lisha* during month of Ramadan.

ạshana *n.f.* Match(es).

ạshâr̃ *n.f.* (*pl.* **ạshàr̃ẹ-ạshàr̃ẹ**) Abusive, obscene language.

ạshạr̃ar̃i *n.m.* (*f.* **ạshạr̃ar̃ịya,** *pl.* **ạshạr̃àr̃ai**) Foul-mouthed, morally degraded person.

ạshe *excl.* 1. Expresses surprise or doubt: *~? haka ne?* really? is that so? 2. Expresses confirmation of sth.: ~ *Audu ne* so it was Audu after all.

ąshįr̃in *n.f. and adj.* Twenty.

ąsįbįtį *n.f.*(*pl.* **ąsįbįtoci**) Hospital, dispensary, clinic.

ąsir̃i *n.m.* (*pl.* **ąsir̃ai**) 1. Secret, sth. private. 2. Magic charm or spell, usu. harmful: *an yi masa* ~ s.o. has harmed him with magic.

ąsir̃ta *v.t.* 1. Confide: *ya* ~ *mini wata magana* he told me sth. secretly. 2. Keep sth. secret: *ya* ~ *maganar da na faɗa masa* he kept secret what I told him.

aska *n.f.* 1. (*pl.* **ąsàke**) Straight razor, scalpel, pen-knife. 2. Marks on face or body which identify person by tribe or profession.

askąr̃awa *pl.* of **bą'askąr̃è.**

askè *v.t.* Shave.

aski *n.m.* 1. Shaving. 2. Pruning (tree, bush).

àssąlatų *n.f.* Dawn, very early morning.

àssha *excl.* What a pity! How distressing! ***aikin*** ~ misdeeds.

ąsųbâ *n.f.* 1. First prayer of the day. 2. Time of day before the first light of dawn. 3. General term for morning: *barka da* ~ good morning!

ąsusų *n.m.* 1. Money box. 2. Treasury, funds, savings. ~***n taimako*** donation(s).

ątąfa *n.f.* Ginned cotton.

ątàmfa *n.f.* (*pl.* **ątamfofi**) Printed manufactured cloth.

ątąsayè *n.m.* Physical exercises, esp. of horses or soldiers.

ątįni *n.m.* Dysentery.

ątishawà *n.f.* Sneezing.

ątòm *n.m.* Atom.

ątonę̀-jąnàr̃ *n.m.* Attorney-General.

àttajįr̃i *n.m.* (*f.* **àttajįr̃a,** *pl.* **àttàjįr̃ai**) Wealthy person.

Àttaur̃a *n.f.* Old Testament.

ątųrè *n.m.* Throwing handful of dust or ash (by children) to shame s.o.

au . . . au *conj.* Either . . . or: ~ *ka ci jarrabawa* ~ *ka koma gida* either you pass the examination or you will be sent home; ~ *ka yi* ~ *ka bari oho* whether you do it or not, I don't care.

audųga *n.f.* Cotton.

aukà *v.t.* (with i.o.) 1. Attack, fall upon s.o.: *sun* ~ *mana da faɗa* they attacked us. 2. Befall: *masifa ta* ~ *musu* a calamity has befallen them. *v.i.* Collapse, cave in (e.g. house or well).

auki *n.m.* 1. Expansion, progress: *tafiya ta yi masa* ~ he made good progress in his journey. 2. Sth. which lasts longer than expected: *kuɗi ya yi mini* ~ my money lasted longer than expected.

àukų *v.i.* Happen, occur, arise.

àuna (į/e) *v.t.* Buy sth. by measureful: *na auni hatsi mudu uku* I bought three measures of grain. **aunà** *v.t.* (*vn.* **ąwò**) 1. Weigh, measure. ~ ***hanya*** survey. 2. Test, examine. ~ ***arziki*** be lucky (used when s.o. has escaped from a dangerous incident). 3. Aim at sth.

àune *n.m.* Awareness, realization.

àunę-àunę *pl.* of **ąwò.**

àura (į/e) *v.t.* (*vn.* **aure**) Marry s.o. **aurà** *v.t.* Arrange for s.o. to marry s.o.: *ya* ~ *wa Audu Ladi* he arranged for Audu to marry Ladi.

àurątayyà *n.f.* Intermarriage.

aure *n.m.* (*pl.* **àurę-àurę**) 1. Marriage. 2. Pair of birds or animals for breeding: *na sayi tantabara* ~ *biyar* I bought five pairs of pigeons. 3. Grafting of plants. 4. *vn.* of **àura.**

àuta *n.m. or f.* Last-born or youngest child.

ąwà *n.f.* (*pl.* **ąwoyi**) Hour.

ąwaki *pl.* of **ąkųyà.**

ąwàr̃tąki *n.m.* Pincers, pliers.

ąwązà *n.m.* (*pl.* **ąwązu**) Rib.

ąwò *n.m.* (pl. **àunę-àunę**) 1. Measure, measurement. 2. Standard measure, measure of one pound weight. 3. Buying daily needs at market. 4. Aiming (of a weapon). 5. Metre of a poem. 6. *vn* of **àuna.**

ayà *n.f.* (*pl.* **ayoyi**) 1. Verse (esp. of Koran). 2. Punctuation mark: ~***r tambaya*** question mark. 3. Stop, pause.

ą̀yą̀bą̀ *n.f.* Banana(s).
ayàn *n.m.* 1. Iron for pressing. 2. Pressing, ironing.
ayą̀ři *n.m.* (*pl.* **ayąřoři**) Caravan.
àyyâ *excl.* How terrible! I'm so sorry! (used for serious misfortune such as bad accident or death). **ayyà** *excl.* What a shame! How terrible! (used after hearing of sth. bad but not really serious, like losing a coin or stubbing one's toe).
ayyųkà *pl.* of **aikì.**
ayyųřųřûi *id.* The sound of *guɗa.*
ązà *v.t.* 1. Put or place sth. on top of sth. 2. Impose (e.g. task or tax). *v.i.* Think: *na* ~ *ba za ka zo ba* I thought you wouldn't come.
ą̀zabà *n.f.* (*pl.* **ą̀zàbu, ązabobi**) Great pain, anguish, torture.
ą̀ząhàř *n.f.* 1. Second prayer of the day. 2. Time of day from about 2 p.m. to 4 p.m.
ą̀zal *adv.* Used in *tun fil* ~ since time immemorial.
ą̀zą̀lįyà *n.f.* Predestined misfortune.
ąząmà *n.f.* Intention, purpose, zeal: *yana da* ~ *a aikinsa* he works conscientiously.
ązanci *n.m.* 1. Sense, meaning. 2. Common sense, intelligence, wit.
ązàřa *n.f.* (*pl.* **ą̀zàřu**) Section of split tree (usu. deleb palm) used for roofing.
ązų̀mi *n.m.* 1. The fast of Ramadan. 2. Fasting.
ązùrfa *n.f.* Silver.
àzzalų̀mi *n.m.* (*f.* **àzzalų̀ma,** *pl.* **àzzàlų̀mai**) Oppressor, bully, cheat.
ązuzųwà *pl.* of **ąjì.**
àzząƙą̀ri *n.m.* Penis.

B

bâ (Alt. form of **babų̀** when obj. expressed) 1. There isn't any, there aren't any: ~ *mai* there isn't any petrol. 2. Without: *ya tashi tafiya* ~ *guzuri* he left on his journey without provisions. 3. Less (in telling time): *ƙarfe uku* ~ *kwata* a quarter to three.
[1]**ba** (vl. and tone vary acc. to use, *see* Appendix 2) Not (general neg. marker).
[2]**ba** *v.t.* (becomes **bâ** before noun obj.) 1. Give, offer: *sun* ~ *mu takardar izni* they gave us a permit. 2. Cause emotion in s.o.: *ya* ~ *ni haushi* he annoyed me; *ya* ~ *Audu dariya* it made Audu laugh.
bą'à *n.f.* Mockery, joke.
bą̀'askąřè *n.m.* (*pl.* **askąřawa**) Soldier.
bàbą *n.m.* 1. Father. 2. Respectful term of address for an old man.
bàba *n.m.* (*pl.* **bàbànni**) Eunuch.
babą̀ *n.f.* Paternal aunt, mother.
baba *n.m.* Indigo: *ya ji* ~ it is dyed well with indigo.
bą̀bambąɗè *n.m.* (*f.* **bą̀bambą-ɗįya,** *pl.* **bambąɗawa**) Professional beggar who attaches himself to praise-singers and musicians.
bą̀barbąrà *n.f.* Good-quality knife or sword made in Borno.
bàbbą *n. and adj.* (*pl.* **mânya**) 1. Big: ~*n doki* big horse; ~*r riga* big gown. 2. Important, great: *su ne manya* they are the most important ones. 3. Elder, senior: *ni ne* ~*nsu* I'm the eldest of them.
babbą̀ka *v.t.* (*vn.f.* **bàbbą̀kà**) Grill, toast, singe.
babbą̀ke *v.t.* Block up space with one's body.
babbąƙu *n.m.* Stage of learning Arabic consonants without vowels.
babè *n.m.* Large locust.
babì *n.m.* 1. Chapter. 2. Category.
babų̀ There isn't any, there aren't any (neg. form corresponding to **ą̀kwai**): *akwai mai? a'a,* ~ is there any petrol? no, there isn't any.
bàbuř *n.m.* (*pl.* **babųřà**) Motorcycle.

ba dą *v.t.* Alt. form of **bąyar̃ dą**.

baddąla *v.t.* Change (clothes, direction, etc.).

bądò *n.m.* Water-lily.

bą̀dukù *n.m.* (*pl.* **dùkàwa**) Leather worker.

bąɗà *v.t.* Sprinkle powdered substance: *ya ~ yaji a tuwo* he sprinkled spices on the *tuwo*.

bą̀ɗį *n.f. and adv.* Next year. **~ *waccan*** the year after next. **~ *baɗaɗa*** the far-distant future.

bąɗì *n.m.* Powdered mixture of spice and groundnut cake sprinkled on *tsire* and *kilishi*.

bą̀fadà *n.m.* (*pl.* **fàdàwa**) Courtier.

baffą̀ *n.m.* (*pl.* **bàffànni**) Paternal uncle.

bą̀gàrųwa *n.f.* Large acacia tree.

bą̀gįdajè *n.m.* (*f.* **bą̀gįdajįya**, *pl.* **gįdàdàwa**) Unsophisticated person, simpleton, rustic.

bą̀gwari *n.m.* (*f.* **bą̀gwarįya**, *pl.* **gwàràwa**) 1. Gwari man. 2. Person who cannot speak Hausa well.

bą̀hągò *n.m.* (*f.* **bą̀hągų̀wa**, *pl.* **bą̀hą̀gwai**) 1. Left-handed person. 2. Difficult person or thing.

bąhą̀si *n.m.* Investigation, inquiry.

bâ-hąyà *n.m.* Latrine.

bą̀hilì *n.m.* (*f.* **bą̀hilįya**, *pl.* **bą̀hìlai**) Miser.

bahò *n.m.* Bathtub, large round basin.

bàì (contr. of neg. marker **bą̀** and pro. **yą̀**) He did not.

bai *v.t.* (with **wą̀**) Alt. form of **[2]ba** before noun obj.: *na ~ wa Musa kuɗin* = *na ba Musa kuɗin* I gave Musa the money.

bàibâi *adv.* Inside-out: *ya sa rigarsa ~* he put on his gown inside-out.

baibą̀ye *v.t.* (*vn.f.* **bàibąyà**) Thatch a house.

bâi ɗąyą *adv.* 1. Level, smooth. 2. Similar, same: *fenti ya tashi ~* the paint came out the same colour.

baiko *n.m.* Betrothal.

baitì *n.m.* (*pl.* **baitoci**) Line of verse, stanza.

bàitùlmalį *n.m.* Treasury.

baiwa *n.f.* 1. Gift, esp. from God. 2. Generosity. 3. Betrothal.

[1]bąjau *n.m.* Cloth on which card players play.

[2]bąjau *adv.* Reddened: *bakinsa ya yi ~ da goro* his mouth is stained with kolanut.

bąjè *v.t.* 1. Make level, flatten. 2. Spread out.

bąję-bą̀ję̀ *id.* Smeared all over (usu. with filth).

bą̀jintà *n.f.* Possessing outstanding, impressive qualities (e.g. bravery or strength).

bajò *n.m.* Badge.

bą̀ka *n.m.* (*pl.* **bąkunkųnà**) 1. Bow. **~*n gizo*** rainbow. 2. Catch of lock. 3. Hacksaw.

bąką̀ *adv.* In the mouth: *ban sami abin da zan sa a ~ ba* I haven't found anything to eat.

baką̀ce *v.t.* (*vn.* **bàką̀ce**) Winnow grain with circular tray.

bą̀kan *n.m.* Pretending to be asleep.

bą̀kanįkè *see* **mą̀kanįkè**.

bàki *n.m.* (*pl.* **bakųnà**) 1. Mouth. ***~ da ~*** face-to-face. 2. Mouth of vessel, opening, entrance: *~n tulu* mouth of pot. 3. Speaking, speech: *sa ~* interfere; *yi ~* curse s.o.; *yi ~ biyu* break one's word. ***~ ɗaya*** unanimously. 4. Edge: *~n kogi* river bank; *~n kasuwa* near the market. ***~ da hanci*** very near. 5. Limit: *na yi ~n ƙoƙarina* I've done all that I can.

bàkin *prep.* 1. In exchange for, as equivalent to: *na ba da sabulu a ~ madara* I gave some soap in exchange for some milk. 2. On the verge of: *suna ~ tashi sai abokansu suka dawo* they were about to leave when their friends returned.

bąkwài *n.f. and adj.* Seven. ***~ biyu*** a fortnight.

[1]bąƙi *n. and adj.* (*f.* **bąƙa**, *pl.* **bąƙàƙe**) 1. Black, dark. ***~n ruwa*** clear drinking water. 2. (in compounds) Sth. bad, negative: *baƙar aniya* evil intentions; *~n ciki* sadness; *~n jini* unpopularity; *baƙar magana* angry, bitter words; *~n rai* evil character; *baƙar zuciya* bad-temperedness.

[2]bąƙi *n.m.* 1. (*pl.* **bąƙàƙe**) Letter

of any alphabet. 2. (*pl.* **babbạƙu**) Consonant in Arabic script.

bàƙo *n.m.* (*f.* **bàƙụwa,** *pl.* **bàƙi**) 1. Guest, stranger, visitor: *mun yi* ~ we have a visitor. *~n dare* burglar. 2. Foreign element: *ido ya yi* ~ dirt has got into my eye.

bàƙon dàuro *n.m.* Measles.

bàƙuntà (cị/ce) *v.t.* Be a guest or visitor of: *na bakunce shi* I was his guest; *ina ~r Kano* I am a stranger in Kano.

bạ̀lạgạ̀ *v.i.* Reach puberty.

bàlagà *n.f.* 1. Eloquent use of language. 2. Rhetoric (subject for study).

bạ̀la'ì *n.m.* Calamity, great misfortune.

bạlàs *n.m.* Balance (in accounting). *yi* ~ settle the score.

bàl-bàl *id.* Flickering or fluttering: *wuta tana ci* ~ the fire is burning brightly.

balbạ̀la *v.t.* Make a bright fire. ~ *bala'i* have a serious row.

bâlbelà *n.f.* (*pl.* **bàlbèlu**) Cattle egret. *yi* ~ dress all in white.

balịgi *n.m.* (*f.* **balịga,** *pl.* **bàlịgai**) Adult.

bàllàntạna *see* **bàlle.**

bàlle 1. (after neg. sentence) How much less: *bàn iya hawan keke ba* ~ *babur* I can't even ride a bicycle, let alone a motorcycle. 2. (after affirmative sentence) How much more: *ni ma na iya* ~ *kai* if I can do it, you certainly can.

bambam *adv.* Different, distinct: *sun yi* ~ they differ. *sha* ~ miss one another on the way.

bambancì *n.m.* Difference, distinctness. *nuna* ~ discriminate against s.o. *~n kabila* tribalism. *~n launi* racialism.

bàmbạ̀ni *n.m.* Raising the voice in anger.

bambànta *v.t.* Differentiate, separate, distinguish. **bàmbantạ̀** *v.i.* Differ, be different.

bàmbạ̀rạ̀kwài *excl.* How strange, abnormal!: ~ *namiji da suna Hajara!* what a peculiar thing for a man to have the name Hajara!

bâmmi *n.m.* Palm wine.

bàn (contr. of neg. marker **bạ̀** and pro. **ìn**) I did not.

ban Form of ²**ba** used in compounds: ~ *girma* showing respect; ~ *haushi* annoyance; ~ *kwana* saying goodbye; ~ *magana* calming down s.o.; ~ *tsoro* frightening.

bạnạ *n.f. and adv.* 1. This year. *ɗan* ~ fresh, cheeky young person. 2. Age (esp. of cattle): *saniya mai* ~ *bakwai* a seven-year-old cow.

bạ̀nạsaȓè *n.m.* (*f.* **bạ̀nạsaȓịya,** *pl.* **nạ̀saȓạ, nạ̀sàȓu**) Christian.

bạnạtị *n.m.* Bayonet.

bànda *n.f.* Drying meat or fish over fire.

bandạ̀ *prep.* 1. Apart from, excluding, besides: ~ *kai wa ya zo?* besides you, who else came?; ~ *ni ba wanda ya zo* no one came except me. 2. Without: *ki ba ni fura* ~ *nono* give me some *fura* without milk.

bandejị *n.m.* Bandage.

bandiȓ *n.m.* Bolt of cloth.

bàndiȓì *see* **màndiȓì.**

bân ɗakì *n.m.* Latrine.

bànga *n.f.* (*pl.* **bangụnà**) Small bowl-shaped drum which is beaten with the fingers (usu. played for traditional rulers).

bàngạ̀-bangà *n.m.* Crowding around s.o.: *an yi wa sarki* ~ the chief is surrounded by his followers.

bangạ̀je *v.t.* Push rudely and forcefully aside.

bango *n.m.*(*pl.* **bangwàye**) 1. Wall (of hut or room). 2. Cover of book.

bànka (ị/e) *v.t.* 1. Collide: *ya banki kofa* he broke the door down with his body. 2. Drink much of. 3. Patch clothing.

bankà *v.t.* (with i.o.) Set big fire to: *an* ~ *wa daji wuta* the bush has been set aflame.

bankạ̀ɗa *v.t.* 1. Lift up edge of mat, cloth, etc. 2. Reveal: *ya* ~ *asirina* he disclosed my secret.

bankạ̀ɗe *v.t.* Push aside.

bankè *v.t.* Knock down or aside with great force: *mota ta* ~ *jaki* the car knocked over the donkey.

¹**bankì** *n.m.* (*pl.* **bankụnà**) Bank, coffers.

²bankì *n.m.* (*pl.* **bànkę-bànkę**) Patch of material.

ban kwana *n.m.* Taking one's leave of s.o., saying good-bye.

banƙąra *v.t.* Twist outwards, warp or bend sth.

bàn-nį-dą̀-mugù *n.m.* Acne in adolescents.

bànte *n.m.* (*pl.* **bantųnà**) Loin-cloth. *yi* ~ circumcise. ***shan*** ~ triangular shape.

banza *n.f.* Useless, foolish person or thing: *aikin* ~ fruitless task; *yaron* ~ foolish boy; *zaman* ~ idleness. *adv.* (with **ą**) 1. In vain. 2. Cheaply, easily, free: *na same shi a* ~ I got it cheaply, free.

bar̃ *see* **bąrì.**

bàrą *n.f. and adv.* Last year. ~ ***waccan*** the year before last.

bàr̃a *n.f.* Aiming at sth., attempting to catch sth.: *abin* ~ target.

bąrà *n.m.* (*f.* **bąranyà**, *pl.* **bąrori**) Servant.

bąr̃à *n.f.* Begging for alms.

bą̀rą̀-gurbį *n.m.* 1. Eggs left unhatched. 2. Sth. or s.o. left after others have gone.

bąram-bą̀ràm *adv.* At variance, in disharmony: *sun rabu* ~ they have become estranged.

bąràndą̀ *n.m.* Buying goods speculatively for resale at a large profit. ***ɗan*** ~ commercial agent, middleman.

bàr̃àsa *n.f.* Any strong alcoholic beverage.

bar̃bąɗa *v.t.* Sprinkle, scatter: *ya* ~ *labari* he spread the news.

bàr̃bąɗi *see* **bùr̃bųɗi.**

bâr̃bąjè *n.m.* A biting fly.

barbąra *n.f.* Mating by animals. ~***r yanyawa*** child from an interracial marriage.

barci *n.m.* 1. Sleep: *ciwon* ~ sleeping sickness. ***wawan*** ~ deep sleep. ***dogon*** ~ death. 2. Solidification of liquids: *nono ya yi* ~ the milk is curdled.

bar̃de *n.m.* (*pl.* **bąr̃àde**) 1. A traditional title held by a mounted warrior. 2. Brave person.

bąre *see* **bàlle.**

bàr̃e *n.m. or f.* Outsider, stranger, one not related by blood.

bą̀rewa *n.f.* (*pl.* **bą̀rèyi**) Gazelle.

bàr̃ga *n.f.* Stable.

bàr̃go *n.m.* (*pl.* **bar̃gųnà**) Blanket.

bąrì *v.t.* (becomes **bar̃** before obj.) 1. Leave, leave off: *ya bar aikinsa* he left his job; *ku bar wannan surutu* stop this chattering! 2. Let, allow: *na bar shi ya shiga* I allowed him to enter; ~ *mu tafi* let's go!

bar̃įkį *n.f.* 1. Barracks, camp, rest house. 2. Township, urban area, city. ***ɗan*** ~ city slicker.

bą̀r̃imà *n.f.* (*pl.* **bą̀r̃imu**) 1. Corkscrew. 2. Thread of screw.

bar̃kà *excl.* General greeting (to which reply is ~ *kadai*). ~ *da rana* good day! ~ *da zuwa* welcome! ~ *da aiki* well done! ~ *da arziki* congratulations! *za ni* ~ I'm off to give congratulations (e.g. on the occasion of a birth).

bàr̃ką̀tài *adv.* In disorder, mess: *ga takardu a teburinsa* ~ look at the mess of papers on his desk.

bàr̃kòno *n.m.* Pepper.

bar̃kwancì *n.m.* Joking.

basasà *n.f.* Usu. used in *yakin* ~ any destructive war, esp. civil war.

bashì *n.m.* (*pl.* **basussųkà**) Debt, buying sth. on credit: *ya ɗauki* ~*n mota* he bought a car on credit; *ya ci* ~ he is in debt.

bashi *n.m.* Bad smell of rotting meat or fish.

bą̀silla *n.f.* (*pl.* **bą̀sillu**) Large needle for sewing leather and stiff materials.

bàsir̃à *n.f.* Insight, quick understanding, intelligence: *da idon* ~ carefully and intelligently; *ɓatan* ~ loss of insight or reason; ~ *ta fado masa* an intelligent solution has occurred to him.

basųkùr̃ *n.m.* (*pl.* **basųkųr̃ori**) Bicycle.

basùr̃ *n.m.* Piles, haemorrhoids.

basussųkà *pl.* of **bashì.**

bata *n.m.* Bundle of grass prepared for thatching.

bà-tą-kashį *n.m.* Coming to blows, physical struggle.

bą̀taljyà *n.f.* (*pl.* **bątaljyoyi**) Battalion.

batir̃ *n.m.* (*pl.* **batųr̃à**) Battery.

batsą *n.f.* Indecent talk.

bątsįyà *n.f.* (*pl.* **bątsįyoyi**) Gambian oribi (gazelle).

battà *n.f.* (*pl.* **battoci**) Small leather or metal container for tobacco, snuff, etc.

bą̀tu *n.m.* (*pl.* **bątutųwà**) 1. Speech, conversation: *~n duniya* discussing things in general. 2. Matter, affair. 3. Motion, proposal.

bą̀tur̃è *n.m.* 1. (*f.* **bą̀tur̃įya**, *pl.* **tù̃r̃àwa**) European. 2. Senior government official: *~n gona* senior agricultural officer.

baucà *n.f.* (*pl.* **baucoci**) Voucher. ***~r iska*** voucher bearing false claim.

bauɗè *v.i.* 1. Swerve, dodge aside. 2. Go astray (in morals).

bauɗįya *n.f.* Evasiveness, being a dodger.

bâuta *v.t.* (with i.o.) 1. Worship: *yana ~ wa iskoki* he believes in spirit-worship. 2. Serve faithfully, work hard for: *yana ~ wa ƙasarsa tsakani da Allah* he serves his country well. ***matasa masu ~ wa ƙasa*** National Youth Service Corps.
bàuta *n.f.* 1. Slavery, servitude. 2. Worship.

bautar̃ (dą̀) *v.t.* Enslave.

bawà *n.m.* (*f.* **bâiwa**, *pl.* **bayi**) Slave. ***~n Allah*** used as term of address to call a stranger's attention.

bąwą̀li *n.m.* Urine.

bawùl *n.m.* Valve.

baya *n.m.* Back. **bayą** *adv.* Behind, backwards: *sun bar shi a ~* they left it behind; *sun koma da ~* they went back, retreated. ***daga ~*** afterwards, the other day.

bą̀yâmma *n.f.* Anaemia.

bayan *prep.* 1. After: *~ haka* after that, then; *~ da kun gama kwa iya tafiya* after you have finished you may go. 2. Behind: *yana ~ sabon gini* it's behind the new building. ***~ gida, ~ gari, ~ ɗaki*** latrine.

bą̀yani *n.m.* (*pl.* **bą̀yànai** Explanation.

bąyar̃ (dą̀) *v.t.* (= **ba dą̀** before d.o.) 1. Give: *ya ~ da kuɗi* he gave away some money; *na ~ da kayana wanki* I gave my clothes to be washed. 2. Betray s.o. ***~ da baki*** persuade, convince s.o.

bàyayyà *n.f.* Giving things to one another, relieving one another in a task.

bàye *n.m.* Copulation by horses.

bayi *pl.* of **bawà.**

bayyą̀na *v.t.* 1. Explain. 2. Reveal, expose. **bàyyąną̀** *v.i.* Be revealed, appear: *Mahdi ya ~ a gabas* the Mahdi appeared in the east.

bą̀za *n.f.* Fringed leather apron or loincloth worn during dancing. ***da ~rsa suke rawa*** they are living off his riches.

bązà *v.t.* Spread (out) sth.

bą̀ząmą̀ *v.i.* Bolt, run away.

bąząra *n.f.* Hot season just before the rains.

bą̀zàr̃-bą̀zàr̃ *id.* Flapping or flowing of ragged clothes or of a gown in the wind.

bà zą̀tą *n.f.* Surprise: *ya yi ~* he did something very unexpected.

bą̀ząwą̀ri n.m. (*f.* **bą̀ząwą̀ra**, *pl.* **ząwąrawa**) Person who is no longer married but still marriageable.

bebànce *v.i.* Become or pretend to be deaf and dumb.

bebe *n.m.* (*f.* **bebįya**, *pl.* **bebàye**) Deaf mute.

bedi *n.m.* Flower bed.

bège *n.m.* Longing, yearning: *ina ~n zuwansa* I am longing for him to come.

begįlą̀ *n.m.* (*pl.* **begįloli**) Bugle.

begųwa *n.f.* Porcupine.

bêl *n.m.* Belt.

bêlbelà *see* **bâlbelà.**

bèlį, bèlų *n.m.* Uvula.

beli *n.m.* Bail: *an yi ~nsa* he was allowed bail.

bencì *n.m.* (*pl.* **bencųnà**) Bench.

bene *n.m.* (*pl.* **benàye**) Upstairs, upper storey.

ber̃à *n.f.* (*pl.* **ber̃or̃i**) Girl whose breasts are not yet formed and who is not marriageable.

bezà *n.f.* A coarse salt.

bį *v.t.* 1. Follow, come next after. 2. Obey: *ya ~ umurnin ubansa* he obeyed his father's instructions. 3. Travel by way of: *ya ~ hanya* he took the road. 4. Be owed something: *ya ~ Audu bashi* Audu owed him some money; *ina binka ziyara* you owe me a visit.

bi-bango *n.m.* Water trickling down wall from leaky roof: ~ *ya ɓata mini ɗaki* the water leaking down the wall has ruined my room.

[1]**bice** *v.t.* Cover with smoke, dust, etc.: *an* ~ *mu da kura* we were covered all over with dust.

[2]**bice** *v.i.* Go out, be extinguished (of fire, lamp).

bidà *n.m.* Thatching needle.

bi da *v.t.* 1. Subdue, force under control: *ya* ~ *doki* he tamed the horse. 2. Lead: *Audu ya* ~ *mu ta mummunar hanya* Audu led us through a rough road.

bî da bî *adv.* One after the other, in order, in sequence: *mun gaisa* ~ we greeted each other in turn.

bìdi *n.m.* 1. Roan horse. 2. Orange-coloured bambara groundnuts.

bidi'à *n.f.* (*pl.* **bidi'o'i**) 1. Innovation in religious practices, heresy. 2. Merrymaking, drumming.

biɗa (i/e) *v.t.* Look for, search.

bîf *id.* Thud: *buhun dawa ya faɗo* ~ the sack of corn has fallen to the ground with a thud.

bigirè *n.m.* (*pl.* **bigirai**) Place.

bìjimi *n.m.* (*pl.* **bijimai**) 1. Large bull. 2. Stalwart fellow.

bijire *v.t.* (with i.o.) Revolt, desert: *matarsa ta* ~ *masa* his wife has deserted him.

bika *n.m.* Baboon.

biki *n.m.* (*pl.* **bukukuwà**) Celebration, festival, feast, ceremony: ~*n aure* marriage celebration.

bikili *n.m.* Bay horse.

bikò *n.m.* Attempt to reconcile runaway wife, enemy, etc.

biƙi *n.m.* Hot baths taken by women lasting up to forty days after delivery of child. *jinin* ~ maternity bleeding.

bîl *n.m.* Bill, invoice.

bila haddin *adv.* Without limit, numerous, many: *mutane sun taru* ~ a large crowd of people were gathered.

bilìmbitùwa *n.f.* Long, aimless, and fruitless search.

bìmbìni *n.m.* Thinking constantly and anxiously about sth.

bincika *v.t.* (*vn.* **bìncike**) Investigate, inquire into: *'yan sanda sun* ~ *maganar* the police have investigated the matter.

bìncike *n.m.* (*pl.* **bìncike-bìncike**) 1. Investigation. 2. Research. 3. *vn.* of **bincika.**

bindigà *n.f.* (*pl.* **bindigogi**) Gun, firearm. *yi* ~ explode: *tayar mota ta yi* ~ the tyre of the car has blown out.

bini-bìni *adv.* Repeatedly, often: *duk abin da ya same shi* ~ *sai ya zo wurina* whatever befalls him, he repeatedly comes to me.

binjima *n.f.* Fulani-style hand-woven shirt, open at the sides.

binne *n.m.* Sowing of seeds in anticipation of the rains.

binnè *v.t.* 1. Bury. 2. Fill in a hole.

bir̃bishi *n.m.* Summit, top.

bir̃gedìyà *n.m.* Brigadier.

birgima *n.f.* Rolling on the ground (animal or child).

birì *n.m.* (*pl.* **birai**) Monkey. ***dattijon*** ~ an elderly man whose behaviour is not suitable to his age.

bir̃is *id.* Ignoring a person, turning a deaf ear: *ya yi* ~ *da shi* he turned a deaf ear towards him.

bìr̃jik *id.* Abundantly: *akwai motoci* ~ there are lots of cars.

bir̃ki *n.m.* Brake(s): *ya ja* ~ he put on the brakes.

birkìce *v.t.* Overturn, turn inside out: *ya* ~ *kunkuru* he turned the tortoise upside down. *v.i.* Become confused, upset, disorganized.

birkìɗa *v.t.* Roll sth. around in liquid or powder to coat it: *tana* ~ *nama a gishiri* she is coating the meat with salt. **bìrkiɗa** *v.i.* Roll about on the ground (animal).

bir̃kìlà *n.m.* (*pl.* **bir̃kiloli**) Brick-layer.

bir̃ni *n.m.* (*pl.* **bir̃àne**) Walled town, city: *babban* ~ capital city.

birò *n.m.* Ball-point pen, biro.

bisà *prep.* 1. On top, above, on: *sa shi* ~ *tebur* put it on the table. 2. Concerning, with reference to: ~ *zancen nan* concerning this matter. 3. In accordance with: ~ *ga yadda suka saba* according to their habit. 4. Used in forming fractions: *biyu* ~ *biyar* two-fifths.

bisa *n.f.* (*pl.* **bisàshe**) Pack animal.

bịsani *adv.* (with **dạ̀gạ̀**) Afterwards, later: *daga ~ muka zo* we came afterwards.

bịshar̃à *n.f.* Good news.

bịshịyà *n.f.* (*pl.* **bịshịyoyi**) Tree.

bịsịmillà *excl.* Used when inviting s.o. to begin a meal, come into a room, sit down, etc.

bịsịmillahì *excl.* Said by s.o. about to begin eating, start work, etc.

bìskît *n.m.* Biscuit.

bît *n.m.* Used in *bakin ~* police beat.

bità *n.f.* Reading again through a text: *na yi ~r karatuna* I have gone through my lesson again.

bịtịnar̃è *n.m.* Veterinary.

[1]**bịyà** *v.t.* Teach or study by reading.

[2]**bịyà** *v.i.* Go via, pass by, call at: *zan ~ ta kasuwa* I will go via the market; *na ~ ta wurinsa* I called at his house.

bịya *v.t.* 1. Pay: *ba a ~ albashi ba* the salary has not been paid; *ya ~ bashi* he repaid the debt. 2. Fulfil: *ya ~ mini bukata* he granted my wish.

bịyar̃ *n.f. and adj.* Five.

bịyayyà *n.f.* Obedience.

bịyụ *n.f. and adj.* 1. Two. 2. Double: *nauyin wannan ya yi ~n wancan* this is twice as heavy as that. ***fuska*** ~ two-faced. ***magana*** ~ double talk: *ya yi mini magana* ~ he went back on his word.

bịyụ̀ bịyû *n.m.* Double loss.

bobụwa *n.f.* A biting fly.

bodì *n.m.* Body of a lorry.

boka *n.m.* (*f.* **bokanyà**, *pl.* **bokàye**) Native doctor, wizard.

bokịtị *n.m.* (*pl.* **bòkịtai**) Bucket.

bokò *n.m.* 1. Western education. 2. Hausa written in Roman script. 3. Mock arrangement: *yakin ~* army manœuvres. 4. Adulteration, fraud, trick.

bokùl *n.m.* (*pl.* **bokụloli**) Buckle.

bolà *n.f.* (*pl.* **bololi**) Refuse pit.

bôm *n.m.* Bomb.

borà *n.f.* A less-favoured wife.

bòr̃e *n.m.* Rebelliousness, disobedience.

bòri *n.m.* The cult of spirit possession. ***ɗan*** ~ a follower of the cult.

bor̃ìs *n.m.* 1. Used in *'ya'yan ~* ball bearings. 2. Intentionally spinning car or motorcycle around in soft sand.

bòrorò *n.m.* Blister.

bôs *n.f.* (*pl.* **bôs-bôs**) Bus.

bòyị *n.m.* (*pl.* **bòyị-bòyị**) Houseboy, steward.

bubụ̀ *n.m.* Mouth disease with rotting of teeth, usu. in children.

budà *n.f.* Dry, windy, harmattan haze.

bụ̀duddụ̀gi *n.m.* (*pl.* **bụ̀dùddụ̀gai**) A large, edible toad.

bụ̀durwa *n.f.* (*pl.* **bụdurwoyi**) 1. Unmarried girl of marriageable age. 2. Girl-friend (of a boy).

buɗà *v.t.* 1. Open slightly. 2. Disclose: *ta ~ mini asirinsa* she has disclosed his secrets to me.

bùɗạ̀-bàkị *n.m.* Taking the first meal of the day during Ramadan.

buɗè *v.t.* Open.

buɗì *n.m.* 1. New opportunities (in trade), progress (in education): *ya sami ~n kasuwa* he has found new trade outlets. 2. Opening a water inlet in an irrigated plot.

bụ̀ga (ị/e) *v.t.* (*vn.* **bụgù**) Beat, strike, hit, thrash: *na bugi yaro* I struck the boy; *rana ta buge su* the sun beat down on them. ***bugi ciki*** get information indirectly.

bụgà *v.t.* Beat, strike sth. ~ ***bindiga*** fire a gun; ~ ***iska*** pump up a tyre; ~ ***littafi*** publish, print a book; ~ ***nakiya*** set off an explosive; ~ ***waya*** send a telegram or make a telephone call.

bụ̀gụ *v.i.* 1. Be thoroughly beaten. 2. Be drunk.

bụgù dạ̀ ƙarì *conj.* Moreover, in addition.

bujè *n.m.* Traditional-style trousers with very wide crotch.

bụ̀hu *n.m.* (*pl.* **bụhunhụnà**) Sack, bag.

bụ̀kar̃i *n.m.* Compass for drawing, drafting.

bụ̀katà *n.f.* (*pl.* **bụ̀kàtu**) Need, requirement: *ina da ~r naira dari in yi wa 'yata aure* I need ₦100 in order to get my daughter married; ~ *ta kama* the need has arisen; *abin da ake* ~ what is required. ***biyan*** ~ wish fulfilment: *ta sami biyan ~rta* her wish has been fulfilled.

bukkà *n.f.*(*pl.* **bukkoki**) Grass hut.

bu̧là *n.f.* Washing blue.

bulalà *n.f.* Whip, lash.

bulbù̧la *v.t.* Pour liquid in or out of vessel with a gurgling sound.

bù̧lô *n.m.* Cement block, brick.

bù̧lotà *n.f.* (*pl.* **bu̧lotoci**) Blotting paper.

bu̧lus *id.* Sth. gotten cheaply or without effort: *sun sami* ~ they got it very cheap.

bùndùm-bundum *id.* Floundering or splashing around noisily while swimming.

bùnƙasa̧ *v.i.* Develop into fullness, grow important, prominent, or serious: *ƙasarmu ta* ~ our country has developed greatly.

bunƙù̧sa *v.t.* Push up or crack ground (by plant).

bunu *n.m.* Old thatch.

bùnsu̧ru *n.m.* (*pl.* **bùnsù̧rai**) He-goat.

buntsù̧ra *v.t.* Used in ~ *baki* purse one's lips; ~ *duwaiwai* walk with hips swaying in sexy manner.

bù̧ra̧ *v.i.* Be ripe.

bùra *n.f.* Penis.

bùr̃bù̧ɗi *n.m.* Crumb, small particle.

bur̃gà *v.t.* Whisk or stir liquid with swizzle stick. **bùr̃ga (i̧/e)** *v.t.* Intimidate s.o. by threats. *n.f.* Intimidation.

burgami *n.m.* (*pl.* **bùrgàmai**) Goatskin bag esp. used by native doctors.

bur̃gè *v.t.* Impress s.o. by one's speech, manner, etc.

bur̃gu *n.m.* (*pl.* **bu̧r̃àge**) Giant male rat or bandicoot.

buri *n.m.* Wish, ambition, goal, aim: *ya cim ma ~nsa* he fulfilled his ambition; *dogon* ~ aiming very high (in bargaining, etc.).

burji̧ *n.m.* Gravel.

burmà *v.t.* (*vn.* **burmi**) Invert small calabash over mouth of larger one to prevent spilling. *v.i.* Cave in (of roof of building).

bu̧r̃odi̧ *n.m.* Bread.

bù̧r̃oshi *n.m.* Brush.

bur̃su̧na̧ *see* **fur̃su̧na̧.**

bur̃su̧na *v.t.* Apply or smear on too much of sth. (e.g. powder).

bur̃ta̧li *n.m.* Hedged road between farms used as cattle track.

bur̃tu *n.m.* Ground hornbill. ***shiga*** ~ disguise oneself, use a clever stratagem.

bùr̃tuntù̧na *n.f.* Fungus affecting guinea-corn.

bu̧r̃ù̧ji *n.m.* 1. Good luck, auspicious day: *ya sami* ~ he has had a stroke of luck. 2. The Milky Way galaxy.

bùs *id.* Extremely unpleasant smell: *da shigowa sai na ji* ~ on entering I smelt a terrible odour.

bùsa (shi̧/she) *v.t.* Winnow. ***ya bushi iska*** he lived like a lord.

busà *v.t.* Blow with mouth. *v.i.* Blow (of wind). *n.f.* (*pl.* **bùshȩ-bùshȩ**) 1. Blowing with mouth. 2. Music made with any wind instrument. 3. Idle talk.

bùshashà *n.f.* Spending money in an extravagant way.

bushè *v.t.* 1. Blow sth. out or away: *ya* ~ *fitila* he blew out the lamp. 2. Winnow. *v.i.* 1. Dry up. 2. Become depleted: *aljihuna ya* ~ I am stone-broke. 3. Stand at attention. 4. Used in ~ *da dariya* burst out laughing.

bushi̧ya *n.f.* Hedgehog. ***~r kara*** collection of cornstalks tied upright, usu. left on the farm. ***ciwon*** ~ rinderpest.

but *id.* Appearing suddenly and quickly: *ya fito* ~ *daga raminsa* he came out suddenly from his hole.

butà *n.f.* (*pl.* **butoci**) Water jug, kettle.

bùtàci *n.m.* Anything floating on surface of liquid (bran, wisps of grass, etc.).

bù̧tù̧lu̧ *n.m. or f.* (*pl.* **bù̧tu̧lai**) Ungrateful person.

bututu *n.m.* 1. Funnel. 2. Watering can.

bù̧wayà (i̧/e) *v.t.* Be beyond one's reach, power. **bù̧waya̧** *v.i.* Become impossible.

bù̧yà-bù̧yà *id.* Walking sloppily in a long flowing gown.

buyagi *n.m.* Small twigs for firewood.

buzu *n.m.* (*f.* **buzụwa,** *pl.* **buzàye**) 1. Tuareg. 2. Undressed goat or sheep skin usu. used as prayer mat.
bụzu-bụ̀zù *id.* Very hairy.
bụzurwa *n.f.* (*pl.* **bụzurwoyi**) Long-haired goat or sheep.
bùzuzù *n.m.* (*pl.* **bùzùzai**) Dung beetle, stag beetle. **~ n taba** large quid of chewed tobacco.

Ɓ

ɓaɓatu *n.m.* Noisy, quarrelsome talk about a small matter.
ɓaɓɓạke *v.t.* Uproot: *iska ta ~ bishiya* the wind has uprooted the tree. *v.i.* Become uprooted, loose: *siminti ya ~* the cement has cracked loose.
ɓaɓɓarkịya *n.f.* Fine sediment used for roofing.
ɓaɓè *v.i.* Break off relations, friendship: *shi da ita sun ~* he and she have severed their relationship.
ɓacị *v.i.* Become damaged, spoiled: *al'amari ya ~* the situation is bad.
ɓad dạ *v.t.* Alt. form of **ɓạtar̃ dạ.**
ɓàd-dạ-sawụ *n.m.* Sth. that deceives, misdirects: *ɓarayi sun sa kayan 'yan sanda don su yi ~* the thieves put on policemen's uniforms to conceal their real intention.
ɓạgas *adv.* (with **ạ**) Cheaply, easily, for next-to-nothing.
ɓạkàne *pl.* of **ɓauna.**
ɓạlakụ̀ce *v.i.* Thin down, waste away, diminish: *jarinsa ya ~* his capital has diminished.
ɓạ̀làu *id.* Emphasizing gaping hole or opening: *ya yi dariya ~* he laughed with his mouth wide open.
ɓàl-ɓàl *id.* Palpitating, beating (esp. of heart): *zuciyata tana bugawa ~* my heart is thumping.
ɓalɓàlce *v.i.* 1. Waste away, diminish, decrease: *na so in yi aiki, na ~ a hira* I wanted to work but instead wasted my time talking. 2. Become idle or lazy: *dansa ya ~* his promising son has come to nothing.
ɓalgạ̀ce *v.i.* Be chipped.
ɓalgạ̀ta *v.t.* Break or chip off piece.
ɓallà *v.t.* Fasten, hook up, button: *ya ~ maɓallin rigarsa* he buttoned his shirt.
ɓallè *v.t.* Break apart, unfasten: *ya ~ maɓallin rigarsa* he unbuttoned his shirt. *v.i.* Break away: *ya ~ daga jam'iyyar* he broke away from the party.
ɓàllị-ɓàllị *n.m.* Severe palpitations of the heart.
ɓạlo-ɓạ̀lò *id.* Clearly and distinctly: *agana ta fito masa ~* smallpox marks have appeared clearly on his face.
ɓam *id.* Popping sound.
ɓamɓạre *v.t.* (*vn.f.* **ɓàmɓạrà**) Tear or strip off: *ya ~ karo daga jikin bishiya* he stripped the gum off the tree.
ɓangạ̀le *v.t. and v.i.* Break or chip off (esp. piece of pot).
ɓàntạrà (ị/e) *v.t.* Break off large piece of sth. hard: *ya ɓantari mazarkwaila* he broke off a large piece of brown sugar.
ɓarà *v.t.* Split into sections: *ya ~ goro* he split up the kolanut.
ɓạ̀rạkà *n.f.* 1. Place where stitching has come undone. 2. Breach of trust, betraying. **ɗinkin ~** mending broken relationships.
ɓạrar̃ (dạ) *v.t.* Cause sth. to spill, drop: *akuya ta ~ gari* the goat knocked over the flour.
ɓạrarrạ̀ka *v.t.* Boil continuously (of liquid).
ɓạ̀rawò *n.m.* (*f.* **ɓạraunịya,** *pl.* **ɓạ̀ràyi**) Thief. **~n zaune** s.o. who receives stolen goods.
ɓàr̃ɓạshi *n.m.* Crumbs, bits, flakes,

sparks: ~n *ƙasa ya zubo mini* bits of earth (from mud roof) fell on me.

ɓarè *v.t.* Peel, strip, shell (groundnuts, fruit, etc.).

ɓargo *n.m.* Bone marrow.

ɓạri *n.m.* 1. Dropping sth. unintentionally: *Bafulatana ta yi ~n nono* the Fulani woman has spilt the milk. 2. Miscarriage: *mai cikin ta yi ~* the woman has had a miscarriage.

ɓạrì *n.m.* Shivering, trembling (e.g. from fear or anger).

ɓarì *n.m.* One of the two halves of sth.: *~n goro* one half section of a kolanut; *~n duwawu na hagu* the left buttock.

ɓarkà *v.t.* Used in *ya ~ tusa* he broke wind.

ɓarkè *v.i.* Become ripped, burst: *madatsar ruwa ta ~* the dam has burst open.

ɓàr̃na *n.f.* 1. Damage, destruction, trouble: *ruwa ya yi ~* the rain has done a lot of damage. 2. Waste, wastefulness: *ta cika ~* she is wasteful.

ɓarzà *v.t.* Grind coarsely.

ɓas *id.* Snapping sound: *ya ɓare gyaɗa ~* he shelled the groundnut with a snap.

ɓạtạ̀ *v.i.* Get lost: *kuɗina sun ~* I lost my money.

ɓatà *v.t.* 1. Spoil, damage: *yaro ya ~ mini riga da dauɗa* the boy dirtied my gown; *ya ~ kansa* he has spoilt his own image; *ya ~ rai* he has become angry; *sun ~ tsakaninsu* they have become estranged. 2. Insult s.o.

ɓạtàn Form of **ɓạtạ̀** used in compounds: *~n basira* being at a loss to do the required thing; *~ ɓakatantan* double loss; *~ dabo* sudden, unexpected disappearance; *~ kai* losing one's way; *~ karatu* forgetting sth. learned; *~ wata* ceasing menstruation due to pregnancy.

ɓạtar̃ (dạ̀) *v.t.* (= **ɓad dạ̀** before d.o.) 1. Lose sth. 2. Lead s.o astray. 3. Spend (money).

ɓauna *n.f.* (*pl.* **ɓạkàne**) Bush-cow

ɓaure *n.m.* Fig tree, fig.

ɓawo *n.m.* Bark, shell, rind.

ɓer̃a *n.m.* (*pl.* **ɓer̃àye**) Mouse, rat.

ɓincịna *v.t.* Break off a small piece of sth.

ɓingịre *v.i.* Topple over, fall over on side.

ɓoyè *v.t.* (*vn.* **ɓoyo**) Hide, conceal.

ɓoyo *n.m.* 1. Concealment. **~n wawa** hiding sth. but leaving traces. 2. *vn.* of **ɓoyè**.

ɓulà *v.t.* 1. Bore hole. 2. Gore (with horn): *sa ya ~ masa ciki da ƙaho* the bull has gored him in the stomach.

ɓulɓul *id.* Excessively fat.

ɓulelè *n. and adj.* (*f.* **ɓulelịya,** *pl.* **ɓula-ɓùlà**) Fat.

ɓullo *v.i.* Appear suddenly or unexpectedly: *rana ta ~ da wuri* the sun has appeared early; *ya ~ masa da wata dabara* he sprang a new plan on him.

ɓuntù *n.m.* Husks of rice or wheat.

ɓurmạ *n.f.* (*pl.* **ɓụràme**) Box-like rat trap.

ɓurmà *v.i.* Cave in (e.g. pit).

ɓụ̀runtu *n.m.* Pilfering, looting in a noisy manner: *ɓera yana ~* the mouse is pilfering noisily.

ɓụsà *v.t.* Bore or make hole in sth.

ɓuyạ *v.i.* Hide oneself. **ɓuya** *n.m.* Concealment.

C

câ *n.f.* (followed by rel. cont. pro.) Thinking: ~ *nake Dauda ne* I thought it was Dauda; ~ *suke ba na nan shi ya sa ba su zo ba* they thought I wasn't home so they didn't come.

caɓà *v.t.* Make slushy or splotchy: *ta* ~ *hoda a fuskarta* she put too much powder on her face. ~ ***magana*** speak indistinctly, speak inappropriately.

càɓi *n.m.* Mud, muddy water, slush.

caɓùla *v.t.* Put sth. into sth. sloppy or messy: *ya* ~ *hannunsa cikin kwatamin* he put his hand into the sump.

caca *n.f.* Gambling: ~*r ƙwallon ƙafa* football pools. ~***r baki*** talking repeatedly or tiresomely about sth.

cafè *v.t.* Catch sth. which has been thrown.

caffà *n.f.* Pledging oneself to a person of influence for his protection.

cajè *v.t.* Search, ransack: *'yan sanda sun* ~ *gidansa* the police searched his house.

cajì *n.m.* 1. Criminal charge. ~ ***ofìs*** police charge-office. 2. Fee, charge.

cak *id.* Stopped stock-still: *ruwa ya ɗauke* ~ the rain has completely stopped.

caka (i/e) *v.t.* Stab, pierce: *ya cake shi da mashi* he stabbed him with a spear.

caka *n.m.* Clubs (suit in playing cards).

caka-caka *id.* Describes pock-marked face: *fuskarta ta yi* ~ *da zanzana* her face is covered with smallpox marks.

caki *n.m.* Small gourd rattle (musical instrument).

cakùɗa *v.t.* Mix thoroughly (solid with liquid).

cakùɗe *v.i.* Be mixed up, confused, entangled.

càkulkùli *n.m.* Tickling.

càkwaikwaiwà *n.f.* 1. Starling 2. Chatterbox.

cali *n.m.* Net bag.

càli-càli *n.m.* Person behaving like a buffoon or clown.

càmfa (i/e) *v.t.* (*vn.* **camfì**) Be superstitious about.

camfì *n.m.* (*pl.* **càmfe-càmfe**) 1. Superstition. 2. *vn.* of **càmfa.**

cân *adv.* Over there (distant but visible). *dem.* (becomes **càn** if preceded by word with final high tone) That, those (distant but visible): *ɗakunan* ~ those rooms over there. **can** *adv.* There (not visible). *dem.* 1. That, those (not visible). 2. That, those (the one(s) referred to): *a* ~ *garin aka gan shi* it was in that town that he was seen.

càncak *id.* Completely gone: *sun tashi* ~ they have gone away for good.

càncantà (ci/ce) *v.t.* Deserve: *ya cancanci yabo* he deserves praise. **càncantà** *v.i.* Be suitable, befit: *ya* ~ *mu ba shi* it is befitting that we give it to him.

canjà *v.t.* (*vn.* **canji**) 1. Change, do sth. over: *sun* ~ *wuri* they have moved to a different place. 2. Exchange goods, money.

canjaràs *adv.* Being equally matched in sports: *sun yi* ~ they had a draw.

canjì *n.m.* (*pl.* **cànje-cànje**) 1. Change (money). 2. Any change (e.g. position, climate, situation). 3. Gears (of car or motorcycle): *babur ɗinka* ~ *nawa ne?* how many gears does your motorcycle have? 4. *vn.* of **canjà.**

cankàcakarè *n.m.* Running short of sth.: *abinci ya zama* ~ the food ran short.

canzà *see* **canjà.**

car̃ *id.* Be vertical, very straight: *hanya ta tsaya* ~ the road is very straight.

caȓa *n.f.* Crowing of cock. ***zakaransa ya yi*** ~ he is lucky.
cạȓabke *n.m.* Game of tossing and catching stones on back of hand.
càȓbi *n.m.* (*pl.* **caȓbụnà**) Rosary.
càȓki *n.m.* (*pl.* **caȓkụnà**) Ox-pecker (bird).
càȓkwai *id.* Very sweet: *wannan rake da zaƙi yake* ~ this sugar-cane is very sweet indeed.
cas *id.* 1. Neatly arranged. 2. Completely: *ya ba ni canjina* ~ he gave me all the change. 3. *See* [2]**kụlẹ̀**.
casà *v.t.* (*vn.f.* **càsa**) 1. Thresh grain. 2. Beat s.o. severely, thrash: *sun* ~ *ɓarawo sosai* they beat up the thief.
cạ̀sạ̀'in *n.f. and adj.* Ninety.
câssa *n.f.* Bow-leggedness.
cạ̀za (jị/je) *v.t.* 1. Charge s.o. a fee. 2. Charge s.o. with a criminal offence.
càzbi *see* **càȓbi.**
cê *v.t.* (*vn.f.* **cêwa**) (with i.o. or **dạ̀**) Say, tell: *na* ~ *masa ya zo* = *na* ~ *da shi ya zo* I told him to come. ***sai ka*** ~ like, as if: *dariya sai ka* ~ *mahaifinsa* he laughs just like his father.
ce *see* **ne.**
ceďịya *n.f.* (*pl.* **ceďịyoyi**) Fig tree.
cèfạ̀ne *n.m.* Buying various ingredients for making *miya*.
cêk *n.m.* Cheque.
cèta (cị/ce) *v.t.* (*vn.* **cèto**) Rescue, save.
cêwa *n.f.* 1. (with verbs of thinking, saying, hearing, etc.) That: *an gaya mana* ~ *za ka zo* we were told that you would come. 2. *See* **câ.** 3. *vn.* of **cê.**
cị *v.t.* 1. Eat. 2. Eat up, consume: *wuta ta* ~ *gida* the fire burned up the house; *ya* ~ *kuďin* he spent the money; *ya* ~ *amanata* he betrayed my trust. 3. Win, overcome: *ya* ~ *jarrabawa* he passed the examination; *sun* ~ *nasara* they were victorious.
cî *n.m.* (*pl.* **cịyẹ-cịyẹ**) Appetite, having great capacity: *dokin nan* ~ *gare shi* this horse has a good appetite; *jakar nan* ~ *gare ta* this bag has a great capacity; *itace* ~*n wuta gare shi* this firewood burns well.
cịbi *n.m.* Teaspoon.
cibì *n.m.* Protruding navel.
cibịya *n.f.* 1. Navel. 2. Central place, hub, centre.
ciccịɓà (ị/e) *v.t.* Lift and carry sth. heavy: *ku taya ni mu cicciɓi wannan kayan* please help me to lift this load up.
ciccìje *v.i.* Exert all one's strength.
cịdà *n.f.* Rumbling of thunder.
ci dạ̀ *v.t.* (= **cishe** before pro. d.o.) Alt. form of **cịyaȓ dạ̀.**
cif *id.* Fully, exactly: *ya ba ni canjina* ~ he gave me all of my change.
cifďì *see* **tabďì.**
cîfjojị *n.m.* Chief judge, magistrate.
cị g̃ạ̀bạ *v.i.* 1. Carry on, continue, keep doing: *ku* ~ *da aiki* continue with your work. 2. Make progress, become developed. **cî g̃ạ̀bạ** *n.m.* 1. Promotion. 2. Progress, civilization.
cịg̃ita *v.t.* (*vn.f.* **cịg̃ịyà**) Search for.
cijè *v.t.* Prevent from moving by gripping with teeth: *kacar keke ta* ~ *rigarsa* the bicycle chain has caught hold of his gown. *v.i.* Become jammed, stuck, stopped: *giyar mota ta* ~ the gears of the car are jammed; *aiki ya* ~ the work has come to a standstill.
cik *id.* Stopped stock-still: *sun tsaya* ~ they came to a complete standstill.
cịkà *v.t.* 1. Fill. 2. Fulfil: *ya* ~ *alƙawari* he kept his promise. 3. Do much of, be characterized by: *ya* ~ *surutu* he is too talkative. ***ya*** ~ he is dead. **cịkạ** *v.i.* Be full, filled up, complete.
cịkạ̀sa *v.t.* 1. Fulfil, complete. 2. Make up a deficiency.
cịkè *v.t.* Fill up completely. *v.i.* Be exhausted, worn out, fed up.
cịkì *n.m.* (*pl.* **cikkụnà**) 1. Stomach. ***kayan*** ~ entrails. ***farin*** ~ happiness. ***baƙin*** ~ sadness. 2. Pregnancy: *tana da* ~ she is pregnant. **cịkị** *adv.* Inside: *tana* ~ she is inside. ~ ***da bai*** inside and out, front and back.
cịkin *prep.* In(side), among: ***mun***

gan shi ~ *mutane* we saw him among the people.

cịkò *n.m.* 1. Balance outstanding. 2. Goods bought intended for resale. 3. Filling (of tooth, hole).

cikò *n.m.* Hairstyle where hair is combed forward to a point over forehead.

cịkowà *n.f.* Overcrowding, overflow: *jirgi ya yi* ~ the train is overcrowded.

cịkwikwịya *v.t.* Crumple (cloth, paper).

cịlạ̀kowà *n.f.* Hornbill.

cim *v.t.* (with i.o.) Catch up with, overtake: *ya* ~ *ma burinsa* he achieved his goal; *na* ~ *masa a hanya* I overtook him on the road.

cìma *n.f.* Staple food: *tuwo* ~*r Hausawa ne* *tuwo* is the staple food of the Hausa people.

cì mà zàunẹ *n.m. or f.* Sponger.

cìncịrindò *n.m.* Dense crowd causing congestion.

cindò *n.m.* Person with a sixth (usu. deformed) finger.

cìngâm *n.m.* Chewing-gum.

cịnịki *n.m.* 1. Trade, trading, bargaining. 2. Habit: ~*nsa zage-zage* his habit is insulting people.

cịnịkayyà *n.f.* Period during harvest season when much trading is done.

cinnà *v.t.* 1. (with i.o.) Set fire to: *ya* ~ *wa ɗaki wuta* he set fire to the house. 2. Set dog onto s.o. or sth.

cìnnakà *n.f.* (*pl.* **cìnnàku**) Small, black biting ant.

cinyà *n.f.* (*pl.* **cinyoyi**) Thigh.

cînye *v.t.* 1. Eat up. 2. Defeat (in competition, war, or gambling).

cir̃ *id.* 1. Very straight, vertical: *soja ya mike* ~ the soldier stood very still. 2. Very full, complete: *kuɗina ya cika* ~ my money is all here.

cịrà *v.t.* Raise, lift up, take off: *ya* ~ *hannu* he raised his arms; *ya* ~ *masa hula* he took off his hat in his honour. *v.i.* Rise, come up high: *dawa ta* ~ the guinea-corn is high.

cir̃à *n.f.* Sore on eyelid.

cì ranị *n.m.* Going away from home during the dry season in search of work or better pasture lands.

cịrè *v.t.* Pull out: *ya* ~ *mini ƙaya* he pulled the thorn out for me.

cịr̃òmạ̀ *n.m.* 1. A traditional title (usu. held by son of an emir). 2. Used in *cikina na kiran* ~ I am feeling hungry.

cishe *see* **ci dạ̀.**

cìta (cị/ce) *v.t.* Guess.

cìttạ *n.f.* Used in ~*r aho* or ~ *mai yatsu* ginger root.

cìttạ̀ *n.f. and adv.* Four days hence.

ciwò *n.m.* (*pl.* **cìwạ̀cẹ-cìwạ̀cẹ**) 1. Illness, disease. ~**n sanyi** gonorrhea. 2. Pain, ache: *ya ji* ~ *a ƙafa* he has a pain in his leg. 3. Sth. disheartening, discouraging: *wannan abu da* ~ *yake* this matter is very discouraging.

cịyar̃ (dạ̀) *v.t.* (= **ci dạ̀** before d.o.) 1. Feed person or animal. 2. Care for, provide for s.o.

cịyawà *n.f.* (*pl.* **cịyàyi**) Grass.

cìza (jị/je) *v.t.* (*vn.* **cizò**) Bite.

cìzga (ị/e) *v.t.* Wrench out, pull out.

cịzìl *n.m.* (*pl.* **cịzịloli**) Chisel.

cokạ̀li *n.m.* (*pl.* **cokụlà**) Spoon. ~ ***mai yatsa*** fork.

cù *id.* Sizzling noise: *ruwan kwai ya zube cikin tafasasshen mai* ~ the egg dripped into the boiling oil with a sizzling noise.

cùɗa (ị/e) *v.t.* Used in *zaman duniya biki ne, cuɗe ni in cuɗe ka* the world necessitates people helping each other. **cuɗà** *v.t.* Scrub s.o.'s body.

cùɗanyà *n.f.* Mixing or mingling with others.

cuɗè *v.i.* Become confused, involved: *magana ta* ~ the matter is very confused.

cụku *n.m.* Cheese.

cụ̀kù-cụku *n.m.* Obtaining things through devious means: *ya yi* ~ *an ba shi kwangila* he got the contract deviously.

cụku-cụ̀kù *id.* 1. Being tangled. 2. Being ragged: *ya yi* ~ *da tsummokara* he was dressed in rags.

cụkwi *see* **cụku.**

¹cunà *v.t.* (with i.o.) Set person or animal on s.o. to catch him: *an* ~ *masa kare* they set a dog on him.

²cunà *n.f.* (*pl.* **cunoni**) Side seam joining lower ends of gown.

cùne *n.m.* Putting person or animal on s.o.'s trail: *an yi masa* ~ someone has informed on him.

cùnkus *id.* In profusion, abundance.

cunkùshe *v.i.* Be dense, compressed, crowded: *hanya ta* ~ the road is crowded.

curà *v.t.* (*vn.* **curì**) Knead into balls.

curì *n.m.* 1. Ball of food formed by kneading: ~*n fura* ball of *fura*. 2. *vn.* of **curà**.

cusà *v.t.* Stuff sth. into sth. **cùsa** *n.f.* Force-feeding a horse with medicinal cake.

cùsàyi *n.m.* Syphilis.

cushè *v.i.* Be completely stuffed: *kwalbati ya* ~ *da ciyawa* the culvert is stuffed up with grass.

¹cùta (cì/ce) *v.t.* Trick, cheat, or deceive s.o. *n.f.* (*pl.* **cùcẹ-cùcẹ**) Deceit, cheating.

²cùta *n.f.* (*pl.* **cututtụkà, cùcẹ-cùcẹ**) Illness, disease.

cwai *id.* Describes sth. very sweet: *yana da zaki* ~ it is very sweet.

D

¹dà̧ *prep. and conj.* 1. With: *ya kewaye gidansa* ~ *zana* he screened off his house with *zana* mats; *ya zo* ~ *kare* he came with a dog; *ka buga shi* ~ *karfi* hit it forcefully; *ya bushe* ~ *dariya* he broke out with laughter. 2. Used in cont. tense to indicate possession: *yana* ~ *kudi* he has money; *ba shi* ~ *kome* he has nothing. 3. Used in cont. tense to form adj. phrases: *yana* ~ *nauyi* it is heavy. 4. And: *ya dauki kwari* ~ *baka* ~ *kibau* he took a quiver, a bow, and some arrows; ~ *ni* ~ *shi duk mun yarda* both he and I agree; *hamsin* ~ *biyu* fifty-two. 5. By, by means of: *na zo* ~ *kafa* I came by foot; *ya rantse* ~ *Allah* he swore by God. 6. (with time words) At, in, during: ~ *safe* in the morning; ~ *karfe uku* at three o'clock. 7. Regarding, in relation to, with respect to: *rigar ta yi kyau* ~ *shi* the gown suits him well; *masallaci yana kudu* ~ *kasuwa* the mosque is south of the market. 8. Than: *gara motsi* ~ *zama* moving about is better than sitting in one place. 9. Used in greetings with *sannu* and *barka*: *sannunka* ~ *aiki* how are you getting along? *barka* ~ *rana* good afternoon!

²dà̧ *conj.* 1. (before rel. clause) That, who, whom, which: *gangar* ~ *maroki ya kada* the drum that the musician beat; *marokin* ~ *ya kada ganga* the musician who beat the drum. 2. Used with certain conjunctions such as **bayan, tun, sai** without changing their meaning: *bayan* ~ *muka tashi* = *bayan mun tashi* after we left; *muna aiki tun* ~ *safe* = *muna aiki tun safe* we've been working since morning. 3. (used to join certain clauses) That: *na yi mamaki* ~ *ka gaya mini haka* I was surprised that you told me that. 4. When, on: ~ *ya jefe ni sai na kauce* when he threw it at me I dodged aside; ~ *zuwa kusa da gida sai dokin ya soma gudu* on arriving close to home the horse began to run. 5. Since, from the time of: *shekara hamsin ke nan* ~ *zuwansa* it has been fifty years since he first came.

³dà̧ There is, there are: ~ *jaridu?* are there any newspapers? *i,* ~ *akwai* yes, there are; *yau* ~ *rikici* today there's going to be trouble.

⁴dà̧ Required before d.o. of verbs of

the type **sąyar̃ dą̀, mai dą̀,** and with certain other verbs such as **ąmìnce** and **mânta.**

dâ *adv.* 1. Formerly, once upon a time: *mutanen* ~ people of long ago; *mutumin* ~ old-fashioned person; *zamanin* ~ in former times; *tun* ~ from earliest times. 2. Just now: ~ *abin da zan gaya maka* that is just what I was about to tell you. **~ ma** 1. Originally, already: ~ *ma na san haka za a yi* I knew beforehand that this would happen. 2. It is well known that: ~ *ma sai an sha wuya akan tuna Allah* it is always the case that one only remembers God when in trouble.

dà 1. If . . . then (past unrealized condition): ~ *ya zo* ~ *ya same mu* had he come he would have found us; ~ *na sani* if I had only known. **~ ma** would that, if only: ~ *ma na gan shi* if only I had seen it. 2. If . . . then (remote possibility): ~ *a tambaye ni* ~ *na yarda* if I were asked, I would agree.

dą̀'ą̀wa *n.f.* 1. Legal claim: *yana ~r yana da gaskiya* he is claiming he is in the right. **mai** ~ claimant, plaintiff. 2. False claim, boast: *kuɗinsa* ~ *ne* his wealth is a myth.

dabà *n.f.* Durḅar.

dąbaibą̀ye *v.t.* 1. Hobble animal's forefeet. 2. Entangle. *v.i.* Become entangled: *maganarsa ta* ~ his statement has become hopelessly entangled.

dą̀baibą̀yi *n.m.* Rope for hobbling animal's feet.

dą̀bam *adv.* Different, distinct, apart from: *ya fita* ~ *da saura* he stands out distinctly from the others; *ware shi* ~ put it aside; *aikina* ~ *da nasa* my job is different from his; *ya dasa itatuwa iri* ~ ~ he planted trees of various kinds.

dą̀bar̃à *n.f.* **(***pl.* **dą̀bàr̃u, dą̀bàr̃cę-dą̀bàr̃cę)** 1. Plan, idea, resourcefulness: ~ *ta faɗo mini* an idea occurred to me; *ba shi da* ~ he is not resourceful. 2. Scheme, device, trick: *ya yi mini* ~ he played a trick on me.

dąbàr̃ce *v.t.* Trick, cheat.

ɗabbà *n.f.* (*pl.* **ɗabbobi**) Beast, animal: **~r** *gida* domestic animal, **~r** *jeji* wild animal.

ɗabbąr̃ę̀-ɗabbąr̃ę̀ *adv.* Spotted, stained with spots.

dab dą̀ *prep.* Very close to, near to, right against: *gidansa yana nan* ~ *titi* his house is very close to the street; ~ *zuwanka ya tafi* he went off just before you arrived. **~ dab** right next to each other.

dabgąja *n.m.* 1. Damaged kolanut. 2. Person with mouth messy from eating kolanut.

dàbge *n.m.* Stew made with a lot of meat. **shan** ~ luxurious living.

dąbinò *n.m.* (*f.* **dąbinų̀wa,** *pl.* **dą̀bìnai**) Date palm, date.

[1]**dąbò** *n.m.* Child's first attempts at standing.

[2]**dąbò** *n.m.* Trick, magic, sleight of hand.

dabùr̃ce *v.i.* Be confused.

dabùr̃ta *v.t.* Confuse.

daɓà *v.t.* 1. Stab, wound: *ya* ~ *masa wuka* he stabbed him with a knife. 2. Do or apply a lot of: *ta* ~ *shuni a ka* she put a lot of indigo on her head.

dąɓą-dąɓą *id.* In large numbers: *sun yi* ~ a lot of them (pimples, ants, etc.) have appeared.

dą̀ɓàs *id.* Sitting heavily, firmly.

dąɓè *v.t.* Beat on earth to make a floor. **dą̀ɓe** *n.m.* Floor.

daɓų̀ri *n.m.* (*pl.* **daɓųrà**) Mouth or gums of cow.

dàce *n.m.* Coincidence, stroke of luck: *sun yi* ~ they met by chance.

dacè *v.i.* 1. Be appropriate, suitable, proper: *wandon ya* ~ *da rigar* the trousers match the gown; *abin da ka yi bai* ~ *ba* what you did was not proper. 2. Prosper: *wane ya* ~ so and so is successful.

dadą̀ra *v.t.* (with i.o.) Cut with a blunt knife or edge.

dàddąrę *adv.* (with **dą̀**) At night.

dàddąwa *n.f.* Black locust-bean cakes.

dąɗà *v.t.* (*vn.* **dąɗì**) 1. Add, increase: *ya* ~ *wayo* he has become wiser. 2. Repeat, do sth. again: *ya* ~ *gaya mata* he told her again.

dą̀ɗai *adv.* Ever, always, (with neg.)

never: *yana ta kallonmu kamar* ~ *bai taɓa ganinmu ba* he was looking at us as if he had never seen us before.

ɗạɗè *v.i.* Be or last long: *ya tafi ya* ~ he went and stayed away for a long time; *na* ~ *ina aiki a nan* I have been working here for a long time.

daɗi *n.m.* Pleasantness, enjoyment: *na ji* ~*nsa* I enjoyed it; *magana mai* ~*n ji* pleasant talk; *cin* ~ *gare shi* he's used to luxury.

dạfà *v.t.* Cook.

dafà *v.t.* 1. Lean on or press with hand: *ya* ~ *mini tsani* he leaned on the ladder to steady it for me. 2. Favour or support s.o.

dạ̀fạ̀-dụkạ̀ *n.m.* Jollof rice.

[1]**daffọ̀** *n.m.* Depot, warehouse.

[2]**daffọ̀** *n.m.* Basic training period for recruits.

dạfì *n.m.* Poison.

dàfifi *n.m.* Large mass, large numbers of sth.: *sojoji sun yi* ~ *a bayan birni* a large number of soldiers have gathered outside the city walls.

dafkà *v.t.* (with i.o.) Apply profusely: *an* ~ *masa kaya* he has been heavily laden.

daftạ̀r̃i *n.m.* (*pl.* **dàftạ̀r̃ai**) Register, ledger: ~*n haraji* tax register book.

dạ̀gạ̀ *prep.* 1. From: ~ *nan zuwa can* from here to there; ~ *yau* from now on, henceforth. 2. By, at: *ya sa shi* ~ *ƙofa* he put it by the door. 3. After, beyond: ~ *nan sai ya mutu* after that he died; ~ *baya* afterwards; ~ *ni sai kai* after me then you.

dạga *n.f.* (*pl.* **dạgàge**) Bangle-charm.

daga *n.f.* Struggle, fight: *an sha* ~ *da shi kafin a kawo shi* it was a struggle to bring him in. ***ja*** ~ prepare for battle. ***bakin*** ~ front line of battle.

dạgạcì *n.m.* (*pl.* **dạ̀gạ̀tai**) Village head.

dạgar̃gạ̀za *v.t.* Crush, destroy: *kura ta* ~ *kan 'yar akuya* the hyena has crushed the head of the young goat.

dagè *v.i.* 1. Strive: *ya* ~ *ya nome gonarsa* he worked hard to hoe his farm. 2. Be obstinate: *ya* ~ *ya ƙi zuwa* he stubbornly refused to come.

dàgi *n.m.* (*pl.* **dagụnà**) 1. Paw of cat or dog. 2. Heraldic design, emblem. 3. Insignia, trade-mark.

dagì *n.m.* (*pl.* **dagogi**) Digging rod.

dạ̀gọ-dạ̀gọ *n.m.* Left-over food.

dagụ̀la *v.t.* Spoil, disturb, upset: *yara sun* ~ *abinci* the children have messed up the food; *ya* ~ *masa rai* he upset him greatly. **dàgụlạ̀** *v.i.* Be spoiled, disturbed.

dagụ̀mi *n.m.* (*pl.* **dagummà**) Man's leather charm worn on upper arm.

dạ̀gwạlò *n.m.* Used-up indigo dye.

dạgwalgwạ̀la *v.t.* Soil food or water.

dạ̀gwàlgwạ̀lo *n.m.* Food or water in a dirty condition.

dahìr̃ *n.m.* Reality, truth: *wannan* ~ *ne* this is definitely so.

dai *prt.* Used to soften abruptness of statement: *ni* ~ *ba na so* I don't happen to like it; *amma* ~ *ba ka kyauta masa ba* but it seems that you haven't been kind to him; *kada* ~ *ka manta* try not to forget it.

daidai *adv.* Correctly, exactly: *ƙarfe goma* ~ ten o'clock precisely; *rigarka ta yi* ~ *da kai* the gown suits you well; *takalmin ya yi masa* ~ the shoes fit him exactly. ~ ***wa daida*** exactly. *prep.* Corresponding to, level with: *albashinsa* ~ *aikinsa* his salary corresponds with his work; ~ *gidansa* right by his house.

dàidaità (cị/ce) *v.t.* 1. Aim at, go straight to. 2. Make sth. coincide with: *mu daidaici lokacin da zai ɗauki albashi mu kai masa kayan* let's take him the goods just at the time that he gets his salary. **daidàita** *v.t.* Make exact, straighten, put right: *ya* ~ *shi* he adjusted it properly. **dàidaitạ̀** *v.i.* Be symmetrical, lined up: *sahu ya* ~ the people are lined up evenly; *sun* ~ *da juna* they have come to an agreement.

daimòn *n.m.* Diamond.

dainà *v.t.* Stop doing, cease:

agogona ya ~ *aiki* my watch doesn't work any more; *ya* ~ *shan taba* he's given up smoking.

da'ɉɍa *n.f.* (*pl.* **da'ɉɍoɍi**) Circle: *sun yi* ~ they have formed a circle.

dajè *v.t.* (*vn.f.* **dajɉya**) Trim or reinforce edges of mat or cloth: *an* ~ *tabarma da ja* the mat has been trimmed in red.

daji *n.m.* (*pl.* **dazuzzụkà**) Bush, uninhabited country, forest. ***ciwon*** ~, ***harbin*** ~ skin disease affecting cattle. ***tashar*** ~ rumour.

dàjɉne *n.m.* Wiping one's nose with back of hand.

dạkà *v.t.* 1. Pound (grain). 2. Beat person or thing: *ya* ~ *ƙofa* he knocked at the door. ***kada ka*** ~ ***tawa*** don't imitate me! ~ ***tsalle*** leap. ***namijin*** ~ well-pounded spicy condiments.

dạ̀kạ̀li *n.m.* Low mud platform outside compound.

dàkarè *n.m.* (*pl.* **dàkàru**) 1. Foot-soldier. 2. Hard worker.

dàkạtà (cɉ/ce) *v.t.* (*vn.* **dakò**) Wait for: *na dakaci zuwansu* I waited for their arrival. **dakạ̀ta** *v.i.* Wait, pause.

dạ̀kau *n.m.* Pounding corn for pay.

dạki-dạki *adv.* In order, item by item, evenly: *sun jeru* ~ they are lined up evenly.

dạko *n.m.* Carrying load for payment. ***ɗan*** ~ porter.

dakụ̀sa *v.t.* Make sth. dull, blunt.

dakụ̀she *v.i.* 1. Become dull, blunt. 2. Lose sharpness (of intelligence, good looks, etc.): *kyansa ya* ~ he has lost his good looks.

dạƙau *id.* Hard and dry: *fadamar ta yi* ~ *saboda rashin ruwa* the swamp is hard and dry due to lack of rain.

dạ̀ƙiƙà *n.f.* (*pl.* **dạƙiƙoƙi**) Second (of time).

dạ̀ƙiƙi *n. and adj.* (*f.* **dạ̀ƙiƙɉya**, *pl.* **dạ̀ƙiƙai**) Stupid, dull.

daƙụ̀na *v.t.* Mess up or dirty sth. by handling: *kada ka* ~ *mini rigata* don't mess up my gown. **dàƙụnạ̀** *v.i.* Become soiled, messed up.

[1]**dạƙụwà** *n.f.* Sweets made from ground tigernuts or groundnuts.

[2]**dạƙụwà** *n.f.* Insulting gesture made by spreading the fingers upwards.

dạƙwa-dạ̀ƙwà *pl.* of **danƙwạlelè.**

dạƙwalwa *n.f.* (*pl.* **dạƙwàle**) 1. Large laying-hen. 2. Beautiful girl with mature figure.

dạlà *n.f.* (*pl.* **dạloli**) 1. Two-shilling piece in old Nigerian currency. 2. Maria Theresa dollar. 3. Five-franc piece in old French currency.

dạ̀lạ̀ki *n.m.* Sediment of dyepit or of gruel.

dạ̀lạ̀lạ̀ *id.* Indicates sth. very slimy or viscous.

dạ̀lalạ̀ *v.i.* Dribble (of saliva).

dạ̀lili *n.m.* (*pl.* **dạ̀lilai**) Cause, reason, excuse: *ina* ~? what's the reason? ***neman*** ~ picking a quarrel.

dalla-dalla *adv.* Clearly, in an orderly manner: *ya gaya mini labarin* ~ he told me the story clearly.

dallạ̀ɍa *v.t.* Dazzle with bright light: *ya* ~ *mini tocilan* he dazzled me with the torch.

dalụma *n.f.* Plump woman.

dam *id.* Squarely, firmly: *ya zauna* ~ he sat down squarely.

dàma (ɉ/e) *v.t.* (*vn.* **damù**) Worry, bother: *ba abin da ya dame shi* nothing bothers him.

damà *v.t.* 1. Mix sth. solid into a liquid. 2. Mix up, confuse: *ya* ~ *magana* he has confused the matter.

damạ *n.f.* Right-hand side, direction: ~ *da hauni* right and left. ***da*** ~ with the right hand, on the right-hand side. ***kwanta*** ~ die, pass away.

dama *n.f.* 1. Chance, opportunity, possibility: *ban sami* ~*r zuwa ba* I didn't get a chance to come; *in ka ga* ~ if you want to. 2. Equal, sth. comparable: *ba ka da* ~ you're great! *abin nan ba* ~ there's nothing like it. 3. Improvement: *ya yi* ~ he is feeling better. 4. (with **dạ**) Quite a lot, many: *mutane da* ~ *suna goyon bayansa* quite a lot of people support him.

damạ-damạ *adv.* In moderate quantity, fairly good.

dàmąna *see* **dàmįna.**
dàmàtsiri *n.m.* Small poisonous green snake.
dàmbàr̃wa *n.f.* Rowdy quarrelling.
dambę *n.m.* Boxing. ***ɗan*** ~ boxer.
dambu *n.m.* Food made of flour, onions, and hemp leaves cooked together.
damè *v.i.* Be mixed up, confused.
dàmfąmi *n.m.* Temporary grass fence.
dàmfąrà (į/e) *v.t.* Cheat, trick.
damfą̀ra *v.t.* 1. Compress, stuff: *ta* ~ *tufafinta a tukunya* she stuffed her clothes into the pot. 2. (with i.o.) Apply or do profusely: *an* ~ *wa mota kaya* the car has been heavily loaded.
dąmi *n.m.* (*pl.* **dą̀mmai, dâmma**) Bundle of grain.
dàmįna *n.f.* The rainy season: ~ *ta faɗi* the rainy season has set in. ~ ***biyu*** quick-growing crop (e.g. beans, maize) of which two harvests can be had in one season. ~ ***kusa*** boiled dried groundnuts.
dàmįsà *n.m. or f.* (*pl.* **damįsoshi, dàmįsu**) Leopard.
dąmo *n.m.* Land-monitor (lizard).
damtsè *n.m.* (*pl.* **dąmàtsa**) Forearm.
dàmų *v.i.* 1. Be fully mixed. 2. Be worried.
damų̀ƙa *v.t.* Clutch with both hands.
dàmųna *see* **dàmįna.**
dàndą *n.m.* Piebald horse.
dandą̀li *n.m.* Central open space in village or town.
dandąmą̀li *n.m.* Raised doorstep.
dandan *id.* Firmly: *ƙofar ta dannu* ~ the door is firmly closed.
dandąɓas *id.* Squatness, dumpiness.
dàndąɓą̀sa *n.f.* (*pl.* **dàndą̀ɓą̀sai**) Squat but well-built girl.
dandą̀ƙa *v.t.* 1. Pound and crush sth. on stone or log: *ta* ~ *kanwa a kan dutse* she pounded the potash on the stone. 2. Mistreat, beat s.o.
dandą̀ƙe *v.t.* Castrate (bull or goat).
dàndį *n.m.* Roaming about leading a loose, carefree life. ***ɗan*** ~ vagabond.
danga *n.f.* (*pl.* **dangogi**) Cornstalk fence.
dangą̀ce *v.t.* Make fence around farm or house.
dàngąną̀ *v.i.* Resign oneself to, depend heavily on: *kada ka* ~ *ga kowa banda Allah* do not depend on anyone except God. **dàngąnà** *n.f.* Resignation: *ya ɗauki* ~ he resigned himself to his fate.
dangą̀na *v.t.* 1. Pledge or pawn sth. 2. Lean, prop, put against: *ya* ~ *tsani da bango* he propped the ladder against the wall; *sun* ~ *mana nauyin aiki* they pushed the responsibility of the work onto us. *v.i.* Extend to, travel up to: *ya* ~ *daga nan har Alkahira* he travelled from here as far as Cairo.
dangąnę̀ dą̀ *prep.* Regarding, relating to: *gwamnati ta kafa doka* ~ *shan ƙwaya* the government has issued a decree regarding the use of drugs.
dàngantà (cį/ce) *v.t.* Be related to, comparable to: *abin da ya yi ya danganci hauka* what he did was close to madness. **dangànta** *v.t.* Associate, relate: *bai kamata a* ~ *wali da aikin assha ba* a saint should not be associated with misdeeds. **dàngantą̀** *v.i.* (with **dą̀**) Depend on, be related to: *zuwana ya* ~ *da samun mota a kan lokaci* my coming depends on my getting a car on time.
dàngàntąkà *n.f.* Relationship.
dangi *n.m.* (*pl.* **dangogi**) Kin, family relation(s), relative(s): *shi ɗan* ~ *ne* he has a lot of relatives.
danjà *n.f.* (*pl.* **danjoji**) 1. Danger. 2. Red danger signal. 3. Tail-lights of car, bicycle, etc.: ~*r motarsa ba ta kamawa* the tail-lights of his car don't work.
dànkąli *n.m.* Potato(es). ~***n turawa*** Irish potato.
danki *n.m.* Display of articles of adornment (decorated calabashes, enamelware, etc.) in a bride's room.
dànƙa (į/e) *v.t.* Grasp with hand, clasp: *ya danƙi ƙeyarsa* he grabbed him by the nape of the neck.
danƙà *v.t.* Hand over, entrust:

ya ~ fayiloli a hannuna he handed the files over to me.

danƙąre *v.t.* Compress, put tightly together.

danƙàrį *excl.* What a huge lot (of packed material)!: *~! motar nan ta ɗauko kaya* wow! this car has brought a large amount of goods.

danƙì *n.m.* Handful.

danƙò *n.m.* 1. Gum, rubber. 2. Stickiness. 3. Sth. long-lasting: *aurensu ya yi ~* their marriage has lasted a long time. 4. Sling (for throwing stones).

danƙwąlelè *n. and adj.* (*f.* **danƙwąleląya**, *pl.* **danƙwal-dànƙwàl, dąƙwa-dąƙwà**) Large and round.

dannà *v.t.* Press down, compress.

dànni *see* **dàr̃ni.**

danshi *n.m.* Dampness, moisture.

dąrà *n.f.* Game like draughts, Ludo game. ***mai gidan*** *~* sth. having coloured squares (e.g. cloth).

dąr̃ąjà *n.f.* (*pl.* **dąr̃ąjoji**) 1. Worth, value. 2. Respect. 3. Rank, standing, nobility.

dąr̃am *id.* Stable, firm: *bangon na nan tsaye ~* the wall is perfectly stable.

dąr̃ąsi *n.m.* (*pl.* **dąr̃ussà**) Lesson.

dąre *n.m.* (*pl.* **dąràre**) 1. Night: *~ ya yi* it is night-time. 2. Eve, the evening before: *~n Jumma'a* Thursday night. **dąrę** *adv.* (with **dą**) At night: *sukan fita da ~* they usually go out at night.

darè *v.i.* Crumble, fall apart, crack (esp. of earthen pot).

dąr̃ektà *n.m.* (*pl.* **dąr̃ektoci**) Director.

dàrįya *n.f.* Laughter, laugh: *ya kece da ~* he burst out laughing.

[1]**darjè** *v.t.* Choose the best from a number of things: *ya ~ mata* he has chosen a very good wife.

[2]**darjè** *v.t.* Graze oneself by falling or sliding: *ya ~ kafarsa a kan dutse* he grazed his leg sliding off the rock.

dar̃mà *n.f.* Lead, tin.

dàr̃ni *n.m.* (*pl.* **dar̃nųkà**) Cornstalk fence.

dąsà *v.t.* (*vn.* **dąshì**) Transplant, plant out seedlings.

dasąshi *n.m.* Gums.

dąshe *n.m.* (*pl.* **dąshę-dąshę**) Young plants for transplanting.

dashì *n.m.* 'Dash', small gift of money.

daskąre *v.i.* Solidify, coagulate.

dątsa (į/e) *v.t.* Intercept (person), block (road), dam up (water).

datsà *v.t.* Chop or cut up into pieces (wood or grass).

dątsįya *n.f.* Damming or cutting off flow of water.

dattakǫ̀ *n.m.* Gentlemanliness, respectability.

dàttį *n.m.* Dirt, filth.

dattijǫ̀ *n.m.* (*f.* **dattijįya,** *pl.* **dàttàwa, dàttijai**) Gentleman, an elder, respected person, a mature person.

dàudąwa *see* **dàddąwa.**

daudų̀ *n.m.* Used in *ɗan ~* a man who behaves like a woman.

dauɗà *n.f.* Dirt, filth.

daujè *v.t. and v.i.* Graze (skin).

daulà *n.f.* (*pl.* **dauloli**) 1. Wealth, abundance. 2. Kingdom, empire.

daurą dą *prep.* Right beside: *ya ɗaga hannunsa ~ kunnuwansa* he raised his hands up close to his ears.

daurè *v.i.* Endure hardship patiently.

dàuri *n.m.* Olden times

dauri *n.m.* Herbal concoction used as tonic, esp. for children.

daurįya *n.f.* Ability to endure hardship or pain.

dàuro *n.m.* Type of millet.

dausąyi *n.m.* Well-watered pastureland.

daushe *n.m.* Last year's kolanuts after new crop has come. ***hawan*** *~* short ride by chief and followers on second day of Sallah festival.

dąwą *n.m.* The bush, woods.

dawà *n.f.* Guinea-corn.

dàwaiwainįya *n.f.* Going back and forth aimlessly.

dąwaki *pl.* of **dokì.**

dàwąra *n.f.* Going around in a circle.

dąwò *n.m.* (*pl.* **dąwâyya**) Ball o *fura* without milk.

dawo *v.i.* Come back, return here.

dawwąma *v.t.* 1. Make permanent, everlasting. 2. Entrust: *na ~*

kuɗin a hannunsa I entrusted the money to him. **dàwwąmą̀** *v.i.* Last forever. ***gidan*** **~** Paradise.

dazà *v.t.* Trim or reinforce edge of sth.

dazuzzųkà *pl.* of **dajì.**

denà *see* **dainà.**

dìddįga *n.f.* Remaining particles, crumbs, dregs.

diddįge *v.i.* Become old, worn out, ragged.

diddįgè *n.m.* (*pl.* **dįgàdįgai**) Heel.

diddįgi *n.m.* Used in *bin* ~ tracing sth. back to its origin, finding the cause of sth.

dįdìmnįya *n.f.* Sound of feet on roof.

dįgà *n.f.* (*pl.* **dįgogi**) Pickaxe.

dįgàdįgai *pl.* of **diddįgè.**

dįgir̃gir̃ *id.* Very short.

dįgįr̃ì *n.m.* (*pl.* **dįgįr̃or̃i**) University degree.

dįla *n.m.* (*pl.* **dįloli**) Jackal.

dilà *see* **ądilà.**

dìllalì *n.m.* (*f.* **dìllalįya,** *pl.* **dìllàlai**) Broker.

dîm *n.m.* Low-beam headlight.

dįmǫkų̀rą̀ɗiyyà *n.f.* Democracy.

dįnà *n.f.* Dinner party.

dinar̃ì *n.m.* (*pl.* **dìnàr̃ai**) Gold coin.

dìndįkwą̀lǫ̀ *n.m.* Small pieces of yam or sweet potato fried in oil.

dìndįmi *n.m.* 1. Night-blindness. 2. Shyness, inexperience: *bako yana da* ~ a stranger always feels awkward.

dindìndin *adv.* Perpetually, forever.

dingà *v.t.* Keep on doing: *ya* ~ *kokari* he kept on trying.

dìntsa (į/e) *v.t.* Take out handful of sth.

dintsì *n.m.* Handful.

dinya *n.f.* Goose.

di'ò *n.m.* (*pl.* **di'ò-di'ò**) D.O. (District Officer).

dįrą *v.i.* Leap down, swoop down.

dįr̃ebą̀ *n.m.* (*pl.* **dįr̃ebobi**) Driver.

dįri *n.m.* Sound of voices or movement.

dįr̃ì *n.m.* Erect posture.

dir̃kà *n.f.* (*pl.* **dir̃koki**) Thick pole with a forked end.

dìrkakà (į/e) *v.t.* Approach with determination: *mun dirkaki aiki* we attacked the work with zeal.

Dįsambà *n.m.* December.

dìsfensà *n.m.* (*pl.* **disfensoshi**) Dispensary attendant.

diwanì *n.m.* (*pl.* **dìwànai**) 1. Register, account book. 2. Anthology.

diyyà *n.f.* 1. Compensation payable for accidental homicide or injury. 2. War indemnity.

dodą̀na *v.t.* Touch lightly with end of sth. long.

dòdo *n.m.* (*f.* **dòdannįya,** *pl.* **dòdànni**) 1. Monster, goblin, evil spirit. 2. Any object inspiring fear.

dodò *n.m.* Forming a line, column.

dòdòrįdò *n.m.* Showing off, attempting to impress or intimidate.

doɗè *v.t.* Stop up mouth or hole.

dogą̀ra *v.t.* Lean on sth. for support while standing or walking. **dògąrą̀** *v.i.* Lean on, depend on, rely on: *ta* ~ *ga Audu* she relied on Audu. **dògąrà** *n.f.* Ability to withstand hardship: *Allah ya nufe shi da* ~ *da abin da ya samu* God has given him the patience to be content with what he has.

dògąrì *n.m.* (*pl.* **dògą̀rai, dogąrawa**) Emir's bodyguard.

dogo *n. and adj.* (*f.* **dogųwa,** *pl.* **dogàye**) Tall, long. *n.m.* Railroad tracks: *jirgi ya goce daga kan* ~ the train jumped off the tracks.

[1]**dòka (į/e)** *v.t.* (*vn.* **dukà**) Beat, hit, thrash.

[2]**dòka** *n.f.* (*pl.* **dokoki**) Rule, law, order. ***ɗan*** **~** Local Authority policeman. ***shirin*** **~** legislative bill.

[1]**dokà** *n.m.* Large tree with shiny leaves, white flowers, and large flat pods.

[2]**dokà** *n.f.* Pad used in women's hairdressing.

dokì *n.m.* (*f.* **godįya,** *pl.* **dąwaki**) Horse. ***~n zage*** saddled horse led by s.o. for use as a spare by a travelling chief.

dokìn Allàh *n.m.* Praying mantis.

dokìn cacą *n.m.* Gambling cowrie, dice.

dokìn ƙofà *n.m.* Raised doorstep.

dokin ryuwa *n.m.* Channel carrying water from irrigation pole.
dokin wyuyà *n.m.* Nape of neck.
dolę̀ Must, necessarily: ~ *mu je mu gaishe shi* we must go to greet him; *ya zama* ~ *ne* it has become necessary; *na* ~ compulsory.
dolo *n.m.* (*f.* **dolywa,** *pl.* **dolàye**) Fool.
dòmin, don *conj.* Because, in order that: *ina jira ne* ~ *in karɓi albashina* I'm waiting in order to get my salary. ~ ***kada*** lest: *na gudu* ~ *kada a gan ni* I ran away lest I be seen. *prep.* Because of, for the sake of, on behalf of: *ina yin wannan* ~*ku* I'm doing this for your sake.
don mè *inter. adv.* Why? What for?
dòrina *n.f.* 1. Hippopotamus. 2. Whip made from hippo hide.
doro *n.m.* 1. Convexity. 2. Being round-shouldered.
dòsa (shi/she) *v.t.* Set out for, face, approach.
dosà *v.t.* Keep on doing.
dòshirò *n.m.* Simpleton, dullard.
doyà *n.f.* Yam(s).
dozin *n.m.* Dozen.
du *see* **duk.**
dy̨'a'i *n.m.* Invocatory prayer, wish.
dùba (i/e) *v.t.* (*vn.* **duba**) 1. Look at, gaze at. 2. Face: *ka dubi gabas sosai in za ka yi salla* face directly eastwards when you pray. **dubà** *v.t.* 1. Visit, look in on sick person. 2. Inspect. 3. Look, look at. 4. Search for, look for. 5. Pay attention to.
duba *n.m.* 1. Fortune-telling. ***malamin*** ~ fortune-teller, sorcerer. 2. *vn.* of **dùba.**
dùbągàri *n.m.* Sanitary inspector.
dybu *n.f. and adj.* (*pl.* **dùbbai**) 1. One thousand. 2. Thousands, many: ~*n gaisuwa* many greetings; *soja dubbai* thousands of soldiers.
dybỳr̃a *n.f.* (*pl.* **dybyr̃or̃i, dybur̃r̃à**) Anus.
du-dù-du *adv.* All in all, at the moment: ~ *ba mu fi awa uku muna aiki ba* all in all we haven't worked more than three hours.
dỳgùnzymą̀ *v.i.* Become emotionally upset, confused.
dygur̃gỳje *v.i.* Be crushed into tiny pieces, disintegrate.
dỳgỳzùm *id.* 1. Thick, unkempt (of hair). 2. Ragged.
dyhù *n.m.* 1. Darkness, dark colour. 2. Shadow, silhouette. 3. Denseness (of forest), closeness (of weave). 4. Ignorance, lack of awareness: *ya shige mini* ~ I'm not clear about the matter.
dyhùnta *v.t.* Darken.
dyhywà *n.f.* (*pl.* **dyhywoyi**) Thickly wooded place in open country.
duk, dykà *adj.* 1. Every, all: ~ *mutum* = *mutum* ~ everyone; ~ *mutane* = *mutane* ~ all the people; ~ *biyar* all five (of them). 2. Every, any, ever (when followed by rel. clause): ~ *inda ya tafi* wherever he went; ~ *wanda ya ba mu* whoever gives it to us. *adv.* Entirely, completely: ~ *ya ɓata mini lokaci* he completely wasted my time. *pro.* 1. All: *sun ba shi* ~ they gave it all to him. 2. The whole, entirety: *dukan jama'a sun goyi bayan gwamnati* the entire population supported the government. ~ ***ɗaya ne*** it's all the same, it doesn't matter. ***duk da haka*** nevertheless. **duk dą̀** *prep.* In spite of, despite: *duk da faɗan da na yi masa bai bari ba* in spite of the quarrel I had with him, he didn't stop it.
dukà *n.m.* Punch, blow. 2. *vn.* of **dòka.**
dukanci *n.m.* Leather-working.
dùkàwa *pl.* of **bą̀dukù.**
dukiya *n.f.* (*pl.* **dukiyoyi**) Wealth, riches, property.
dukkà *see* **duk.**
dyky-dyky *adv.* Very early dawn.
duƙà *v.i.* 1. Stoop, bend down. 2. Be determined: *sun* ~ *sai dai sun gama aiki* they were determined to finish the work.
dỳƙyfą̀ *v.i.* Do with great determination.
dyƙunƙỳne *v.i.* Be crumpled, dirty.
dyƙus *id.* Very short.
dỳƙyshi *n.m.* (*f.* **dỳƙysa,** *pl.* **dỳƙỳsai**) Colt, foal

dùlmụyạ̀ *v.i.* Sink deep into sth. (water, affair, studies, etc.).
dụmà *v.t.* 1. Put mouth deeply into sth.: *akuya ta ~ bakinta a cikin hatsi* the goat put its mouth deep into the grain. 2. (with i.o.) Strike s.o. with sth.
dụma *n.m.* Gourd, pumpkin.
dùmbụzà (jị/je) *v.t.* Take by the handful or mouthful (kolanuts, grain, coins, etc.).
dumɓu *n.m.* (*pl.* **dumɓàye**) Any worn-out tool.
dùmfarà (ị/e) *v.t.* Approach directly.
dụmu-dụ̀mù *id.* 1. Being messy. 2. Red-handed: *an sami ɓarawo ~ da kayan sata* the thief was caught red-handed with stolen goods.
dunà *n.m.* Very black person or thing.
dùndu *n.m.* Punch or thump on back.
dùndufà *n.f.* Long, narrow drum.
dùndụmi *see* **dìndịmi.**
dundunịya *n.f.* (*pl.* **dundunịyoyi**) Heel.
dundụ̀rusù *n.m.* (*pl.* **dùndụ̀rùsai**) Large adze.
dunɗè *v.i.* Used in *gari ya ~* the sky is overcast.
dùngu *n.m.* (*pl.* **dungụnà**) 1. Stump of maimed arm. 2. Stub of receipt, cheque-book.
dùngụrà (ị/e) *v.t.* Bump into.
dunịyà *n.f.* The world. ***shiga ~*** leave one's home to see the world. ***~ ta yi daɗi*** all's right with the world. ***ɗan ~*** profligate person. ***sha ~*** be well travelled.
dunƙụ̀la *v.t.* 1. Knead into balls. 2. Clench (fist).
dunu *n.m.* Used in *na ci ~nsa* I seized him round the waist (in wrestling).
dur̃gu *n.m.* (*f.* **dur̃gụwa**, *pl.* **dur̃gwàye**) Short-legged person, bird, or animal.
durƙụ̀sa *v.i.* (*vn.* **dùrƙụso**) Kneel down.
[1]**dụ̀r̃ô** *n.m.* Petrol or kerosene drum.
[2]**dụ̀r̃ô** *n.m.* Draw in a game.
dụr̃obạ̀ *n.m.* (*pl.* **dụr̃obobi**) Prison warder.
dụrụ̀mi *n.m.* (*pl.* **dụrụmà**) A fig tree.
dùsa *n.m.* 1. Bran. 2. Metal filings.
dusạ̀ *n.m.* Spades (suit in playing cards).
dụshè *v.i.* Become dim, dark, faded.
dụshị-dụshị *adv.* 1. Almost blind. 2. Barely visible.
duskụ̀re *v.i.* Become blunt.
dutsè *n.m.* (*pl.* **dụwàtsu**) 1. Stone, mountain, hill. 2. Flint, grindstone.

'D

ɗa *n.m.* (*f.* **'ya**, *pl.* **'ya'ya**) 1. Son, daughter: *ni ~nsa ne* I am his son; *Kande 'yar Talatu ce* Kande is Talatu's daughter. 2. Free-born or freed person. 3. Well-bred person. 4. Fruit: *'ya'yan itace* fruit of tree.
ɗa'à *n.f.* Etiquette: *yana da ~* he is well-bred.
ɗabbạ̀'a *v.t.* (*vn.* **ɗab'ì**) Print, publish.
ɗạ̀bi'à *n.f.* (*pl.* **ɗạ̀bi'u**) Behaviour, custom, trait, character: *muguwar ~* bad habit.
ɗaci *n.m.* Bitterness, bitter taste: *gaskiya ~ gare ta* truth is bitter. ***mai ~n rai*** one with an unpleasant disposition.
ɗaɗà *v.t.* (with i.o.) 1. Strike a blow: *ta ~ masa mari* she slapped him. 2. Set fire to sth.: *ya ~ wa jinka wuta* he set fire to the thatch.
ɗaɗạ̀r̃a *v.t.* (with i.o.) Brand with fire: *an ~ wa saniya wuta* the cow has been branded.
ɗâɗɗoyà *n.f.* A fragrant herb.
ɗạfà *v.t.* 1. Stick onto: *ya ~ takarda jikin bango* he stuck the

piece of paper on the wall. 2. (with i.o.) Accuse s.o. falsely of sth.: *ya ~ masa sata* he accused him of theft.

ɗa̧fè *v.t.* (usu. with i.o.) Stick close or cling to: *jinjiri ya ~ mata* the baby stayed close to her and wouldn't leave her; *biri ya ~ a reshe* the monkey clung to the branch.

ɗà̧ga, ɗà̧gawà̧ *n.f.* Arrogance.

ɗa̧gà̧ *v.t.* 1. Raise, lift: *ta ~ muryarta* she raised her voice. *~ kai* put on airs. 2. Postpone: *an ~ bikin* the celebration has been postponed. *v.i.* 1. Rise, become higher (moon, price, crops, etc.). 2. Set off, leave, go away: *ba zan ~ daga nan ba sai ka biya* I won't budge from this place until you pay me.

ɗa̧gȩ *n.m.* Standing on tiptoe: *sai da ya yi ~ sa'an nan ya hango su* he didn't see them until he stood on his toes.

ɗa̧gè *v.t.* Raise up: *ya ~ ƙafa* he lifted his (sore) foot off the ground. *v.i.* Shrink, become short: *rigarsa ta ~* his gown shrank.

ɗà̧gogo̧ *adv.* In a shaky, uncertain position: *kujera tana ~* the chair is shaky.

ɗa̧gwas *id.* Well-formed, symmetrical: *yarinya ce 'yar ~ da ita* she is a small well-built girl.

ɗai-ɗai *adv.* One by one, separately, singly, one after another: *an yi ~ da takardun* the papers have been scattered one by one; *sun shigo ~ da ~* they came in one after the other.

ɗaiɗàita *v.t.* Scatter, spread. **ɗàiɗaità̧** *v.i.* Become scattered, spread.

ɗa̧kà̧ *adv.* In the room: *kullum yana ~ ba ya fita* he is always inside and never goes out.

ɗakì *n.m.* (*pl.* **ɗaky̧nà**) Room, hut. *mai ~* woman of the house, wife.

ɗalįbi *n.m.* (*f.* **ɗalįba,** *pl.* **ɗàlįbai**) Student at secondary school or university.

ɗà̧ma̧rà *n.f.* (*pl.* **ɗà̧mà̧ru**) 1. Belt. *ja ~* screw up one's courage. 2. Act of tying sth. around waist. 3. Tail side of a coin.

ɗàmba *n.f.* 1. Bog. 2. Deception.

ɗamè *v.t.* Tighten, straighten, make taut: *ya ~ baka* he pulled the bow taut.

[1]ɗan *gen.* of **ɗa.**

[2]ɗan *n.m.* (*f.* **'yar̃,** *pl.* **'yan**) 1. Used to indicate a person's origin: *~ arewa* northerner; *~ Fulani* person of Fulani descent; *'yar Kano* Kano woman; *'yan ƙasa a Nijeriya* Nigerian citizens. 2. Used to indicate a person's profession or activity: *~ kallo* spectator; *~ kasuwa* market trader; *'yan kwangila* contractors.

[3]ɗan *adj.* (*f.* **'yar̃,** *pl.* **'yan**) Used to form diminutive of noun: *~ yaro* little boy; *'yar akuya* young goat; *mai ~ nauyi* sth. slightly heavy; *wasu 'yan kaya* a few small things. *adv.* A little bit: *ka ~ dakata* wait a little while; *na ~ taɓa aiki* I worked just a little bit; *muna ~ hutawa* we're taking a little rest.

ɗa̧nà *v.t.* Set, adjust, cock (trigger, bow, etc.): *an ~ tarko* the trap has been set; *kunama ta ~ harbi* the scorpion raised its stinger.

ɗanà *v.t.* 1. Borrow sth. for temporary use: *na ~ sabon keken Sule* I borrowed Sule's new bicycle. 2. (with i.o.) Apply sth. to: *kunama ta ~ mini harbi* the scorpion stung me.

ɗan Ą̇dàm *n.m.* (*pl.* **'yan Ą̇dàm**) Human being.

ɗanɗà̧na *v.t.* Taste, experience: *ya ~ talauci* he experienced poverty.

ɗàngà̧r̃a̧fai *n.pl.* Elevated wooden shoes used during rainy season.

[1]ɗanì *n.m.* Borrowing or using sth. temporarily: *don Allah ka ba ni ~n kekenka* can I use your bike for a while? *mai mota ya ba mu ~* the motorist gave us a lift.

[2]ɗanì *n.m.* Measurement of distance from tip of thumb to outstretched middle finger.

ɗànkà̧ɗa̧ɓi *n.m.* 1. Crab-lice. 2. Plant with prickly burrs.

ɗankwali *n.m.* Square nylon kerchief, head-tie.

ɗan'y̧wa *n.m.* (*f.* **'yar̃'y̧wa,** *pl.*

'yan'ụwa) 1. Brother, cousin, relative. 2. The second of a pair of things: *kawo mini* ~*n takalmin nan* bring me the other shoe of this pair.

ɗan wake *n.m.* Small dumplings made of bean flour and cooked in water.

ɗanye *n. and adj.* (*f.* **ɗanya,** *pl.* **ɗànyu**) 1. Raw, fresh, unripe. 2. Inexperienced.

ɗar̃-ɗar̃ *id.* Palpitating.

ɗạrà *v.t.* Exceed slightly: *ya* ~ *ta tsawo* he is a little taller than her.

[1]**ɗạ̀ri** *n.f. and adj.* (*pl.* **ɗạrurrụwà**) Hundred.

[2]**ɗạ̀ri** *n.f.* (*pl.* **ɗạrurrụkà**) Halfpenny in old Nigerian currency.

ɗari *n.m.* 1. Coldness due to wind, usu. during harmattan season. 2. Chills due to illness.

ɗata *n.f.* Small green bitter tomato-like fruit.

ɗàtànnịya *n.f.* Gall-bladder.

ɗàu *id.* Emphasizes intense heat or pain: *kunama ta harbe ni* ~ the scorpion stung me badly.

ɗau *v.t.* Alt. form of **ɗaukà** before i.o. or noun d.o.

ɗaukà (ɗàukị/ɗàuke) *v.t.* 1. Take (up), carry: *ya dauki buhun hatsi* he took up the bag of corn. ***ɗauki wuta*** catch fire. ***ɗauki fansa*** take revenge. 2. Overcome: *barci ya dauke shi* he fell asleep; *fitila ta dauki idonsa* the lamp dazzled him. 3. Bear responsibility for: *na dauki nauyin saukar da bakon* I was responsible for putting up the guest. 4. Assume, regard, view: *an* ~ *Audu dattijo ne* Audu was assumed to be a gentleman. 5. Accept, consent: *abin da ya* ~, *ni ban* ~ *ba* I won't put up with what he does.

ɗàukạci *n.m.* The whole of: *duk* ~*n dalibai sun tafi hutu* all of the students went on holiday.

ɗaukạ̀ka *v.t.* Honour, promote, or help s.o. **ɗàukạkà** *n.f.* 1. Honour, glory. 2. Promotion.

ɗâuke *v.t.* 1. Remove, carry all away: *sun* ~ *mana kuɗinmu* they stole all of our money. 2. Wean. *v.i.* Be dried up, stop flowing: *ruwa ya* ~ the rain has stopped.

ɗàuke *n.m.* Suppository, usu. for children.

ɗâuki *n.m.* Powerful act, military operations.

ɗàuki *n.m.* Distributing share of food due to each member of the household.

ɗauko *v.t.* 1. Lift up and bring. 2. Begin to deteriorate (animal, plant): *ya* ~ *mutuwa* it is dying; *ya* ~ *tsufa* it is getting old.

ɗàukụ *v.i.* Be misunderstood or confused.

ɗaurà *v.t.* Tie sth. onto sth.: *na* ~ *sirdi ga doki* I saddled the horse. ~ ***aure*** perform the marriage ceremony.

ɗaurạ̀ye *v.t.* Rinse.

ɗaurè *v.t.* (*vn.* **ɗaurì**) 1. Tie up sth. 2. Imprison s.o.: *ba a taɓa* ~ *shi ba* he has never been in prison before.

ɗaurì *n.m.* 1. Bundle. 2. Imprisonment, prison sentence: *an yi masa* ~*n shekara uku* he was given a three-year sentence. 3. *vn.* of **ɗaurè.**

ɗạ̀wafì *n.m.* Circling the Ka'aba at Mecca.

ɗạ̀wàinịya *n.f.* Struggling with one's tasks.

ɗạyạ *n. and adj.* 1. One. 2. The same: *duk* ~ *ne* it's all the same to me; *aikinsu* ~ *ne* their function is identical; *shawararsu ta zo* ~ they made a unanimous decision. 3. The other: ~ *littafin* the other book.

ɗàya (ị/e) *v.t.* (*vn.f.* **ɗaya**) Strip (bark, skin, etc.).

ɗàzụ *adv.* A moment ago, a while ago, just now.

ɗebè *v.t.* 1. Remove, set aside, take out of: *ya* ~ *wani abu daga cikin albashinsa* he set aside a portion of his salary. 2. Give up, relinquish (hope, interest): *na* ~ *ƙauna daga abin nan* I stopped having any interest in this matter.

ɗèfi *n.m.* Edge, tip.

ɗibà (ɗèbị/ɗèbe) *v.t.* Dip out, scoop up (liquid, grain): *ta debi ruwa daga rijiya* she drew water from the well.

ɗibbụ̀ *see* **tsubbụ̀.**

ɗibgà *v.t.* Do much of, experience a lot of: *ya ~ hasara* he suffered a great loss.
ɗịgà *v.t.* Pour out by drops: *likita ya ~ masa magani a ido* the doctor put eye-drops in his eye. **ɗịgạ** *v.i.* Drip.
ɗịgil *id.* Very short.
ɗịgìrgịre *n.m.* Balancing load on head without holding it.
ɗịgo *n.m.* (*pl.* **ɗịgẹ-ɗịgẹ**) 1. Drop, drip. 2. Dots placed above or below Arabic consonants. 3. Full stop.
ɗîm *id.* Thud.
ɗimà *v.t.* (with i.o.) Hit, strike: *ya ~ mini dundu* he struck me with his fist.
ɗịmàma *v.t.* Warm up, heat up (food).
ɗimàuce *v.i.* Become nervous, confused, overcome by fear.
ɗimbi *n.m.* Superabundance: *~n mutane* hundreds of people.
ɗịmi *n.m.* Warmth.
ɗịmì *adv.* Abundantly: *ya tara littattafai ~* he collected a lot of books.
ɗimụwa *n.f.* Losing one's way or bearings.
ɗin *gen. link* (used with nouns ending in a consonant) Of, possessed by, belonging to, part of: *kwas ~su* their course. **ɗîn** *dem.* The very one referred to: *uku ~* the three in question; *mutumin nan ~* this very man; *haka ~* exactly so; *wannan ~* that very one.
ɗìngịshi *n.m.* Limping.
ɗinkà *v.t.* (*vn.* **ɗinki**) Sew.
ɗinki *n.m.* 1. Embroidery. 2. *vn.* of **ɗinkà.**
ɗinya *n.f.* Black plum tree or its fruit.
ɗir̃kà *v.t.* 1. (with i.o.) Do violence to: *na ~ masa wuka* I stabbed him with a knife. 2. Poke hand into hole. *v.i.* Enter unexpectedly: *sun ~ cikin ofis a guje* they entered the office without warning.
ɗis *id.* Sound of dripping.
ɗịsà *v.t.* Pour out by drops, sprinkle.
ɗiwà *n.f.* Pus.
ɗịya *see* **'ya.**
ɗofà *v.t.* Stick onto, affix.
ɗòki *n.m.* 1. Eagerness, keenness. 2. Throbbing pain.
ɗorà *v.t.* (*vn.* **ɗori**) 1. Put on, place onto: *na ~ Ali a kan doki* I put Ali on the horse. 2. Set, bind broken limb.
ɗòrạwà *n.f.* (*pl.* **ɗòrạ̀yi**) Locust-bean tree. **ruwan ~** light yellow colour.
ɗòre *n.m.* Going without pre-dawn meal during Ramadan.
ɗori *n.m.* 1. Increasing length or width of sth. (as in adding a row of bricks to wall). 2. *vn.* of **ɗorà.**
ɗorịya *n.f.* Stacking things one on top of the other.
ɗosạ̀na *v.t.* Set fire to sth.
ɗòyi *n.m.* Stench.
ɗụmàma *see* **ɗịmàma.**
ɗụ̀mi *n.m.* 1. *See* **ɗịmi.** 2. Hum of conversation, hubbub.
ɗunɗu *n.m.* Thorny shrub.
ɗùngum *adv.* Entirely, completely: *ya kare ~* it is completely finished.
ɗùngụmạ̀ *v.i.* Start off in a large group.
ɗurà *v.t.* (*vn.* **ɗuri**) Pour liquid through narrow opening.
ɗuri *n.m.* 1. Piping seam of gown by inserting threads. 2. *vn.* of **ɗurà.**
ɗurịyà *n.f.* Information, news from a distant place: *tun tafiyarsa har yanzu ko ~rsa babu* since his departure there is no trace of news about him.
ɗụwàwu, ɗụwàiwai *n.m.* Buttocks.

E

e *excl.* 1. Yes. 2. Well . . .
ẹdịtạ̀ *n.m.* (*pl.* **ẹdịtoci**) Editor.
ehò *see* **ihù.**
ekà *n.f.* (*pl.* **ekoki, ekà-ekà**) Acre.
el'ê *n.f.* (*pl.* **el'è-el'è**) L.A. (Local Authority).
ẹlẹ̀mantạr̃ẹ̀ *n.f.* Elementary school.
emtì *n.m.* Any empty container.
en'è *n.f.* (*pl.* **en'è-en'è**) N.A. (Native Authority).
erịyạ̀ *n.f.* (*pl.* **erịyoyi**) Radio or television aerial.

F

fạ̀ *inter. prt.* How about? What about?: *ni ~?* well, how about me? *wannan ~?* how about this one?
fạ *prt.* Used for contrast or emphasis: *ni ~ zan tafi* as for me, I'm going; *su ne ~* they are certainly the ones.
fa *n.m.* Flat rock: *na yi shanya a kan ~* I spread out my clothes to dry on a flat rock.
Fạ̀bȓairụ̀ *n.m.* February.
fạcạ-fạcạ *id.* Spattered all over with liquid.
fàcàka *n.f.* Squandering: *yana ~ da kudi* he is squandering money.
fạcàl *id.* Sound of sth. falling into shallow water.
fàce *prep.* Except, with the exception of: *babu abin bautawa da gaskiya ~ Allah* nothing deserves devout worship except God.
facè *see* **fyacè.**
facì *n.m.* Patch, patching (of punctured tyre).
fàda *n.m.* Father (priest).
fadạ̀ *n.f.* 1. Court of chief or king. 2. Favour: *ya sami ~ gurinka* he easily got your favour.
fạ̀dạmà *n.f.* (*pl.* **fạdạmomi, fạ̀dạ̀mu**) Marshy low-lying land.
fadanci *n.m.* Obsequiousness, flattery.
fàdàwa *pl.* of **bạ̀fadà.**
fạ̀ɗa (ị/e) *v.t.* (*vn.* **fạɗì**) Tell, say, utter.
fạɗà *n.m.* (*pl.* **fạ̀ɗàcẹ-fạ̀ɗàcẹ**) Quarrel, squabble, nagging.
faɗà *v.t. and v.i.* 1. Fall into, onto, descend on: *ya ~ rijiya* he fell into a well. 2. Throw oneself into, onto. 3. Attack: *ya ~ ni da fada* he shouted at me.
faɗạ̀ɗa *v.t.* Broaden. **fàɗạɗạ̀** *v.i.* Become broad.
fạɗạkar̃ (dạ̀) *v.t.* Teach, tell, cause to realize.
fàɗà-wụtạ *n.m.* Moth.
fạɗẹ̀ *n.m.* Sandals, slippers.
fàɗe *see* **fyàɗe.**
fạɗì Alt. form of **fạ̀ɗa.**
faɗị *v.i.* (*vn.f.* **faɗụ̀wa**) 1. Fall, descend: *rana ta ~* the sun set. 2. Fail. 3. Become cheaper. 4. Lose (profit, heart).
faɗi *n.m.* Width, breadth, broadness. **~n kai** overrating one's abilities. **~n rai, ~n zuciya** conceitedness.
fàɗị-kạ̀-mụtụ̀ *n.m.* Chinaware, crockery.
faɗụ̀wa *n.f.* 1. Failure, loss. **~r gaba** disappointment. 2. *vn.* of **faɗì.**
fàfa *n.f.* Scraping out insides of gourd, pumpkin.
fàfạrà (ị/e) *v.t.* Chase, pursue furiously, drive away.

fa̧fa̧r̃andà *n.f.* 1. Verandah. 2. Large sweet mango.
fafàta *v.i.* Struggle, have a hard time with: *sai da muka ~ kafin ya ba ni kuɗina* only after some struggle did he give me my money.
fafè *v.t.* Scrape out insides of gourd or pumpkin.
fàfu̧r̃àtan *adv.* Entirely, completely: *ya ƙi ~* he completely refused.
fa̧gàci *n.m.* (*pl.* **fàga̧tai**) A traditional title.
fa̧ge *n.m.* (*pl.* **fa̧gàge**) 1. Open space, arena, course. 2. Furlong.
fa̧hàmi *n.m.* 1. Intelligence. 2. Intelligence-producing charm or medicine.
fa̧hàr̃i *see* **àlfa̧hàr̃i.**
fàhintà, fàhimtà (ci̧/ce) *v.t.* Understand. *n.f.* Intelligence, understanding.
fa̧hintar̃ (dà) *v.t.* Teach, cause to understand.
fa'i̧dà *n.f.* (*pl.* **fa'i̧doji**) Usefulness, gain, benefit.
faifà *n.f.* (*pl.* **faifofi**) Currency note, paper money.
faifai *n.m.* (*pl.* **fa̧yàfa̧yai**) 1. Small round mat used for covering vessels and for winnowing. 2. Phonograph record. 3. Any disc-like thing.
fa̧ka (i̧/e) *v.t.* (*vn.* **fa̧ko**) 1. Lie in wait for. 2. Eavesdrop on.
fa̧ka̧ra *n.f.* (*pl.* **fa̧kàru**) Francolin, bush-fowl.
fa̧kè *v.i.* 1. Take shelter or refuge. 2. (with **dà**) Use sth. as excuse: *ya ~ da ciwo ya ki zuwa aiki* he used illness as an excuse for not coming to work.
faki̧ti̧ *n.m.* (*pl.* **faki̧toci**) Packet: *~n taba* pack of cigarettes.
fa̧ko *n.m.* 1. Ambush. 2. *vn.* of **fa̧ka.**
fa̧ku̧ *v.i.* Die (of prophets, saints).
fa̧ƙir̃i *n. and adj.* (*f.* **fa̧ƙir̃i̧ya,** *pl.* **fa̧ƙir̃ai**) Poor, destitute.
fa̧ƙò *n.m.* Hard, barren ground.
fal *id.* Chock-full.
fa̧la̧la *n.f.* Abundance, fortune, prosperity.
fa̧la̧lȩ *n.m.* Large flat rock.
fa̧lȩ-fa̧lȩ *id.* Thin and flimsy.
falla̧sa *v.t.* Disclose s.o.'s secret to cause shame.
fallè *v.t.* Hit s.o. hard: *ya ~ ta da mari* he slapped her very hard.
falle *n.m.* Sheet of paper, single thickness of cloth.
falle-falle *adv.* Singly, one by one: *an ɓaɓɓalle tebur an mai da shi ~* they dismantled the table piece by piece.
falma̧r̃àn *n.f.* Waistcoat.
falò *n.m.* Parlour: *ɗaki ne ciki da ~* it is a house with two rooms (bedroom and parlour).
fâm *n.f.* (*pl.* **fàmfa̧mai**) 1. Pound in currency (esp. old Nigerian currency). 2. The equivalent of two Naira (used unofficially in quoting prices).
famà *v.t.* (*vn.* **fami**) Hurt an already existing wound, reopen a painful matter.
fama *n.f.* 1. Struggle, striving: *tana ~ da aiki* she has a lot of work to do; *fagen ~* battlefield. 2. Suffering due to hardship or illness: *yana ~ da mura* he is suffering from a cold.
fàmfa̧rà *n.f.* Losing baby teeth.
famfàra *v.i.* Flee, escape quickly.
famfò *n.m.* (*pl.* **famfu̧nà**) 1. Pump, pumping. 2. Incitement: *an yi musu ~ su yi tawaye* they were incited to rebel. 3. Enema.
fàmît *n.m.* Permit.
fa̧nar̃i̧tè *n.m.* Penalty in sports.
fancà *n.f.* Puncture, flat tyre.
fanɗa̧re *v.i.* Stray or turn away from: *ya ~ daga layi* he got out of line; *zamansa a Ikko ya sa ya ~* living in Lagos has led him astray.
fanga̧li *n.m.* (*pl.* **fangu̧là**) Irrigation bed.
fànjamà *n.m.* Loose, pyjama-like trousers.
fankà *n.f.* (*pl.* **fankoki**) Electric fan.
fanka̧ma *n.f.* Boastfulness, conceitedness.
fankàshali *n.m.* (*f.* **fankàshali̧ya,** *pl.* **fànka̧shàlai**) Person lacking in common sense.
fànke *n.m.* Fried cake made of wheat flour.
fankèkȩ *n.m.* 1. Pancake. 2. Powder for make-up.

fànko *n.m.* (*pl.* **fankųnà**) 1. Empty container. 2. Matchbox. 3. Penniless person.
fannì *n.m.* (*pl.* **fannoni**) 1. Branch of knowledge, subject. 2. Group, type, category.
fànsa (shį/she) *v.t.* 1. Redeem s.o. from slavery. 2. Ransom s.o. 3. Buy sth. from s.o. who no longer needs it. 4. Buy a holy text (esp. Koran). **fansa** *n.f.* 1. Redemption, ransom. 2. Revenge: *ya dau* ~ he took his revenge.
fansar̃ (dą̀) *v.t.* 1. Sell (polite term used when buyer is highly respected person or does not really want to sell item). 2. Sell a holy text (esp. Koran).
fantsą̀ma *v.t.* Splash, scatter, spread (liquid, flour, crowd of people, etc.). **fàntsąmą̀** *v.i.* Be scattered, spread: *mutane sun* ~ *cikin daji* the people have dispersed into the bush.
fąrą *n.f.* Anaemia.
fàra *n.f.* (*pl.* **fàri**) Grasshopper, locust.
farà *v.t.* Begin, start: *sun* ~ *samun sauƙi* they have begun to recover.
fąr̃ą'à *n.f.* Cheerful disposition, geniality.
fąr̃abįtį *n.m.* Private (army or police).
fą̀r̃agà *n.f.* 1. Opportunity. 2. Leisure, spare time.
fąr̃ą̀li *see* **fą̀r̃illà.**
fąrànta *v.t.* 1. Gladden, please: *ya* ~ *mini zuciya* he made me happy. 2. Whiten.
fą̀r̃antì *n.m.* (*pl.* **fą̀r̃àntai**) Plate, tray.
fąrar̃-hùla *n.f.* Civilian.
fąrar̃-ƙąyà *n.f.* Gum arabic tree.
fą̀r̃ashì *n.m.* Price.
fąr̃at *id.* At once, suddenly: *ya yi* ~ *ya gudu* he suddenly ran off. ~ ***ɗaya*** instantly, immediately.
fąr̃atį *n.m.* Parade.
fąrau-fąrau *n.m.* Water mixed with a little flour or sour milk.
fą̀rautà (cį/ce) *v.t.* Hunt. *n.f.* Hunt, hunting.
farcè *n.m.* (*pl.* **fąràta**) Fingernail.
fàr̃ɗa (į/e) *v.t.* Hoe up underground crops, esp. groundnuts.
far̃faɗįya *n.f.* Epilepsy.
far̃fąɗo *v.i.* Recover from unconsciousness or illness.
fàr̃fajįya *n.f.* Open space in front of compound.
farfąra *n.f.* White variety of guinea-corn.
fâr̃felà *n.f.*(*pl.* **far̃feloli**) Motor fan, propeller.
fàr̃fèsu *n.m.* Pepper-soup.
far̃gą *v.i.* Realize: *ya* ~ *daga laifinsa* he realized his mistake.
fàr̃gą̀ba *n.f.* Dread, fear.
fąrì *n.m.* Drought.
[1]**fąri** *n. and adj.* (*f.* **fąra**, *pl.* **fąràre**) 1. White. 2. Strips of hand-woven white cloth. 3. Shroud. 4. (in compounds) Sth. good, positive: ~*n ciki* happiness; ~*n jini* popularity; *farar zuciya* mild-temperedness.
[2]**fąri** *n.m.* (*pl.* **farfąru**) Vowel sign in Arabic script.
farį *n.m.* Beginning, start, origin: *shi dan* ~ *ne* he is the first-born child. ***da*** ~ first of all, in the first place. ~***n farko***, ~***n farawa*** right from the start.
fą̀r̃illà *n.f.* (*pl.* **fą̀r̃ìllai**) Obligatory duty (religious).
fàr̃įyà *n.f.* Boastfulness, showing off.
farjì *n.m.* Vagina.
fàrka *n.m. or f.* (*pl.* **fąrèkąni**) Paramour.
far̃kà *v.i.* 1. Wake up, gain awareness: *ya* ~ *daga barci* he woke up. 2. Revive (fainted person, drooping plant).
[1]**far̃kè** *v.t.* Rip open stitching of seam. *v.i.* Become unstitched.
[2]**far̃kè** *v.i.* Retaliate for having been cheated: *ya cuce ni naira goma amma sai na* ~ he cheated me out of ten Naira but I got even with him.
far̃ke *n.m.* (*pl.* **fątàke**) Itinerant trader.
farko *n.m.* Beginning: *da* ~*n zuwansa* when he first arrived; *yarinya ta* ~ the first girl. ***da*** ~ at first, in the beginning. ***na*** ~ firstly, first of all.
fàr̃mąkì *n.m.* Sudden attack.
fàrsa *n.f.* Poultice.
farsa *n.f.* Kolanut which has accidentally split into sections.

faṙtanyà *n.f.* (*pl.* **fa̧ṙètta̧ni**) Small hoe.

fàrụ *v.i.* Happen, occur.

fâs *n.m.* Being first in competition, examination: *wannan dalibi ya yi* ~ this student was first in his class.

fa̧sà *v.t.* (*vn.* **fa̧shi**) 1. Break, shatter. 2. Disperse.

fasà *v.t.* Postpone, give up idea of doing sth. *v.i.* Used in *tafiya ta* ~ plans for the trip have been cancelled.

fà̧sahà *n.f.* 1. Cleverness, skill. 2. Art, artistry.

fa̧sà̧li *n.m.* 1. Orderliness, arrangement, symmetry. 2. Chapter, section. 3. Season.

fàsfô *n.m.* Passport.

fa̧shè *v.i.* 1. Be broken. 2. Used in ~ *da dariya* burst out laughing; ~ *da kuka* burst out crying. 3. Be scattered, dispersed.

fa̧shì *n.m.* 1. Highway robbery. 2. *vn.* of **fa̧sà**.

fashì *n.m.* Postponement, delay: *mu tafi babu* ~ let's go without delay.

fasịƙi *n. and adj.* (*f.* **fasịƙa**, *pl.* **fàsịƙai**) Profligate, immoral.

fasil *n.m.* (*pl.* **fasịloli**) Parcel.

fasinjà̧ *n.m.* (*pl.* **fasinjoji**) Passenger.

fàska̧rà (ị/e) *v.t.* Be beyond one's control: *wannan yaro ya faskare su* this boy is beyond their control. **fàska̧rà̧** *v.i.* Be or prove impossible: *ɓarawo ya* ~ *kamuwa* the thief is impossible to catch.

faskà̧ra *v.t.* (*vn.* **fàskà̧re**) Split firewood.

faskịlà̧ *n.m.* First-class accommodation (usu. on train).

fà̧so *n.m.* Chapped or cracked skin of foot.

fa̧sà̧'ofis *n.m.* Post office.

fassà̧ṙa *v.t.* 1. Translate. 2. Explain. **fassa̧ṙà** *n.f.* (*pl.* **fassa̧ṙoṙi**) 1. Translation. 2. Explanation.

fastò *n.m.* (*pl.* **fastoci**) Pastor.

fat *id.* Emphasizes whiteness: *fari* ~ pure white.

fatà *n.f.* (*pl.* **fatu**) 1. Skin (of person or animal). 2. Leather. 3. Membrane (e.g. of drum).

fata *n.m. or f.* Hope, wish: *ya yi musu* ~*n alheri* he wished them well; *muna* ~ *zai dawo gobe* we hope he will return tomorrow.

fa̧ta̧-fa̧ta̧ *id.* Helter-skelter, in disorderly haste: *ya kore su* ~ he chased them away helter-skelter.

fa̧ta-fà̧tà *id.* Wide, broad: *kunnuwansa* ~ he has large ears.

fà̧ta̧kà *n.m.* Two-shilling piece in old Nigerian currency.

fa̧tàke *pl.* of **faṙke.**

fa̧ta̧là *n.f.* (*pl.* **fà̧tà̧lu**) Woman's kerchief, head-tie.

fà̧tà̧li *n.m.* 1. Disregard for s.o.'s advice: *ya yi* ~ *da zancena* he disregarded what I said. 2. Throwing sth. aside carelessly.

fa̧talwa *n.f.* (*pl.* **fa̧talwoyi**) Ghost.

fa̧tanyà *n.f.* (*pl.* **fà̧tànyu**) *see* **faṙtanyà.**

fa̧ta̧ṙa *n.f.* Lack, want (esp. of money): *yau muna* ~*r kuɗi* today we are out of money.

fàtàri *n.m.* Woman's underskirt.

fà̧tàtta̧kà (ị/e) *v.t.* Rout, scatter (in battle).

fa̧taucì *n.m.* Trading.

fà̧tà̧wa *n.f.* Request (usu. for information): *ina da* ~ *a kan wannan aiki* I have a question regarding this work.

fà̧tè-fa̧te *n.m.* A mushy food made of flour and vegetables.

fa̧tsa̧ *n.f.* Fish-hook, fishing with hook.

fàu *id.* Describes sudden bright flash of light: *sai na ga haske* ~ *a gabana* then I suddenly saw a flash of light in front of me.

faucè *see* **fyaucè.**

fàufau *adv.* Completely, entirely (always with neg. meaning): ~ *ya ki zuwa gurina* he absolutely refused to come to me; ~ *ba zan yarda ba* I will never ever agree.

fawà *n.f.* Butchering.

fà̧yàfà̧yai *pl.* of **faifai.**

fa̧yè *v.t.* Be characterized by: *ya* ~ *katsarandan da yawa* he is always interfering.

fayil *n.m.* (*pl.* **fayịloli**) Correspondence file.

fayyà̧ce *v.t.* Explain thoroughly.

fedà *n.f.* (*pl.* **fedoji**) Bicycle pedal.

feɗè *v.t.* (*vn.f.* **fiɗà**) Flay or skin an animal.
fegi *n.m.* (*pl.* **fegųnà**) 1. Peg. 2. Plot of land.
feƙè *v.t.* Sharpen to a point.
feleƙe *n.m.* Affectation.
fenshò *n.m.* Pension.
fensir̃ *n.m.* (*pl.* **fensįr̃or̃i**) Pencil.
fentà *n.m.* Painter.
fenti *n.m.* Paint: *an shafe ɗaki da* ~ the room has been painted.
ferè *v.t.* (*vn.f.* **firà**) Pare.
fesà *v.t.* Spray.
fèshi *n.m.* Splashing of rain into house.
fetò *n.m.* Short trousers.
fetùr̃ *n.m.* Petrol, petroleum.
fį *v.t.* 1. Exceed, surpass: *sun* ~ *ashirin* there are more than twenty; *ya* ~ *ƙarfina* it is beyond my ability. ~ ***kyau*** be better: *ya* ~ *kyau mu tashi yanzu* it would be better for us to leave now. ~ ***dacewa*** be more suitable. ~ ***son*** prefer: *na* ~ *son wannan da wancan* I prefer this one to that. 2. Used to form adjectives of comparison: *hular nan ta* ~ *taka tsada* this hat is more expensive than yours; *ya* ~ *dukansu tsawo* he is the tallest one of them.
fįcè *v.i.* Go out and away.
fidą̀bur̃di *n.m.* P.W.D. (Public Works Department).
fįda'ù *n.m.* Prayers for the dead.
fid dą̀ *v.t.* (= **fisshe** before pro. d.o.) Alt. form of **fįtar̃ dą̀**.
fiddau *n.m.* Sth. which has been rejected or which is no longer useful.
fiɗà *n.f.* 1. Surgical operation. 2. *vn.* of **feɗè**.
fįɗįye *v.t.* (*vn.f.* **fįɗįyà**) Castrate an animal.
fiffįka *n.f.* Flapping wings.
fiffįkè *n.m.* (*pl.* **fįkàfįkai**) Wing.
fifikò *n.m.* Showing one's superiority over others.
fifita *v.t.* (*vn.f.* **fifita**) 1. Fan food to cool it. 2. Promote s.o.: *an* ~ *matsayinsa* he was promoted to a new position.
figè *v.t.* Pluck (feathers, hair).
fį'įli *n.m.* (*pl.* **fį'įlai**) 1. Verb. 2. Affected speech or behaviour.
fįkàfįkai *pl.* of **fiffįkè**.
fikò *see* **fifikò**.
fiƙà *n.f.* Canine tooth.
fiƙè *see* **feƙè**.
fįƙįhų̀ *n.m.* Islamic jurisprudence.
fil *n.m.* Safety-pin, pin.
fįlàfįli *n.m.* (*pl.* **fįlàfįlai**) Canoe paddle.
fįlakǫ̀ *n.m.* Bashfulness, modesty.
fįlâs *n.m.* Flask, thermos bottle.
fįlastą̀ *n.f.* 1. Plastering. 2. Plaster bandage.
fįlayà *n.f.* (*pl.* **fįlayoyi**) Pliers.
fil ą̀zal *adv.* Used in *tun* ~ since time immemorial.
filfįlò *n.m.* 1. Butterfly. 2. Children's kite.
fili *n.m.* (*pl.* **filàye**) 1. Open space, field. 2. Plot of land for building. 3. Chance, opportunity: *ba ni* ~*n yin magana* give me a chance to speak. ***a*** ~ frankly, openly.
filla-filla *adv.* Step by step, item by item (of speech or writing): *ka yi bayani* ~ explain it clearly, step by step.
fillè *v.t.* Sever or lop off with one stroke.
fįlò *n.m.* (*pl.* **fįloli**) Pillow.
filtà *n.f.* (*pl.* **filtoci**) Filter.
fîm *n.m.* 1. Roll of film. 2. Cinema.
fincę *n.m.* Meat trimmings given to butcher's assistants.
fìncįkà (į/e) *v.t.* Pull out suddenly with force.
fįr̃âm *n.m.* Frame.
fįr̃amą̀r̃è *n.f.* Primary school.
firgįgit *id.* Describes startled or frightened movement: *ya tashi* ~ he got up with a start.
firgįta *v.t.* Frighten, scare, startle.
firgįtą̀ *v.i.* Become frightened, startled.
fįr̃ijį *n.m.* Fridge, refrigerator.
fįr̃imįyà *n.m.* (*pl.* **fįr̃imįyoyi**) Premier.
fisshe *see* **fid dą̀**.
fįtą *v.i.* 1. Go out. 2. Turn out well: *ya wanke taguwa ta* ~ *tas* he washed the gown and it came out very clean.
fįtacce *adj.* (*f.* **fįtaccįya**, *pl.* **fįtàttu**) Outstanding, famous.
fįtar̃ (dą̀) *v.t.* (= **fid dą̀** before d.o.) 1. Take out, remove. 2.

Dismiss, depose s.o. 3. Display sth.
fi̜ti̜ki *n.m.* Grass cutting.
fi̜ti̜là *n.f.* (*pl.* **fi̜ti̜lu**) 1. Lamp. 2. Light, electricity: *gidan nan da ruwa da* ~ this house has water and electricity.
fi̜ti̜nà *n.f.* (*pl.* **fi̜ti̜nu**) Trouble, mischievousness, quarrelsomeness.
fi̜to *n.m.* Palm wine, native beer.
fi̜tò *n.m.* Ferrying.
fitò *n.m.* Whistling.
fi̜tsari *n.m.* Urine.
fi̜yayye *n.m.* Superior person (usu. applied to the Prophet Muhammad).
fi̜ye̜ da̜ *prep.* 1. More than, exceeding: *na yi* ~ *awa biyar ina karatu* I have been studying for more than five hours; ~ *koyaushe* more than ever. 2. Better than: *ba ni wani* ~ *wannan* give me one better than this one.
fìzga (i̜/e) *v.t.* Grab: *ya fizgi fensir daga hannuna* he grabbed the pencil from my hand.
fu̜ka *n.f.* Bronchitis, asthma, or similar lung disease.
ful *id.* Used in *sabo* ~ brand-new.
fu̜lawà *n.f.* 1. Wheat flour. 2. Flower, blossom of plant.
fu̜logi̜ *n.m.*(*pl.* **fu̜logogi**) Sparking-plug.
fu̜loti̜ *n.m.* Buying-station for cash crops.
fùnkàso *n.m.* Wheat-cake eaten with *miya* or honey.
fu̜ra *n.f.* 1. Balls made of cooked millet. 2. Gruel made by mixing these balls with sour milk or, less often, with water and tamarind.
fu̜re *n.m.* (*pl.* **fu̜rànni**) Flower, blossom.
furfu̜ra *v.t.* Barter, exchange. **fùrfu̜ra̜** *v.i.* Be bartered, exchanged.
furfu̜ra *n.f.* Grey hair.
fu̜r̃ofa̜gandà *n.f.* Propaganda.
fur̃sù̜na̜ *n.m.* (*pl.* **fur̃su̜noni**) Prisoner.
fur̃tà *v.t.* Utter, mention: *ko magana daya ban* ~ *ba* I didn't utter a word.
fur̃tù̜mi *n.m.* (*pl.* **fur̃tu̜mà**) Bullock.
fu̜rù̜ci *n.m.* Utterance, declaration, statement.
furzà *v.t.* Spit out.
fu̜sàta *v.t.* Make s.o. angry. **fù̜sata̜** *v.i.* Become angry.
fu̜shi *n.m.* Anger, bad temper, irritability, touchiness.
fuskà *n.f.* (*pl.* **fuskoki**) 1. Face. 2. Direction: ~*r gabas* eastward. 3. Geniality: *yana da ban* ~ he is easy to get along with. **cin** ~ humiliation.
fùskantà (ci̜/ce) *v.t.* 1. Face, head for. 2. Have an opinion, point of view: *na fuskanci zancen duk rashin gaskiya ne* my view of the matter is that it is completely false.
fu̜tuk *id.* Used in *shi bagidaje ne* ~ he is a complete country bumpkin.
fyacè *v.t.* Blow one's nose.
fyaɗà *v.t.* 1. Whip, flog: *ta* ~ *masa bulala* she hit him with a whip. 2. Knock down: *keke ya* ~ *shi da ƙasa* a bicycle knocked him down.
fyàɗe *n.m.* Rape: *ya yi mata* ~ he raped her.
fyaucè *v.t.* Swoop down on.

G

ga̜ *prep.* (becomes **ga̜re** before pro.) 1. In, on, near: *suna dauke da kaya* ~ *kawunansu* they are carrying goods on their heads; *ya soka tsire* ~ *tukuba* he stuck the *tsire* into a mound for cooking. 2. In the presence of: *je ka* ~ *sarki* go to the chief; *suna gare shi* they are in his presence. 3. To s.o.: *ya yi kira* ~ *mutane da su ƙara ƙokarinsu* he appealed to the people to increase their efforts. 4. In the possession of: *da kobo goma* ~ *Audu* Audu has ten kobo. 5. On the side of, in the care of, dependent on: *muna* ~ *Allah* we depend on God. 6. With reference to, regarding: ~ *gudu ya fi ni ba* ~ *tsalle ba* he is better than me in running but not in jumping. 7. Alt. means of forming locative phrases: *muna gabas gare shi* = *muna gabas da shi* we are east of it; *ina baya* ~ *Audu* = *ina bayan Audu* I am behind Audu. 8. In, of (with dates): *ran biyar* ~ *watan Mayu* the fifth of May.

ga̧ *see* **ga̧ni.**

gà Here it is, there it is: ~ *kuɗinka* here's your money; ~ *ni* here I am; ~ *su can a zaune* there they are, seated.

gą̀ba *n.m.* 1. Front part of body of person or animal. ~ ***ɗaya*** simultaneously, all together, all at once. ***faɗuwar*** ~ losing heart. 2. Male or female genitals. 3. The distance of outstretched arms from fingertip to fingertip. **gą̀ba̧** *adv.* In front, forward, ahead: *yana* ~ he is in front. ***nan*** ~ in the future, henceforth.

gàba *n.f.* Enmity, hostility. ***abokin*** ~ enemy.

gą̀ban *prep.* 1. In front of, before: *ya faɗi* ~ *sarki* he prostrated himself before the chief. 2. Beyond, on the other side of: *yana* ~ *kogi* he is on the other side of the river; *ya fi* ~ *lissafi* it is beyond calculation.

gą̀bàni, gą̀bànni *n.m.* The time just before, the eve: ~*n zuwansa an yi faɗa* just before his arrival there was fighting.

gą̀bàrųwa *see* **bą̀gàrųwa.**

ga̧bàs *n.f.* East.

ga̧ba̧shin *prep.* East of.

gą̀batà (cį/ce) *v.t.* 1. Lead, be leader of: *ya gabace mu* he is our leader. 2. Approach: *yanzu jirgin nan ya gabaci Kano* this train must now have drawn near to Kano. 3. Precede: *Sarki Sanusi ya gabaci Sarki Ado* Emir Sanusi preceded Emir Ado.

ga̧batar̃ (dą̀) *v.t.* 1. Promote, elect as leader. 2. Introduce: *ya* ~ *da su gaban alkali* he presented them to the judge.

ga̧batâr̃wa *n.f.* Preface, introduction.

ga̧bato *v.t. and v.i.* Approach, draw near.

gabcè *v.t. and v.i.* 1. Collapse, cause to collapse. 2. Bite off much of, break off large piece.

gab dą̀ *prep.* Near, next to: *gidanmu yana* ~ *na Audu* our house is next to Audu's.

gàbta (cį/ce) *v.t.* Bite into, bite off sth. **gabtà** *v.t.* (with i.o.) Bite into s.o.

gàbta̧rà (į/e) *v.t.* Bite off a large piece from.

gàbza (jį/je) *v.t.* 1. Strike with force. 2. Do a lot of: *na gabji aiki* I worked very hard.

ga̧ɓà *n.f.* (*pl.* **ga̧ɓoɓi, gàɓɓai**) 1. Joint of limb, nodule of corn-stalk or sugar cane. 2. Section between joint. 3. Syllable: *kalma mai* ~ *biyu* a disyllabic word.

gaɓà *n.f.* River bank.

gaɓò *n.m.* (*f.* **gaɓų̀wa**) Simpleton, fool.

ga̧ci *n.m.* Edge of river: *ya kai* ~ he has reached the other side of the river.

gą̀da *n.f.* Duiker. ~***r kurmi*** red-flanked duiker.

gàda (jį/je) *v.t.* (*vn.* **gadò**) Inherit, inherit from, succeed to official position: *ya gaji halin ubansa* he took on the character of his father.

ga̧dà *n.f.* (*pl.* **ga̧doji**) Bridge.

gą̀dar̃à *n.f.* Haughty behaviour brought about by wealth, good fortune, etc.

gadar̃ (dą̀) *v.t.* Bequeath.

gaddą̧mà *see* **gar̃dą̧mà.**

gadì *n.m.* Guarding, night-watch. ***mai*** ~ night-watchman.

gadįną̀ *n.m.* 1. Gardener. 2. Garden.

ga̧do *n.m.* (*pl.* **ga̧dàje**) Bed. ~***n sarauta*** throne.

gàdo *n.m.* (*pl.* **gadųnà**) Spotted weaverbird.

gadò *n.m.* 1. Inheritance. 2. ***vn.*** of **gàda.**

gą̀du *n.m.* Wart-hog.

gaɗą *n.f.* Girls' game of clapping and singing.

gąfąkà *n.f.* Satchel.

gafąr̃à *n.f.* Pardon, forgiveness: *na roƙe shi* ~ I asked his pardon. *excl.* Excuse me.

gàfar̃tà (cį/ce) *v.t.* Pardon, forgive: *ya gafarce ni* he forgave me. **gafàr̃ta** *v.t.* (with i.o.) Pardon, forgive: *ya* ~ *mini* he forgave me. ***Allah ya*** ~ ***malam*** polite form of address to a *malam.*

gafi *n.m.* Taste of raw beans.

gąfįyà *n.f.* (*pl.* **gąfįyoyi**) Giant rat, bandicoot.

gągài *n.m.* Aphrodisiac.

gągànįya *n.f.* Struggling with task or person.

gàgąrà (į/e) *v.t.* Be impossible for, be beyond one's capabilities: *lissafin nan ya gagare ni* this calculation is too much for me. 2. Be impossible to do: *ƙulli ya gagari ƙuncewa* it is not possible to untie the knot. 3. Behave rebelliously towards: *jaki ya gagare shi* his donkey is out of control. **gàgąrą** *v.i.* 1. Be impossible: *ƙunce ƙullin nan ya* ~ untying this knot is not possible. 2. Be uncontrollable, rebellious.

gagąra *v.t.* (with i.o.) Cut with blunt instrument: *ya* ~ *masa wuka a wuya* he cut his neck with a blunt knife.

gàgąrarre *n. and adj.* (*f.* **gàgąrarrįya,** *pl.* **gàgąràrru**) Rebellious person or animal.

gàgarųmi *adj.* (*f.* **gàgarųma,** *pl.* **gàgàrųmai**) Big, important, impressive.

gaggàuta *v.i.* Hurry: *mun* ~ *mun gama aikin* we hurried and finished the work.

gaggawa *n.f.* Haste, quickness.

[1]**gagò** *n.m.* (*pl.* **gâgga**) Mighty person.

[2]**gagò** *n.m.* Large calabash ladle with straight handle.

gaibį *n.m.* Sth. hidden, invisible, or unknown: *sanin* ~ *sai Allah* only God knows the unknown.

gai dą *v.t.* (= **gaishe** before pro. d.o.) Alt. form of **gąyar̃ dą.**

gàigąyà (į/e) *v.t.* (*vn.* **gàigąye**) Gnaw, nibble.

gair̃ą *n.m.* Without, minus, lacking: *arba'in* ~ *ɗaya* thirty-nine. ***ba*** ~ ***ba dalili*** without rhyme or reason.

gaisà *v.i.* Exchange greetings: *mun* ~ *da Ali* Ali and I greeted each other.

gaishe *see* **gai dą.**

gaisųwa *n.f.* (*pl.* **gàishę-gàishę**) 1. Greeting, paying one's compliments: ~*r mutuwa* condolences given on a death. 2. Gift presented to a superior.

gâiwa *n.f.* (*pl.* **gaiwoyi**) Lunged mudfish.

gąjàrta *v.t.* Shorten: *ya* ~ *zamansa* he shortened his stay. **gąjartà** *n.f.* Shortness.

gąjere *n. and adj.* (*f.* **gąjerįya,** *pl.* **gąjèru**) Short.

gąjį *v.i.* (*vn.f.* **gąjįyà**) Be tired.

gàjįmàre *n.m.* White, fleecy clouds.

gąjįyà *n.f.* 1. Tiredness. 2. Used in greetings: *ina* ~*?* how are you? *ba* ~ I'm fine. 3. *vn.* of **gąjį.**

gąjįyayye *n. and adj.* (*f.* **gąjįyayyįya,** *pl.* **gąjįyàyyu**) 1. Tired, weary. 2. Destitute: *a taimaki* ~ help the poor.

gąƙè *v.t.* Hem in, prevent movement from a place.

gąląbà *n.f.* Getting the better of, overcoming.

gąlàbaitą *v.i.* Deteriorate due to personal hardships. **gąlàbaità** *n.f.* Aimless wandering: *ba ya ƙome sai* ~ he does nothing but roam about aimlessly.

gąlądimà *n.m.* A traditional title.

[1]**gąlàn** *n.m.* 1. Gallon. 2. Gallon-sized container.

[2]**gąlàn** *n.m.* 1. Ruts in surface of road: *motar ta faɗa* ~ *sifirin ya karye* the car went into a rut, causing a spring to break. 2. Jerky movements of vehicle travelling over rutted road.

gąlątsi *n.m.* Mistakes in pronunciation.

galįbi *n.m.* Most of, majority: ~*n mutanen garin nan suna da kirki* most of the people in this town are kind. *adv.* Usually.

galihų *n.m.* Used in *yana da* ~ he

has parents or guardians who support him.
galla *n.f.* A small bee.
gàlląbà (į/e) *v.t.* Worry, pester s.o.
gąluřà Used in *dan* ~ one who begs by rattling stones in a small tin.
gâm *n.m.* Gum.
gam *id.* Firmly.
[1]**gąmà** *v.t.* Finish doing: *ta ~ kitso* she finished plaiting her hair.
[2]**gąmà** *v.t.* Join, combine: *sun ~ kansu* they co-operated.
gąmą̀-ɗiɗį *n.m.* Insect, male and female of which travel joined together.
gąmą̀-fąɗą̀ *n.m.* A type of cassia tree or its pods.
gambà *n.f.* Tall grass used in making *zana* mats, etc.
gàmbąrà *n.f.* Performance in which conduct of individuals is ridiculed and made fun of, esp. by use of obscene language and sexual innuendoes. **ɗan** ~ Person who performs *gambara.*
gąmè *v.t.* (with i.o.) Conspire against: *mun ~ masa kai* we conspired against him.
gąmę dą̀ *prep.* Concerning, having to do with: *zancen da muka yi ~ tafiyata ya tabbata* the talk we had about my trip has been confirmed.
gamji *n.m.* Gutta-percha tree.
gammo *n.m.* (*pl.* **gammàye**) Head pad used by porters.
gąmo *n.m.* Meeting, encounter.
gamsař (dą̀) *v.t.* (= **gamshe** before pro. d.o.) Please, satisfy s.o.: *aikin da suka yi ya ~ da ni* I was pleased with the work they did.
gamshe *see* **gamsař dą̀.**
gàmshèƙa *n.f.* Black-hooded cobra.
gąmų *v.i.* Meet: *mun ~ a hanya* we met on the road.
gàmzaki *n.m.* Morning star.
gan *see* **gąni.**
ganà *v.i.* Talk privately: *ya ~ da sarki* he had a private audience with the chief. *v.t.* (with i.o.) Cause to experience some sort of difficulty: *ya ~ wa yaronsa azaba* he treated his son badly.
ganàwa *n.f.* Private discussion, chit-chat.
gànda *n.f.* Stew made from feet and head of a cow, cooked esp. on the occasion of a birth.
gândįřobą̀ *n.m.* (*pl.* **gandįřobobi**) Prison warder.
gandu *n.m.* (*pl.* **gandàye**) Big farm.
gànɗa *n.f.* Roof of the mouth.
ganɗò *n.m.* Dam, banked up earth for holding back water.
gànɗòkį *n.m. or f.* Person who does foolish things through over-eagerness.
ganè *v.t.* 1. Understand. 2. Find lost thing, discover: *na ~ littafinka da ya ɓata* I've found your book that was lost.
gànga *n.f.* (*pl.* **gangųnà**) 1. Any cylindrical drum with membrane at both ends. 2. Cylindrical or barrel-shaped container. **~r** ***jiki*** trunk of the body.
gàngan *adv.* (with **dą̀**) 1. Intentionally, deliberately: *da ~ ya zuba ruwa a shimfidata* he purposely spilled some water on my mat. 2. In a joking manner: *da ~ kake* you must be joking.
ganganci *n.m.* Acting in a careless or reckless way: *wannan direba yana ~* this driver is reckless.
gàngànimà *n.f.* Spying. **ɗan** ~ spy.
gangą̀ra *v.i.* Descend down slope, roll down, flow down: *shanu sun ~ rafi su sha ruwa* the cattle went down into the stream to drink.
gàngąrà *n.f.* Sloping ground, depression in ground: *zaman duniya hawa da ~* life has its ups and downs. ***sami*** ~ surmount one's obstacles.
gangąrè *n.m.* Bottom of a slope.
gangàrįyà *n.f.* Pure, unmixed state: *wannan zance gaskiya ne ~rta* what has been said is the absolute truth.
gąni *v.t.* (becomes **gą** before noun d.o. and **gan** before pro. d.o.) 1. See: *mun gan su a kasuwa* we saw them at the market; *mun ga doki* we saw a horse. 2. Look at, watch: *ina ~ sa'ad da suka tashi* I was looking on as they left. *n.m.* Opinion: *a ~nsa* in his opinion.

gą̀nimà *n.f.* Booty.
ganįyà *n.f.* Acme, peak: *yana ~r kuruciyarsa* he is in the prime of his youth.
gànsą̀kuką̀ *n.f.* Green slime collecting on stagnant water.
gàntą̀lį *n.m.* Aimless wandering.
gantsą̀ra *v.i.* 1. Be arched (of back). 2. Sag (of thatched roof). **gàntsąrà** *n.f.* Curvature of back.
gantsą̀re *v.t.* Arch one's back.
ganųwa *n.f.* Town wall.
ganye *n.m.* (*pl.* **ganyàye**) 1. Leaf, foliage. 2. Indian hemp. 3. Counterfeit money.
gą̀ra *n.f.* Termite(s).
gąr̃à *v.t.* Roll circular object along ground. *v.i.* Speed along: *yaro ya ~ a guje a kan kekensa* the boy sped off on his bicycle.
garą It would be better to: *~ mu tafi da wuri* we had better go early.
gara *n.f.* Presents of grain and other foodstuffs given by parents of bride to parents of groom.
gą̀ràje *n.m.* Quick action, haste.
gąr̃ą̀li *n.m.* Doing whatever one pleases.
gą̀rarà *n.m. or f.* Partially blind person.
gą̀rą̀ri *n.m.* Aimless wandering.
gąr̃ą̀r̃i *n.m.* Trouble: *Tanko ɗan ~ ne* Tanko is a troublesome person.
gą̀r̃às-gą̀r̃às *id.* Noise of chewing crunchy food: *yana tauna karas ~* he is munching carrots.
gą̀r̃ą̀tutè *n.m.* Pay given to s.o. leaving civil service.
gąrau *adv.* Clearly: *tana gani ~* she sees clearly.
gą̀raya *n.f.* (*pl.* **gą̀ràyu**) Two-stringed, plucked musical instrument, played esp. for hunters and at *bori* ceremonies.
gar̃dąmà *n.f.* (*pl.* **gar̃dàndąmi**) Dispute, disagreement, argument.
gar̃dì *n.m.* (*pl.* **gàr̃dàwa**). 1. Person who gives performances with snakes or hyenas. 2. Novice studying to become Islamic teacher.
gar̃ɗi *n.m.* Nutty flavour of roasted groundnuts, roasted millet, etc.
gą̀re *see* **gą̀.**
gąr̃ę, gąr̃er̃ę, *n.m.* Any circular object used by children to roll along ground.
gàr̃ę̀ *n.f.*(*pl.* **gar̃ųkà**) Type of small *riga* without embroidery.
gar̃ejį *n.m.* Garage.
gar̃gąda *n.f.* Corrugation on road.
gàr̃gąɗà (į/e) *v.t.* (*vn.* **gàr̃gą̀ɗi**) Warn.
gàr̃gą̀ɗi *n.m.* 1. Warning. 2. *vn.* of **gàr̃gąɗà.**
gar̃gajįya *n.f.* Olden times, traditional things.
gą̀ri *n.m.* 1.(*pl.* **gąrurųwà**) Town. ***mai*** *~* village head. ***ci*** *~* win (e.g. game or race). 2. Atmospheric change: *~ ya waye* it has dawned; *~ ya lumshe* it has become cloudy.
gàri *n.m.* 1. Flour. 2. Any substance in powdered form: *~n madara* powdered milk.
gą̀rin *conj.* In trying to, in the course of: *~ gugar rigata na ƙona ta* while ironing my gown I scorched it.
garjì *excl.* What a hot day!
garka *n.f.* (*pl.* **gąràke**) Small fenced-in garden.
garkè *n.m.* (*pl.* **gąrukkà**) Herd, flock.
gàrkųwa *n.f.* (*pl.* **garkųwoyi**) Shield.
gàr̃ma *n.f.* (*pl.* **gąr̃èmąni**) 1. Large hoe with wide blade. 2. Plough.
gàr̃mą̀hô *n.m.* Gramophone, record-player.
gàr̃u *n.m.* (*pl.* **gar̃ųkà**) Wall around town or compound.
gą̀r̃ur̃à *n.f.* Bright pink dye.
garwa *n.f.*(*pl.* **gąrèwąni**) 1. Kerosene tin. 2. Drum-like container for whitewash. 3. Sth. old, worn out: *~r mota* a dilapidated car.
garwashi *n.m.* Hot embers.
gâs *n.m.* 1. Diesel fuel. 2. Butane gas.
gąsà *v.t.* (*vn.* **gąshì**) Roast, grill directly before fire.
gàsa *n.f.* Competition.
gasà *excl.* Gosh!
gasą̀ya *n.f.* Herb used in making *miya.*
gashì *n.m.* (*pl.* **gasu**) 1. Hair. ***~n baki*** moustache. 2. Feather(s).

ɠaskạta *v.t.* 1. Believe. 2. Verify. **ɠàskạtạ̀** *v.i.* Be borne out, prove to be true: *labarin nan ya* ~ this news has proved to be true.

ɠàskę *adv.* Used in *da* ~ truly, really; *ƙwarai da* ~ very much so, definitely; *da yawan* ~ in great numbers.

ɠàskịya *n.f.* Truth. ***ba da*** ~ believe in, trust in: *ya ba da* ~ *ga Allah* he believes in God.

ɠatạ̀ *n.f. and adv.* Three days hence.

ɠata *n.m.* 1. Caring for, pampering: *Garba ɗan* ~ *ne* Garba is a pampered child. 2. Guardian, protector: *Allah* ~*n kowa* God is the protector of everyone.

ɠatancì *n.m.* Favoured treatment.

ɠàtạri *n.m.* (*pl.* **ɠatụrà**) Axe.

ɠạtò *n.m.* Female genitals.

ɠàtsa (ị/e) *v.t.* Bite off: *na gatsi rake* I bit off a piece of sugar cane. **ɠatsà** *v.t.* (with i.o.) Bite s.o.: *yaro ya* ~ *mini ɗan yatsa* the boy bit me on the finger.

ɠạ̀tse *n.m.* Sarcasm.

ɠàtsịne *n.m.* Sneering grimace.

ɠauɗè *n.m.* Thorny shrub.

ɠàuƙa *n.f.* Haste.

ɠaula *n.m. or f.* (*pl.* **ɠaulàye**) Fool.

ɠàurakà *n.m.* (*f.* **ɠàurakịya**, *pl.* **ɠàuràki**) Crownbird.

ɠaurạya *v.t.* Mix together: *na* ~ *gero da dawa* I mixed the millet and guinea-corn together. **ɠàurạyạ̀** *v.i.* Be uniformly mixed together.

ɠauta *n.m.* Dried form of the bitter tomato *ɗata*.

ɠautsi *n.m.* 1. Disrespectful behaviour. 2. Brittleness.

ɠawa *n.f.* (*pl.* **ɠawàwwạki**) Corpse.

ɠạwạ̀yi *n.m.* Charcoal.

ɠàwo *n.m.* Large acacia tree.

ɠàwur̃tạ̀ *v.i.* Become great, important.

ɠạyà *v.t.* (with i.o.) Tell: *na* ~ *masa ya zo* I told him to come.

ɠayà *n.f.* Extreme end: *ciwonsa ya kai* ~ he is desperately ill.

ɠaya *n.m.* 1. Sth. in unaccompanied, bare, or naked state: *ya kira sunana* ~ he called out my name without any form of address. ~***n tuwo*** plain *tuwo* without *miya*. 2. Small solid bits in *fura*, *koko*, or *kunu* not mixed into solution with milk or water.

ɠạyar̃ (dạ̀) *v.t.* (= **ɠai dạ̀** before d.o.) Greet, pay one's respects to.

ɠạ̀yauna *n.f.* (*pl.* **ɠạ̀yàuni**) Small patch or plot of land given to a young boy to farm on.

ɠayè *n.m.* Used in *ɗan* ~ cocky young person who wears Western dress.

ɠàyya *n.f.* 1. Communal work. 2. Invitation, esp. to communal work.

ɠayyà *n.f.* Thing done or said intentionally to annoy or embarrass someone.

ɠàyyạtà (cị/ce) *v.t.* Invite: *ya gayyace ni suna* he invited me to a naming ceremony.

ɠạzà *v.t.* 1. Fail to do, be unable: *na* ~ *tura mota ni kaɗai* I couldn't push the car alone. 2. Fall short of, be less than: *tsawonsa ya* ~ *ƙafa shiɗa* he is less than six feet tall. *v.i.* Fall short, not be enough: *kuɗina sun* ~ my money wasn't enough.

ɠạ̀zêt *n.f.* Gazette.

ɠefè *n.m.* (*pl.* **ɠyâffa**) Side, edge: ~*n kogi zai yi kyau da noman albasa* land by the side of the river is good for farming onions.

ɠèfen *prep.* Just before, just prior to: ~ *azahar* just before the 2 p.m. prayer.

ɠèga (ị/e) *v.t.* Rub along, scrape along: *kwalekwalena ya gegi gefen kogi* my canoe rubbed along the river bank.

ɠejì *n.m.* Gauge.

ɠemù *n.m.* Beard.

ɠero *n.m.* Millet.

ɠewạya *v.t.* Make tour of, make one's rounds: *gwamna ya* ~ *sojoji* the Governor made an inspection tour of the troops. *v.i.* 1. Go round. 2. Go to the latrine. **ɠèwạyà** *n.f.* Farm inspection.

ɠewạye *v.t.* Surround, encircle: *na* ~ *gonata da shinge* I put a fence around my farm. **ɠewạyè** *n.m.* 1. Enclosure. 2. Latrine.

ɠèza *n.f.* Mane, fringe.

ɠezà *n.f.* (*pl.* **ɠezoji**) Shrub with white flowers.

giɓi *n.m.* (*pl.* **giyaɓu**) 1. Gap from loss of tooth. 2. A shortage or gap in something: *ya kawo mini kuɗi da* ~ he brought the money to me with some missing.

giccìya *v.t.* Lay one thing across another: *ya* ~ *sanda a ƙofar gida* he placed a stick across the doorway. *v.i.* Lie across: *maciji ya* ~ *a hanya* a snake lay across the road.

gida *n.m.* (*pl.* **gidàje**) 1. House, compound. ***mai*** ~ head of a household. ***yaya*** ~? how's your family? ~***n gaskiya*** the Next World. 2. Building: ~*n abinci* hotel, restaurant; ~*n waya* post office. 3. Beehive, hornets' next. 4. Container: ~*n agogo* watch case; ~*n ruwa* car radiator; ~*n sauro* mosquito net. 5. Portion, section: *an kasa goro* ~ *biyu* the kolanuts were divided into two portions.

giftà *v.i.* Cross in front.

gîggiwà *n.f.* Acting wilfully, esp. a child.

gigice *v.i.* Be flustered.

giginyà *n.f.* (*pl.* **giginyu**) Deleb-palm.

gigita *v.t.* Upset, fluster: *labarin mutuwar Jatau ya* ~ *kowa* the news of Jatau's death upset everybody.

gijì *adv.* To home: *za ni* ~ I'm going home.

gilâs *n.m.* Glass.

gillà *n.f.* Used in *kisan* ~ treacherous killing.

gilmà *v.i.* Cross quickly in front.

gilò *n.m.* Aimless wandering.

gimbìya *n.f.* (*pl.* **gimbìyoyi**) Princess, daughter of a chief.

ginạ *n.f.* Flying termite(s).

ginà *v.t.* (*vn.* **gini**) 1. Build (with mud, cement, or bricks). 2. Make pottery. 3. Dig a hole.

gìndi *n.m.* 1. Bottom, base. 2. Buttocks. 3. Person's private parts.

gindi *n.m.* (*pl.* **gindàye**) Rope used to attach animal to stake or to hobble front and back feet on same side.

gìndin *prep.* At the foot of: *yaro na zaune* ~ *bishiya* the boy is seated at the foot of the tree.

gini *n.m.* (*pl.* **ginẹ-ginẹ**) 1. Building made of mud or cement. 2. *vn.* of **ginà**.

ginsa (shi/she) *v.t.* Have as much as one can stand of a particular food. *n.f.* Quality of a food which one cannot eat much of: *wainar kwai tana da* ~ one cannot eat a lot of egg-*waina*.

ginshiƙi *n.m.* (*pl.* **ginshiƙai**) Pillar supporting a roof.

gira *n.f.* Eyebrow, eyelash.

girâm *n.m.* Gramme.

girbè *v.t.* (*vn.* **girbi**) Reap corn.

gir̃giɗe *v.t.* Uproot by shaking: *yaro ya* ~ *itacen da aka kafa* the boy pulled up the tree that had been planted.

gir̃gije *v.t. and v.i.* (*vn.f.* **gir̃gizà**) Shake off, shake to and fro: *doki ya* ~ the horse shook itself off (after rolling in dirt).

gir̃gijè *n.m.* (*pl.* **gizàgizai**) Rain-cloud.

giri *n.m.* Deceit.

gir̃îs *n.m.* Grease.

girkà *v.t.* (*vn.* **girki**) Put a pot on the fire.

girka *n.f.* Initiation of a person into *bori* cult.

girma (i/e) *v.t.* Be older than: *Musa ya girme ni da shekara shida* Musa is six years older than me. **girmạ** *v.i.* Grow up, become grown up. **girma** *n.m.* 1. Bigness, size. ~***n kai*** pride, conceit. 2. Importance, prestige. ***ban*** ~ respect. ***mai*** ~ the honourable . . .

girmạma *v.t.* Honour, show respect to: *yana* ~ *na gaba da shi* he respects his elders.

gishiri *n.m.* Salt.

giwa *n.f.* (*pl.* **giwàye**) Elephant.

giwar-ruwạ *n.f.* Nile perch.

[1]**giyà** *n.f.* Any alcoholic drink.

[2]**giyà** *n.f.* Gear.

gizàgizai *pl.* of **gir̃gijè**.

gizàgo *n.m.* Adze.

gizo *n.m.* Full bushy head of hair on man: *ɗan gaye ya tare* ~ the dandy has a bushy hair style.

gizọ̀ *n.m.* Trickster figure in folk-tales. ***bakan*** ~ rainbow. **gizò** *n.m.* Inspiring fear in s.o. by means of tricky changes in one's appearance.

gịzọ̀gịzọ̀ *n.m.* Spider.
gobà *n.f.* Guava.
gòbạr̃a *n.f.* Conflagration, fire.
gòbẹ *n.f. and adv.* Tomorrow. *watan* ~ next month.
gocè *v.t.* Displace, knock away. *v.i.* 1. Swerve aside, swerve off road or track: *jirgi ya* ~ *daga kan dogo* the train derailed. 2. Become displaced, drop away: *sandar da na tokare taga da ita ta* ~ the stick with which I propped the window up fell away.
gocịya *n.f.* 1. Swerving aside, dodging. 2. Being dodgy, evasive: *Audu ya cika yawan* ~ Audu is very evasive.
godè *v.t. and v.i.* Thank, be thankful.
gòdịya *n.f.* Thanks, gratitude.
goɗịya *n.f.* (*pl.* **goɗịyoyi**) Mare.
gogà *v.t.* (with i.o.) Rub on: *ya* ~ *mini gawayi a riga* he rubbed charcoal on my garment.
goga *n.m.* 1. An experienced, capable person in whom others place their confidence. 2. Favourite friend or literary character.
gògagge *n. and adj.* (*f.* **gògaggịya,** *pl.* **gògàggu**) Experienced, skilled.
gòge *n.m.* Large one-stringed, bowed musical instrument.
gogè *v.t.* (*vn.f.* **gugà**) 1. Scrape dirt off, rub sth. to clean or polish: *kafinta ya* ~ *katako* the carpenter scraped the plank clean. 2. Iron clothes. 3. Belittle s.o. publicly.
[1]**goho** *n.m.* Bending forward with elbows on ground and buttocks in air.
[2]**goho** *n.m.* An all-grey donkey.
golà *n.m.* Goalkeeper.
golo *n.m.* (*pl.* **golàye**) Testicle(s).
gomà̧ *n.f. and adj.* Ten.
gòmịya *n.f.* Multiple of ten used with higher numbers: ~ *tara* ninety.
gona *n.f.* (*pl.* **gònà̧ki**) Farm.
gòra *n.m.* (*pl.* **gorụnà**) 1. Large, round gourd used by fishermen. 2. Large bottle gourd.
gorà *n.f.* (*pl.* **gorori**) 1. Bamboo, cane. 2. Stripe in cloth. 3. Crease, pleat in clothes.
gorì *n.m.* Embarrassing or belittling s.o. by recalling favours done for him in the past.
gori *n.m.* Children's toy top.
gòr̃ịya *n.f.* Biggest and best kolanuts.
gor̃ọ̀ *n.m.* 1. Kolanut. 2. Any small gift or reward.
gòrụbà *n.f.* (*pl.* **gòrụ̀bu**) Dum-palm.
gòshi *n.m.* 1. Forehead. 2. Foremost part of sth.: ~*n mota* front grill of car. 3. Person or thing whose arrival brings good luck: *amarya ta yi* ~ the bride brought good luck to the house. **ɗan** ~ a favourite.
gòshin *prep.* Just prior to: ~ *azahar* just before two o'clock; ~ *kaka* time just before harvest.
gotà *v.t.* Be a little more or longer than: *tsawon wandonka ya* ~ *na Audu* your trousers are a little longer than Audu's.
gòya (ị/e) *v.t.* (*vn.* **goyo**) 1. Care for a child: *ta goye shi har ya girma* she cared for him until he grew up. 2. (with **baya**) Concur with, support: *na goyi bayanka* I am in agreement with you. **goyà** *v.t.* Carry, usu. on the back: *ta* ~ *ɗanta* she carried her child on her back; *ya* ~ *ni a kekensa* he carried me on his bicycle.
goyo *n.m.* 1. Thing or person carried on back. 2. Infant, baby. 3. *vn.* of **gòya.**
gû *see* **wụri.**
gụbà *n.f.* Poison.
[1]**gụ̀da (ị/e)** *v.t.* (*vn.* **gụdù**) Run away from: *yaro ya guji gidansu* the boy ran away from home.
[2]**gụ̀da** *n.m.* (*pl.* **gụ̀dàji**) 1. One: *ta ba da kobo* ~ she gave one kobo. 2. Unit of one: ~ *nawa?* how many? ~ *ashirin* twenty. 3. Lumps in *tuwo, fura,* etc.
gụ̀danà̧ *v.i.* 1. Flow (of water). 2. Progress (of work, etc.)
gụdanar̃ (dà̧) *v.t.* Run, administer: *Garba ne yake* ~ *da ayyukan ma'aikatar nan* Garba is the one who administers this factory.
gụdàwa *n.f.* Diarrhoea: *yana* ~ he has the runs.

gỵdỳ *v.i.* Run, run away. **gỵdù** *n.m.* 1. Running, running away: *doki ya yi* ~ the horse ran away. *da* ~ quickly, fast. 2. *vn.* of **gỳda** and **gỵdỳ.**

gỳdỵmà *n.f.* (*pl.* **gỵdỵmomi**) Hammer.

gỵdùmmạwa *n.f.* Help, assistance.

gỵdun-gỳdùn *id.* Very big: *na sayi doya* ~ I bought great big yams.

gỵdùn-zucịya *n.f.* Tact.

guɗà *n.f.* (*pl.* **gùɗẹ-gùɗẹ**) Shrilling done by women to express joy.

gùga *n.m.* (*pl.* **gugỵnà**) Bucket for drawing water from well.

gùgỵwà *n.f.* Whirlwind.

gỵjè *v.i.* (with i.o.) Run away from: *ya* ~ *masa da kekensa* he ran off with his bicycle.

gỵjịya *n.f.* Bambara groundnuts.

gulbi *n.m.* (*pl.* **gỵlàbe**) River.

gulmạ *n.f.* Setting one person against another through gossip, etc.

gỳlôb *n.m.* Globe, light-bulb for torch or headlamp of car.

gỳmàgỳmai *pl.* of **gungỵmè.**

gỵmàka *pl.* of **gunkì.**

gùmba *n.f.* Sweet pounded millet mixed with water.

gỳmi *n.m.* 1. Perspiration, sweat. 2. Hot weather.

gûn *see* **wỵrin.**

gỵnà *n.f.* Plant with bitter round fruit.

gỵnàgỵni *n.m.* Complaining.

gundà *n.f.* (*pl.* **gundoji**) Young fruit, esp. pumpkin.

gùndỵmà *n.f.* (*pl.* **gundỵmomi**) Administrative district.

gundỳma *v.t.* Do much of evil act: *an* ~ *masa sata* he was heavily robbed; *ya* ~ *ashar* he swore profusely.

gùndỵrà (ị/e) *v.t.* Lose interest in, be tired of: *hutun nan ya gundure ni* I've had enough of this vacation. **gùndỵrạ̀** *v.i.* Become bored, fed up.

gundỵwa *n.f.* Slice of sth.

gunɗà *n.f.* Wood-boring insect.

gungỵmè *n.m.* (*pl.* **gỳmàgỳmai**) Log.

gùngỳni *n.m.* Grumbling to oneself, complaining.

gunjì *n.m.* Growling by animal.

gunkì *n.m.* (*pl.* **gỵmàka**) Idol, fetish.

guntu *n. and adj.* (*f.* **guntỵwa,** *pl.* **guntàye**) 1. Short. 2. Stub: *guntuwar taba* cigarette butt.

guntỳle *v.t. and v.i.* Cut short: *jelar kare ta* ~ the dog's tail is cut short.

gunya *n.f.* Light greyish-brown horse.

gỳr̃asà *n.f.* Baked wheat-cake.

gurbì *n.m.* (*pl.* **gỵràba**) 1. Shallow hole in ground, rock, etc. *~n ido* eye socket. 2. Place where person or thing is usually to be found.

gurɓàce *v.t. and v.i.* Stir up sediment in water: *shanu sun* ~ *ruwa* the cattle have stirred up mud in the water.

gur̃ɗè *v.t.* Cause a sprain or dislocation: *na ka da shi har na* ~ *shi* I threw him down with such force that I sprained his foot. *v.i.* Become sprained or dislocated.

gur̃fàna *v.i.* Kneel with front legs or elbows on ground, such as by camel or by woman crouching in childbirth.

gurgù *n. and adj.* (*f.* **gurgỳwa,** *pl.* **gỵràgu**) Lame, cripple.

gurgùnce *v.i.* Become lame.

gurgùnta *v.t.* Make lame: *ciwon ƙafa ya* ~ *shi* the injury to his foot has lamed him. **gùrguntạ̀** *v.i.* Go badly, not turn out as planned (e.g. work).

gùrgỵrà (ị/e) *v.t.* Gnaw.

gur̃gỵzu *n.m.* A crowd or mass composed entirely of one kind of thing: *waɗancan mutanen makafi ~nsu* that group of people are all blind; *wake* ~ beans cooked alone.

gỵri *see* **wỵri.**

gỵrin *see* **wỵrin.**

gỵringuntsi *n.m.* Cartilage, gristle.

gurjè *v.t.* Gin cotton.

gùrji *n.m.* Small cucumber-like vegetable.

gùr̃nàni *n.m.* Growling (e.g. of lion or dog).

gur̃u *n.m.* (*pl.* **gur̃àye**) Large leather belt usu. containing charms.

gỵsà *v.i.* Move aside, move a little

gų̀shè *v.i.* 1. Pass by, move on. 2. Die.

gųtsų̀ra *v.t.* Break piece off.

gųtsų̀re *v.t.* (with i.o.) Break off piece of sth. belonging to s.o.: *gatari ya* ~ *mini ɗan yatsa* a piece of my finger was taken off by the hoe. *v.i.* Become broken off: *wutsiyar ƙadangare ta* ~ the lizard's tail broke off. **gųtsųrè** *n.m.* Fragment, piece.

gųzà *n.m.* Lizard, water-monitor.

gųzųma *n.f.* (*pl.* **gų̀zų̀mai, gųzàme**) 1. Old cow. 2. Old woman.

gų̀zųri *n.m.* 1. Provisions for a journey. 2. Travel allowance.

gwaɓi *n.m.* Being thick-set, sturdy (of person).

gwąda̍ *v.t.* (*vn.* **gwąjì**) 1. Measure, measure out. 2. Test, try. 3. Compare: *na* ~ *aikin jiya da na yau* I compared yesterday's work with today's. 4. (with i.o.) Show, demonstrate: *ya* ~ *mini yadda ake kunce taya* he showed me how to take off the tyre.

gwą̀dǫ̀ *n.m.* (*pl.* **gwaddųnà**) Handwoven heavy cotton blanket worn over shoulder by men.

gwaɗąre *n.m.* Acting or dressing in a conspicuous manner in order to attract attention.

gwą̀fa *n.f.* (*pl.* **gwą̀fànni, gwąfofi**) Forked end of a stick. *~r danƙo* catapult.

[1]**gwaggǫ̀** *n.m.* Usu. used in *~n biri* baboon.

[2]**gwaggǫ̀** *n.f.* 1. Paternal aunt. 2. An old woman.

gwagwàgwa *n.f.* Struggling with difficulty.

gwągwarcì *n.m.* Bachelorhood.

gwągwàrmąyà *n.f.* Struggling, as in wrestling, etc.

gwàgwįyà (į/e) *v.t.* Gnaw at.

gwaibà *see* **gobà.**

gwaidų̀wa *n.f.* Egg-yolk.

gwaiwa *n.f.* Testicle(s).

gwąjì *n.m.* 1. Experiment, test: *gonar* ~ experimental farm. 2. Demonstration: *~n kayayyakin amfanin gona* agricultural show. 3. *vn.* of **gwąda̍.**

[1]**gwâl** *n.m.* Goal (football, etc.).

[2]**gwâl** *n.m.* Gold.

gwą̀làn-gwąlan *n.m.* 1. Speaking unintelligibly. 2. Speaking in a language which is foreign to listener.

gwąlè *v.t.* Embarrass or hurt s.o.'s feelings by purposely snubbing or interrupting him.

gwalè *v.t.* Open eyes widely.

gwalę̀-gwalę̀ *n.m.* Fatigue duties assigned to soldier, student, etc.

gwalo *n.m.* Grimace.

gwambą̀za *n.f.* Western waterbuck.

gwàmmą̀ Rather, it would be better if: ~ *mu tafi yau* we had better go today.

gwammą̀ce *v.i.* Be preferable: *ya* ~ *mu tafi Amirka da Ingila* we would prefer going to America than to England.

gwamnà *n.m.* (*pl.* **gwamnoni**) Governor. ***gwamna-janar*** governor-general.

gwamnątį *n.f.* (*pl.* **gwamnątoci**) Government.

gwamų̀tsa *v.t.* Mix or gather together an assortment of things.

gwàmųtsą̀ *v.i.* Be crowded closely together.

gwąnànce *v.i.* Be or become an expert: *ya* ~ *da ɗinki* he has become an expert tailor.

gwàndą̀ *see* **gwàmmą̀.**

gwandà *n.f.* (*pl.* **gwandoji**) Pawpaw. ***~r dawa*** custard-apple.

gwangwąni *n.m.* (*pl.* **gwangwąnàye**) Small tin.

gwą̀ni *n.m.* (*f.* **gwą̀na,** *pl.* **gwąnàye**) Expert, highly skilled person.

gwànjo *n.m.* Auction sale.

gwanki *n.m.* (*pl.* **gwankàye**) Roan antelope.

gwàno *n.m.* Stink-ant. ***jerin*** ~ in a single file, in succession.

gwàr̃gwądo *n.m.* Proportion, moderation: *ya yi taimako daidai* ~ he helped moderately.

gwàr̃gwądon *prep.* In proportion to: *kowa ya ba da taimako* ~ *ikonsa* each should contribute according to his ability.

gwarį *n.m.* Yard engine used to shift railroad cars around.

gwàrje *n.m.* Bell, usu. hung round neck of donkey.

gwar̃zo *n.m.* (*f.* **gwar̃zụwa**, *pl.* **gwar̃zàye, gwạr̃àje**) Person of great energy and pluck.

gwatsò *n.m.* Twisting motion of hips in dancing.

gwauro *n.m.* (*f.* **gwaurụwa**, *pl.* **gwagwàre, gwauràye**) Now unmarried person who was formerly married.

gwaza *n.f.* Koko-yam.

gwàzarmà *n.f.* Grub found in refuse heaps.

gwiɓà *n.m.* Sediment at bottom of water pot.

gwiwà *n.f.* (*pl.* **gwiwoyi**) Knee.

gyạ̀ɗa *n.f.* Groundnut(s).

gyạ̀lẹ̀ *n.m.* (*pl.* **gyạloli**) Woman's shawl.

gyàmbo *n.m.* (*pl.* **gyambụnà**) Ulcerated wound.

gyàngyạɗi *n.m.* Nodding due to drowsiness.

gyangyạ̀re *v.i.* Fall down dead.

gyarà *v.t.* Repair, straighten up, make neat. **gyara** *n.m.* 1. Repairs. 2. Small amount of corn, meat, etc. added by seller to that which is actually paid for. 3. Amendment to constitution, etc.

gyàre *n.m.* Large cricket which buzzes loudly.

gyârta *v.t.* Repair.

gyartai *n.m.* Calabash mender.

gyàtsa *n.f.* Belching.

gyàtụma *n.f.* (*pl.* **gyàtụ̀mai**) 1. An old woman. 2. Polite term for referring either to one's mother or to s.o. else's mother.

gyàuro *n.m.* Plants growing in farm from seeds unintentionally dropped or left in ground.

gyautò *n.m.* (*pl.* **gyautụnà**) Woman's large wrapper.

H

hạbạ̀ *excl.* 1. Used in negative persuasion or coaxing: ~ *kyale ni* come, come, leave me alone! ~ *yi shiru mana* please stop crying! 2. Used when sth. is finally understood: ~ *yanzu na ji magana* now I understand this matter. 3. Used in contradicting: ~ *wa zai yarda da wannan?* come on, who would agree with that?

hạba-hạba *n.f.* Taking good care of s.o. or sth., looking after: *yana ~ da amaryarsa* he is taking good care of his bride.

hạbaici *n.m.* Innuendo, hint, indirect reference.

hạɓà *n.f.* (*pl.* **hạɓoɓi**) Chin.

hạ̀ɓạkạ̀ *v.i.* Expand, swell: *kogi yana ~* the river is swelling; *arzikin Audu yana ~* Audu's wealth is increasing.

hạɓàr̃ kạdà *n.f.* Cotton cap with pointed flaps which cover ears, worn esp. by Fulani.

haɓẹ̀ *n.m. or pl.* Hausa person who has no Fulani ancestry.

hạɓò *n.m.* Nose-bleed.

hạ̀dà-hạda *n.f.* Buying season for cash crops.

hạdạri *n.m.* Storm.

haddà *n.f.* Memorization.

haddạ̀ce *v.t.* Memorize: *ya ~ shi a ka* he learned it by heart.

haddạ̀sa *v.t.* Cause, bring about.

haddi *n.m.* (*pl.* **haddodi**) 1. Fixed punishment for transgressing Islamic law: *~n sata* punishment for theft. 2. Limit: *ya wuce ~* he went over the limit.

hạ̀disi *n.m.* (*pl.* **hạ̀disai**) Practices, traditions, sayings of the Prophet Muhammad.

hạɗà *v.t.* 1. Join, unite: *sun ~ kai suna ciniki* they amalgamated their business; *~ kai shi ne ƙarfi* unity is strength. ~ **baki** conspire. 2. Introduce: *na ~ shi da manaja* I introduced him to the manager.

hạɗaka *n.f.* Sth. shared by many: *garin nan na* ~ *ne* this town is made up of many tribes.
hạɗạmà *n.f.* Greed.
hạɗạr̃i *n.m.* (*pl.* **hạɗạr̃ur̃r̃ụkà**) 1. Danger, risk. 2. Accident, serious calamity.
haɗɗì *n.m.* Fortune-telling.
hạɗì *n.m.* 1. Mixing or putting together things of different quality (e.g. gowns or perfumes). 2. Causing mischief, setting other people to quarrel.
hạɗịye *v.t.* (*vn.f.* **hạɗịyà**) Swallow.
hạɗụ *v.i.* 1. Be joined, meet. 2. Be full-blown: *taron ya* ~ the crowd has gathered fully; *hadari ya* ~ the storm is at its height.
hafsà *n.m.* (*pl.* **hafsoshi**) Army officer.
hạga (ị/e) *v.t.* Borrow without intention to pay back: *Audu ya hagi Bala naira goma* Audu borrowed ten Naira from Bala with no intention to repay him.
hạgụ, hạgun *adv.* 1. Left: *yana ɓarin* ~ it is on the left-hand side. 2. Contrary to expectation: *harkokin sun zo ta* ~ the affairs are not in our favour.
haibà *n.f.* Appearance which inspires respect.
hàifa (ị/e) *v.t.* Give birth to, beget: *ta haifi 'ya'ya uku* she had three children; *sauri ya haifi nawa* haste makes waste.
haifụ̀ *v.i.* (*vn.f.* **haifụwa**) Give birth, be capable of giving birth: *ba ta* ~ *ba tukuna* she has not had any children yet.
haiƙàn *adv.* Very much, exceedingly.
hailà *n.f.* Menstruation, monthly period.
ha'incị *n.m.* Fraud, deceit.
hair̃àn *n.m.* Good deed: *abokina ya yi mini* ~ my friend has done me a good turn.
hajà *n.f.* (*pl.* **hajoji**) Merchandise, goods.
hạjịjịyà *n.f.* 1. Dizziness. 2. Act of turning round and round to make oneself dizzy.
hàjjạtu *n.m.* Learning to read in syllables.
hajjị, hạjị *n.m.* The Greater Hajj.
hạkạ *adv.* Thus: *kamar* ~ like this; *saboda* ~ therefore. ***duk da*** ~ nevertheless. ~ ***nan*** just like that, that's how. ***haka-haka*** so-so, not quite right, not properly done.
hạki *n.m.* Panting, gasping.
hạkì *n.m.* (*pl.* **hạkukụwà**) 1. Grass. 2. Reed mouthpiece of an *algaita*.
hạkikà *see* **hakkàn.**
hạkikànce *v.i.* Be certain about sth.: *na* ~ *za su dawo gobe* I'm positive that they will return tomorrow.
hakìmce *v.i.* Put on airs of self-importance.
hakịmi *n.m.* (*pl.* **hàkịmai**) 1. District head. 2. Any traditional title-holder.
hạkịyà *n.f.* Leucoma (eye disease).
hakkàn *adv.* Undoubtedly, surely, really.
hakkì *n.m.* (*pl.* **hakkoki**) Due, right: *an ba shi* ~*nsa* he was given his due respect; *ya ɗauki* ~*n matarsa* he deprived his wife of her rights.
hạƙà *v.t.* Dig.
hạƙàrƙạri *n.m.* Rib(s).
hạƙiƙà *see* **hakkàn.**
hạƙilo *n.m.* Giving much effort for little gain: *yana ta* ~*n neman kudi* he's going to more trouble than it is worth looking for a job.
haƙƙàn *see* **hakkàn.**
hạƙò *n.m.* Trap, plan to get sth.
hạƙori *n.m.* (*pl.* **hạƙòra**) Tooth.
hạƙụrạ *v.i.* Be patient, withstand hardship.
hạƙụri *n.m.* Patience, resignation.
hạlâ *adv.* Possibly: ~ *bai zo ba* perhaps he has not come.
hạlạka *v.t.* Destroy. **hạlạkạ** *v.i.* Perish, be destroyed.
hạlâl *n.m.* Any lawful act acc. to Islamic law and religion. ***ɗan*** ~ an honourable person, legitimately-born child.
hạlàlta *v.t.* Declare sth. lawful acc. to Islamic law and religion: *an* ~ *auren mata hudu* Islam allows a man to have four wives. **hạlaltạ** *v.i.* Be legal, legitimate.
hạlamà *see* **ạlamà.**

hạlaftà (cị/ce) *v.t.* Attend (meeting, party).
hạli *n.m.* (*pl.* **halàye**) Character, temperament, disposition.
hali *n.m.* Condition, circumstances, situation: *a ~n da ake ciki yanzu* under the present circumstances; *kana da ~n ranta mini naira goma?* are you in a position to lend me ten Naira?
hạlittà *n.f.*(*pl.* **hạlittu**) 1. Creature, creation. 2. Form, shape: *mai kyan ~* well-formed. ***labarin ~*** nature study.
hàllạfạ̀ *v.i.* Appear, arrive.
halwà *n.f.* Religious solitude, retreat: *ya shiga ~ ta wata ɗaya* he has gone into retreat for one month.
hâm *n.m.* Horn of car or lorry: *yi ~* honk the horn.
hạmadà *n.f.* Desert (esp. the Sahara Desert).
hạmạ̀mi *n.m.* Sth. which tastes or smells acrid or astringent.
hạmayyà *n.f.* Rivalry, opposition (political). ***abokin ~*** rival, political opponent.
hàmbụɗà (ị/e) *v.t.* Throw powdered or ground thing into the mouth.
hàmɓạrà (ị/e) *v.t.* Kick.
hamdạlà *n.f.* Giving thanks, showing gratitude to God.
hạmilạ̀ *n.f.* (*pl.* **hạmìlu**) Sword-sling.
[1]**hammà** *n.f.* Act of yawning.
[2]**hammà** *n.f.* 1. Hammer. 2. Distributor points in car or motorcycle engine.
hammạ̀ta *n.f.* (*pl.* **hammạtoci**) Armpit.
hamsà *n.f. and adj.* Five thousand.
hàmsạ̀mịyà *n.f. and adj.* Five hundred.
hàmsin *n.f. and adj.* Fifty. ***ɗan ~*** man who dresses and behaves like a woman.
hạnà *v.t.* 1. Prevent, deter. 2. Forbid, make illegal. 3. Refuse: *na ~ shi 'yata* I refused him my daughter (in marriage).
hancì *n.m.* (*pl.* **hantụnà**) 1. Nose. ***~n allura*** eye of a needle. 2. Bribe: *cin ~* accepting a bribe.
hancị *adv* (with **ạ̀**) In the nose.
hàndụmà (ị/e) *v.t.* Eat a lot of.
hàndụ̀mau *n.m. or f.* Glutton.
hànga (ị/e) *v.t.* (*vn.* **hànge**) 1. See sth. from afar, in the distance. 2. Foresee.
hàngum *n.m.* Mumps.
hạnì *n.m.* Prohibition: *na yi masa ~n yawon banza* I forbade him to go wandering around foolishly.
hànị'àn *n.m.* Satisfaction, contentment.
hạ̀ninịyà *n.f.* Neighing.
hanji *n.m.* Intestines, guts. ***~n agogo*** mainspring of watch. ***~n fitila*** lamp wick.
hankạ̀ɗa *v.t.* 1. Push s.o. or sth. forward. 2. Lift up edge of mat, cloth, etc.
hànkakà *n.f.* (*pl.* **hànkàki**) 1. Pied crow. 2. Fool.
hankạ̀li *n.m.* (*pl.* **hankụlà**) 1. Sense, intelligence. 2. Attention: *ba ni ~nka* pay attention to me. 3. Care: *ka yi ~ da shi* be careful with it; *a ~* slowly, carefully.
hankịcị *n.m.* (*pl.* **hankịtoci**) Handkerchief.
hànƙoro *n.m.* Showing impatient eagerness.
hannu *n.m.* (*pl.* **hannụwà, hannàye**) 1. Hand. ***~n baiwa*** generous hand. ***~n giwa*** elephant's trunk. ***~n riga*** sleeve. 2. Control, authority: *ba shi da ~ a kanmu* he has no authority over us. 3. Possession, share: *ya shiga ~na* it is in my possession.
hantà *n.f.* (*pl.* **hantoci, hantụnà**) Liver.
hantsà *n.f.* 1. Udder. 2. Breast(s). 3. Crotch of trousers.
hàntsạki *n.m.* (*pl.* **hàntsạ̀kai, hantsụkà**) Pincers, tongs, tweezers.
hàntsi *n.m.* Time of day from about 7 a.m. to 11 a.m.
hanyà *n.f.* (*pl.* **hanyoyi**) 1. Road, path: *~r ruwa* watercourse, canal. 2. Way, means, method: *ya sami ~* he found a means of getting his way; *ba ~ a yi* there is no way of doing it.
hanzạri *n.m.* 1. Speed, haste: *ka komo da ~!* come back quickly! 2. Excuse, pretext: *na faɗa masa ~na* I told him my excuse.

haȓ *conj.* 1. As far as, up to: *an yi hanya daga Kano* ~ *Dau*ȓ*a* a road has been built all the way from Kano to Daura; *abin ya kai mu* ~ *ga sarki* the affair has led us right to the chief. 2. Up until: *tun jiya ake yin ruwa* ~ *yau da safe* it has been raining from yesterday up until this morning; *zan iya tsayawa* ~ *ka gama* I can wait until you have finished; *sun yi aiki* ~ *sun gaji* they worked until they got tired. 3. Even, including: *na gaya wa kowa* ~ *sarki* I told everyone, even the chief; *Audu ya zo* ~ *da ɗan'uwansa* Audu has come with his brother as well; *mun sauka* ~ *mun yi wanka* we've arrived and have even bathed. 4. Even though, even with, in spite of: ~ *taimakon da aka yi masa bai ci ba* in spite of the help that he was given, he didn't pass. 5. So much so that: *ciwo ya ci ƙarfinsa* ~ *ya kashe shi* the illness weakened him so much that it killed him.

hạra (ị/e) *v.t.* Try to attain a position or reach a place: *ya hari gadon sarauta* he attempted to win the chieftaincy.

hạȓabà *n.f.* (*pl.* **hạȓabobi**) Area closed off for privacy.

hạȓạfi *n.m.* (*pl.* **hạȓụfà, hạȓạfai**) Any letter of alphabet.

hạȓaji *n.m.* Tax.

hạȓâm *n.m.* Any unlawful act acc. to Islamic law and religion.

hạȓạmà *n.f.* Intending to, on the point of: *ina* ~*r tafiya gobe* I am getting ready to go tomorrow.

hạȓàmta *v.t.* Declare sth. unlawful acc. to Islamic law and religion: *an* ~ *shan giya* drinking is forbidden. **hạȓamtạ** *v.i.* Be unlawful: *karɓar hanci ya* ~ it is illegal to accept a bribe.

hạrarà (ị/e) *v.t.* (*vn.f.* **hạrara**) Glare at s.o.

hạrawà *n.f.* Leaves or stalks of beans, groundnuts, etc. used for fodder.

hàȓba (ị/e) *v.t.* (*vn.* **haȓbi**) 1. Shoot. 2. Sting: *kunama ta harbe shi* the scorpion stung him. 3. Kick (by animal): *yi hankali kada jaki ya harbe ka* be careful lest the donkey kick you. 4. Infect s.o. **haȓbà** *v.t.* Fire a weapon. *v.i.* 1. Be spoiled (chance, image, etc.): *koren zare a kan farar riga ya* ~ green embroidery clashes with a white gown. 2. Begin to ripen (fruits).

haȓdà *see* **haddà.**

haȓɗè *v.i.* 1. Become entangled 2. Sit cross-legged.

hàrgàgi *n.m.* Uproar.

hàrgịtsi *n.m.* Disagreement, argument, dissension.

hạri *n.m.* (*pl.* **hạrẹ-hạrẹ**) Raid: *sun kai wa Kano* ~ they raided Kano.

haȓkà *n.f.* (*pl.* **haȓkoki**) 1. Business, affair. 2. Movement: *ba ya* ~ *da hannunsa* he can't move his hand.

hàrƙịya *n.f.* A common grass used for fodder.

[1]**hàȓsashi** *n.m.* Bullet, cartridge, shell. ~ ***mai linzami*** guided missile.

[2]**hàȓsashi** *n.m.* Foundation of building: *sarki ya sa* ~ *ginin masallaci* the Emir laid the foundation for the mosque.

harshè *n.m.* (*pl.* **harsụnà, hạràsa**) 1. Tongue. 2. Tip of sth. (flame, sword, whip, etc.). 3. Language.

hàȓzụƙạ *v.i.* Become suddenly angry, lose one's temper.

hạsạlạ *v.i.* Become angry. **hạsạlà** *n.f.* Anger.

hasạli 1. In fact: ~ *ma dai Audu yana cikin wadanda suka tafi* Audu, in fact, is among those who went. 2. It would be best: ~ *ma dai ka taho da shi gobe* you had better bring it tomorrow.

hạsaȓà *n.f.* (*pl.* **hạsaȓoȓi**) Misfortune, loss.

haskà *v.t.* Illuminate, make light: *farin wata ya* ~ *ɗakin* the moon lit up the room.

haske *n.m.* 1. Light, brightness. 2. Quick intellect. 3. Hint.

hassạdà *n.f.* Envy.

hạsumịyà *n.f.* Minaret, tower.

hatịmi *n.m.* (*pl.* **hàtịmai**) 1. Seal, official stamp. 2. Badge.

hạtsạbibi *n.m.* (*f.* **hạtsạbibịya,** *pl.* **hạtsạbibai**) 1. Person with extraordinary ability. 2. Magician.

hạtsànịya *n.f.* Loud argument, wrangling.
hạtsạ̀r̃i *see* **hạɗạ̀r̃i.**
hatsi *n.m.* Corn, grain.
hàtta *conj.* Even: *kowa ya zo wajen taro* ~ *sarki ma ya zo* everyone came to the gathering, even the Emir.
hattạr̃à *n.f.* Alertness, attentiveness.
hau *v.t.* (*vn.* **hạwa**) 1. Mount, climb, ride. ~ ***gado*** succeed to office. 2. Begin: *mu* ~ *kan karatu* let's start reading. *v.i.* 1. Be in excess: *guda uku sun* ~ there are three too many. 2. Go up, increase in price.
hàuka *n.m.* 1. Madness, being possessed by spirits, being out of self-control. ***ciwon*** ~ = ~***n kare*** rabies. 2. Roughness (of lake, river).
haukạ̀ce *v.i.* Become mad.
haunị 1. *See* **hạgụ.** 2. *n.m.* Executioner.
haur̃à *v.t.* 1. Climb over. 2. Exceed: *kuɗin da ya samu sun* ~ *naira ɗaya* he got more than one Naira.
hàur̃e *n.m.* Low place in town wall where people cross in and out.
haurè *n.m.* 1. Tooth. 2. Tusk, ivory.
hausạ *n.f.* 1. Hausa language. 2. Any language. 3. Meaning: *ban gane* ~*rka ba* I don't understand what you mean.
hàusàncẹ *adv.* (with **ạ̀**) 1. In Hausa. 2. Clearly, frankly: *ka bayyana mini a* ~ explain it to me in straightforward language.
haushì *n.m.* Barking of dog.
haushi *n.m.* Annoyance: *na ɗan ji* ~*nsa* I was a bit annoyed with him.
hautsụ̀na *v.t.* 1. Mix together, esp. materials for making mud bricks. 2. Muddle things up.
hauya *n.f.* (*pl.* **hauyoyi**) Small hoe.
hạwa *vn.* of **hau.**
hạ̀wa'i *n.m. or f.* Irresponsible person.
hạ̀wainịya *n.f.* Chameleon.
hạwàye *n.pl.* Tears.
[1]**hạyà** *v.t.* Cross over, traverse.
[2]**hạyà** *v.t.* Hire, rent.
hạyaƙi *n.m.* Smoke.
hạ̀yàm-hạ̀yàm *id.* Gobbling up food: *yana cin abinci* ~ he is gobbling up his food.
hạ̀yànịya *n.f.* Uproar, tumult, din.
hạyì *n.m.* 1. Side of a river, valley, town. 2. Thatched roof of a room.
haza wassạ̀lam Formula for closing a letter or saying good-bye.
[1]**hazbịya** *n.f.* (*pl.* **hazbịyoyi**) Speckled pigeon.
[2]**hazbịya** *n.f.* Stye.
hazịƙi *n. and adj.* (*f.* **hazịƙa,** *pl.* **hàzịƙai**) Intelligent, sharp.
hạzo *n.m.* 1. Haze, mist. 2. Shortsightedness: *idona ya yi* ~ my sight is not good.
hê *excl.* Hey, you! Pay attention!
hêdkwạtà *n.f.* Headquarters. ~***r ƙasa*** capital.
helụ̀mạ̀ *n.m.* (*pl.* **helụmomi**) Headman, foreman.
hịdịma *n.f.* (*pl.* **hịdịmomi**) Service, business.
hịjịr̃a *n.f.* 1. Year of the Prophet Muhammad's flight from Mecca, from which the Muslim calendar begins. ***gudun*** ~ forced migration. ***'yan gudun*** ~ refugees.
hịkayà *n.f.* Tale, narrative (usu. with moral).
hịkịmà *n.f.* (*pl.* **hịkịmomi**) Wisdom, talent.
himmà *n.f.* (*pl.* **himmomi**) Perseverance, determination, energy.
hìmmạ̀tụ *v.i.* Strive, do one's best.
hinjì *n.m.* Hinge(s).
hir̃ *excl.* Warning against doing sth.: ~ *kada ka yi* don't do it!
hir̃ạ *n.f.* Chatting, conversation.
hịsabì *n.m.* Reckoning up the good and bad deeds of a person on Judgement Day. ***malamin*** ~ soothsayer, fortune-teller.
hịzịfi *see* **ịzịfi.**
hoɓɓàsà *excl.* Up with it! (as in picking up a load). ***aikin*** ~ valueless work.
hodà *n.f.* Powder.
hoɗịjàm *excl.* Fancy! What a pleasant surprise!
hogè *n.m.* (*pl.* **hôgga**) Sod, clod.
hohọ̀ *excl.* What a pity! What bad luck!
hokị *n.m.* Hockey.

holè *v.t. and v.i.* Relax, be at ease, enjoy sth.
hòlį *n.m.* Falling in (as in marching or drilling).
holò *n.m.* Polo.
holoƙo *n.m.* 1. Harvest season dust storm without rain. 2. Kernel-less groundnuts, grainless corn ears.
homà *n.f.* Boastfulness.
homàn *n.m.* Foreman.
hòra (į/e) *v.t.* (*vn.* **hòro**) Discipline, train, punish.
hòtêl *n.m.* (*pl.* **hotęloli**) Hotel, bar, restaurant.
hòto *n.m.* (*pl.* **hotųnà**) 1. Photograph. 2 Illustration, picture in book.
hubbar̃ę̀ *n.m.* Tomb of religious leader (esp. that of Shehu Usman dan Fodio).
hucè *v.i.* Cool off (temper, food, weather).
hùci *n.m.* Difficulty in breathing.
hùda *n.f.* Bud, blossom.
hudà *v.t.* (*vn.* **hujì**) Pierce, bore a hole.
huɗà *v.t.* (*vn.f.* **hùɗa**) Bank up soil to form ridges.
hųɗų *n.f. and adj.* Four.
hųɗųbà *n.f.* Sermon.
hùhu *n.m.* Lung(s).
huhù *n.m.* (*pl.* **huhųnà**) Wrapping made of grass, leaves and rope for keeping kolanuts.
hujì *n.m.* 1. Hole pierced in nose or ear for inserting ornament. 2. Inoculation. 3. Advance (of pay). 4. *vn.* of **hudà.**
hujjà *n.f.* (*pl.* **hujjoji**) Reason, excuse.
hų̀kumà *n.f.* (*pl.* **hųkumomi**) Governing body, authority, public board: *~r Hausa* The Hausa Board.
hųkuncì *n.m.* (*pl.* **hų̀kùncę-hų̀kùncę**) Verdict, sentence (of a court).
hųkùnta *v.t.* Give a verdict or sentence, pass judgement.
hùla *n.f.* (*pl.* **hulųnà**) Cap. ***~r sarauta*** crown.
hulɗà *n.f.* Transactions: *~r ciniki* trade relations.
hųlu-hų̀lù *id.* Swollen, puffed up (of face): *kuncinsa ya yi ~* his cheeks are puffed up.
hųlųlų *id.* Abundantly.
hų̀lur̃ì *n.m.* Religious ecstasy.
hųmùsi, hųmùshi *n.m.* One fifth of sth., a share.
hùnhų̀na *n.f.* Mildew.
huntu *n.m.* (*f.* **huntųwa,** *pl.* **huntàye**) Poor person, naked person.
hùntur̃ù *n.m.* Cold season, harmattan.
hurà *v.t.* Blow on sth., inflate. ***~ wuta*** start a fire, do sth. quickly or intensively.
hùrau *n.m.* Larva of digger-wasp.
hùr̃de *n.m.* Grey horse.
hųr̃ų̀mi *n.m.* Open space surrounding a compound used for grazing, burial ground, etc.
hùrwa *n.f.* Repentance shown by the gesture of throwing earth over one's head or shoulders.
hus *n.m.* 1. Used in *ba shi da ~* he has no energy. 2. Lint at bottom of pocket.
hų̀sufì *n.m.* Eclipse of sun or moon.
hųsumà *n.f.* (*pl.* **hųsumomi**) Quarrel, enmity.
hutà *v.i.* 1. Rest, relax, be free from sth. 2. Die: *Allah ya sa ya ~* may he rest in peace.
hutsu *n. and adj.* (*f.* **hutsųwa,** *pl.* **hutsàye**) Cantankerous, ill-tempered.
hutu *n.m.* Rest, holiday.

I

[1]i *see* **e.**
[2]i *see* **im.**
įbadà *n.f.* Serving God through prayer and good life.
įblîs *n.m.* Satan.
į̀bųrò *n.m.* Cereal similar to *acca.*
įcè *n.m.* Wood, tree, stick: *~n wuta* firewood.
i dą̀ *v.t.* Alt. form of **įyar̃ dą̀.**
į̀dan *conj.* If: *~ ka zo da wuri, za mu tafi tare* if you come early, we'll go together.
įdar̃ dą̀ *see* **įyar̃ dą̀.**
iddà *n.f.* 130-day period during which a woman may not remarry.
idì *n.m.* Any major Muslim festival.
įdò *n.m.* (*pl.* **įdànu**) Eye. ***a ~n jama'a*** publicly. ***~n sau*** ankle. ***ɗauka ~*** glitter. ***kashe ~*** wink. ***sa ~*** wait expectantly. ***yi ~ cikin karatu*** learn fast in school. ***zuba ~*** look intently at, watch out for. **įdǫ** *adv.* (with **ą̀**) In the eye: *ya tsone ni a ~* he poked me in the eye.
įgįyà *n.f.* (*pl.* **įgįyoyi**) 1. Rope. 2. Chevron, stripe indicating rank in army or police.
į̀gwa *n.f.* (*pl.* **įgogi**) Artillery gun.
ihù *n.m.* Yelling.
i'ìna *n.f.* Stuttering, stammering.
įjabà *n.f.* Fulfilment of a wish.
įjar̃à *n.f.* 1. Wages, commission. 2. Fee for sending court messenger for a witness. 3. Agreement as to rate of pay: *sun yi ~* they have agreed on the wages.
įjè *v.t.* 1. Put aside, store, reserve. 2. Push aside.
ikò *n.m.* Power, control, authority: *muna cikin ~n sarki* we are under the authority of the Emir.
įkwaità *n.f.* Equator.
įlahįr̃i *n.m.* Whole, entirety.
ilgazì *n.m.* Allegory.
ilhamì *n.m.* Inspiration.
illà *n.f.* (*pl.* **illoli**) Blemish, fault, weakness.
ilmì, įlįmi *n.m.* 1. Knowledge (esp. of Muslim theology). 2. Branch of knowledge or learning: *~n kimiya* science.
im *v.t.* (with i.o.) Overcome, persuade s.o. to one's own viewpoint: *da ƙyar muka ~ ma mutanensa* it was only with difficulty that we overpowered his men.
imanì *n.m.* 1. Faith in Islam. 2. Strong belief.
imma *conj.* Either . . . or : *~ dai su biya ni yanzu ko kuma mu yi rigima* either they pay me right now or we'll have a fight over it.
ìn *pro.* (subjun. tense subj.) I.
in *see* **įdan.**
įnâ *see* **ą̀nâ.**
įna *inter. adv.* 1. Where?: *~ suka tafi?* where did they go? 2. Used in general greetings: *~ aiki?* how are you getting along? *~ gajiya?* how are you? *~ labari?* how are things? 3. Used in *~ sunanka?* what is your name?
įnà *pro.* (cont. tense subj.) I.
įną̀bi *n.m.* Grape(s).
incì *n.m.* Inch.
indą̀ *rel. adv.* Where: *ban san ~ suka tafi ba* I don't know where they went.
indà-inda *n.f.* Behaving or talking indecisively.
ìndąr̃ąr̃o *n.m.* (*pl.* **ìndąr̃ąr̃ai**) Metal roof drain.
ingànta *v.t.* Make durable, strengthen, reinforce.
ìngar̃mà *n.m.* 1. Large stallion. 2. Big, burly person.
ingįlishì *n.m.* 1. Englishman, English people. 2. The English language.
ingįrįci *n.m.* Hay.
įnįfàm *n.m.* Uniform (clothing).
injì *n.m.* (*pl.* **injųnà**) Engine.
injįnįyà *n.m.* (*pl.* **injįnįyoyi**) Engineer.
inkar̃ì *n.m.* Denial.

innạ *n.f.* 1. Mother, maternal aunt. 2. Polite form of address to one's mother, maternal aunt, or any woman of comparable age. 3. Disease causing paralysis, polio.

innanạha *n.f.* Furthest limit, extreme degree: *gwani ne na* ~ he is the foremost expert.

innạr̃ịdịdị *id.* Large and unruly (of crowd): *taron* ~ *gayyar wofi* crowd of useless hangers-on.

innàtû *n.m.* Inner tube of a tyre.

in sha Àllahụ *excl.* God willing.

ìnshoṟà *n.f.* Insurance.

intạha *n.f.* Used in *kai* ~ reach the limit, become extreme: *abin ya kai* ~ the matter became serious.

ịnụwà *n.f.* 1. Shade. 2. Shadow. 3. Protection: *yana* ~*r sarkin kasuwa* he is under the protection of the head of the market.

ìnzalì *n.m.* Orgasm.

ịrì *n.m.* 1. Seed(s). 2. Stock, offspring (of people or animals). 3. Type, kind, sort: ~ *uku* three types; *babu* ~*nsa* there aren't any like it. **ịrì-ịrì** *adv.* Of different kinds: *na ga tsuntsaye* ~ I saw various kinds of birds.

ịr̃ịli *n.m.* Respect, honour, image: *an keta* ~*nsa* he has been put to shame.

ịrin *prep.* Like: *ka ɗinka mini riga* ~ *wannan* make me a gown like this one.

ịsa (shị/she) *v.t.* Suffice: *wannan ba zai ishe mu ba* this will not be sufficient for us. *n.f.* Arrogance, conceit: ~*rsa ta yi yawa* his pride in himself is extreme. ***mai*** ~ person of rank, authority. **ịsạ** *v.i.* 1. Reach, arrive at: *ya* ~ *gida* he reached home. 2. Be sufficient, adequate: *ya* ~ that's enough, that's fine. 3. Be authoritative: *Allah ya* ~ may God deal sternly with you (for your wrong-doing). 4. Reach puberty.

ịsar̃ (dạ) *v.t.* Convey or deliver news or message: *ya* ~ *da sako wurin sarki* he delivered the message to the chief.

ịshar̃à *n.f.* (*pl.* **ịshar̃or̃i**) Sign, indication (often negative).

ịshè *v.t.* Overtake.

ịshịr̃in *see* **ạshịr̃in.**

iskà *n.f.* 1. Air, breeze, wind. ***ɗan*** ~ idler, loafer. ***harbin*** ~ being in nimble form. ***wayar*** ~ rumour, false report. 2. (*pl.* **iskoki**) Spirit, usu. ref. to *bori* cult.

iskancì *n.m.* Profligacy, loose living.

iskè *see* **ịshè.**

ịsò *n.m.* Announcing arrival of a visitor: *a yi mana* ~ *wurin Audu* let Audu know we have arrived.

istịhar̃à *n.f.* Seeking Divine counsel.

istịmàt *n.m.* Estimate.

ịtạ *pro.f.* (ind.) She, her.

ịtàce *n.m.* (*pl.* **ịtatụwà**) Tree, wood, stick.

ịwa *see* **yạ.**

ịyạ *n.f.* Term of address for one's maternal aunt.

ịyà *v.t.* Be able to do: *ya* ~ *tuki* he knows how to drive.

ịya *conj.* Up to, as far as: *rigarsa ta tsaya* ~ *gwiwa* his gown only came down to his knees.

ịyàka *n.f.*(*pl.* **ịyakoki**) 1. Frontier, border, boundary. 2. Limit: *ya kai* ~ he has reached the limit, he's fed up; *ya duba* ~*r ganinsa* he looked as far as he could see.

ịyakạce *v.t.* Restrict, limit: *na* ~ *masa abin da zai yi* I set limits on what he was allowed to do.

ịyakạci *n.m.* The whole: ~*n abin da na sani ke nan* that's all I know about it.

ịyàkwàndịshàn *n.f.* Air conditioner.

ịyalì *n.f.* One's family, dependants.

ịyar̃ (dạ) *v.t.* (= i **dạ** before d.o.) Accomplish, complete: *bari in* ~ *da salla kafin mu tafi* let me do my prayers before we leave.

ịyàwa *n.f.* Ability, mastery: *ya fi ni* ~ he is more capable at it than I; *yana da wuyar* ~ it is a difficult thing to do well.

ịyàye *n.pl.* Parents.

ịyò *n.m.* Swimming.

ịzà *v.t.* Push ahead, onto: *ta* ~ *wuta* she pushed the firewood closer to the fire.

izga *n.f.* 1. Tail used as fly-switch. 2. Bow for playing stringed musical instruments (such as *goge* or *kukuma*).

ìzgịli *n.m.* Being presumptuous, boastful.

izịfi *n.m.* One of the sixty sections into which the Koran is divided.

ịznì, ịzịni *n.m.* Permission. ***takardar*** ~ permit, warrant.

izzà *n.f.* Haughtiness, contemptuous indifference.

J

[1]**ja** *v.t.* 1. Pull, drag: ***na gan shi*** *yana* ~***n rago*** I saw him pulling a ram along. 2. Draw (water from well). 3. Attract (attention). 4. (with **dà̧**) Compete with s.o.: *kowa ya* ~ *da mai ƙarfi zai fadi* whoever tries to compete with a strong man will lose.

[2]**ja** *n. and adj.* (*pl.* **jajàye**) Red. ~***n aiki*** hard work. ~***r wahala*** severe trouble. ~***r zuciya*** bravery.

jabbà *n.f.* (*pl.* **jabbobi**) Loose-fitting sleeveless robe worn over a *kufta* or *jamfa*.

jà̧bụ *n.m.* Counterfeit, fake. ***ɗan*** ~ anything counterfeit or fake (e.g currency).

jaɓa *n.f.* Stinking shrew-mouse.

jạdạwà̧li *n.m.* (*pl.* **jà̧dạwà̧lai**) Multiplication table.

jaddà̧da *v.t.* Reform, revive (esp. religion).

jà̧fa'ì *n.m.* Slander, abusive language.

jafi *n.m.* Ceremonial greeting in which horsemen draw up sharply before the chief and salute with clenched fist.

jạgab *id.* Very wet, damp.

jà-gà̧bạ *n.m. or f.* Guide, leader.

jà-gorà̧ *n.m. or f.* 1. Usu. used in *ɗan* ~ blind person's guide. 2. Guide, instruction book. 3. Leader.

jạgwalgwà̧la *v.t.* Soil, spoil, botch: *yarinya duk ta* ~ *abinci* the girl made a mess of the food.

jạhà *see* **jịhà.**

jà̧hadì *see* **jịhadì.**

jahilcì *n.m.* Ignorance, illiteracy.

jahịli *n.m.* (*f.* **jahịla**, *pl.* **jàhịlai**) Ignorant or illiterate person.

ja'ịbà *n.f.* Misfortune, calamity.

ja'ịr̃i *n.m.* (*f.* **ja'ịr̃a**, *pl.* **jà'ịr̃ai**) Shameless, disrespectful person.

jaje *n.m.* 1. Sympathy: *ta yi musu* ~ she expressed her sympathy to them. 2. Regret over sth. lost.

jajịbèr̃ẹ *n.m.* Day before a festival day.

jâk *n.m.* Automobile jack.

jà̧ka *n.f.* (*pl.* **jạkunkụnà**) 1. Any kind of bag. 2. The sum of one hundred pounds in old Nigerian currency.

jà̧kadà *n.m.* (*f.* **jà̧kadịya**, *pl.* **jà̧kàdu**) 1. Chief attendant, go-between at a chief's court. 2. Ambassador, consular official.

jakèt *n.m.* Jacket.

jàki *n.m.* (*f.* **jàka**, *pl.* **jàkai**, **jakụnà**) 1. Donkey, ass. 2. Stupid person.

Jallà̧ *excl.* Praise God!

jàllo *n.m.* Gourd water-bottle.

jà̧mạ'à̧ *n.f.* (*pl.* **jạmạ'o'i, jà̧mà̧'u**) 1. The public, a public gathering, crowd. ***a idon*** ~ in public. 2. Community or its inhabitants.

jambạɗȩ̀ *n.m.* Abscess under arm-pit.

jamf̣à *n.f.* (*pl.* **jamfofi**) Long-sleeved jumper worn as inner garment with either *gare* or *shakwara*.

jàmhur̃ịyà *n.f.* Republic.

jàmhur̃ù *n.m.* Intrigue, conspiracy: ***sun yi masa*** ~ ***sun ɗafa*** ***masa sata*** they conspired against him and accused him of stealing.

jam'ì *n.m.* 1. Congregation of people for joint prayer. 2. Plural (in grammar).

jamị'à *n.f.*(*pl.* **jamị'o'i**) University.

jamị'i *n.m.* (*f.* **jamị'a,** *pl.* **jàmị'ai**) Leader, director.
jàm'iyyà *n.f.* (*pl.* **jam'iyyoyi**) Political party, club, society, association.
jạ̀nạbà *n.f.* Impurity (religious).
Jạ̀naiř̀ụ *n.m.* January.
jạ̀na'ịzà *n.f.* Funeral.
jạnàř *n.m.* General (military).
jạ̀nạ̀řetò *n.m.* Generator.
jàn-bàkị *n.m.* Lipstick.
jangạ̀li *n.m.* Cattle-tax.
jan ɡwada *n.m.* Orange-headed male lizard.
jàngwam *n.m.* Misfortune, trouble: *kada ka ja wa kanka* ~ don't bring trouble on yourself.
janjạ̀mi *n.m.* (*pl.* **jànjạ̀mai**) 1. Woven cloth or leather strap tightened around body of horse to keep saddle in place. 2. Military sash.
jànjàni *n.m.* Slowness in eating: *ya cika* ~ he eats very slowly.
jantẹ̀ *n.m.* Cold accompanied by fever.
jânye *v.t.* 1. Drag away: *ya* ~ *kura daga hanya* he moved the hand-truck away from the road. 2. Withdraw: *ya* ~ *ra'ayinsa* he withdrew his opinion.
jạ̀řạbà *n.f.* 1. Excessive desire: *taba ta zama* ~ *gare shi* he is addicted to smoking. 2. Calamity.
jàřfa *n.f.* Facial markings.
jaři *n.m.* 1. Capital for business. 2. Asset.
jạ̀řidà *n.f.* (*pl.* **jạ̀řidu**) Newspaper.
jàrìrai *pl.* of **jinjịri** and **jàrìrì.**
jàrìrì *n.m.* (*f.* **jàrìrìya,** *pl.* **jàrìrai**) Infant.
jařřạ̀ba *v.t.* Test, examine, try.
jařřạ̀bâwa *n.f.* Examination, test. ***ci*** ~ pass an examination.
jař̀ụmi *n. and adj.* (*f.* **jař̀ụma,** *pl.* **jàř̀ụmai**) Brave.
jařumtạkà *n.f.* Bravery.
jauje *n.m.* Drum similar to but larger than *kalangu.*
jauřạ *n.f.* Peddling, petty trading.
jạ̀wabì *n.m.* (*pl.* **jạ̀wàbai**) 1. Message, speech. 2. Reply or opinion regarding a matter.
jàyayyà *n.f.* Dispute, controversy.
jạ̀za'i *n.m.* Retribution.
je *v.i.* (*vn.* **zụwà**) 1. Go to: *mun* ~ *Katsina mun dawo* we went to Katsina and returned. ~ ***ka,*** ~ ***ki*** go! 2. Arrive at: *sa'ad da muka* ~ *Katsina mun ga sarki* when we arrived at Katsina we saw the chief.
jèfa (ị/e) *v.t.* (*vn.* **jifà**) Throw at: *an jefe mu da dutse* someone threw a stone at us. **jefà** *v.t.* 1. Throw: *ya* ~ *dutse* he threw a stone. 2. Post (letter).
jefì-jefì *adv.* Often.
jegò *n.m.* Suckling of infant.
jejì *see* **dajì.**
jèla *n.f.* Tail.
jemà *v.t.* (*vn.f.* **jimà**) Tan (leather).
jemaɡè *n.m.* (*pl.* **jèmàɡu**) Fruit-bat.
jerà *v.t.* Arrange in a row.
jerì *n.m.* Row, line.
jewa *n.f.* 1. Going to and fro. 2. Hovering.
jị *v.t.* 1. Hear. ***in*** ~ ***wane*** so-and-so said . . . 2. Understand: *ba ya* ~*n turanci* he doesn't understand English. 3. Listen: ~ *mana!* listen! 4. Feel, taste, smell: *ina* ~*n yunwa* I'm hungry; *na* ~ *kamshinsa* I can smell its fragrance. ~ ***gari*** feel the pinch, be short of money. ~ ***jiki*** feel out of sorts.
jibɡà *v.t.* Pile loads on top of one another.
jibị *n.f. and adv.* Day after to-morrow. ***watan*** ~ month after next.
jibì *n.m.* Any meal.
jịɓa *n.m.* Small anthill.
jịɓi *n.m.* Perspiration, sweat.
jịda (ị/e) *v.t.* Remove goods or people from one place to another in several trips: *gafiya ta jidi hatsi* the rat has removed all of the grain.
jịdalì *n.m.* Struggle, combat, trouble.
jiddîn *adv.* Used in ~ *wala hairin* always, at all times.
jido *n.m.* Removal of things to another location.
jifà *vn.* of **jèfa.**
jịɡạ *n.f.* Jigger insect.
jịɡịda *n.m.* (*pl.* **jịɡịdu**) String of ornamental beads worn around hips by women.

jigila *n.f* Going back and forth: *Hukumar Alhazai tana shirin kawar da wahaloli wajen* ~*r alahazai* the Pilgrims Welfare Board is making plans to ease the difficulties regarding the transport of pilgrims.

jigò *n.m.* 1. One of two supporting poles of an irrigation device. 2. Pole used to support roof of hut. 3. Theme (in literature).

jihà *n.f.* 1. Region, state. 2. Direction: *a* ~*r gabas* eastward.

jihadì *n.m.* Holy war to spread Islam.

jijiya *n.f.* (*pl.* **jijiyoyi**) Vein, artery, muscle, nerve. ~***r itace*** roots of a tree.

jijjiga *v.t.* Shake to and fro, up and down: *mota ta* ~ *su* the lorry bounced them up and down.

jikà *adv.* (with **à**) On the body: *an soke shi da mashi a* ~ a spear pierced his body.

jikà *n.m. or f.* (*pl.* **jikoki**) Grandchild.

jiki *n.m.* (*pl.* **jikunà**) Body. ***yi*** ~ become fat. ***ji*** ~ experience difficulty, tiredness. ***janye*** ~ withdraw from activity.

jikin *prep.* Against, embedded in: *kusa tana* ~ *bango* the nail is stuck in the wall.

jiƙà *v.t.* Soak, moisten. **jiƙa** *v.i.* Be soaked, wet.

[1]**jiƙò** *n.m.* Medicinal tonic made by soaking herbs and roots.

[2]**jiƙò** *n.m.* Used in *wani* ~ sometimes. **jiƙò-jiƙò** *adv.* From time to time.

jim Used in ~ *kaɗan* = *jimawa kaɗan* after a while, shortly.

jimà *v.i.* Spend some time: *za su* ~ *a Kano* they will stay a while in Kano; *sai an* ~ see you later!

jimà *n.f.* 1. Tanning. 2. *vn.* of **jemà.**

Jimada Lahir̃ *n.m.* Sixth month of the Muslim calendar.

Jimada Lawwàl *n.m.* Fifth month of the Muslim calendar.

jima'i *n.m.* Sexual intercourse.

jimillà *n.f.* Sum total: *ya ba ni* ~*r naira ashirin* he gave me the sum total of twenty Naira.

jimina *n.f.* (*pl.* **jiminu**) Ostrich.

jimiri *n.f.* Endurance, patience.

jimlà *n.f.* 1. Amount. 2. Sum, total: *za a kashe* ~*r kuɗin da suka kai naira miliyan* a sum of one million Naira will be spent.

jîn Form of **ji** used in compounds: ~ *baki* quarrelsomeness; ~ *kai* arrogance; ~ *magana* being obedient; ~ *rai* conceit.

jìnga *n.m.* Wages, agreed amount of payment for a contract.

jìngim *id.* Plentifully, abundantly: *akwai kaya* ~ *a kasuwa* there is plenty of merchandise in the market.

jìnginà *n.f.* Pawn or deposit given as a pledge for money borrowed: *ya ba da hularsa* ~ he pawned his cap.

jingina *v.t.* Prop against: *na* ~ *tsani a bango* I propped the ladder against the wall. **jìnginà** *v.i.* Lean against: *na* ~ *da bango* I leaned against the wall.

jini *n.m.* 1. Blood. 2. Menstruation. 3. Popularity: *yana da* ~*n mutane* he is popular; *farin* ~ popularity; *bakin* ~ unpopularity.

jìniyà *n.f.* Siren.

jinjimi *n.m.* White ibis (bird).

jìnjinà *n.f.* Saluting a superior by shaking raised fist.

jinjina *v.t.* 1. Test the weight of something: *ya* ~ *buhun ya ga ba zai iya ɗauka ba* he tested the weight of the sack and found that he couldn't lift it.

jinjiri *n.m.* (*f.* **jinjinniya,** *pl.* **jiràjirai, jàrìrai**) Infant.

jinka *n.f.* Thatch, act of thatching.

jinkè *v.t.* Thatch.

jìnkiri *n.m.* Delay, procrastination, tardiness: *ya sa mun yi* ~ he caused us delay.

jinyà *n.f.* 1. Nursing, tending sick person. 2. Being a patient.

jira *n.f.* Black-throated weaver-bird.

jira *v.t.* Wait for: *na* ~ *shi har awa ɗaya* I waited for him for an hour.

jirgà *v.i.* Move a short distance away.

jirgi *n.m.* (*pl.* **jiràge**) Any type of vehicle (except automobile): ~*n danƙaro* road-roller; ~*n ƙasa* train; ~*n ruwa* ship; ~*n sama* aeroplane.

jịri *n.m.* Dizziness, seeing double: *mashayi yana ganin* ~ the drunkard is feeling dizzy.

jirkịce *v.t. and v.i.* Tilt, fall over on side.

jitạ-jitạ *n.m.* Rumour: *ya baza* ~ he spread rumours around.

jịtụ *v.i.* Be on good terms with s.o.: *mun* ~ *da juna* we got along with each other.

jịyậ *n.f. and adv.* Yesterday. ***shekaran*** ~ last year. ***watan*** ~ last month. ***mazan*** ~ the older, conservative generation.

jiyyà *see* **jinyà.**

jojị *n.m.* (*pl.* **jojị-jojị**) Judge, magistrate.

jụ̀gum *id.* Despondently: *tana zaune* ~ she sat dejectedly.

juji *n.m.* Rubbish-heap. ***garwan*** ~ garbage can.

jùju *n.m.* 1. Fetish, spirit. 2. Slightly daft person.

Jummạ'à *n.f.* Friday.

juna *n.m.* Each other: *sun ga* ~ they have seen each other. ~ ***biyu*** pregnancy.

jurè *v.t.* Endure: *ba ya iya* ~ *wahala* he can't tolerate hardship.

jụ̀wa *n.f.* Giddiness.

jùya (ị/e) *v.t.* Copy sth. written.

juyà *v.t.* 1. Turn round: *ya* ~ *kansa gabas* he turned his head to the east. 2. Turn into, transform.

jùyàyi *n.m.* 1. Anxiety about sth. 2. Sympathy, feeling pity.

juyì *n.m.* Change of state, position, climate, etc.

jụzụ̀'i *n.m.* Portion, section, part (esp. of Koran).

K

[1]ka *pro.m.* (vl. and tone vary acc. to use, *see* Appendix 1) You, your.

[2]ka *adv.* On the head: *ya ɗauki kaya a* ~ he carried the load on his head.

kạbà *n.f.* Fronds of dum-palm.

kabạr̃ai *n.m.* A yellow weaver-bird with black head.

kậbậr̃i *n.m.* (*pl.* **kạbur̃bụr̃à**) Grave, tomb.

kạbàt *n.m.* Cupboard.

kabejị *n.m.* Cabbage.

kậbewà *n.f.* (*pl.* **kậbèyi**) Pumpkin.

kậbịdò *n.f.* (*pl.* **kậbịdu**) Double-matting worn for protection against rain.

kậbilà *see* **ƙậbilà.**

kabòyị *n.m.* Cowboy.

kạɓè *v.t.* Flip, flick away: *ya* ~ *kansa* he quickly turned his head to the side.

kạcà *n.f.* Chain (esp. of bicycle). ***haƙoran*** ~ sprockets.

kạcạ-kạcạ *id.* 1. In a messy or disorderly state: *ɗakin ya yi* ~ *da takardu* papers are scattered all over the room. 2. In a mutilated or ruined condition: *sun ɓata shi* ~ they spoiled it completely.

kạcal *id.* Emphasizes contempt and smallness of value: *kobo* ~ *ya ba ni* he gave me a mere kobo.

kậcịɓis *adv.* Meeting suddenly: *mun yi* ~ *da su* we met them suddenly.

kàcịyà *n.f.* Circumcision.

kạdậ 1. Indicates negative command or order: ~ *ka tafi gobe* don't go tomorrow; ~ *yara su shigo nan* no children should come in here; ~ *mu yi gardama* let's not argue. 2. (often preceded by **don** or **dòmin**) Lest: *na ajiye shi* (*domin*) ~ *ya fadi* I put it aside lest it fall.

kạdà *n.m.* (*pl.* **kậdànni, kạdoji**) Crocodile.

ka dậ *v.t.* (= **kashe** before pro. d.o.) Alt. form of **kayar̃ dậ.**

kạdàfkạr̃à *n.m.* White-bellied bustard (bird).

kậdai Used after **sànnụ** or **bar̃kà** when replying to these greetings.

kạdạrà *n.f.* Property, goods.
kạdạ̀ri *n.m.* Value, price: *ya karya masa* ~ he sold it to him at a cheap price.
kạ̀darkò *n.m.* (*pl.* **kạ̀dàrkai, kạ̀dàrki**) Small bridge.
kạdò *see* **kạdà.**
kạɗà *v.t.* 1. Beat (drum). 2. Spin (cotton). 3. Churn, whisk, stir. 4. Shake, sway, wave: *ya* ~ *kai* he shook his head in disagreement, he nodded in agreement; *kare ya* ~ *wutsiya* the dog wagged its tail; *iska ta* ~ *bishiya* the wind made the tree sway.
kạɗai *adv.* Only, alone: *mun gan shi shi* ~ we saw only him; *su* ~ *suka sani* they alone know.
kạɗàita *v.t.* Used in ~ *Allah* believe in the oneness of God. **kạ̀ɗaitạ̀** *v.i.* Be alone, be apart.
kạ̀ɗan *adv.* 1. A few, a little: *mutane* ~ a few people. 2. A little bit, slightly: *dakata* ~ wait a little while; *ta iya* ~ she can do it slightly. ***saura*** ~ almost, just a bit more: *saura* ~ *da na taka shi da mota* I almost ran him over with my car. ***yi*** ~ be too little, not enough. ***kaɗan-kaɗan*** very slightly.
kạɗanyà *n.f.* Shea tree or its fruit.
kạɗè *v.t.* 1. Hit and knock away or knock down: *mota ta* ~ *yaro* the car knocked the boy down; *na* ~ *hannunsa* I knocked his hand away. 2. Shake or knock dust from garment. 3. Shed leaves: *bishiyar nan ta* ~ *ganyenta* this tree has shed its leaves. *v.i.* Be in trouble.
kạɗì *n.m.* 1. Spinning. 2. Churning.
kaɗọ̀ *n.m.* (*f.* **kaɗụ̀wa,** *pl.* **haɓẹ̀**) Hausa person who has no Fulani ancestry.
kaf *id.* Completely: *na cinye shi* ~ I ate it all up.
kạfà *v.t.* 1. Erect, put up: *sun* ~ *laima* they erected a tent. 2. Stick sth. into: *ya* ~ *kusa a bango* he hammered a nail into the wall. 3. Found, establish (e.g. club). 4. Proclaim, issue a law.
kạfa *n.f.* (*pl.* **kạfofi**) 1. Small hole, opening, crack. **~*r allura*** eye of a needle. 2. Loophole, means of escape: *ba ka da* ~*r fita* you have no way out.
kàfạɗà *n.f.* (*pl.* **kàfạ̀ɗu**) Shoulder.
kạ̀farà *n.f.* Penalty to atone for breaking certain Islamic laws.
kạfè *v.t.* Fasten sth. onto: *an* ~ *sanarwa a jikin bishiya* a notice was stuck on the trunk of the tree. *v.i.* 1. Become stuck. 2. Persist, be obstinate: *yaron nan ya* ~ *sai ya bi mu* this boy insists on following us.
kạfì *n.m.* Charm buried in front of doorway or hung inside house for protection against misfortune.
kàfin, kàfin *conj.* Before: ~ *in dawo, ya gama* before I return, he will have finished; *tun* ~ *su iso, muka tashi* we had left before they arrived.
kafintạ̀ *n.m.* (*pl.* **kafintoci**) Carpenter.
kàfịrètò *n.m.* Carburettor.
kafịri *n.m.* (*f.* **kafịra,** *pl.* **kàfịrai**) Infidel, non-Muslim.
kaftà *v.t.* Dig ground up.
kàftanì *n.f.* Caftan, type of *taguwa* with wide sleeves.
kafùr *n.m.* Camphor.
kạgò *n.m.* Round house with thatched roof.
¹kâi *n.m.* (*pl.* **kawụnà,** *gen.* **kân**) 1. Head. ***sha*** ~ get ahead of, outflank s.o. 2. Top, tip, starting point: *kan dutse* top of mountain; *kan rafi* source of the stream; *kan littafi* beginning of the book. 3. Intelligence: *ba shi da* ~ he doesn't use good sense. 4. Self: *ni da* ~*na na yi* I did it by myself; *shi kansa* he himself. 5. Unit, bundle: *kan kara* bundle of cornstalks; *kan itace* load of wood. 6. Used in *'yan* ~ a little extra, a little bit more: *hamsin da 'yan* ~ a few more than fifty. ~ ***tsaye*** at once, immediately.
²kâi *excl.* Used to express mild disapproval, doubt, or surprise.
¹kai *pro.m.* (ind.) You.
²kai *v.t.* Take, take to: *an* ~ *shi asibiti* he was taken to the hospital; *sun* ~ *mana yaki* they made war on us. *v.t. and v.i.* 1. Reach, arrive, attain: *yanzu ya* ~ *Makka* by now he has arrived at Mecca;

mutane sun ~ *hamsin* the number of people came to fifty; *abin ya* ~ *har ya sake ta* the matter reached the point that he finally divorced her; *Bello ya* ~ *ubansa tsawo* Bello is as tall as his father. 2. Suffice: *kuɗin nan za su* ~ *ku mako biyu* this money will last you two weeks; *tsawon igiyar nan bai* ~ *ba* this rope is not long enough.

kaicọ *excl.* What bad luck! What a pity! *kome ya same shi ba* ~ whatever happens to him will serve him right.

kaidì *n.m.* (usu. used in neg.) Limit, restriction: *yana aiki ba* ~ he is working non-stop.

kaifạ̀fa *v.t.* Sharpen.

kaifi *n.m.* 1. Sharpness: *wuƙar nan ba ta da* ~ this knife is not sharp. 2. Sharp edge: *takobi* ~ *biyu* double-edged sword. 3. Alertness, intelligence.

kaigạmạ̀ *n.m.* A traditional title.

kàikàicẹ *adv.* (with **ạ̀**) In a roundabout way: *ya zage mu a* ~ he abused us indirectly.

kaikàita *v.t. and v.i.* Slant, tilt, tip.

kaitọ *see* **kaicọ.**

kaiwa *n.f.* Gift for which an equivalent return-gift is expected at a later date.

kàji *pl.* of **kàza.**

[1]**kàka** *n.f.* Harvest season.

[2]**kàka** *n.m. or f.* (*pl.* **kàkànni**) Grandfather, grandmother. ***kakannin-kakanninmu*** our ancestors.

kàkabì *n.m.* Surprise, wonder.

kàkàki *n.m.* 1. Long metal horn blown in honour of an Emir. 2. Funnel. 3. Spokesman: *haka ne wani* ~*n gwamnati ya bayyana mana* that is how a government spokesman explained it to us.

kạkàn *pro.m.* (hab. tense subj.) You.

kakari *n.m.* 1. Loud snoring. 2. Gasping noises made by animal whose throat has been cut.

kạkè *pro.m.* (rel. cont. tense subj.) You.

[1]**kàki** *n.m.* Phlegm from throat.

[2]**kàki** *n.m.* Khaki cloth.

kakì *n.m.* Used in ~*n zuma* beeswax, empty honeycomb.

kàkịdè *n.m.* Meat fat drippings.

kakkạ̀ɓe *v.t.* Shake dust off sth. *v.i.* Shed leaves.

kàkkạr̃ai *n.m.* Disease of fingers.

kalạ *n.m.* Gleaning. ~***n faɗa*** looking for a fight.

kàlàci *n.m.* Any meal.

kạ̀lami *n.m.* Words, speech.

kàlandà *n.f.* Calendar.

kạ̀làngu *n.m.* (*pl.* **kạlangụnà**) Hourglass-shaped variable-tone drum.

kàlạtà (cị/ce) *v.t.* Glean.

kallạ̀bi *n.m.*(*pl.* **kallụbà**) Woman's head-tie.

kallạ̀fa *v.t.* (with i.o.) Impose sth. on s.o.

kàllạtà (cị/ce) *v.t.* Look at.

kallo *n.m.* Watching, looking at: *mun sha* ~ *a filin idi* we saw a lot at the prayer-grounds.

kalmà *n.f.* (*pl.* **kalmomi**) Word.

kalmạ̀ɗa *v.t.* Bend over edge of sth., usu. metal. **kàlmạɗạ̀** *v.i.* Be bent over.

kalmạ̀sa *v.t.* Fold over or tuck in edge of cloth or paper. **kàlmạsà** *n.f.* Hem of garment.

kaltịbetà *n.f.* (*pl.* **kaltịbetoci**) Cultivator tractor.

kàlulụwà *n.f.* Swollen glands, esp. in armpit or groin.

kalụ̀ma *v.t.* Pass tongue around inside mouth after eating.

kalwa *n.f.* Seeds of locust-bean tree (used in making locust-bean cakes for *miya*).

kàm *prt.* Used for emphasis: *ni zan tafi* ~ I will definitely go; *wannan yaro* ~ *ba ya ji* this boy is really naughty.

kam *id.* Securely.

kạ̀ma *n.m. or f.* (*pl.* **kạ̀mànni, kạ̀mànnu**) 1. Similarity, resemblance: *sun yi* ~ they look alike. 2. Appearance, image: *ya sake* ~ he changed his appearance. 3. Equivalent, counterpart: *in ka kawo naira biyu zan ƙara maka* ~*rsu* if you give two Naira I will add the equivalent sum.

kamà *v.t.* (*vn.* **kamù**) 1. Catch, seize, take hold of. ~ ***baki*** abstain from eating in deference to a fast. 2. Capture, arrest s.o. 3.

Start: *ya* ~ *aiki jiya* he started working yesterday. *v.i.* Catch hold, take (e.g. of fire or dye).

kạman *see* **kạmar̃.**

kạmànta *v.t.* Compare: *kada ka* ~ *ni da Audu* don't try to compare me with Audu.

kạmar̃ *prep.* Like, about: ~ *haka* thus, like this; *ya yi* ~ *shekara goma* he was about ten years old. *conj.* As if, as though: *na ji* ~ *zan yi amai* I felt as though I would vomit.

kạmạshò *n.m.* Commission on thing sold.

kạmatà (cị/ce) *v.t.* Be fit or suitable for s.o.: *rigar nan ta kamaci Audu* this gown is just right for Audu. **kạmatạ** *v.i.* Be seemly, necessary: *ya* ~ *mu yi shi da kanmu* we ought to do it ourselves.

kambi *n.m.* Crown.

kàmbu *n.m.* (*pl.* **kambụnà**) Man's charm worn around the arm.

kamɓori *n.m.* Shell of egg, nut, etc.

kamè *v.i.* Become stuck, adhere.

kamfạni *n.m.* (*pl.* **kamfạnoni**) Company.

kamfàs *n.m.* Compass.

kàmfạtà (cị/ce) *v.t.* Take much of (esp. grain, water).

kamịli *n.m.* (*f.* **kamịla,** *pl.* **kàmịlai**) Perfect, gentle person.

kàmìn, kàmin *see* **kàfìn.**

kam-kam *adv.* Tightly: *na rike igiya* ~ I held the rope tightly.

kammạla *v.t.* Complete, finish up: *ya* ~ *aikinsa* he completed his work. **kàmmạlạ** *v.i.* Be complete, finished.

kàmụ *n.m.* 1. Ball of dough made of guinea-corn or millet flour used in *koko.* 2. Gruel made from such balls of dough.

[1]**kamù** *n.m.* Measurement of distance from elbow to tip of middle finger.

[2]**kamù** *vn.* of **kamà.**

kamụwa *n.f.* Seizing property as settlement for unpaid debt.

[1]**kân** *prep.* 1. On, on top of: *ya zauna* ~ *kaya* he sat on top of the loads. ***a* ~ *kari*** exactly on time, at the agreed-upon time. 2. About, regarding: *mun tattauna a* ~ *wannan matsala* we debated about that matter. 3. Because of, on account of: *a* ~ *faɗan da suka yi da Bello, Tanko ya bar gida* Tanko left home because of the fight he had with Bello.

[2]**kân** *gen.* of [1]**kâi**: ~*sa* his head; ~ *allura* point of a needle.

kàn Hab. tense marker (*see* Appendix 1): *jirgin sama* ~ *tashi ƙarfe bakwai na safe* the airplane leaves at seven o'clock in the morning.

kạnà *pro.m.* (cont. tense subj.) You.

kanạ *conj.* After that, then: *sai ya gaya musu* ~ *ya tashi* after he has told them he can then leave.

kạnànzîr̃ *n.m.* Kerosene.

kạnàr̃ *n.m.* Colonel.

kạnạr̃i *n.m.* Canary.

kàndạgàrkị *n.m.* Protection.

kân gạdo *n.m.* Common sense.

kàngạrạ *v.i.* Rebel, become difficult to control: *yaran sun* ~ the children were uncontrollable.

kangar̃wa *n.f.* 1. Thing rendered useless due to some essential part missing: ~*r fitila* a lamp without its glass. 2. Rim of bicycle wheel.

kangè *v.t.* Pen up, lock in.

kango *n.m.* (*pl.* **kangàye**) Old deserted building in ruined condition.

kankambà *n.f.* Putting on airs, showing off.

kankạna *n.f.* Watermelon.

kankạre *v.t.* Scrape, remove dirt weeds, bark, etc.

kankạrẹ *n.m.* 1. Concrete. 2. Well with a concrete rim.

kankì *n.m.* West African hartebeeste.

kân ƙụda *n.m.* The tiniest amount.

kannè *v.t.* Close one eye: *ya* ~ *mini ido a asirce* he winked slyly at me.

kạnomạ Used in *dan* ~ severe dysentery.

kân sarki *n.m.* 1. Postage stamp. 2. Head side of a coin.

kantà *n.f.* Counter, shelf.

kanta *n.f.* Callus.

kantạre *v.t. and v.i.* Make or be crooked.

kànti *n.m.* (*pl.* **kantųnà**) Shop, store.
kàntomà *n.m.* (*pl.* **kantomomi**) Local Authority administrator.
kantù *n.m.* Block of salt, sugar, etc.
kanu *n.pl.* Used in *~n labarai* news headlines, topics.
kànumfàri *n.m.* Clove(s).
kanwa *n.f.* Potash.
kanyà *n.f.* Ebony tree.
kâr̃ *see* **kądą̀**.
kąrà *v.i.* (*vn.* **kąrò**) Clash, collide: *sojojin gwamnati sun ~ da 'yan sunƙuru* the government forces clashed with the guerrillas.
kąra *n.m.* (*pl.* **kąràre**) Stalk of corn, sugar cane, etc. ***~n hanci*** bridge of the nose. ***~n jiki*** trunk of the body, figure. ***~n taba*** one cigarette.
kàra *n.f.* 1. Mutual respect, courtesy: *Audu ba shi da ~* Audu is disrespectful. 2. Being screened off.
karà *v.t.* 1. Put sth. near: *na ~ hannu a wuta* I put my hands close to the fire. 2. (with i.o.) Approach closely in vehicle: *ya ~ mini mota* his car came very close to me.
kąr̃af *id.* Suddenly: *~ ɗaya muka tarar da su* suddenly we came upon them.
ką̀r̃ągà *n.f.* (*pl.* **ką̀r̃ą̀gu, ką̀r̃ą̀gai**) 1. Bed made of stalks or sticks. 2. Throne.
ką̀r̃ahįyà *n.f.* An act or thing which is disfavoured by Islam but not actually forbidden.
ką̀r̃amà *n.f.* (*pl.* **kąr̃amomi**) 1. Generosity, kindly disposition: *ya yi mini ~* he was very kind to me. 2. Marvel, something wonderful: *Audu da ~ yake* Audu can do marvellous things.
ką̀r̃àmbàni *n.m.* Meddlesomeness.
kąr̃àmbątà *n.f.* Black-crested hawk-eagle.
ką̀rammiskì *n.m.* 1. Small bright-red spider. 2. Velvet.
kąr̃ànta *v.t.* 1. Read. 2. Study.
kąr̃antar̃ (dą̀) *v.t.* Teach, educate.
kąr̃às *n.m.* Carrot(s).
ką̀r̃àtu *n.m.* (*pl.* **ką̀r̃àncę-ką̀r̃àncę**) 1. Reading. 2. Learning, education: *~n Muhammadiyya* Islamic studies; *~n boko* Western education.
kar̃aukà *n.f.* (*pl.* **kàr̃àuku**) Highway.
kąrayà *n.f.* 1. Loss of heart, despair. 2. Being weak-willed, spineless.
kàr̃bu *n.m.* Selvedge, edge of cloth.
kàrɓa (į/e) *v.t.* 1. Receive, accept, take: *na ~ daga gare shi* I accepted it from him; *ya karɓi maganarka* he believes you. 2. Suit, befit s.o.: *hula ta karɓe shi* the cap suited him.
kar̃cè *v.t.* Abrade, scrape (skin): *itace ya ~ masa jiki* he got scraped by the tree.
ką̀re *n.m.* (*f.* **kàrya**, *pl.* **kar̃nųkà**) Dog.
karè *v.t.* 1. Shield or screen from view: *ya ~ hasken fitila da takarda* he screened off the light with a piece of paper. 2. Guard, protect.
kąren motà *n.m.* Driver's mate.
karfąsa *n.f.* Perch (fish).
karfą̀ta *n.f.* (*pl.* **kàrfą̀tu**) Shoulder of meat.
kar̃go *n.m.* A tree whose bark is used as rope.
[1]**kąrì** *n.m.* 1. Fold, crease in cloth. 2. Gain, benefit: *a kan ~* at the right moment. 3. Rhythm, metre of song or poem. 4. Act which invalidates ceremonial ablutions.
[2]**kąrì** *n.m.* Frond of palm tree.
kàrįkįtai *n.pl.* Odds and ends.
ką̀r̃imì *n. and adj.* (*f.* **ką̀r̃imįya**, *pl.* **ką̀r̃imai**) Generous.
kąrìn mą̀gąnà *n.f.* Proverb.
kàrįyà *n.f.* Carrier on bicycle.
karįyà *n.f.* 1. Approaching closely by. 2. Screen, shield.
kar̃kącè *v.i.* 1. Be bent, crooked. 2. Go astray in morals.
kar̃kàndą̀ *n.m. or f.* Rhinoceros.
kàrkąra *n.f.* Rural area which is settled and farmed.
kar̃kar̃wà *n.f.* Trembling, shivering.
kar̃kąshi *n.m.* Herb used in making a slimy type of *miya*.
kar̃ką̀ta *v.t.* Twist out of shape, cause sth. to swerve, veer towards. **kàr̃kątą̀** *v.i.* Be crooked, swerve.
karmą *n.m.* (*pl.* **kąrèmąni**) Crafty and shameless person.

karmami *n.m.* Leaves of guinea-corn or millet.
karmą̀tsa *v.t.* Do work quickly and carelessly.
kàrmą̀tse *n.m.* Work done hurriedly and carelessly.
kạrò *n.m.* 1. Collision. 2. *vn.* of **kạrà.**
kạrofi *n.m.* Dye-pit.
kàr̃o-kàr̃o *n.m.* Seeking contributions from a number of people to help s.o.: *mun yi* ~ *mun saya masa riga* we all contributed and bought him a gown.
kàr̃sạna *n.f.* (*pl.* **kàr̃są̀nu**) Heifer, young cow who has not yet given birth.
[1]**kar̃tà** *v.t.* Scrape, scratch.
[2]**kar̃tà** *n.f.* 1. Card-playing. 2. Playing cards.
kàr̃tushì *n.m.* Cartridge case.
kar̃ụ̀wą̀ *n.f.* (*pl.* **kàr̃ụ̀wai**) 1. Harlot, prostitute. 2. *n.m. or f.* A crafty, underhanded person.
kàrya *n.f.* 1. Bitch. 2. Harlot, prostitute.
karyà *v.t.* 1. Break (e.g. stick, bone). 2. Fold (e.g. cloth, paper). 3. Violate, invalidate, break (e.g. promise, fast).
karyè *v.i.* 1. Break, snap, be broken. 2. Become invalid: *alwala ta* ~ the ablutions were nullified.
kạsà *v.t.* Arrange, sort out, classify: *na* ~ *su kashi-kashi* I sorted them into different heaps. ~ ***kunne*** pay attention.
kasà *v.t.* 1. Fall short, be insufficient: *kudinsa sun* ~ *sayen rigar* his money is not enough to pay for the gown. 2. Be unable or fail to do: *ya* ~ *gama aikinsa* he was unable to finish his work.
kasa *n.f.* Puff-adder.
ką̀sạdà *n.f.* Risk, bet: *ya yi cinikin* ~ he bought the thing at a risk.
kasą̀fi *n.m.* 1. Preoccupation: *yana* ~*n gabansa* he's minding his own business; *ina da wani ɗan* ~ *a gida* I've got something at home to keep me busy. 2. Allocating, dividing out: *shekarar* ~*n kuɗi* fiscal year.
ką̀sala *n.f.* Lethargy, lack of energy.
kạsànce *v.i.* Become, happen, turn out that: *zancensa ya* ~ *gaskiya* what he said turned out to be true; *zai* ~ *sun dawo* it may happen that they have returned.
kasą̀ye *v.t.* Defile with excrement.
kàsêt *n.m.* Cassette tape.
kash *excl.* Oh dear!
kạshè *v.t.* 1. Kill. 2. Divorce. 3. Withdraw sth. from use, cancel: *an* ~ *hanyar Wudil* the road to Wudil has been closed off. 4. Extinguish (light, fire). 5. Spend (money). 6. Defeat s.o. in competition: *ya* ~ *ni a neman Kande* he won out over me in seeking marriage with Kande. 7. Do a lot of sth. to s.o.: *sun* ~ *shi da tsada* they made him pay a lot of money for it.
kashe *see* **ka dą̀.**
ką̀shedì *n.m.* Warning.
kàshègą̀ri *see* **wàshègą̀ri.**
kạshì *n.m.* 1. Small heap, pile. 2. Chapter, section. 3. Part, portion, fraction. 4. Suggested price on sth. given out to sell. **kạshì-kạshì** *adv.* In heaps.
kashi *n.m.* Excrement. ***na ba shi*** ~ I gave him a bad time.
ką̀shìngịɗą̀ *v.i.* Recline on one's side: *in kana so ka* ~ *sa matashi* if you want to recline on your side, use a pillow!
kàshịyà *n.m. or f.* Cashier.
kaskà *n.f.* Tick.
kasko *n.m.* (*pl.* **kạsàke**) Small earthen bowl.
kàsụwa *n.f.*(*pl.* **kasụwoyi**) Market. ***ɗan*** ~ trader.
katako *n.m.* Timber, plank of wood.
ką̀tangà *n.m.* Large fragment of broken pot.
kạtanga *n.f.*(*pl.* **ką̀tàngi, ką̀tàngu**) Mud wall of house or compound.
ką̀tantanwà *n.f.* Snail-shell.
kạtạrà *n.f.* (*pl.* **kạtạrori**) Outside of thigh.
ką̀tạr̃i *n.m.* Good luck: *Allah ya yi mana* ~ may God bring us luck.
kạtar̃she *v.t.* Used in *Allah ya* ~ *shi* he had good luck.
katì *n.m.* (*pl.* **katụnà**) 1. Gambling at cards. 2. Any card.
katịbi *n.m.* (*f.* **katịba**, *pl.* **kàtịbai**) Scribe.

kạ̀tifà *n.f.* (*pl.* **kạ̀tifu, kạ̀tifai**) Mattress.
kạtsạlandàn *n.m.* Intrusiveness, meddlesomeness.
kạtsè *v.t.* 1. Cut off. 2. Interrupt: *ya ~ mini hanzari* he interrupted what I was doing. *v.i.* 1. Snap in two, be cut in two. 2. Run short.
katsè *v.t.* Scrape clean by running finger, stick, etc. around surface.
kau *v.i.* Move out of the way: *~ daga nan* clear out of here!
kaucè *v.i.* Dodge, avoid, step aside: *ga mota nan, ka ~* there's a car coming, get out of the way!
kauci *n.m.* A parasitic plant which grows on trees.
kaucịya *n.f.* Dodging, stepping to one side.
kau dạ̀ *v.t.* (= **kaushe** before pro. d.o.) Alt. form of **kạwar̃ dạ̀.**
kàu-dạ̀-bàr̃ạ *n.m.* Charm to avoid being wounded.
kauɗi *n.m.* Verbosity, talkativeness.
kaurà *v.t.* Collide hard with s.o.: *mun ~ karo da shi* we collided with him; *na ~ masa mari* I slapped him hard.
kauri *n.m.* Thickness, fatness (of humans).
kaushe *see* **kau dạ̀.**
kaushi *n.m.* Roughness.
kạwài *adv.* 1. Only, merely, just: *Audu ~ ya iya wannan aiki* only Audu can do this work. 2. Without reason, without warning: *haka ~ ka zage ni* you abused me like that for no reason. 3. Quietly: *na same shi zaune ~* I found him seated quietly.
kạwaici *n.m.* Reticence, being taciturn.
kạ̀wali *n.m.* (*f.* **kạ̀walịya,** *pl.* **kạ̀wàlai**) Pimp.
kạwar̃ (dạ̀) *v.t.* (= **kau dạ̀** before d.o.) 1. Put aside, remove to another place. 2. Shift, alter position: *ya ~ da kai* he averted his glance.
[1]**kawo** *v.t.* Bring. *v.i.* Reach, arrive.
[2]**kawo** *n.m.* A mahogany tree with large black seeds.
kàwụ *n.m.* (*pl.* **kàwụ̀nai**) Maternal uncle.
kawụnà *pl.* of [1]**kâi.**
kaya *n.m.* (*pl.* **kayàyyạki**) 1. Load(s). 2. Goods associated with other things or activities: *~n aiki* tools; *~n ɗaki* room furnishings; *~n ƙira* smithing implements; *~n miya* soup ingredients. 3. Clothes, clothing.
kayar̃ (dạ̀) *v.t.*(= **ka dạ̀** before d.o.) 1. Knock down, fell: *iska ta ~ da itace* the wind blew the tree down. 2. Defeat, overcome: *mun ~ da su a zaɓe* we defeated them in the election.
kayyạ *excl.* I doubt . . .: *~, ba na zaton zai zo yau* I doubt if he would come today.
kayyà *excl.* A call for help in catching a thief or animal.
kạ̀za *adv.* Such and such, so and so, so forth and so on: *ya sayi abu ~* he bought such and such a thing; *ya yi ~ da ~* he did this and that.
kàza *n.f.* (*pl.* **kàji**) Hen, chicken.
kạzàf *n.m.* False accusation.
kạzạgi *n.m.* Small hourglass-shaped drum which is hung from the neck and beaten with flexible beaters made of cloth or leather.
kạzàllạhà *n.f.* Meddlesomeness, inquisitiveness.
kazganyà *n.f.* Mature young sheep which has not yet given birth.
kè Rel. cont. tense marker (*see* Appendix 1): *ina mutumin da ~ girbe gero?* where is the man who is harvesting the millet?
ke *pro.f.* (ind.) You.
keɓè *v.t.* Keep or set aside: *ya ~ mana wuri dabam* he reserved a special place for us.
kecè *v.t. and v.i.* Tear, be torn.
keji *n.m.* (*pl.* **kejoji**) Bird-cage.
kèkẹ̀ *n.m.* (*pl.* **kekụnà**) 1. Bicycle. 2. Machine: *~n ɗinki* sewing machine; *~n hannu* wheelchair.
kesò *n.m.* (*pl.* **kesụnà**) Worn-out palm-leaf mat.
ketà *v.t.* Split, tear off, cut through: *ƙusa ta ~ rigata* the nail has torn my gown.
kewa *n.f.* Feeling of solitude or grief after the departure or death of s.o.

kewạ̀ya *v.i.* Go around a place, make a circuit.
kewạ̀ye *v.t.* Surround: *ya* ~ *gidansa da zana* he fenced his compound with *zana* mats. **kewạyè** *n.m.* 1. Enclosure. 2. Environs, surroundings: *Kano da* ~*nta* Kano and its environs.
ki *pro.f.* (vl. and tone vary acc. to use, *see* Appendix 1) You, your.
kịbịyà *n.f.* (*pl.* **kịbịyoyi, kịbau**) Arrow.
kịcicịyà *n.f.* A small beetle which bores into wood.
kịcìn *n.m.* Kitchen.
kịdahụ̀mi *n.m.* (*f.* **kịdahụ̀ma,** *pl.* **kịdàhụ̀mai**) Bumpkin, simpleton.
kịɗà *n.m.* (*pl.* **kạ̀ɗẹ-kạ̀ɗẹ**) 1. Beating (drum), plucking or bowing (stringed instrument). 2. Music.
kịɗịme *v.i.* Be upset, confused, flustered.
kịfà *v.t.* Turn upside down: *ta* ~ *ƙwarya ta zauna a kai* she turned over a calabash and sat on it.
kịfar̃ **(dạ̀)** *v.t.* Tip over: *garin sauri ta* ~ *ƙwaryar nononta* in trying to hurry she tipped over her calabash of milk.
kịfè *v.i.* Tip over.
kifi *n.m.* (*pl.* **kifàye**) Fish.
kịkà *pro.f.* (rel. past tense subj.) You.
kịkàn *pro.f.* (hab. tense subj.) You.
kịkè *pro.f.* (rel. cont. tense subj.) You.
kịlakị *n.m.* (*pl.* **kịlakawa**) Modern-dressed harlot.
kịlîf *n.m.* Paper clip.
kịlisà *n.f.* Horse-riding for pleasure.
kịlịshi *n.m.* Thin strips of meat coated with pounded groundnuts and spices and dried in the sun.
kịlịyà *n.f.* 1. Parking car off the road to the side. 2. Shifting to side of road to give room for a passing car.
killạ̀ce *v.t.* Screen or fence off place to protect from view or entry.
kịlô *n.m.* 1. Kilogramme. 2. Kilometre.
kịlògịrâm *n.m.* Kilogramme.
kịlòmità *n.f.* Kilometre.
kimà *n.f.* 1. A moderate amount: *ya sha ruwa* ~ he drank a little water. 2. Judicial appraisal of goods or property for settlement of debt in lieu of payment.
kimànta *v.t.* Evaluate, assess, estimate: *ka* ~ *kuɗin gyaran motarka?* have you estimated what it will cost you to repair your car?
kimba *n.f.* A small pepper.
kimsà *v.t.* 1. Stuff sth. untidily into a container. 2. (with i.o.) Stab or punch s.o.: *sun* ~ *masa wuƙa a ciki* they thrust a knife into his stomach. ~ ***kai*** rush into.
kin *pro.f.* (past tense subj.) You.
kịnà *pro.f.* (cont. tense subj.) You.
kìndir̃mo *n.m.* Sour milk with its full curd and cream, yoghurt.
kịni *n.m.* One's equal: *ni ba* ~*nki ba ce* I am not your equal.
kịnịbibì *n.m.* 1. Divulging secrets, tale-telling. 2. Hiding one's real feelings or thoughts or giving a wrong idea of them.
kìnkịmà **(ị/e)** *v.t.* Carry heavy thing with hands.
kìntatà **(cị/ce)** *v.t.* Estimate sth. quantitative: *na kintaci lokacin da zai iso, sai na je don mu sadu* I calculated the time of his arrival and went to meet him.
kìntsà *v.t.* Pack up for a journey. *v.i.* 1. Tidy up, put one's affairs in order. 2. Sit properly.
kìntsattse *n. and adj.* (*f.* **kìntsattsịya,** *pl.* **kìntsàttsu**) Polite.
kịra *v.t.* 1. Call, summon. 2. Invite.
kịrarì *n.m.* Praise-epithet: '*sarki zaɓen Allah*' ~*n sarakai ne* 'A chief is God's choice' is a praise-epithet for chiefs.
kirɓà *v.t.* (*vn.* **kirɓì**) Pound wet or cooked substance (e.g. cooked yam).
kirci *n.m.* Eczema.
kịri *n.m.* Peddling house to house or village to village.
kịrịgà *n.f.* Raised platform for stacking farm produce or firewood to prevent them from getting damp.
Kịr̃istà *n.m.* Christian.
kir̃kì *n.m.* 1. Kindness: *ya yi mini* ~ he was kind to me. 2. Excellence, good quality: *ya ba ni abin* ~ he gave me sth. of good quality.
Kir̃sịmạtị *n.m.* Christmas.

kiȓtanì *n.m.* Heavy string.

kịsà *n.m.* 1. Killing: *~n kai* murder; *~n gilla* brutal killing. 2. Cancellation: *~n aure* divorce. 3. Defeat.

kishì *n.m.* Jealousy. ***~n zuci*** competitive spirit, ambition.

kịshìngịɗạ̀ *v.i.* Rest on one's elbow while reclining.

kishịya *n.f.* (*pl.* **kishịyoyi**) 1. Co-wife. 2. Opposite of sth.: *an sa ka abu kana yin ~rsa* you have been asked to do sth. but you are doing the opposite.

kìskadì *n.m.* Diligently studying the Koran to memorize it.

kissạ̀ *n.f.* (*pl.* **kissoshi**) Using clever or deceitful means for some purpose: *ta yi masa ~ ta raba shi da kuɗinsa* she deprived him of his money through guile.

kịtịkạ̀ *n.f.* Kit-car.

[1]**kịtsè** *v.t.* Plait, braid.

[2]**kịtsè** *n.m.* Suet, fat on meat.

kịtsò *n.m.* Coiffure, hair-do.

kiwạ̀ta *v.t.* (*vn.* **kiwò**) Tend, feed animal.

kiwò *n.m.* 1. Tending animals at pasture. 2. Grazing or feeding by any animal or bird. ***~n lafiya*** hygiene. 3. *vn.* of **kiwạ̀ta.**

kịya-kịya *n.f.* Usu. used in *~ bos* small bus used for commercial transportation.

kịyamà *n.f.* Used in *ranar ~* the Day of Resurrection.

kịyashi *n.m.* (*pl.* **kịyàsai**) Small ant.

kịyayà (ị/e) *v.t.* Be on guard against, avoid: *ka kiyayi yawan gantali da dare don kada ɓarayi su tare ka* don't go roaming around at night lest you meet up with thieves.

kịyàye *v.t.* 1. Protect, take care of, look after: *Allah ya ~ mu* may God protect us. 2. (with **dạ̀**) Observe, take notice of: *ya ~ da abin da na faɗa masa* he heeded what I told him.

kò *prt.* Used for emphasis: *na ~ gode* I really thank you; *za su zo ~ gobe* they will really come tomorrow.

ko *prep. and conj.* 1. Or: *kana son wannan ~ wancan?* do you want this one or that one? 2. Whether, if: *na tambaye shi ~ Bala ya zo* I asked him whether Bala had come; *duba cikin akwatin can ~ littafin yana nan* look in that box to see whether the book is there. 3. Used to form polite question: *~ za ka ara mini bironka?* I wonder whether you would lend me your biro? 4. (often used in *~ ba haka ba*) Isn't that so?: *shi ne abin da ya faɗa, ~ ba haka ba?* that is what he said, isn't it? 5. Even: *~ ƙaramin maciji tsoronsa nake ji* even a little snake frightens me; *bai ~ yi mana sallama ba* he didn't even say good-bye to us. 6. (with **dạ̀** or **dạ̀ yạkẹ̀**) Even if, though, although: *~ da yake ya zo ba zan gan shi ba* even though he has come, I will not see him.

koɗà *v.t.* (*vn.f.* **kuɗà**) 1. Sharpen blade or surface of grinding stone by beating. 2. (with i.o.) Hit s.o. with a sharp blow.

koɗè *v.i.* Fade (of colour).

kòfạtò *n.m.* (*pl.* **kòfạ̀tai**) Hoof.

kọfè *n.m.* Copy.

kòfi *n.m.* Coffee.

kofùȓ *n.m.* Corporal.

kògi *n.m.* (*pl.* **kogụnà**) River.

kògo *n.m.* (*pl.* **kògwànni, kogụnà**) Cavity: *~n bishiya* hollow of tree; *~n dutse* cave.

ko'ịna *adv.* 1. Everywhere, (with neg.) anywhere. 2. Wherever: *~ muka duba, ba ma ganin kome sai ruwa* wherever we looked we could see nothing but water.

kòkạwà *n.f.* 1. Wrestling. 2. Struggling with task.

kòkẹ-kòkẹ *pl.* of **kuka.**

kòko *n.m.* Cocoa.

kokọ *n.m.* Gruel made from guinea-corn flour which has been soaked in water for two or three days.

kòkwanto *n.m.* Doubt: *da na gaya masa maganar bai yi ~ ba* When I told him the matter, he didn't doubt it.

koƙàƙà *see* **koyàyà.**

kọlẹjị̀ *see* **kwạlẹjị̀.**

kolì *n.m.* Peddling of small wares: *ɗan ~ ya baza ~nsa* the petty trader has spread his wares for sale.

[1]kolo *n.m.* (*pl.* **kolàye**) Drum similar to *jauje*, with which it is usu. combined, but with fixed pitch.

[2]kolo *n.m.* Dog (abusive term).

komà *v.i.* 1. Go back, return. 2. Turn into, become.

koma *n.m.* (*pl.* **komàye**) Fishing net.

kome *pro.m.* 1. Everything. 2. (with neg.) Anything, nothing: *ban sayi* ~ *ba* I bought nothing. 3. Whatever, anything which: ~ *ya yi zafi maganinsa Allah* whatever difficulties arise, put your faith in God.

komi *n.m.* (*pl.* **komàye**) 1. Small fishing boat for one person. 2. Boat-shaped watering trough made of wood or concrete.

[1]komo *v.i.* Come back, return here.

[2]komo *n.m.* 1. Misshapen calabash. 2. Alt. name for the large *garaya* played esp. for hunters.

kòra (i̧/e) *v.t.* Chase, drive away.

kora *n.f.* Scalp disease.

kòrarre *n.m.* (*f.* **kòrarri̧ya**, *pl.* **kòràrru**) Fugitive, runaway.

kor̃è *n. and adj.* (*f.* **kor̃i̧ya**, *pl.* **kwâr̃r̃a, kor̃àye**) Green.

[1]kôs *n.m.* Course, training.

[2]kôs *n.m.* Trump card.

kòtso *n.m.* Open-ended, hourglass-shaped variable-tone drum which is beaten with the fingers.

kotù̧ *n.m.* (*pl.* **kotu̧nà**) Court.

kowa *pro.m.* 1. Everyone, everybody. 2. (with neg.) Anyone, no one, nobody: *ba mu ga* ~ *ba* we didn't see anyone. 3. Whoever, anyone who: ~ *ya rena gajere bai taka kunama ba* whoever has contempt for anything small has never stepped on a scorpion.

kowàcce *f.* of **kowànne.**

kowà̧cȩ̀ *f.* of **kowà̧nȩ̀.**

kowà̧ɗànnȩ̀ *pl.* of **kowà̧nȩ̀.**

kowà̧ɗànne *pl.* of **kowànne.**

kowà̧nȩ̀ *dem.* (*f.* **kowà̧cȩ̀**, *pl.* **kowà̧ɗànnȩ̀**) 1. Every, each. 2. (with neg.) Any. 3. Whatever, any: ~ *irin abinci ka samu, ka ci* whatever kind of food you get, eat it.

kowànne *pro.m.* (*f.* **kowàcce**, *pl.* **kowàɗànne**) 1. Everyone, each one. 2. (with neg.) None, any: *ba na son* ~ *daga cikinsu* I don't like any of them. 3. Whichever one: ~ *ka ba ni ina so* I will like whichever one you give me.

kòya (i̧/e) *v.t.* (*vn.* **kòyo**) Learn.

koyà *v.t.* (with i.o.) Teach s.o.

koyà *n.f.* Red earth used in making facial powder or dye.

koyar̃ (dà̧) *v.t.* Teach (a subject): *ina* ~ *da labarin ƙasa* I teach geography.

koyàushȩ̀ *adv.* 1. Always. 2. (with neg.) Never. 3. Whenever: ~ *ka zo nan za ka sami goro* whenever you come here you will get a kolanut.

koyàyà *adv.* 1. No matter how, in whatever way. 2. (with neg.) In any way at all. 3. However: ~ *ka taɓa makunnin fitilar nan sai ta kama* no matter how you touch that light switch it will work.

koyì *n.m.* Imitating: *ta yi* ~ *da babarta* she followed the example of her mother.

kòyo *vn.* of **kòya.**

ku *pro.pl.* (vl. and tone vary acc. to use, *see* Appendix 1) You, your.

kubà *n.f.* (*pl.* **kubobi**) Door lock. **ɗan** ~ large-sized key.

kubbi̧ *n.m.* Hearts (suit in playing cards).

kubcè *see* **ku̧ɓù̧ce.**

kù̧be *n.m.* (*pl.* **kù̧bànni**) Sheath for sword or knife.

kù̧bubu̧wà *n.f.* 1. Viper. 2. Quick-tempered person.

ku̧ɓèwa *n.f.* Okra.

ku̧ɓù̧ce *v.i.* 1. Escape. 2. (with i.o.) Escape from, get lost: *ya* ~ *mini* he escaped from me.

kù̧caki *n.m.* (*f.* **kù̧caka**, *pl.* **kù̧càkai**). Slovenly person.

ku̧dancin *prep.* South of.

ku̧dù̧ *n.m.* South, southwards.

kù̧duddu̧fi *n.m.* (*pl.* **kù̧dùddù̧fai**) Burrow-pit.

kuɗà *v.n.* of **koɗà.**

ku̧ɗè *v.i.* Withdraw into a hole.

ku̧ɗi *n.m. or pl.* (*pl.* **ku̧ɗàɗe**) 1. Money. 2. Cost, price.

ku̧ɗin-cizò *n.m.* Bed bugs.

ku̧fai *n.m.* Site of abandoned town.

kuftà *n.f.* A three-quarter-length

taguwa with embroidery around the neck and sleeves.

kụ̀fụlạ̀ *v.i.* Be quick-tempered: *in an yi masa abu kadan sai ya* ~ if you do any little thing to him he becomes angry.

kụ̀ge *n.m.* Pair of metal bells joined together and beaten with a small horn (musical instrument).

kujè *v.t. and v.i.* Abrade, scratch, be abraded, be scratched.

kụjèra *n.f.* (*pl.* **kụ̀jèru, kụ̀jèri**) 1. Chair, stool. 2. Seat in legislature.

kụkạ̀ *pro.pl.* (rel. past tense subj.) You.

kukạ *v.i.* Used in expressions such as *zai* ~ *da kansa* he will have only himself to blame.

kukà *n.f.* (*pl.* **kukoki**) Baobab tree or its fruit or leaves.

kuka *n.m.* (*pl.* **kòkẹ-kòkẹ**) 1. Weeping, crying. 2. Any high-pitched cry of animal or bird. 3. Complaining.

kụkàn *pro.pl.* (hab. tense subj.) You.

kụkè *pro.pl.* (rel. cont. tense subj.) You.

kukụ̀ *n.m.* Cook.

kukumà *n.f.* Small one-stringed, bowed musical instrument.

kul *see* **ạ̀kul.**

kụlà *v.t.* 1. (usu. with **dạ̀**) Pay attention. 2. Care: *ko ya tafi ko bai tafi ba, ba zai* ~ *ba* he doesn't care whether he goes or not. **kụ̀la** *n.f.* Attentiveness, alertness.

kulɓạ̀ *n.f.* Skink lizard.

[1]**kụlẹ̀** *n.f.* Cat.

[2]**kụlẹ̀** *n.m.* Challenge: *an yi masa* ~ he was challenged. *excl.* I challenge you! to which the answer is *cas*.

kulki *n.m.* (*pl.* **kụlàke**) Cudgel, club.

kullè *v.t.* Lock, lock in, lock up: *ya* ~ *ta* he locked her in (kept her in purdah); *alkali ya* ~ *mai kisan kai* the judge locked up the murderer.

kullum *adv.* 1. Always, every day. 2. Every (followed by noun indicating unit or period of time) ~ *shekara* every year; ~ *safiya* each morning. ***aikin yau da*** ~ day-to-day affairs.

kụ̀lôb *n.m.*(*pl.* **kụ̀lôb-kụ̀lôb**) Social or sports club.

kụmạ *prt.* Also, too, likewise: *ni* ~ *zan tafi* I too will go; *in ka gama wannan sai* ~ *ka yi wancan* when you finish this, you should do that as well.

kụmà *v.t.* Repeat, do again.

kụ̀mallo *n.m.* Vomiting from hunger. ***ji*** ~ feel nauseous. ***karya*** ~ eat breakfast.

kụ̀mama *n.m. or f.* (*pl.* **kụ̀màmai, kụ̀màmu**) Person of weak physical constitution.

kụmànta *v.t.* Enfeeble, make weak. **kụ̀mantạ̀** *v.i.* Become feeble.

kụmàtu *pl.* of **kuncì.**

kumbò *n.m.* (*pl.* **kumbụnà**) 1. Flat tray-like calabash used as eating bowl. 2. Space-ship, satellite.

kumbụ̀ra *v.t.* Cause to swell. **kùmbụrạ̀** *v.i.* Become swollen.

kùmbụri *n.m.* Swelling, swollen area.

kumfa *n.f.* Froth, foam, suds.

kụ̀murci *n.m.* Black-hooded cobra.

kun *pro.pl.* (past tense subj.) You.

kụnà *pro.pl.* (cont. tense subj.) You.

kụ̀namà *n.f.* (*pl.* **kụ̀nàmu**) Scorpion.

kuncè *see* **kwancè.**

kuncì *n.m.* (*pl.* **kụmàtu**) Cheek.

kundi *n.m.* (*pl.* **kundàye**) A malam's bundle of loose papers containing his secret prayers and charms.

kùngẹ-kùngẹ *n.m.* Going here and there, involving oneself in various affairs.

kụ̀nî *n.m.* Quinine.

kùnkunnịya *n.f.* Soot which collects on ceiling of a kitchen.

kùnkụru *n.m.* (*pl.* **kùnkụ̀rai**) Tortoise.

kunnà *v.t.* Light (fire, lamp). ~ ***kai*** enter without excuse or permission: *ta* ~ *kanta ɗakinsa* she entered his room without permission.

kûnne *n.m.* (*pl.* **kunnụwà**) Ear. ***'yan*** ~ ear-rings. **kunnẹ** *adv.* (with **ạ̀**) In the ear: *na zuba masa* *ruwa a* ~ I poured some water in his ear.

kùntįgì *n.m.* Small one-stringed, plucked musical instrument.

kùntu *n.m.* (*pl.* **kuntųnà**) Brown blanket used by army personnel.

kuntųkųru *n.m.* Small bowl-shaped drum which is hung from the neck and beaten with small flexible sticks.

kų̀nu *n.m.* Gruel made of flour, usu. guinea-corn or millet, cooked in water and flavoured with tamarind, potash, or pepper.

kunyà *n.f.* 1. Embarrassment, shame, modesty, sense of propriety: *tana da* ~ she is modest; *ba shi da* ~ he has no shame; *ya ba ni* ~ he embarrassed me. 2. Avoidance relationship (e.g. between a man and his in-laws).

kunya *n.f.* (*pl.* **kunyoyi**) Ridge-row on farm.

[1]**kura** *n.f.* (*pl.* **kuràye**) 1. Hyena. 2. A child's noise-maker swung around on a string. **cin** ~ cheating, esp. taking more than one's share in a business transaction.

[2]**kura** *n.f.* Hand-pushed truck.

kųràda *n.f.* Small axe.

kùràri *n.m.* Intimidation.

kųrą̀tandu *n.m.* Small hide container for antimony.

kùrɓa (į/e) *v.t.* Sip.

kurcįya *n.f.* (*pl.* **kurcįyoyi**) Small dove.

kur̃ɗà *v.i.* Crawl through, pass underneath.

kurè *n.m.* (*pl.* **kuràye**) Male hyena.

kų̀rege *n.m.* (*pl.* **kų̀règu**) Ground-squirrel.

kur̃gą *n.f.* Diarrhoea in children.

kuri *n.m.* Bluster, boasting.

kûr̃kųdų̀ *n.m.* Sand lice.

kûr̃kųkù *n.m.* Prison.

kùr̃kųnu *n.m.* Guinea-worm.

kurkų̀re *v.t.* Rinse (mouth).

kurma *n.m. or f.* (*pl.* **kųrâme**) Deaf person.

kurmę *n.m.* Playing in water.

kurmì *n.m.* 1. Thick forest, jungle. 2. Used in *san* ~ prison warder.

kur̃nà *n.f.* A thorny tree with edible berries.

kùr̃tu *n.m.* (*pl.* **kur̃tųnà**) Small, round gourd.

kųrùm *adv.* 1. Only, merely: *wannan aikin* ~ *na ce ka yi* it was only this work that I told you to do. 2. Silently, motionlessly: *na same shi zaune* ~ I found him quietly seated.

kų̀rumbò *n.m.* Bicycle chain-case.

kųrurùta *v.t.* Exaggerate.

kų̀rurųwà *n.f.* Shouting, loud call.

kùrwa *n.f.* Ghost, spirit, soul: *maye ya kama* ~*rta* the sorcerer has trapped her spirit.

kurya *n.f.* Drum similar to but smaller than *ganga*.

kųsą *adv.* Near: *matso* ~ come closer to me; *yana* ~ *da tasha* it is near the lorry park. *v.i.* Be about to do sth., be close to doing sth.: *ya* ~ *isa Kano* he is nearing Kano; *mun* ~ *gamawa* we are almost finished.

kų̀satà (cį/ce) *v.t.* Approach.

kushè *v.t.* Find fault with: *ya* ~ *mini adona* he found fault with my dress.

kų̀shewa *n.f.* (*pl.* **kų̀shèyi**) Grave.

kųshìn *n.f.* Cushion.

kùskųrą̀ *v.i.* Misbehave: *kar ka* ~ *ka dade* you better not misbehave and dawdle.

kuskų̀re *v.t.* Miss (target, chance, etc.): *na* ~ *samun wane a gida* I missed finding so-and-so at home.

kuskųrè *n.m.* 1. Miss, failure. 2. Mistake, error.

kusù *n.m.* (*pl.* **kusa**) Rat, mouse.

kų̀sumburwà *n.f.* Corn-stalk flute.

kųsùrwa *n.f.* (*pl.* **kųsurwoyi**) Corner. ~**r huɗu** the four points of a compass.

kutsà *v.t.* 1. Squeeze through tight opening or crowded place. 2. Barge into place or matter, interfere in matter: *Tanko ya* ~ *kansa cikin zancen da ba nasa ba* Tanko interfered in a matter that did not concern him.

kųtų̀r̃i *n.m.* Hindquarters of animal.

kų̀turtą̀ *v.i.* Become a leper.

kųturtà *n.f.* Leprosy.

kųtųru *n.m.* (*f.* **kųturwa**, *pl.* **kųtàre**) Leper.

kų̀tuttųrè *n.m.* (*pl.* **kų̀tùttų̀rai**) Tree-stump.

kụwą *prt.* Used to affirm sth.: *Musa ~ ya zo* Musa has certainly come; *ita ce ta yi shi ~* it was she who did it, in fact.

kuwwà, kuwà *n.f.* 1. Shouting. 2. *See* **àmsą-kuwwą.**

kụyanga *n.f.*(*pl.* **kụyàngi**) Female slave.

kụzą *n.m.* Tin.

kuzà *v.t.* Pour much water or liquid into: *ta ~ ruwa a miya* she used too much water in the soup.

kụzari *n.m.* Showing energy.

kwa *pro.pl.* (tone varies acc. to tense, *see* Appendix 1) You.

kwąbò *n.m.* (*pl.* **kwàbbai, kwabbụnà**) Penny, pence in old Nigerian currency.

kwąɓa (į/e) *v.t.* Warn, prevent from doing: *ta kwaɓi yaronta ya bar tsokanar faɗa* she warned her child to stop causing trouble.

kwąɓà *v.t.* Haft, insert tool blade into its handle.

kwaɓà *v.t.* (*vn.f.* **kwàɓa**) Mix sth. into paste.

kwąɓè *v.t. and v.i.* 1. Unhaft. 2. Knock sth. out of hand or knock hand away.

kwaɗà *v.t.* Knock down, hit hard, do forcefully.

kwąɗàita *v.t.* (with i.o.) Make s.o. want sth.: *na ~ masa tafiya haji* I got him interested in going on the Hajj. **kwąɗaitą** *v.i.* Have great desire: *na ~ da tafiya karatu* I was very keen to go on for higher studies.

kwąɗąyi *n.m.* Yearning, craving, greed, covetousness: *ina jin ~n nama* I crave meat.

kwąɗọ *n.m.* Cold sauce made of pounded groundnuts or *daddawa* and various condiments.

kwàɗo *n.m.* (*pl.* **kwàɗi**) 1. Frog, toad. 2. Padlock. 3. Embroidery in half-moon design on back edge of neck of gown.

kwâf *n.m.* (*pl.* **kwafụnà**) Cup.

kwàfsa *see* **kwàsfa.**

kwàikwąyà (į/e) *v.t.* (*vn.* **kwaikwąyo**) Imitate: *yaro ya kwaikwayi kukan jaki* the boy imitated the cry of a donkey.

kwaikwąyo *n.m.* Imitation. ***wasan ~*** play, drama.

kwajįri, kwagįri *n.m.* Walking-stick with curved handle.

kwakì *n.m.* Black-hooded cobra.

kwaki *n.m.* Cassava flour.

kwàkkwąfa *n.f.* Cantering (of horse).

kwakkwąfa *v.t.* 1. Knock sth. into hole. 2. Tap bottom of calabash to knock flour out, tap stack of papers on surface to line up the edges.

kwakwà *n.f.* 1. Oil-palm tree, palm kernel. 2. Coconut palm tree, coconut.

kwakwąrẹ *see* **kankąrẹ.**

kwàkwazò *n.m.* Loud fuss.

kwâl *n.m.* Coal.

kwal *id.* Used in *raina ~* I am very happy.

kwąlà *n.f.*(*pl.* **kwąloli**) Collar.

kwąląba *n.f.* (*pl.* **kwąlàbe**) 1. Glass bottle. 2. Crowbar.

kwąlàshât *n.f.* Shirt with collar.

kwalbątį *n.m.* (*pl.* **kwalbątoci**) Culvert.

kwąlejį *n.f.* College.

kwąlẹkwąlẹ *n.m.* Canoe.

kwali *n.m.* (*pl.* **kwalàye**) Cardboard, carton.

kwâlli *n.m.* Antimony (applied in powdered form as a cosmetic).

kwallįya *n.f.* Dressing up: *ta ci ~ ta tafi wurin biki* she dressed up and went to the ceremony.

kwąlò-kwąlo *n.m.* Offering less than the agreed-on price (in trading).

kwàltâ *n.m.* Tarred road, tar.

kwąmandà *n.m.* (*pl.* **kwąmandoji**) Commander.

kwąmįnis *n.m.* Used in *ɗan ~* Communist.

kwąmįshįnà *n.m.* (*pl.* **kwąmįshįnoni**) Commissioner.

kwąmįtî *n.m.* (*pl.* **kwąmįtoci**) Committee.

kwąnà *n.f.* Corner, bend: *yi ~* turn a corner.

kwaną *v.i.* 1. Spend the night: *na ~ ina karatu* I spent the whole night reading. 2. Spend a 24-hour period: *mun ~ uku a hanya* we spent three whole days on the road. ***mu ~ nan*** let's stop here, 'to be concluded' (written formula indicating continuation of a series).

kwana *n.m.* (*pl.* **kwànąki**) 1.

Spending the night: *ina ~?* how are you? 2. Spending a 24-hour period: *na yi ~ uku a Ikko* I was in Lagos for three days. **~ *biyu*** a few days time, a while. ***~n baya*** the other day.
kwaną-kwaną *n.m.* Fire-fighting.
kwànce *n.m.* Second-hand goods: *ya ba ni ~n riga* he gave me a second-hand gown.
kwancè *v.t. and v.i.* Untie, unfasten, become untied, unfastened.
kwàncịya *n.f.* 1. Lying down, prone position. 2. *vn.* of **kwânta.**
kwàndo *n.m.* (*pl.* **kwandụnà**) Basket.
kwanğịla *n.f.* Contract (for construction). ***ɗan*** **~** contractor.
kwànğịrị *n.m.* Large head-pan for carrying earth.
kwanğwąla *n.f.* Long pole used for canoeing or as roof pole of house.
kwànkwąɗà (ị/e) *v.t.* Gulp, drink quickly.
kwànkwąsò *n.m.* Area of back above buttocks.
kwanò *n.m.* (*pl.* **kwanụkà, kwanoni**) 1. Metal or enamel bowl. **~n *sarki*** head-pan. 2. Corrugated iron sheeting.
kwânta *v.i.* (*vn.f.* **kwàncịya**) 1. Lie down. 2. Be settled or at rest, subside: *hankalinsa ya ~* his mind is at rest.
kwantai *n.m.* Perishable foodstuffs which have been left unsold.
kwàntą̀-ràfị *n.m.* Reedbuck.
kwanto *n.m.* Hiding oneself for ambush, out of fear, etc.: *maharbi ya yi ~ ya harbi gada* the hunter hid himself so that he could shoot the duiker.
kwantsà *n.f.* Mucus that collects in the eye during sleep.
kwanya *n.f.* 1. Skull. 2. Brains.
kwar̃à *v.t.* Do sth. excessively or with force: *ta ~ masa ruwa* she poured water all over him.
kwą̀ra-kwą̀ra *n.f.* Stilts.
kwąràm *adv.* Suddenly.
kwą̀ràmnịya *n.f.* Any loud noise: *magina suna ~ saboda buge-buge* the builders are making a lot of noise by their hammering.
kwą̀ranga *n.f.* Ladder.
kwą̀r̃ankwątsą *n.f.* Thunder, sound of thunder.
kwąràra *v.t.* Do much of, esp. rain: *an ~ ruwa a Kano jiya* it rained heavily in Kano yesterday.
kwą̀rarą̀ *v.i.* Flow, flood.
kwąrąrọ *id.* Describes round thing being too large or wide: *zoben nan ya yi mini ~* this ring is too big for me.
kwąrąro *n.m.* Alley, narrow street.
kwarè *v.t.* Lift and expose: *iska ta ~ rufin ɗaki* the wind tore the roof off the hut.
kwą̀ri *n.m.* (*pl.* **kwąrurụwà**) Quiver (for arrows).
kwąrì *n.m.* Valley, depression in ground.
kwàrjịni *n.m.* Dignity, of dignified appearance.
kwar̃kwąr̃o *n.m.* 1. Spindle for thread. 2. Bobbin in sewing machine.
kwàr̃kwąsà *n.f.* Flirting.
kwar̃kwàsa *n.f.* Driver ant.
kwàr̃kwą̀shi *n.m.* Dandruff.
kwâr̃kwątà *n.f.* Louse, lice.
kwàrmątò *n.m.* Blabbing, disclosing a secret.
kwar̃tancì *n.m.* Adultery.
kwar̃to *n.m.* (*f.* **kwar̃tụwa,** *pl.* **kwar̃tàye**) Lover, mistress.
kwą̀sa-kwą̀sa *n.f.* Pink-backed pelican.
kwàsfa *n.f.* Shell or outer covering (e.g. eggshell, skin of orange, cartridge case).
kwashè *v.t.* 1. Dip out completely (food). 2. Collect and remove: *ɓarayi sun ~ mana kaya duka* the robbers stole all of our goods.
kwastàn *n.m.* Customs, import duties.
kwât *n.f.* Coat.
[1]**kwątà** *n.f.* Sewage drain leading away from compound to cesspit.
[2]**kwątà** *n.f.* 1. A quarter of a yard of cloth. 2. One quarter of an hour.
kwąta *n.f.* Slip of the tongue.
kwàta *n.f.* 1. Abattoir, slaughterhouse. 2. Quay.
kwątą-kwątą *id.* Completely.
kwą̀tą̀masta *n.m.* Quartermaster.
kwą̀tąmi *n.m.* Cesspit.

kwą̀tànce *n.m.* Directions (how to get to a place).
kwątancì *n.m.* Illustration, example.
kwątànta *v.t.* Compare, explain by illustration: *ya* ~ *mini girman dutsen* he gave me an idea of the size of the stone.
kwą̀tar̃nįya *n.f.* Large, wide-mouthed earthenware pot.
kwą̀tąshì *n.m.* Upper storey of house.
kwazari *n.m.* Very heavy first rains of the rainy season.
kwą̀zazząbò *n.m.* (*pl.* **kwą̀zàzzą̀bai**) Water-cut channel or gorge.
kwiɓì *n.m.* (*pl.* **kwįyàɓa**) Side of the body between thorax and hips.
kwikwįyò *n.m.* Puppy.
kya *pro.f.* (tone varies acc. to tense, *see* Appendix 1) You.
kyaftìn *n.m.* Captain.
kyàkkyawa *adj.* (*pl.* **kyawàwa**) Beautiful, handsome.
kyąmąr̃ą̀ *n.f.* (*pl.* **kyąmąr̃or̃i**) Camera.
kyân *gen.* of **kyâu**.
kyandìr̃ *n.m.* (*pl.* **kyandįr̃or̃i**) 1. Candle. 2. Fluorescent light bulb.
kyànkyąsò *n.m.* (*pl.* **kyànkyą̀sai**) Cockroach.
kyânwa *n.f.* (*pl.* **kyanwoyi**) Cat.
kyar̃ *adv.* (with **dą̀**) With difficulty, only with difficulty: *da* ~ *na dauko shi* only with difficulty did I carry it.
kyar̃kyąr̃a *n.f.* Cackling of hen before laying eggs.
kyarma *n.f.* Shivering, trembling (from fear or cold).
kyât *n.m.* Cake.
kyâu *n.m.* (*gen.* **kyân**) 1. Goodness, fine appearance, beauty: *wannan zane mai* ~ *ne* this cloth is beautiful; *tana da kyan gani* she is good-looking, pretty. 2. Used in *da* ~ all right, fine, very well.
kyauro *n.m.* (*pl.* **kyauràye**) Arrow shaft.
kyâuta *v.i.* 1. Be kind: *Audu bai* ~ *wa matarsa ba* Audu is not kind to his wife. 2. Reduce price or increase amount (in bargaining). **kyàuta** *n.f.* Gift, present.
kyautą̀ta *v.t.* 1. Improve: *an* ~ *hulɗar ciniki tsakanin Nijeriya da Amirka* trade relations have been improved between Nigeria and America. 2. (with i.o.) Be generous to s.o. **kyàutątą̀** *v.i.* Improve, become better.
kyàutų *v.i.* Be suitable, should be, ought to: *ya* ~ *su dawo yanzu* they ought to come back now.

Ƙ

ƙà *see* **yàyà.**
ƙaba *n.m.* General name for pain felt in various parts of body: ~*n ciki* indigestion; ~*n ƙashi* rheumatism.
ƙą̀bilà *n.f.* (*pl.* **ƙą̀bìlu**) 1. Tribe, ethnic origin. 2. One's relatives, followers.
ƙą̀dandonįya *n.f.* Large millipede.
ƙą̀dangąrè *n.m.* (*f.* **ƙą̀dangąrų̀wa**, *pl.* **ƙą̀dàngą̀ru**) Lizard.
ƙaddą̀r̃a *v.t.* Predestine: *Allah ya* ~ *sai Audu ya yi arziki* God has ordained that Audu will be a rich man. *v.i.* Estimate, reckon: *mun* ~ *kudinsa za su kai naira hudu* we estimate its price to be four Naira. **ƙàddąrà** *n.f.* Fate: ~ *ta riga fata* fate overrides hope.
ƙąfà *n.f.* (*pl.* **ƙąfàfu, ƙąfafųwà**) 1. Foot, leg. *da* ~ on foot. 2. Foot (unit of measurement). 3. Foot (in poetry). 4. Wheel. 5. Tripod.
ƙąfè *v.i.* Dry up: *rijiya ta* ~ the well has dried up.

ƙagà *v.t.* Invent. ~ ***ƙarya*** accuse s.o. falsely.

ƙą̀gautą̀ *v.i.* Be eager: *ya* ~ *da ya tafi* he is eager to go.

ƙągè *v.i.* Become temporarily stiff (of body): *na daɗe ina karatu wuyana har ya* ~ I was reading for such a long time that my neck got stiff.

ƙagę *n.m.* False accusation: *an yi masa* ~*n satar kuɗi* he was falsely accused of stealing money.

ƙą̀ho *n.m.* (*pl.* **ƙą̀hòni**) 1. Horn. 2. Blood-letting (done by sucking through horn).

ƙai *n.m.* (*gen.* **ƙan**) Used in *jin* ~ mercy, pity: *Allah ya ji ƙansa* may God have mercy on his soul.

ƙa'įdà *n.f.* (*pl.* **ƙa'įdodi**) 1. Regulation, standard: *an ajiye* ~*r rubutun Hausa* standards have been set for Hausa orthography. 2. Etiquette, rules of social behaviour: *ya san* ~ he knows what is expected of him; *ya wuce* ~ he exceeded the limits of good behaviour.

ƙaimi *n.m.* 1. Spur of cock. 2. Spur for urging on horse: *ya yi wa dokinsa* ~ *ya ruga da gudu* he spurred his horse on and made it run.

ƙa'įmi *n.m.* (*f.* **ƙa'įma**, *pl.* **ƙà'į-mai**) Householder, leader.

ƙàiƙą̀yi *n.m.* 1. Chaff from winnowing. 2. Itching.

ƙàƙà *see* **yàyà.**

ƙaƙąlę *n.m.* Being over-fastidious.

ƙaƙƙàutâwa *n.f.* (used only in neg.) Without stopping: *tana ta aiki ba* ~ she kept on working incessantly.

ƙalą̀ *n.m.* Word, speech: *da ya gan su bai ce musu* ~ *ba* when he saw them he didn't say a word to them.

ƙąlau *id.* Very: *ai wannan shayi ya yi sanyi* ~ this tea is much too cold; *lafiya* ~ very well (used as greeting in answer to *kana lafiya?* how are you?).

ƙallą̀ *see* **ą̀ƙallą̀.**

ƙallą̀fa *v.t.* 1. Be eager or keen about: *ta* ~ *ranta sai ta je* she is keen on going. 2. Accuse falsely: *an* ~ *masa sata* he has been falsely accused of stealing.

ƙąmè *v.i.* 1. Dry out and become stiff. 2. Stand stiffly (at attention or from fear).

ƙamfa *n.f.* Lack, shortage, failure: *an yi* ~*r ruwa a wurare da yawa* there is a shortage of water in many areas.

ƙan *gen.* of **ƙai.**

ƙamshi *n.m.* Fragrant smell: *wannan turare yana da* ~ this perfume smells very good.

ƙamùs *n.m.* Dictionary.

ƙąnanà *pl.* of **ƙànƙąnè** and **ƙą̀rąmi.**

ƙandą̀re *v.i.* Become rigid or dry: *ƙurjin ya bushe ya* ~ the boil has dried up.

ƙandas *id.* Lacking in oil: *an ba ni waina* ~ *da ita* I was given dried-out *waina.*

ƙąnè *n.m.* (*f.* **ƙanwà**, *pl.* **ƙânne**) Younger brother, younger sister.

ƙanją̀me *v.i.* Become thin.

ƙànjįkį *n.m.* Unhealthy state of body hindering healing of sores.

ƙànƙąnè *n. and adj.* (*f.* **ƙànƙąnų̀wa**, *pl.* **ƙąnanà**) Small.

ƙanƙąmo *n.m. or f.* Stinginess, stingy person.

ƙanƙànce *v.i.* Become small.

ƙanƙancì *n.m.* Humiliation.

ƙànƙąr̃a *n.f.* 1. Flint. 2. Ice, hail, snow.

ƙanƙą̀ra *v.t.* Make sth. very well: *ta* ~ *tukunya* she made a fine pot.

ƙanwà *f.* of **ƙąnè.**

ƙanzo *n.m.* Scraps of *tuwo* which have stuck to the pot.

ƙarą *v.i.* Cry out. **ƙara** *n.f.* Complaint, grievance.

ƙarà *v.t.* (*vn.* **ƙari**) 1. Do again, repeat: *kada ka* ~ *yin haka* don't do that again. 2. Increase, add to: *an* ~ *masa aiki* they have increased his work.

ƙar̃aji *n.m.* Crying out in pain.

ƙą̀ra-ƙą̀ra *n.f.* Eating snack between meals.

ƙàràmbau *n.m.* Chickenpox.

ƙą̀rąmi *n. and adj.* (*f.* **ƙą̀rąma**, *pl.* **ƙąnanà**) 1. Small. 2. Young, younger: *shi ne* ~*nsu* he is the younger of them. ~***n mutum*** mean-minded person.

ƙąranci *n.m.* Shortage: *an yi* ~*n ruwa* there was a shortage of water.

ƙạràngịya *n.f.* Grass with prickly burrs.

ƙạrànta *v.t.* Diminish. **ƙạrantạ** *v.i.* Become insufficient. **ƙạrantà** *n.f.* Mean-mindedness: *ya nuna mana halin* ~ he was very inconsiderate to us.

ƙạrarrạwa *n.f.* Bell.

ƙarạsa *v.t.* Finish.

ƙarè *v.t. and v.i.* Complete, finish: *na* ~ *aikina tun da wuri* I finished my work early; *wahalarsa ta* ~ his troubles are over.

ƙarfạfa *v.t.* 1. Strengthen. 2. Encourage. 3. Emphasize. **ƙàrfạfạ** *v.i.* Become strong or encouraged.

ƙàr̃famfạna *n.f.* Dirt or lint inside pocket. ***ba shi da ko*** ~ he has no money.

ƙarfè *n.m.* (*pl.* **ƙạràfa**) 1. Metal. 2. O'clock: *ya iso nan da* ~ *tara* he came here at 9 o'clock.

ƙarfi *n.m.* 1. Strength, power. 2. Potency (of medicine). ***yi*** ~ come into vogue, be popular.

ƙạrì *n.m.* Sting of bee, scorpion, or wasp.

ƙarì *n.m.* 1. Increase, addition: *ma'aikata sun sami* ~*n albashi* there has been a pay rise for workers. 2. Appendix (of book). 3. *vn.* of **ƙarà.**

ƙàr̃ƙạshi *n.m.* Underside, underneath: ~ *ya fi fili* there's more room underneath.

ƙàr̃ƙạshin *prep.* Under, beneath: *na sa shi* ~ *tebur* I put it under the table.

ƙarƙo *n.m.* Durability.

ƙar̃nì *n.m.* (*pl.* **ƙar̃nụkà**) Century.

ƙaro *n.m.* Gum, resin.

ƙàrshe *n.m.* 1. End: *zai zo* ~*n watan nan* he's coming at the end of this month. 2. Last, final: *wannan ita ce saɗuwarmu ta* ~ that was our final meeting. 3. Tip: ~*n Afirka* the tip of Africa.

ƙàrụ *v.i.* 1. Increase, become increased. 2. Benefit: *na karanta littafin nan na* ~ I read this book and benefited from it.

ƙàrụwa *n.f.* Used in *sami* ~ have an additional child.

ƙarya *n.f.* (*pl.* **ƙạràirai, ƙàryạcẹ-ƙàryạcẹ**) Lie, falsehood.

ƙaryạta *v.t.* 1. Deny. 2. Contradict.

ƙạsa *n.f.* (*pl.* **ƙạsàshe**) 1. Earth, soil, ground. ***farar*** ~ whitewash. 2. Country, state. ***labarin*** ~ geography. **ƙạsạ, ƙas** *adv.* On the ground, below: *ta yar da kobo a* ~ she threw a kobo on the ground; *kina* ~ *da ni* you are junior to me; *ka yi* ~ *da shi* lower it!

ƙàsaitạ *v.i.* Become important, full grown: *sabuwar ma'aikatar nan ta* ~ *da wuri* the new factory has developed rapidly. **ƙàsaità** *n.f.* 1. Development. 2. Importance. 3. Pomposity.

ƙạsạ-ƙạsạ *adj.* Earth-coloured, brownish.

ƙạsàn *prep.* At the bottom of: *dauda ta yi yawa a* ~ *tankin* there is too much dirt at the bottom of the tank.

ƙạshi *n.m.* (*pl.* **ƙạsusụwà, ƙassà**) 1. Bone. 2. Plot (in drama or novel).

ƙạsidà *n.f.* (*pl.* **ƙạsidu**) Ode.

ƙatò *n. and adj.* (*f.* **ƙatụwa,** *pl.* **ƙâtta**) Huge, big.

ƙàuna *n.f.* Affection, love.

ƙàunạtà (cị/ce) *v.t.* Beg, plead.

ƙaurạ *v.i.* 1. Move to another town. 2. Emigrate. **ƙaura** *n.f.* Migration.

ƙaurà *n.f.* Red guinea-corn.

ƙaurạce *v.t.* (with i.o.) Stop visiting place or person: *ya* ~ *mana kwana biyu* he hasn't visited us for some time.

ƙauri *n.m.* 1. Smell of burnt rags, hair, etc. 2. Cooked feet and parts of head of cow distributed two days before naming ceremony.

ƙauyè *n.m.* (*pl.* **ƙauyụkà**) Village.

ƙạwa *n.f.* (*pl.* **ƙạwàye**) 1. Female friend of a girl or woman. 2. Adornment.

ƙawà *n.f.* Fondness, great desire (esp. for food).

ƙạwanyà *n.f.* (*pl.* **ƙạwànyu**) 1. Any metal ring. 2. Circle around sth.: *soja sun yi wa abokan gaba* ~ the army has encircled the enemy.

ƙạwàta *v.t.* Make beautiful: *ta* ~ *ɗakinta* she furnished her room well. **ƙạwatạ** *v.i.* Be, become beautiful.

ƙą̀wà-zucį *n.m.* Greed: *~nsa ya jawo masa kunya* he was brought to shame as a result of his greed.

ƙą̀yà *n.f.* (*pl.* **ƙą̀yoyi**) 1. Thorn. 2. Small fish bone. 3. Quill of hedgehog or porcupine.

ƙayè *n.f.* Showing off one's stylishness of dress.

ƙayyą̀de *v.t.* 1. Pass order, rule, agreement: *an ~ musu lokacin zuwa aiki* they were given a fixed time for coming to work. 2. Estimate a number, price, wage: *ba su ~ yawan mutanen da suka ɓata ba* they haven't estimated the number of people who got lost.

ƙą̀zàf *see* **ką̀zàf.**

ƙą̀zami *n. and adj.* (*f.* **ƙą̀zama,** *pl.* **ƙą̀zàmai**) 1. Dirty. 2. Excessive: *yana da ~n karfi* he is too strong (for his own good).

ƙą̀zânta *n.f.* Dirtiness, filth.

ƙazwa *n.f.* Scabies.

ƙeƙą̀sa *v.t.* Dry: *rana ta ~ ganye* the sun dried the leaves. **ƙèƙąsą̀** *v.i.* Be dried.

ƙememe *id.* Used to emphasize **ƙį** or **hąnà**: *ya ki ~* he flatly refused; *ubanta ya hana aurensu ~* her father absolutely refused to consent to their marriage.

ƙerà *v.t.* (*vn.f.* **ƙirà**) Forge, smith, manufacture.

ƙèrèrè *id.* Used in *ta tsaya a gabansa ~* she stood in front of him disrespectfully.

ƙèta *n.f.* Being malicious for its own sake: *raba makaho da sandarsa ~ ce* taking away the stick of a blind person is a malicious act.

ƙetą̀ra *v.t.* 1. Cross (road, river, border, etc.). 2. Emigrate.

ƙetą̀re *v.t.* Cross over. **ƙetąrè** *n.m.* The other side: *yana ~n kogi* he is on the other bank of the river.

ƙeyà *n.f.* 1. Nape of the neck. 2. Hindsight.

ƙį *v.t.* Refuse.

ƙįbà *n.f.* Fatness.

ƙįdàya *v.t.* Count, reckon. **ƙįdaya** *n.f.* Counting, enumeration: *~r jama'a* population census.

ƙįdìddįgà *n.f.* 1. Reflection, pondering. 2. Counting.

ƙifce *n.m.* Blinking, winking.

ƙįfil *n.m.* Love-potion smeared on the eyes.

ƙiftà *v.t.* 1. Blink. 2. (with i.o.) Wink: *ta ~ mini ido* she winked at me.

ƙiƙàm *id.* Used in *ya tsaya a kaina ~* he stood in front of me silently and listlessly.

ƙil *id.* Emphasizes smallness.

ƙilą̀ *see* **wątąƙilą̀.**

ƙirà *vn.* of **ƙerà.**

ƙįràre *n.m. or pl.* Twigs for firewood.

ƙirgà *v.t.* Count up: *ya ~ su duka* he counted them all up; *ya ~ daga ɗaya har zuwa goma* he counted from one to ten.

ƙirgì *n.m.* (*pl.* **ƙįràga**) Tanned cowhide.

ƙįri *n.m.* Being wide-eyed. ***~ da muzu*** outright, bluntly.

ƙirì *n.m.* Rope made of hide.

ƙįrin *id.* Emphasizes blackness: *baki ~* jet black.

ƙįrìnįya *n.f.* Playful mischievousness, esp. by children.

ƙįris *id.* A little bit: *sauran ~ keke ya kade yaron* the bicycle almost bumped into the boy.

ƙìrji *n.m.* Chest.

ƙirƙįra *v.t.* 1. Invent. ***~ laifi*** blame s.o. falsely. 2. Create, bring forth into existence.

ƙis *see* **ƙįris.**

ƙishì *n.m.* Thirst, craving: *yana jin ~* he is thirsty; *yana ~n taba* he is craving a cigarette.

ƙįshin-ƙįshin *n.m.* Rumours: *na ji ~ an ce za su zo gobe* it is rumoured that they are arriving tomorrow.

ƙįshirwa *n.f.* 1. Thirst. 2. Need.

ƙissà *n.f.* (*pl.* **ƙissoshi**) Story, anecdote.

ƙįyasì *n.m.* Analogy.

ƙįyàsta *v.i.* Consider carefully, weigh opinion: *idan ka ~ a ranka za ka ga cewa bai kyauta ba* if you think it over carefully, you will conclude that he has done wrong.

ƙįyayyà *n.f.* Mutual hatred.

ƙodà *n.f.* (*pl.* **ƙodoji**) Kidney.

ƙòdą̀gò *n.m.* The nut of dum-palm or deleb-palm trees.

ƙodągo *n.m.* Any work for wages, esp. farming.
ƙofà *n.f.* (*pl.* **ƙofofi**) 1. Doorway, gate. **~*r fada*** open space in front of Emir's palace. 2. Opening in fence, hole in roof. 3. Opportunity, means. 4. Way out, loophole.
ƙofi *n.m.* Causing fear, esp. by person or animal thought to have the ability to cast spells.
ƙòƙąri *n.m.* Effort, trying hard: *~nsa ne ya ba shi* he got it by his own efforts; *ina ~na* I'm doing my best.
ƙoƙàrta *v.i.* Try hard, exert oneself.
ƙoƙè *v.i.* Fade (of colour).
ƙoƙį *n.f.* Wife of Gizo, a trickster hero in Hausa folklore.
ƙoƙįƙoƙį *n.m.* Praying mantis.
ƙòƙo *n.m.* (*pl.* **ƙoƙųnà**) Small calabash. **~*n kai*** skull. **~*n gwiwa*** knee-cap.
ƙoƙųwa *n.f.* Top of cap, straw hat, or round thatched roof.
ƙolį *n.m.* Top, summit. ***taron ~*** summit conference.
ƙonè *v.t.* Burn. *v.i.* 1. Be burnt. 2. Dry up (e.g. of well).
ƙorąfi *n.m.* Fussing, fretting.
ƙôrai *pl.* of **ƙwarya.**
ƙòrąmà *n.f.* (*pl.* **ƙòràmu**) Stream.
ƙosà *v.i.* 1. Become exasperated. 2. Become ripe.
ƙosai *n.m.* Fried cakes made of bean flour.
ƙòshį *v.i.* Be replete: *ya ci har ya ~* he ate until he was full.
ƙòshįyà *n.f.* (*pl.* **ƙoshįyoyi**) Wooden ladle.
ƙotà *n.f.* (*pl.* **ƙotoci**) Handle (of hoe, axe, etc.).
ƙòto *n.m.* Feeding, pecking.
ƙozo *n.m.* Large edible toad.
ƙubąkà *n.f.* Hem at top of trousers for trouser string.
ƙųda *n.m.* (*pl.* **ƙųdàje**) Fly. **~*n zuma*** bee. **~*n tsando*** tsetse fly.
ƙųdundų̀ne *v.i.* Lie curled up, be rolled up.
ƙųdų̀ra *v.t.* 1. Knot. 2. Decide: *ya ~ niyyar tafiya* he has decided to travel.
ƙųdųr̃à *excl.* My word! Fancy!
ƙugì *n.m.* Groaning, moaning.
ƙugįya *n.f.* (*pl.* **ƙugįyoyi**) Hook.
ƙugù *n.m.* Lower back.
ƙujè *v.t. and v.i.* Scrape, abrade.
ƙųƙų̀mi *n.m.* Shackling s.o. by tying hands around neck.
ƙųƙut *id.* 1. Shortness, compactness: *mutum gajere ne ~ da shi* he is a very short person; *'yar rumfa ce ~ da ita* it's a very narrow stall. 2. Closeness (of relationship): *Kande yar'uwata ce ~* Kande is my close relation.
ƙuƙùta *v.i.* Try hard.
ƙųlè *v.i.* Fly into a rage.
ƙųliƙųli *n.m.* Fried groundnut balls.
ƙullà *v.t.* 1. Knot: *ya ~ bakin zare* he knotted the end of the thread. 2. Plot against: *sun ~ mini dabara* they conspired against me.
ƙùlli *n.m.* Punching.
ƙùllu *n.m.* Mixture of flour and water used to make *waina* or *koko.*
ƙùllutù *n.m.* (*pl.* **ƙùllùtai**) Swelling from sting or bite.
ƙųlu-ƙų̀lù *id.* Large and round (of eyes, onions or fruit).
ƙùlulù *n.m.* Swelling or lump on body due to illness.
ƙulųmi *n.m.* (*f.* **ƙulųma,** *pl.* **ƙùlų̀mai**) Stingy person.
ƙų̀ma *n.m.* Flea.
ƙùmba *n.f.* 1. Mussel shell. 2. Fingernail.
ƙùmbįyà-ƙumbįya *n.f.* Refusal, inability to come to the point.
ƙunà *n.f.* Great heat: *ranar nan tana da ~* the sun is very hot today.
ƙuna *n.m.* Scar on skin or hole in clothing resulting from being burnt.
ƙunci *n.m.* 1. Bad temper. 2. Narrow, constricted area: *ɗakin ya yi masa ~* the room is too small for him.
ƙùndu *n.m.* Gizzard.
ƙundų̀me *v.t.* Cut off branches of tree to produce new branches. **~ *kai*** shave head of female (because of scalp disease).
ƙungįya *n.f.* (*pl.* **ƙungįyoyi**) Society, union, association. ***yi ~*** travel together.
ƙungurmi *n.m.* Bare state: **~*n***

ɗaji thick bush or forest far from inhabited area; ~*n matsiyaci* destitute person.

ƙùnsa (shị/she) *v.t.* Contain, deal with: *ga alama maganarsa ta ƙunshi gaskiya* it seems that what he said contains an element of truth. **ƙunsà** *v.t.* (*vn.* **ƙunshì**) Wrap sth. up: *ta ~ kuɗi a ɗankwalinta* she wrapped the money in her head-tie.

ƙunshì *n.m.* (*pl.* **ƙùnshẹ-ƙùnshẹ**) 1. Parcel. 2. *vn.* of **ƙunsà.**

ƙùntạtạ̀ *v.i.* Be restricted (of area).

ƙuntạ̀ta *v.t.* (with i.o.) Pester or badger s.o.

ƙunzụgu *n.m.* Tucking loincloth into waistband.

ƙụrà *v.t.* (with i.o.) Stare: *ya ~ mata ido* he stared at her.

ƙùra *n.f.* Dust.

ƙụrè *v.t. and v.i.* Corner, restrict: *wuri ya ~ masa* he was hemmed in (and couldn't escape); *lokaci ya ~* there is little time left.

ƙụrèwa *n.f.* Extremity: *ya ajiye kayansa can ~r ɗaki* he kept his things at the extreme end of the room.

ƙụ̀r̃ị'à *n.f.* (*pl.* **ƙụr̃ị'o'i**) 1. Vote, ballot: *sun jefa ~rsu* they cast their votes. 2. Drawing lots, divination.

ƙurji *n.m.*(*pl.* **ƙụràje**) Pimple, boil.

ƙùr̃mus *id.* Used in *ƙone ~* burn up completely.

ƙụ̀rụ *n.m.* Taking a risk, reckless courage.

ƙurù *n.m.* Pony.

ƙụ̀rùcịya *n.f.* Youthfulness.

ƙụ̀rungụ̀ *n.m.* Spotted catfish.

ƙur̃yạ̀ *n.f.* Wall of room facing door: *ya shiga ~r ɗaki* he has entered the innermost part of the room.

ƙusà *n.f.* (*pl.* **ƙusoshi**) 1. Nail. ~ ***mai tiredi*** screw. 2. Rapping s.o. on head with middle knuckle. 3. Ruining s.o.'s chances indirectly: *an yi masa ~ a wurin neman kwangila* there was a plot to prevent him from getting the contract.

ƙụ̀sumbi *n.m.* Hump on back (due to spinal deformity). ***mai ~*** hunchback.

ƙụ̀ta *n.f.* Clicking noise made in the throat to indicate annoyance.

ƙwacè *v.t.* Take by force. *v.i.* Behave rebelliously: *kan mota ya ~* the steering went out of control. **ƙwàce** *n.m.* Plundering.

ƙwadạgo *see* **ƙodạgo.**

ƙwạdọ̀ *n.m.* Type of draughts.

ƙwạ̀fa *n.f.* Clicking sound made in throat to indicate anger.

ƙwafà *v.t. and v.i.* Squeeze into crowded place: *ya ~ cikinsu ya zauna* he squeezed himself between them and sat down.

ƙwafì *n.m.* Re-sowing farm where seeds did not germinate.

ƙwai *n.m.* (*pl.* **ƙwạyàye,** *gen.* **ƙwan**) 1. Egg. 2. Electric bulb, globe. ***ƙwan fitila*** lamp glass.

ƙwàinanụ̀wa *n.f.* Wise young girl.

ƙwaƙụ̀le *v.t.* Scrape out from inside: *yaro ya ~ kunnensa* the boy scraped dirt out of his ear.

ƙwàƙwa *n.f.* Being inquisitive, inclined to persistent questioning.

ƙwạƙwalwa *n.f.* Brain.

ƙwal *id.* Alone: *sai shi ɗaya ~* he is completely alone.

ƙwạ̀lạ *n.f.* Bulb of water-lily.

ƙwalà *v.t.* Resound: *ya ~ musu kira* he called them in a loud voice; *sun ~ shi da sanda* they hit him with a resounding blow.

ƙwạ̀lele *n.m.* Teasing by offering sth. and then refusing to give it.

ƙwallo *n.m.* (*pl.* **ƙwallàye**) 1. Stone of any fruit. 2. Ball. 3. Ball game: *~n raga* basketball. ***ci ~*** win race or contest.

ƙwambò *n.m.* Boastfulness.

ƙwan *gen.* of **ƙwai.**

ƙwànƙwàmai *n.pl.* Evil spirits causing madness.

ƙwanƙwạ̀sa *v.t.* Knock or tap on.

ƙwànso *n.m.* Pod, shell, nut, cotton-boll.

ƙwàra (ị/e) *v.t.* Cheat.

ƙwarà *n.f.* Shea nuts.

ƙwạr̃ai *adv.* Very much, indeed: *yana da kuɗi ~* he is very rich.

ƙwạ̀r̃àngwal *n.m.* Skeleton.

ƙwarbai *n.m.* Difficulty: *an sha ~ da su* there was a lot of trouble with them.

ƙwạr̃è *v.i.* Become expert: *ya ~*

da dinki he became an expert tailor.

ƙwarè *v.t. and v.i.* Choke: *tuwo ya* ~ *shi* he choked on the *tuwo*.

[1]**ƙwari** *n.m.* Soundness, strength of construction.

[2]**ƙwari** *n.m.* Spell (cast on a person).

ƙwârƙwạrà *n.f.* (*pl.* **ƙwạ̀ràƙwạ̀rai**) Concubine.

ƙwârƙwạtà *see* **kwârkwạtà.**

ƙwàrnạ̀ƙi *n.m.* Flatulence.

ƙwàro *n.m.* (*pl.* **ƙwàri**) 1. Insect. 2. Thief.

ƙwarya *n.f.* (*pl.* **ƙôrai**) Calabash.

ƙwàrzạbà (i̧/e) *v.t.* Pester, annoy. *n.f.* Pestering, being a nuisance.

ƙwàrzạnà (i̧/e) *v.t.* Scratch.

ƙwạsai-ƙwạsai *id.* Very clean: *ya wanku* ~ it is well washed.

ƙwàuri *n.m.* (*pl.* **ƙwaurụkà**) Calf, shin.

ƙwaurò *n.m.* Insufficient supply, niggardliness: *an yi mana* ~*n abinci* we weren't given enough food.

ƙwàya *n.f.* (*pl.* **ƙwayoyi**) 1. Grain (e.g. of corn). 2. Tablet, pill. ***shan*** ~ taking dangerous drugs.

ƙwàzo *n.m.* Diligence, hard work: *Musa ya nuna* ~ *a aikinsa* Musa has really worked hard.

ƙyafè *v.t.* 1. Grill on fire. 2. Dry oneself near fire.

ƙyalè *v.t.* Ignore (person or thing).

ƙyạlì *n.m.* Adornment, make-up.

ƙyali̧ya *n.f.* Ignoring people: *yana da yawan* ~ he ignores people a lot.

ƙyalƙyạ̀la *v.t.* Used in ~ *dariya* laugh loudly.

ƙyàlƙyạ̀li *n.m.* Twinkling, glittering.

ƙyallà *v.t.* Catch a glimpse of: *ya* ~ *ido ya ga ɓarawo* he caught a glimpse of the thief.

ƙyalle *n.m.* (*pl.* **ƙyallàye**) Any small piece of cloth.

ƙyàlli *n.m.* Shininess.

ƙyàma *n.f.* Feeling of aversion or abomination: *yana* ~*r kutare* he has an aversion to lepers.

ƙyânda *n.f.* Measles.

ƙyanƙyạ̀she *v.t.* Hatch (eggs).

ƙyar̃ *see* **kyar̃.**

ƙyas *id.* (used with neg.) Nothing at all: *ba su ba mu ko* ~ *ba* they gave us absolutely nothing. ***ji*** ~ hear rumour.

ƙyasà *v.t.* Admire.

ƙyàsƙi *n.m.* Skin disease affecting face, neck, and chest.

ƙyàshi *n.m.* Jealousy, covetousness.

ƙyastà *v.t.* Strike match or flint to make fire.

ƙyàstu *n.m.* Flint.

ƙyasụwa *n.f.* A tall coarse grass.

ƙyaure *n.m.* (*pl.* **ƙyạmàre**) Door.

ƙyûya *n.f.* 1. Laziness. 2. Uncooperativeness.

L

lạ̀'ạdà *n.f.* Commission on a business transaction.

lạ̀'ạkạ̀ri *n.m.* Care, consideration: *ka yi* ~ *da zancen da na fada maka* consider what I have told you.

lạ̀'ạllạ̀ *adv.* Perhaps.

lạ̀'ạnà *n.f.* Crime, sin, fault, curse: *ya sha* ~ *kan abin da ya yi* he has been cursed for what he has done.

lạ̀'antà (ci̧/ce) *v.t.* 1. Reprimand, shame. 2. Curse.

lạ̀'ạsàr̃ *n.f.* 1. Third prayer of the day. 2. Time of day from about 4 p.m. till shortly before sunset. ~ ***sakaliya*** the latter part of *la'asar.* ~ ***lis*** the very end of *la'asar.* 3. Weakness, apathy: *jikinsa ya yi* ~ he feels weak.

labà *n.f.* Pound (weight).

làbarì *n.m.* (*pl.* **làbàru, làbàrai**) 1. News, information: *na sha* ~ I heard a lot of news; *ina* ~? what's

new? (greeting to which the answer is ~ *sai alheri*). 2. Story, narrative.
labì *n.m.* Track, cattle path through bush.
labtà *v.t.* Do sth. to excess: *an ~ ruwa jiya* it rained heavily yesterday; *ya ~ wa motarsa kaya* he overloaded his car.
làbuddạ̀ *adv.* Undoubtedly, definitely.
labụle *n.m.* Curtain.
labụ̀r̃ar̃è *n.f.* Library.
lạɓàɓa *v.i.* Approach stealthily: *ya ~ ya sace musu kaya* he sneaked up on them and stole their clothes.
lạɓè *v.i.* Crouch behind sth. or lean against wall to eavesdrop: *ya ~ yana jin abin da muka faɗi* he hid and overheard what we were talking about.
laccà *n.f.* (*pl.* **laccoci**) Lecture.
lada *n.m.* Wages, reward.
lạdạ̀bi *n.m.* Politeness, obedience, good manners.
lạdàbta *v.t.* Discipline.
làdân, làdanì *n.m.* (*pl.* **làdànai**) Muezzin.
Ladị̀ *see* **Lạhạ̀dị̀.**
lạfà *v.i.* Die down (fire, wind, dispute).
lạ̀fafà *see* **lịfafà.**
lạfạ̀zi *n.m.* Speech, pronunciation.
lafịyà *n.f.* 1. Health, good condition, state of general well-being. **mutum mai ~** easy-going person. 2. Used in greetings: *kana ~?* how are you? *~ ƙalau* very well, thank you. *adv.* Safely: *sun zo ~?* did they arrive safely?
làftạnàn *n.m.* (*pl.* **laftạnoni**) Lieutenant.
lạ̀gwạ̀ni *n.m.* Lamp wick.
Lạhạ̀dị̀ *n.f.* Sunday.
lạhạ̀ni *n.m.* 1. Blemish, flaw. 2. Injury, damage.
lạhànta *v.t.* Maim.
Lahịr̃à *n.f.* The Next World.
lâifì *n.m.* (*pl.* **laifuffụkà, laifụkà**) 1. Crime, wrong, fault: *ba shi da ~* he is not to blame. 2. Blemish, defect.
lạ̀'ifì *n.m.* (*pl.* **lạ̀'ifai**) Sexually impotent man.
lailạ̀ya *v.t.* 1. Knead into balls. 2. Knead sth. round to soften it. 3. Massage (a bump or bruise).
¹laimà *n.f.* Dampness.
²laimà *n.f.* (*pl.* **laimomi**) 1. Tent. 2. Umbrella. 3. Parachute. 4. Shade: *bari in yi maka ~* let me shade you (e.g. with the sleeve of my gown).
lạka *n.f.* Spinal cord.
laka *n.f.* Mud found in ponds and marshy areas.
lạƙạ̀bi *n.m.* Name(s) used in addition to or in place of one's given name: *sunansa Idi ~nsa Sakatare* his name is Idi but his nickname is 'Secretary'.
lalàce *v.i.* Spoil, deteriorate.
lalacì *n.m.* Laziness.
lalàta *v.t.* 1. Spoil sth. 2. Disgrace s.o., ruin s.o.'s reputation. 3. Lead s.o. astray. **làlatà** *n.f.* Immoral act, bad conduct.
làlê *excl.* Welcome!
lalè *v.t.* Shuffle cards.
lallạ̀ɓa *v.t.* 1. Soothe, flatter. 2. Repair or tie sth. temporarily or roughly.
lallạmi *n.m.* Cajolery, coddling.
làllasà (shị/she) *v.t.* Persuade, coax.
lallè *n.m.* Henna.
lalle, lallai *adv.* For sure, certainly, necessarily: *~ na gan shi a hanya* I definitely saw him on the way.
làlụbà (ị/e) *v.t.* Grope: *ya lalubi aljihunsa bai sami ko kobo ba* he searched around in his pocket but couldn't find even a kobo.
lambà *n.f.* (*pl.* **lambobi**) 1. Sign, distinguishing mark, trademark. 2. Registration number (on vehicle). 3. Vaccination. 4. Scratch on enamel-ware.
làmbạ̀tû *n.m.* 1. Gutter, drain. 2. Second (in race, exam, etc.).
làmbạ̀wân *n.m.* 1. First (in race, exam, etc.). 2. Poison.
lambo *n.m.* Complaining, fussing about minor injury or inconvenience.
làmbu *n.m.* (*pl.* **lambụnà**) Garden, irrigated land.
lami *n.m.* Insipidness, tastelessness.
¹lạ̀mir̃ì *n.m.* Opinion.

²lạmiři *n.m.* Pronoun (in grammar).
lamụ̀ni *n.m.* Credit in trading: *ya yi mini ~n naira goma* he gave me ten Naira's worth of goods on credit.
làmuntà (cị/ce) *v.t.* Extend s.o. credit in trading: *ya lamunce ni naira goma* he extended me credit of ten Naira.
lamụ̀she *v.t.* Eat quickly, devour: *ya ~ abincinsa* he gobbled up his food.
làngạ *n.f.* A children's game played by holding one foot with opposite hand, and trying to push s.o. else down.
lànga *n.f.* (*pl.* **langụnà**) Lidded dish, usu. of painted enamelware, used for serving *tuwo*.
langạ̀ɓe *v.i.* 1. Become soft or mushy from overcooking or over-ripeness. 2. Droop, flop.
làngạ̀-langạ̀ *n.m.* 1. Strips of iron used for tying bales. 2. Cutlass for cutting grass.
lanƙwạ̀me *v.t.* Eat greedily.
lanƙwạ̀sa *v.t.* Bend (metal).
lànƙwạsà *n.f.* Place where sth. is bent.
làntařkì *n.m.* Electric light, electricity.
Làřạ̀ba *n.f.* Wednesday.
lařdì *n.m.* 1. District, division. 2. Province.
lạ̀řuřà *n.f.*(*pl.* **lạřuřoři**) Necessity: *wata ~ ce ta hana shi zuwa jiya* an unavoidable circumstance prevented him from coming yesterday.
lạ̀řuři *n.m.* Used in *~n magariba* the last few minutes before sunset.
làsa (shị/she) *v.t.* Lick, lick up.
lasạ̀fikà *n.f.* Loudspeaker.
lasàfta *v.t.* Reckon up, count up, enumerate.
làshẹ-làshẹ *n.m.* Snacks served at a party or ceremony.
lasìn *n.m.* Licence.
lâskofùř *n.m.* Lance-corporal.
lasọ̀ *n.m.* Remains from dye-pits used for sealing roofs and cementing surfaces.
lạtàs *n.m.* Lettuce.
latsà *v.t.* Squeeze, press, squash.
lattị *n.m.* Lateness: *kada ka yi ~* don't be late!
latụ̀'addụ̀ *adv.* Abundantly.
lau *id.* Used in *lafiya ~* very well (used as greeting in answer to *kana lafiya?* how are you?).
làuje *n.m.* (*pl.* **laujụnà**) Small sickle.
lâulawà *n.f.* Bicycle.
laulạ̀yi *n.m.* Prone to sickness: *yaro ya cika yawan ~* the boy is always sick.
laumà *see* **lomà**.
launì *n.m.* (*pl.* **launụkà**) 1. Colour. 2. Tune, pattern.
laushi *n.m.* Soft, fine, flexible: *garin nan yana da ~* this flour is very finely ground.
làusuř *n.m.* Garden cress.
¹lauyà *v.t.* 1. Bend to make round. 2. Turn (steering wheel).
²lauyà *n.m.* (*pl.* **lauyoyi**) Lawyer.
lawạ̀li *n.m.* (*pl.* **làwạ̀lai**) Cattle path, usu. between hedges bordering farms.
lạwạ̀shi *n.m.* Onion tops.
làwùřje *n.m.* Trouser-string.
layà *n.f.* (*pl.* **layu**) Charm (usu. religious texts wrapped in leather). ***cin*** *~* swearing on the Koran.
layì *n.m.* (*pl.* **layụkà**) 1. Line, row. 2. Lane, street. 3. Village court of justice.
layyạ *n.f.* Sacrificing a ram during the festival of Id-el-Kabir.
lạ̀zimtà (cị/ce) *v.t.* 1. Frequent a place. 2. Repeat sth., persevere: *in ka lazimci shan madara za ka yi lafiya* if you keep drinking milk you will be healthy.
lazzà *n.f.* Nice, pleasant taste.
lebùř *n.m.* Levelness, flatness.
lebụ̀řạ̀ *n.m.* (*pl.* **lebụřoři**) Labourer.
leɓè *n.m.* (*pl.* **leɓụnà, lâɓɓa**) Lip.
lèfe *n.m.* 1. Basket made of palm fronds. 2. Clothes given to bride by bridegroom before wedding ceremony.
leƙà *v.t.* 1. Peep at. 2. Call on s.o. for visit.
lèmo *n.m.* (*pl.* **lemụnà**) 1. Orange. ***~n tsami*** lemon, lime. 2. Soft drink.
libà *n.m.* (*pl.* **libobi**) Lever.
lịbařbà *n.m.* Revolver, pistol.
lịfafà *n.m.* Shroud.

lifì *n.m.* Leave, furlough.
lịfịdi *n.m.* Protective quilting for horses.
lịkịmo *n.m.* Keeping still, being unobtrusive: *na yi kwance* ~ *sai ya yi tsammani barci nake yi* I was lying down being very quiet so that he thought I was sleeping.
lịkịtą̀ *n.m. or f.* (*pl.* **lịkịtoci**) Doctor.
lìkkafà *n.f.* (*pl.* **lìkkàfu**) Stirrup.
lìkkąfą̀ni *n.m.* Shroud.
liƙà *v.t.* Stick together, gum, cause to adhere.
liƙì *n.m.* Mending or stopping up a hole.
lịlịmàn *n.m.* Liniment.
lịlìn *n.m.* Linen cloth.
lịlis *id.* Thoroughly ground or beaten.
lilò *n.m.* Dangling, swinging.
lìmân *n.m.* (*pl.* **lìmàmai**) Imam.
Lìnjila *n.f.* New Testament.
lìnzamì *n.m.* (*pl.* **lìnzàmai**) 1. Bridle, bit. 2. Triangular openwork embroidery on front of neck opening of gown.
lis *see* **lą̀'ąsàr̃.**
lìsha *n.f.* 1. Fifth prayer of the day. 2. Time of day from darkness until midnight.
lìssafì *n.m.* 1. Arithmetic. 2. Counting, reckoning. 3. List.
lità *n.f.* Litre.
Lìtịnîn *n.f.* Monday.
littafì *n.m.* (*pl.* **lìttàttàfai, lìttàfai**) Book.
lịyafà *n.f.* 1. Hospitality. 2. Party.
lodì *n.m.* Loading.
lofè *n.m.* Smoking-pipe.
logà *n.f.* Careful investigation of sth.: *ya sha* ~*rsa ya sami asirin zancen* he fully investigated the matter and got to the secret.
loką̀ci *n.m.* (*pl.* **lòką̀tai**) Time, period. **loką̀ci-loką̀ci** *adv.* Sometimes, occasionally. **loką̀cîn dą̀** *rel. adv.* When: *ban san* ~ *ya iso ba* I don't know when he arrived.
lokò *n.m.* Recess, nook, corner: *na bi* ~ ~ *ina nemanka* I looked for you in every nook and cranny.
lomà *n.f.* (*pl.* **lomomi**) Morsel of food, mouthful.
lotò *n.m.* Time. **lotò-lotò** *adv.* From time to time.
lotsà *v.t. and v.i.* Cause to sag, sag: *kabewa ta* ~ *dakinsa* the (weight of the) pumpkins made the roof of his house sag; *bayan jaki ya* ~ the donkey's back sagged (under the weight of its loads).
ludą̀yi *n.m.* (*pl.* **lỵwàdu, ludąyà**) 1. Small oblong gourd. 2. Ladle.
luɗų̀ *see* **lỵwaɗì.**
lų̀gų̀de *n.m.* Several women pounding in one mortar at the same time.
lųgwigwìta *v.t.* Knead to soften (e.g. fruit): *ya* ~ *lemo* he squeezed the orange to make it soft.
lulà *v.i.* Flee, go far away.
lullų̀ɓa *v.t.* Cover body with cloth.
lų̀manà *n.f.* Friendship, goodwill: *suna zaman* ~ they live peacefully.
lumshè *v.t.* Close one's eyes (usu. due to drowsiness). *v.i.* Become overcast, cloudy: *rana tana lumshewa* the sun is clouding over.
lùmshi *n.m.* Cloudiness, being overcast.
lungù *n.m.* (*pl.* **lungųnà**) Recess, nook, corner.
lùr̃ą *v.t.* (usu. with **dą̀**) Notice, pay attention: *ya* ~ *da aikinsa* he paid attention to his work.
lur̃u *n.m.* (*pl.* **lur̃àye**) Black or blue and white striped native cloth.
lusą̀r̃i *n.m.* (*f.* **lusą̀r̃a**, *pl.* **lùsą̀r̃ai**) Lazy, good-for-nothing person.
lỵwaɗì *n.m.* Sodomy.

M

(The symbols *, †, and ‡ indicate words formed with the prefix **mą-**. See Appendix 3 for their formation and meaning.)

mą̀ 1. Form of i.o. marker before nouns used after verbs with final **-m** such as **cim, tasam,** etc. 2. In certain dialects, i.o. marker before nouns used in place of **wą̀**: *sun gaya* ~ *sarki labari* = *sun gaya wa sarki labari* they told the news to the chief.

[1]**ma** *prt.* Also, too, even: *zan tafi* ~ I will also go; *yanzu* ~ *ana yi* it is still being done; *da* ~ *na san haka za a yi* I knew even beforehand that this would happen.

[2]**ma** *pro.pl.* (tone varies acc. to tense, *see* Appendix 1) We.

mą̀'abbą̀ *n.m.* Used in *ɗan* ~ a praise singer who praises other praise singers.

***mą'àiką̀ci** *n.m.* Worker.

†**mą'aikąta** *n.f.* (*pl.* **mą̀'àikątu**) Factory, place of work.

mą'àiki *n.m.* Messenger of God (usu. applied to the Prophet Muhammad).

mą'ąjį *n.m.* Traditional title held by the treasurer.

†**mą'ąjįyi** *n.m.* Storeroom.

mą̀'amąlà *n.f.* (*pl.* **mą'amąloli**) 1. Transaction, business. 2. Economic alliance.

mą̀'ą̀na *n.f.* Meaning, sense: *zancensa bai yi* ~ *ba* his speech didn't make any sense.

mą̀'asi *n.m.* Adultery.

†**mą'auna** *n.f.* Place where grain is sold.

‡**mą'auni** *n.m.* Measuring device, scales.

***mąbàr̃ci** *n.m.* Creditor.

***mąbįyi** *n.m.* 1. A follower (esp. religious). 2. Younger brother or sister.

‡**mąbuɗi** *n.m.* Key.

†**mąbųga** *n.f.* Log or flat stone on which washed or dyed clothing is beaten.

***mąbų̀kàci** *n.m.* Needy person.

mąbùnƙų̀sa ƙąsa *n.m.* Any root crop.

‡**mąbur̃gi** *n.m.* Swizzle stick, stick for stirring soup.

***mąbùshi** *n.m.* Horn blower.

‡**mąɓalli** *n.m.* Button, fastener.

mą̀cę̀ *n.f.* (*pl.* **mata**) 1. Woman. 2. Female.

mącè *v.i.* 1. Die. 2. Wear out completely.

***mącèci** *n.m.* Rescuer.

mąci Used in ~ *amana* he who betrays one's trust; ~ *mutunci* one who is disrespectful of others.

maci *n.m.* Marching (e.g. of soldiers).

mąciji *n.m.* (*f.* **mącijįya,** *pl.* **mą̀cizai**) Snake.

†**mącįya** *n.f.* Small wayside market.

mądą̀din *prep.* In place of, instead of: *Zolai ya aura a* ~ *Jummai* it was Zolai he married instead of Jummai.

†**mądąfa** *n.f.* Kitchen, cooking area.

†**mądafa** *n.f.* 1. Place to lean on. 2. Means of support: *ya sami* ~ he has found s.o. to depend on.

***mądàidàici** *n. and adj.* Medium-sized.

mâdaki *n.m.* A traditional title.

madàlla *excl.* General expression of thanks or approval.

mądąr̃a *n.f.* Fresh milk.

†**mądątsa** *n.f.* Place for damming water, dam.

***mądàwwàmi** *n. and adj.* Permanent, everlasting: *Allah* ~ God the Eternal.

‡**mądogąri** *n.m.* 1. Prop, support. 2. One's means of support, livelihood.

‡**mądoshi** *n.m.* 1. Punch (tool). 2. Branding iron.

‡**mądubi** *n.m.* Glass, mirror.

màdųgu *n.m.* (*f.* **màdųga,** *pl.* **màdų̀gai**) Caravan leader.

mąɗabą'a *n.f.* (*pl.* **mąɗabą'o'i**) Press, printing company.

mąɗàci *n.m.* (*pl.* **mą̀ɗàtai**) Mahogany tree.

mạɗacịya *n.f.* Gall bladder.
mạɗàukạ̀ki *n.m.* Used in *Allah ~n Sarki* God the Almighty.
‡**mạɗauri** *n.m.* 1. Anything used for tying. 2. Seat belt.
‡**mạɗebi** *n.m.* Ladle, any implement for dipping out sth.
maɗì *n.m.* Sweet drink made from the fruit of the *ɗinya* tree.
***mạɗìnki** *n.m.* Tailor.
***mạɗòri** *n.m.* One who sets broken bones.
‡**mạɗori** *n.m.* Wooden splint.
†**mạfạka** *n.f.* Shelter.
***mạfạ̀ràuci** *n.m.* Hunter.
†**mạfạrauta** *n.f.* Hunting grounds.
‡**mạfari** *n.m.* 1. Origin, beginning. 2. Reason, cause.
mạfařki *n.m.* (*pl.* **mạ̀fàřkẹ-mạ̀fàřkẹ, mạ̀fàřkai**) Dream.
***mạfạ̀shi** *n.m.* Highway robber.
mạfì Used to form comparative and superlative constructions: *~ yawan mutanen sun san gaskiya* most of the people know the truth; *na ga wata yarinya ~ kyan halitta a ƙofar fada* I saw the most beautiful girl in the world in front of the Emir's palace.
‡**mạfịci, mạfịfịci** *n.m.* Hand-held fan.
***mạfìfìci** *n. and adj.* Superior.
†**mạfịta** *n.f.* 1. Exit, way out. 2. Excuse: *ya shiga rigima ya rasa ~* he got into trouble and found no way out of it.
mạfịtsara *n.f.* Bladder.
***mạgàbci** *n.m.* Enemy.
màgàgi *n.m.* Dazed manner, grogginess on awakening.
***mạgàji** *n.m.* Heir.
mạgàjin gạ̀ri *n.m.* A traditional title.
mạ̀gạnà *n.f.* (*pl.* **mạ̀gàngạ̀nu**) 1. Speech, talk: *ya yi mini ~* he spoke to me. 2. Matter, affair: *~ mai muhimmanci* an important matter.
mạ̀gạ̀naɗisọ̀ *n.m.* Magnet.
mạgànce *v.t.* Bewitch, put a charm on s.o.
magạ̀ni *n.m.* (*pl.* **magungụnà**) 1. Medicine, remedy, treatment: *ya je asibiti ya karɓo ~* he was treated at the hospital. 2. Magic spell or charm: *an yi masa ~* he was bewitched.
mạ̀gạ̀řịbà *n.f.* 1. Fourth prayer of the day. 2. Time of day just at sunset.
mạgarya *n.f.* Jujube tree.
mạgàtạkàřda *n.m.* Traditional title held by the chief scribe.
màgẹ *n.f.* (*pl.* **magụnà**) Cat.
mạgewạyi *see* **mạkewạyi.**
***mạgịni** *n.m.* Builder, potter.
‡**mạgirbi** *n.m.* Harvesting tool.
magịyà *n.f.* Reiterating God's name while making request: *ya yi mini ~ in ba shi rancen kuɗi* he begged me in God's name to lend him some money.
mạgọ *n.m.* Cream-coloured horse.
‡**mạgogi** *n.m.* 1. Grater. 2. Brush. 3. Eraser.
***mạgòri** *n.m.* Peddler of herbs and love potions.
†**mạgụda** *n.f.* Asylum, refuge.
†**mạgụdana** *n.f.* Watercourse.
màgụɗi *n.m.* Dishonesty, carelessness in work.
***mạguɗịya** *n.f.* Woman who makes the shrilling noise *guɗa* during festivities.
***mạgụ̀ji** *n.m.* 1. Fugitive. 2. Fast runner.
‡**mạgwạji** *n.m.* Measuring rod, any measuring device.
mạgwàs *n.m.* Bad-smelling belch.
***mạhàddạ̀ci** *n.m.* One who has memorized the Koran.
†**mạhaifa** *n.f.* 1. Birthplace. 2. Womb. 3. Afterbirth, placenta.
***mạhàifi** *n.m.* Parent.
***mạhàjjạ̀ci** *n.m.* Pilgrim intending to go to Mecca.
‡**mạhạƙi** *n.m.* Pointed or narrow bladed tool for digging holes.
mạ̀hâlli *n.m.* Context, place where sth. belongs: *kome yana da ~nsa* everything has its right place.
***mạhàřbi** *n.m.* Hunter.
***mạhàuci** *n.m.* Butcher, meat-seller.
***mạhàukạ̀ci** *n.m.* Mad person, idiot.
†**mạhauta** *n.f.* 1. Abattoir. 2. Place where meat is sold.
mạ̀hawạřà *n.f.* Debate, formal discussion.
***mạhạ̀yi** *n.m.* Rider, jockey.
mạhò *n.m.* Patch, mend (e.g. on clothing, shoes, fences).

mąhųci *see* **mąfįci.**
***mąhùkùnci** *n.m.* 1. Judge. 2. Administrator.
†**mąhųkunta** *n.f.* Law court.
mâi *n.m.* (*gen.* **mân**) 1. Oil, fat, grease: *man gyaɗa* groundnut oil; *man shafawa* ointment, skin cream. ***man shanu*** butter. ***man ja*** palm oil. 2. Petrol. ***baƙin*** ~ engine oil.
mài (*pl.* **màsų**) 1. Having or being characterized by: ~ *gida* householder; ~ *doki* horseman; ~ *hula* the person with a hat; *yaro* ~ *hankali* a sensible boy; *tebur* ~ *ƙwari* a strong table. 2. Doer of: ~ *sayarwa* seller; ~ *tafiya* traveller; ~ *gyara* repairman.
mai dą̀ *v.t.* (= **maishe** before pro. d.o.) Alt. form of **mąyar̃ dą̀.**
màiġįda *n.m.* 1. Head of household. 2. Respectful form of address for a man.
maiƙò *n.m.* Greasiness, oiliness.
maimai *n.m.* Repeating any act (esp. second weeding of farm).
maimàita *v.t.* Repeat doing or saying sth.: *na* ~ *masa saƙo* I repeated the message to him; *Allah ya* ~ *mana* may God bring back this occasion for us.
màimąkon *prep.* In place of, as substitute for: *ya ba ni kuɗi* ~ *rigar da na nema* he gave me money instead of the gown I asked for.
maishe *see* **mai dą̀.**
mâita *n.f.* Witchcraft.
màiwa *n.f.* Type of millet.
mą̀jajjąwa *n.f.* Sling for throwing stones.
mą̀ją̀lįsà *n.f.* (*pl.* **mą̀ją̀lįsu**) 1. Council, legislative body. ~***ɗinkin duniya*** United Nations. 2. Law court.
mą̀jamį'à *n.f.* (*pl.* **mą̀jàmį'u**) Church.
mą̀ją̀nuni *n.m.* (*f.* **mą̀ją̀nunįya,** *pl.* **mą̀ją̀nùnai**) Madman, crazy person.
mąjanyi *n.m.* (*pl.* **mą̀jànyu**) Long piece of hand-woven cloth used to tie child on one's back.
‡**mąjayi** *n.m.* Girth strap for horse.
†**mąjema** *n.f.* Tannery.
***mąjèmi** *n.m.* Tanner.
majįġi *n.m.* Open air film show.
màjįna *n.f.* Mucus, phlegm: *ya fyace* ~ he blew his nose.
mąjįnacįya *n.f.* Artery, vein.
majistą̀r̃è *n.m.* (*pl.* **majistąr̃or̃i**) Magistrate.
†**mąjįya** *n.f.* Reliable source for news.
***mąjìyyą̀ci** *n.m.* 1. Patient. 2. Nurse.
mą̀jor̃ątę̀ *n.m.* Majority.
mąką̀ *pro.m.* (i.o.) You, to you, for you.
makà *v.t.* 1. Knock s.o. down with a single blow. 2. Knock sth. down (e.g. fruit from tree). 3. (with i.o.) Do wrong to s.o.: *ya* ~ *mini ɗan jabu* he passed a counterfeit coin off on me.
mą̀ką̀buli *n.m.* (*f.* **mą̀ką̀bulįya,** *pl.* **mą̀ką̀bùlai**) Religious souvenir brought back from the Hajj.
mąką̀ɗàici *n.m.* Used in *Allah* ~*n Sarki* The One and Only God.
***mąką̀ɗi** *n.m.* Drummer, musician.
‡**mąkąɗi** *n.m.* 1. Drumstick. 2. Spindle.
mą̀kahò *n.m.* (*f.* **mąkaunįya,** *pl.* **mą̀kàfi**) 1. Blind person. 2. Ignorant person.
mąkàma *n.m.* A traditional title.
†**mąkama** *n.f.* 1. Handle. 2. Supporting reason, excuse: *ya rasa* ~ he failed to give a valid reason.
***mąką̀mànci** *n. and adj.* Similarity, likeness: *na ga agogo* ~*n nawa* I saw a watch that looked like mine.
mąkamąshi *n.m.* 1. Twigs, paper, etc. used as kindling. 2. Fuel.
‡**mąkamfąci** *n.m.* Big calabash ladle used for dipping out gruel.
‡**mąkami** *n.m.* Weapon.
mąkànce *v.i.* Become blind.
mą̀ką̀nezà *n.f.* Vulcanizing.
mą̀ką̀ni *n.m.* Type of coco-yam.
mą̀kanįkè *n.m.* (*pl.* **mą̀kànįkai**) Mechanic.
‡**mąkankąri** *n.m.* Utensil for scraping out food.
mąkantà *n.f.* Blindness.
mą̀ką̀ra *n.f.* Bier, usu. made of raffia.
mą̀kąrą̀ *v.i.* Be late, delayed.
mą̀kàrai *n.pl.* Spirits.
***mąką̀r̃ànci** *n.m.* Well-read person (usu. in Koran).

†**mąkąranta** *n.f.* (*pl.* **mą̀ką̃ràntu**) School, schooling. **ɗan ~** pupil, student.
‡**mąkąri** *n.m.* Antidote.
mąkąr̃ų *n.m.* Magic spell, charm.
†**mąkąsa** *n.f.* Vital place in body: *ɗan dambe ya san ~* a boxer knows where to hit a person to cause the most pain or death.
***mąką̀shi** *n.m.* Killer.
‡**mąkąshi** *n.m.* Any weapon.
mą̀kassą̀r̃i *n.m.* (*f.* **mą̀kassą̀r̃a**,- *pl.* **mą̀kàssą̀r̃ai**) Person disabled from illness.
mąkąwa *n.f.* Used in *ba ~* no doubt, no way of avoiding it.
mą̀kerò *n.m.* Ringworm.
†**mąkewąya, mąkewąyi** *n.m.* 1. Screened-off latrine. 2. Path around place.
[1]**makì** *n.m.* 1. Mark, sign. 2. School marks.
[2]**makì** *n.m.* Wrongdoing, trickery.
makir̃cì *n.m.* Cunning, craftiness, wiliness.
makį̄r̃i *n. and adj.* (*f.* **makį̄r̃a**, *pl.* **màkį̄r̃ai**) Cunning, crafty, wily.
***mąkįtsįya** *n.f.* Hairdresser.
†**mąkįyaya** *n.f.* Pasture, grazing land.
***mąkįyàyi** *n.m.* Herdsman.
makò *n.m.* (*pl.* **makò-makò**) Week.
‡**mąkoɗi** *n.m.* Stone for roughening surface of grinding stone.
mąkoki *n.m.* Used in *zaman ~* three-day mourning period during which condolences are received.
†**mąkoma** *n.f.* The Next World.
màkųbà *n.f.* Paste made from locust bean pods used for plastering wall or floor.
‡**mąkulli** *n.m.* Key, lock.
†**mąkur̃ɗa** *n.f.* Narrow path or passage.
mąkusa *n.f.* Blemish, fault (usu. used in negative): *ba shi da ~* it's faultless.
mąkųwa *n.f.* Going astray, being confused: *ya yi ~ ya rasa gabas da yamma* he was confused and didn't know east from west.
***mąkwą̀ɗàici** *n.m.* Greedy person.
mąkwąfi *n.m.* (*pl.* **mą̀kwą̀fai**) Post vacated by s.o.: *an sa Audu a ~n Bello* Audu has been appointed in Bello's place.
†**mąkwąrara** *n.f.* Channel or drain through which water flows.
mąkwarwa *n.f.* (*pl.* **mąkwàre**) Bush fowl.
mą̀ƙa *n.f.* Getting along in the world, managing.
mąƙà *v.t.* Fix or stick sth. into: *ya ~ bajo a ƙirji* he pinned a badge on his chest.
mą̀ƙą̀ƙi *n.m.* Ticklish feeling in throat after eating or smelling sth. pungent.
mąƙą̀la *v.t.* Lodge sth.: *ya ~ kobo a kunnensa* he stuck a kobo in his ear.
mąƙą̀le *v.i.* Become lodged, fixed, stuck.
mą̀ƙamì *n.m.* 1. Post, position of authority. 2. Status, influence.
maƙą̀ra *v.t.* 1. Fill sth. to the brim. 2. Do much of: *an ~ ruwa jiya* it rained heavily yesterday.
†**mąƙari** *n.m.* Place or space for increasing size of sth.
mąƙar̃ƙąshįya *n.f.* Betrayal, plot against s.o.
mą̀ƙàr̃r̃ą̀bai *n.pl.* 1. Chief's retinue. 2. Trusted friends.
***mąƙàryą̀ci** *n.m.* Liar.
mą̀ƙą̀sudi *n.m.* Aim, meaning, purpose.
mą̀ƙątà *n.f.* (*pl.* **mą̀ƙą̀tai**) Hooked stick, crook.
mąƙè *v.t.* Hide or tuck sth., usu. under arm. *v.i.* Hide oneself.
†**mąƙera** *n.f.* Blacksmith's shop, metal factory. **uwar ~** anvil.
***mąƙèri** *n.m.* Blacksmith.
mą̀ƙèsų *n.m.* Firefly.
***mąƙètą̀ci** *n.m.* Malicious person.
†**mąƙetąra** *n.f.* Crosswalk, ford.
mąƙì Used in *~ sake* one who hates slackness; *~ gudu* he who doesn't run from danger.
màƙil *adv.* Abundantly: *dakin ya cika ~ da mutane* the room is crowded with people.
***mąƙį̀yi** *n.m.* Enemy.
mąƙǫ̀ *n.m. or f.* 1. Stinginess. 2. Stingy person.
mą̀ƙogwą̀ro *n.m.* 1. Throat, windpipe. 2. Neck of jar, bottle.

màƙoƙò *n.m.* Goitre, swelling on neck.
mạƙoshi *n.m.* Oesophagus.
maƙụ̀re *v.i.* Strangle, choke.
***mạƙwàbci** *n.m.* Neighbour.
mạƙwàrwa *n.f.* Gulp of water.
***mạƙyùyạ̀ci** *n.m.* Slacker, lazy person.
mạ̀lạ̀fa *n.f.* (*pl.* **mạ̀lạ̀fu**) Wide-brimmed straw hat.
mạlạhà *n.f.* (*pl.* **mạlạhohi**) Sole of shoe.
mạ̀la'ịkà *n.m.* (*pl.* **mạ̀là'ịku**) Angel.
mạlàla *v.t.* Pour into, onto, over: *ta ~ mai kan abinci* she poured oil over the food. **mạ̀lalạ̀** *v.i.* Flow, spread: *ruwa ya ~ cikin ɗakinsu* water flowed into their house.
***mạlàlàci** *n.m.* Lazy person.
†**mạlallauta** *n.f.* Place for performing religious ablutions.
malàm *n.m.* 1. Form of address corresponding to Mr. 2. *See* **malạ̀mi.**
malàm-bùɗẹ-littafì *n.m.* Butterfly.
malạ̀mi *n.m.* (*f.* **malạ̀ma**, *pl.* **màlạ̀mai**) 1. Teacher, instructor. 2. Learned person, scholar. 3. Officer, official: *~n asibiti* health supervisor, medical supervisor.
malantà *n.f.* Used in *aikin ~* teaching, educational profession.
mạlasa *n.f.* Usefulness, utility.
malejị̀ *n.m.* Speedometer.
malƙwạ̀sa *v.t.* Bend sth. metallic: *ya ~ wuka* he bent the knife.
màllạkà (ị/e) *v.t.* 1. Possess, own: *bai mallaki ko kobo ba* he doesn't even have a kobo. 2. Rule, govern, have authority over.
mallạ̀ki *n.m.* Property: *gidan nan ~nka ne* this house is yours.
malmạla *n.f.* (*pl.* **mạ̀làmạ̀lai**) A mound of *tuwo.*
màlolò *n.m.* 1. Bird's crop. 2. Double chin.
màlùm-malum *n.f.* Type of large *riga* with circular embroidery design.
màmạ *n.m.* Breast. *n.f.* Mother.
***mạmạ̀ci** *n.m.* Deceased person.
màmakì *n.m.* Wonder, surprise.
màmạ̀re *n.m.* (*pl.* **màmạ̀rẹ-màmạ̀rẹ**) Groping about, doing sth. in roundabout way: *yana ~n nemun labari* he is trying to find out the information indirectly.
màmạyà (ị/e) *v.t.* Attack by surprise.
mân *gen.* of **mâi.**
mạ̀nạ̀ *excl.* For sure, well, indeed: *zo ~!* come along now! *ina so ~!* of course I want it!
mạnạ̀ *pro.pl.* (i.o.) Us, to us, for us.
mạnạjạ̀ *n.m.* (*pl.* **mạnạjoji**) Manager.
mânce *v.t.* Forget.
manda *n.f.* Dark salt from Borno used as medicine.
mandạƙo *n.m.* Food made of pounded cassava, salt, *ƙuliƙuli*, and pepper.
màndạwạ̀ri *n.m.* Braid trimming on neck of gown.
màndiřì *n.m.* (*pl.* **màndiřai**) Tambourine-like drum beaten by members of the Qadiriya sect of Islam.
mangạlà *n.f.* (*pl.* **mangạloli**) Twin bags for carrying loads on donkey.
màngạrà (ị/e) *v.t.* Hit or kick hard.
màngạ̀řịbà *see* **mạ̀gạ̀řịbà.**
màngûl *n.m.* Rock salt from Borno.
mangwạ̀rộ *n.m.* (*pl.* **mangwạrori**) Mango tree, mango.
manhạjà *n.f.* Syllabus.
manjạ̀gạrà *n.f.* (*pl.* **mànjạ̀gạ̀ru**) Rake.
manjộ *n.m.* (*pl.* **manjoji**) Major.
mannà *v.t.* Glue sth. onto sth., fasten with gum: *ya ~ kan sarki a jikin ambulan* he fixed a stamp on the envelope.
mannè *v.i.* Become stuck, adhere to: *ɗanko ya ~ mini a riga* the gum has stuck to my gown.
***mạnòmi** *n.m.* Farmer.
mânta *v.t.* (usu. with **dạ̀**) Forget: *na ~ kuɗina = na ~ da kuɗina* I forgot my money.
mantùř *n.m.* Mantle (for lamp).
mantụwa *n.f.* Forgetfulness.
mânya 1. *pl.* of **bàbbạ.** 2. Adults. 3. (= **mânyạ-mânyạ**) Important people, dignitaries.

mànyantą *v.i.* 1. Become old. 2. Become important.
mànzo *n.m.* (*pl.* **mànzànni**) Messenger.
mąrą *see* **mąràs.**
màra (į/e) *v.t.* (*vn.* **marì**) Slap.
marà *n.f.* Lower part of abdomen.
mara *n.f.* Piece of calabash for dipping out *tuwo.*
†**mąrąba** *n.f.* A point of difference: *ina* ~*r molo da garaya?* what is the difference between a *molo* and a *garaya*?
mąr̃àbą *excl.* Welcome!
mą̀ràice *n.m.* Late afternoon.
mąrairàice *v.i.* Wheedle, ask for sth. in pitiful manner: *ya zo wurina ya* ~ *wai in ba shi kuɗi* he came to try to wheedle a loan out of me.
mą̀rąƙi *n.m.* (*f.* **mą̀rąƙa,** *pl.* **mąrųƙà**) Calf.
‡**mąrarąki** *n.m.* Coarse-meshed sieve for liquids.
†**mąrarrąba** *n.f.* 1. Fork in road. 2. Place where tree branches.
mąràs (*pl.* **mąrą̀sa**) Lacking in, not having: ~ *amfani* useless; ~ *lafiya* one who is not well; *magana* ~ *kan gado* senseless talk.
‡**mąratąyi** *n.m.* Strap or peg for hanging sth.
mą̀r̃awwà *n.f.* Respectfulness.
mą̀rayà *n.m.* (*f.* **mą̀rainįya,** *pl.* **mą̀ràyu**) Orphan.
†**mąraya** *n.f.* Settled area outside town wall.
marą̀ya *n.f.* (*pl.* **marąyoyi**) Western cob (a long-legged striped antelope).
màr̃ga *n.f.* A cassia tree commonly known as *gama-faɗa.*
màr̃hąbìn *excl.* Welcome!
mą̀ri *n.m.* Shackle.
marì *n.m.* 1. A slap. 2. *vn.* of **màra.**
***mąrįƙi** *n.m.* Guardian.
‡**mąrįƙi** *n.m.* Handle.
mą̀r̃ilì *n.m.* (*f.* **mąr̃ilįya,** *pl.* **mą̀r̃ilai**) Person disabled from prolonged illness.
†**mąrįna** *n.f.* Dyeing place, dye-pit.
***mąrįni** *n.m.* Dyer.
màrirì *n.m.* (*f.* **màrirįya,** *pl.* **màrìrai**) White oryx (antelope).
Mar̃is *n.m.* March.
màr̃ka *n.f.* Period of constant rain during rainy season.
marką̀ɗa *v.t.* Grind into puree or pulp (e.g. tomatoes, groundnuts, fresh peppers).
marke *n.m.* Chew-stick tree.
mar̃mą̀ɗa *v.i.* Wink at s.o. in coquettish manner.
màr̃màr̃ *id.* Blinking, fluttering (of eyes, heart): *tana* ~ *da ido* she is fluttering her eyelids.
marmąra *n.f.* Laterite.
marmąri *n.m.* Desire, longing, craving: *ina* ~*n shan fura* I feel like eating *fura.*
marmąro *n.m.* Spring gushing out of rocky area.
***mąròƙi** *n.m.* Professional beggar, praise-singer.
***mąròwą̀ci** *n.m.* Miser, stingy person.
mar̃sà *n.m.* Large kolanuts, esp. of good quality.
mar̃tąbà *n.f.* High rank. ***mai*** ~ the honourable, his excellency.
***mąr̃ų̀bùci** *n.m.* Writer.
màrurù *n.m.* Boil on buttocks or thigh.
mąsą̀ *pro.m.* (i.o.) To him, for him.
masà *n.f.* Fried cake, similar to but larger than *waina.*
mąsaba *n.f.* (*pl.* **mą̀sàbai**) Blacksmith's hammer.
‡**mąsąɓi** *n.m.* Steel used with flint and tinder.
mąsai *n.m.* Cesspit.
mąsąki *n.m.* (*pl.* **mą̀są̀kai**) Large calabash.
†**mąsaƙa** *n.f.* (*pl.* **mą̀sàƙu**) Weaving place, textile factory.
***mąsàƙi** *n.m.* Weaver.
†**mąsallaci** *n.m.* (*pl.* **mą̀sàllàtai**) Mosque.
***mąsą̀ni** *n.m.* Knowledgeable person, scholar.
mąsą̀r̃a *n.f.* Maize.
†**mąsąrauta** *n.f.* Seat of government, town where chief resides.
‡**mąsassąbi** *n.m.* Harvesting tool.
†**mąsassąƙa** *n.f.* Carpenter's work area.
***mąsàssą̀ƙi** *n.m.* Carpenter.
†**mąsauki** *n.m.* (*pl.* **mą̀sàukai**) Lodging place, overnight quarters

masha'ą *n.m.* Profligacy.
mà sha Àllahų *excl.* Expression of approval, agreement, appreciation.
‡**mąshafi** *n.m.* Duster.
mąshąhuři *n. and adj.* (*f.* **mąshąhuřįya**, *pl.* **mąshąhùřai**) Well-known, famous.
màshaƙò *n.m.* Bronchitis.
mąshasshąřa *n.f.* High fever, feverishness.
***mąshàwàřci** *n.m.* Advisor, counsellor.
†**mąshaya** *n.f.* 1. Watering place. 2. Drinking place, bar, hotel.
***mąshàyi** *n.m.* Heavy drinker or smoker.
†**mąshekąri** *n.m.* Place where rainy season is spent (esp. by nomadic groups or Koranic students).
mashì *n.m.* (*pl.* **masu**) Spear.
†**mąshįgi** *n.m.* (*pl.* **mąshįgai**) 1. Ford in river. 2. Opening, doorway.
‡**mąshimfįɗi** *n.m.* Cloth placed over horse, camel, or donkey's back before saddle is put on.
màshîn *n.m.* 1. Machine. 2. Motorcycle.
***mąshįririci** *n.m.* One who makes empty promises.
mąsifà *n.f.* (*pl.* **mąsifu**) Misfortune, calamity.
mąsilla *see* **bąsilla.**
masinją *n.m.* (*pl.* **masinjoji**) Messenger.
mąsò Used to indicate intermediate points of the compass: *arewa* ~ *gabas* north-east; *kudu* ~ *yamma* south-west.
mąsokįya *n.f.* Pleurisy (lung disease).
‡**mąsomi** *n.m.* 1. Origin, beginning. 2. Reason, cause.
mąsořọ *n.m.* Whole black pepper.
‡**mąsoshi** *n.m.* Thick metal or bone pin used by women for hairdressing or scratching head.
***mąsòyi** *n.m.* Lover.
***mąsùnci** *n.m.* Fisherman.
mątą *pro.f.* (i.o.) Her, to her, for her.
màta *n.f.* (*pl.* **mata**) 1. Woman. 2. Wife.
***mątàbbąci** *n. and adj.* 1. Permanent, enduring. 2. Reliable.
***mątąfįyi** *n.m.* Traveller.
***mątàimąki** *n.m.* Helper, deputy, assistant.
mątakąla *n.f.* (*pl.* **mątàkąlu**) Flight of steps, stairway.
‡**mątaki** *n.m.* 1. Step, stair. 2. Stage, step (in development). 3. Small piece of leather on which a spindle is spun.
***mątàmbąyi** *n.m.* One who asks questions, inquirer.
‡**mątankąɗi** *n.m.* Large round tray woven from palm fronds used to separate out coarse grain or sand.
‡**mątari** *n.m.* 1. Large spindle for winding hand-spun cotton thread. 2. Container for collecting sth.
***mątàshi** *n.m.* Adolescent, youth.
‡**mątashi** *n.m.* 1. Usu. used in ~*n kai* pillow. 2. In Arabic manuscripts, writing the last word of a page at the top of the next page.
matò *see* **motà.**
‡**mątoshi** *n.m.* Stopper, cork.
mątsà *v.t.* 1. Pinch, squeeze together: *takalma sun* ~ *ni* the shoes pinched me. 2. Press against, hem in s.o. 3. (with i.o.) Worry, pester s.o. *v.i.* Approach, get close to: *sun* ~ *kusa da ƙauye* they got up close to the village.
matsà *v.t.* Squeeze, press liquid out: *ta* ~ *zane* she wrung out the cloth.
***mątsàfi** *n.m.* Fetish-worshipper.
***mątsąkàici** *n. and adj.* Medium-sized.
mątsąlà *n.f.* (*pl.* **mątsąloli**) Problem, affair: ~*r kuɗi ta dame ni* the problem of money bothers me.
***mątsàrkąki** *n. and adj.* Pure, clean.
mątsarmąma *n.f.* Gall bladder.
mątsàttsąkų *n.m.* Leech.
mątsąwař *conj.* (followed by neg.) Provided that, as long as: ~ *dai bai dawo ba mu ci gaba da aiki* as long as he doesn't come back, let's keep on working.
†**mątsąyi** *n.m.* 1. Position, post. 2. Status. 3. One's proper place: *kowa ya zauna a* ~*nsa* everyone should sit down in his own place.
mątsefątà *n.f.* (*pl.* **mątsèfątai**) Tweezers.

‡**mạtsefi** *n.m.* Comb.
***mạtsègùnci** *n.m.* Gossiper.
mạtsi *n.m.* 1. Food shortage. 2. Being crowded in a small area: *wurin nan yana da tsananin* ~ this place is extremely narrow. 3. Pestering.
***mạtsìwậci** *n. and adj.* Insolent.
***mạtsịyàci** *n. and adj.* Poor, destitute.
‡**mạtsokạci** *n.m.* Mirror.
***mạtsòrậci** *n.m.* Coward.
***mạtsùbbậci** *n.m.* Magician, sorcerer.
matuci *n.m.* Femininity.
***mạtùfki** *n.m.* Rope-maker.
mạtụƙa *n.f.* Limit, utmost extent, extremity: *ya yi* ~*r ƙokarinsa amma ya kasa* he tried with all his might but he failed; *mun gode masa* ~*r godiya* we thanked him profusely. *adv.* Extremely: *ya yi aiki* ~ he worked exceedingly hard.
mạtụƙar̃ *conj.* As long as: ~ *ka yi aiki sosai za ka ci nasara* as long as you keep up the good work, you will succeed.
***mạtùƙi** *n.m.* One who drives or propels a vehicle (e.g. airplane pilot, train engineer).
‡**mạtuƙi** *n.m.* 1. Steering wheel, paddle. 2. Stirring stick, pole.
màuludì *n.m.* Date of prophet's birthday (esp. that of the Prophet Muhammad).
mautạre *v.t.* Strike s.o. hard, usu. with sth. heavy and thick: *ya* ~ *su da dirka* he struck them with a large heavy stick.
***mạwậdàci** *n.m.* Wealthy person.
***mạwàƙi** *n.m.* Singer, poet.
***mạwànki** *n.m.* 1. Washer-man. 2. One who washes a corpse before burial.
***mạwụ̀yàci** *n. and adj.* Difficult, troublesome.
mậya (ị/e) *v.t.* Replace, succeed s.o.: *Sule ne ya mayi makwafina* it was Sule who took over my position.
‡**mạyafi** *n.m.* Large cloth for covering head or body.
***mạyàƙi** *n.m.* Warrior.
***mạyàlwậci** *n. and adj.* 1. Abundant. 2. Extensive (of area).
†**mạyanka** *n.f.* 1. Abattoir. 2. Place on throat where cut is made in slaughtering.
mạyani *n.m.* (*pl.* **mậyànai**) Kerchief.
mạyar̃ (dạ̀) *v.t.* (= **mai dạ̀** before d.o.) 1. Return, restore sth. to its place: *na* ~ *da hular da na ara* I returned the cap I borrowed. 2. Change into, convert: *ya* ~ *da ita jamfa* he made it into a *jamfa*. 3. Apply, exert one's efforts: *ku* ~ *da himma* do your best! 4. Transfer s.o. to a different place.
mậyatà *n.f.* Pestering s.o. to give sth. (usu. food or money): *ya dame ni da* ~ he keeps bothering me for money.
***mạyàudậr̃i** *n.m.* Trickster, deceiver.
***mạyàwậci** *n.m.* Stroller, wanderer.
màye *n.m.* Intoxication.
mayè *n.m.* (*f.* **mâyya**, *pl.* **mayu**) Sorcerer, witch, wizard.
Mayù *n.m.* May.
***mạyùnwậci** *n.m.* Person suffering from starvation.
mạzạ *adv.* Quickly. ***maza-maza*** very quickly, as quickly as possible.
mạza *pl.* of **mịjì**.
†**mạzaɓa** *n.f.* Polling station, voting place.
‡**mạzagi** *n.m.* Trouser-string.
mạzàje *pl.* of **mịjì.**
mậzàkụtà *n.f.* 1. Manliness, virility. 2. Being energetic.
***mạzàmbậci** *n.m.* Cheat, cheater.
‡**mạzạri** *n.m.* Spindle.
mậzàrƙwailà *n.f.* Locally made brown sugar.
***mạzàuni** *n.m.* Dweller, settler, inhabitant.
†**mạzauni** *n.m.* Seat, dwelling-place.
mạzàwạrì *n.m.* Large intestine.
mazgè *v.t.* Beat and knock over: *ya* ~ *shi a kunci* he hit him on the cheek and knocked him down.
màzo *n.m.* (*f.* **màzụwa**) Bushbuck (antelope).
†**mạzụrara** *n.f.* Gully, place where water flows out or away.
‡**mạzụrari** *n.m.* Funnel.
mè *inter. pro.* (*pl.* **sụ mè**) What?:

~ suka gani? what did they see? **don** *~?* why? what for?
mèce cè *f.* of **mène nè.**
mêl *n.m.* Mail, letters.
mele *n.m.* Loss of pigment.
mène nè *inter. pro.* (*f.* **mèce cè**, *pl.* **sų mène nè**) What? What is it?: *~ suka gani?* what did they see? *~ wannan?* what is this?
mesà *n.f.* (*pl.* **mesoshi**) 1. Python. 2. Rubber hose.
mesìn *n.m.* Mason.
mètan *n.f. and adj.* Two hundred.
mèyê *inter. pro.* What is it? Why is it?
mịdìl *n.f.* Middle school.
mịjì *n.m.* (*pl.* **mąza, mązàje**) Husband.
mịkị *pro.f.* (i.o.) You, to you, for you.
mikì *n.m.* Ulcer.
miƙ**à** 1. Stretch out, extend. *~* ƙ*afa* go for a stroll. 2. (with i.o.) Hand over to s.o.: *kar*ɓ*i wannan ka ~ wa Audu* take this and pass it to Audu. *v.i.* Extend, spread.
miƙ**è** *v.i.* Go straight, stretch out ahead: *hanyar ta ~ gabas sak* the road leads straight to the east. ***ya ~ tsaye*** he stood up.
mîl *n.m.* (*pl.* **miloli**) Mile.
mịlịmità *n.f.* Millimetre.
mịlịyàn *n.f. and adj.* (*pl.* **mịlịyoyi**) Million.
mịnị *pro.* (i.o.) Me, to me, for me.
mịnistą̀ *n.m.* (*pl.* **mịnistoci**) Minister (political): *~n tsimi da tanadi* Minister of Economic Planning.
minjirya *n.f.* Electric catfish.
minshari *n.m.* Snoring.
[1]**mintì** *n.m.* (*pl.* **mintoci**) Minute (of time).
[2]**mintì** *n.m.* Mint, peppermint.
minų *n.m.* Small kolanuts, dates, or groundnuts.
mirgịna *v.t.* Roll sth. along ground. **mìrgịną̀** *v.i.* Roll along ground.
mịsalì *n.m.* (*pl.* **mịsàlai**) Example, instance, pattern: *ba ni ~* give me an example. ***wuce ~*** be beyond description. *adv.* Around, about: *ya zo ~n* ƙ*arfe biyu* he came around two o'clock.
mịsàlta *v.t.* Compare: *ya ~ girmanka da nawa* he compared your size with mine.
mịshàn *n.m.* Mission (Christian). **ɗan** *~* missionary.
miskì *n.m.* Musk perfume.
miskịlancì *n.m.* Contrariness.
miskịli *n.m.* (*f.* **miskịla,** *pl.* **mìskịlai**) Contrary or difficult person.
miskinì *n.m.* (*f.* **mìskinịya,** *pl.* **mìskìnai**) Destitute person.
[1]**mità** *n.f.* (*pl.* **mitoci**) Electric meter.
[2]**mità** *n.f.* 1. Metre. 2. Metre band of radio.
[3]**mità** *n.f.* Grumbling.
mịtsịli *n.m.* (*f.* **mịtsịla,** *pl.* **mịtsil-mịtsil**) Very tiny thing or person.
mitsitsi *id.* Emphasizes smallness.
mịyà *n.f.* Soup, sauce made with meat, vegetables, and various condiments and eaten with *tuwo*: *~r ku*ɓ*ewa* okra sauce.
mịyàgu *pl.* of **mugù.**
moɗa *n.f.* (*pl.* **moɗàye**) Gourd or cup used for dipping water out of pot.
moɗị *n.f.* Gambling game involving tossing a coin for 'heads' or 'tails'.
molo *n.m.* (*pl.* **molàye**) Three-stringed, plucked musical instrument, similar to *garaya*.
mọnị'odà *n.f.* Money order.
mòra (ị/e) *v.t.* (*vn.* **mòro**) Use, benefit from sth.
morè *v.i.* Enjoy, feel pleasure: *na ~ cikin hutuna* I enjoyed myself during my holiday.
mòrị *n.m.* Type of white guinea-corn.
morì *n.m.* Used in *dan ~* a favourite.
mòrịya *n.f.* Value, usefulness.
mòro *vn.* of **mòra.**
motà *n.f.* (*pl.* **motoci**) Motor-car, vehicle. ***babbar ~*** lorry.
motsà *v.t.* 1. Stir. 2. Exercise (body). *v.i.* Move: *kada ka ~ nan da can* don't move even a little bit.
mòtsattse *n. and adj.* (*f.* **mòtsat-tsịya,** *pl.* **mòtsàttsu**) Mad, insane.
motsì *n.m.* 1. Movement, motion: *ina jin ~ a waje* I hear a noise

outside; *hakorina yana* ~ my tooth is loose.
mòtsų *v.i.* 1. Be well stirred. 2. Become mad.
mowà *n.f.* Favourite wife.
mu *pro.pl.* (vl. and tone vary acc. to use, *see* Appendix 1) We, us, our.
mù'amąlà *see* **mą̀'amąlà.**
mùbayą'à *n.f.* Homage paid to new chief.
mùbazzą̀r̃i *n.m.* (*f.* **mùbazzą̀r̃a,** *pl.* **mùbàzzàr̃ai**) Spendthrift.
mucįya *n.f.* (*pl.* **mucįyoyi**) Stick for stirring *tuwo.*
mudą̀nąbi *n.m.* Standard measure of corn given as alms at end of *azumi.*
muddìn *conj.* So long as, provided that: ~ *yana zuwa gidan nan ba za a rabu da tashin hankali ba* so long as he keeps coming to this house, there will always be trouble.
mudù *n.m.* (*pl.* **mudàye**) Measuring-bowl of a standard size used in selling guinea-corn, rice, etc.
mùdùƙuƙì *n.m.* (*f.* **mùdùƙuƙįya,** *pl.* **mùdùƙùƙai**) Dirty, unkempt, sullen person.
mùfùti *n.m.* (*pl.* **mùfùtai**) Judicial assessor.
mugù *n. and adj.* (*f.* **mugùwa,** *pl.* **mugàye, mįyàgu**) Evil, bad.
mugùn dąwą̀ *n.m.* Wart-hog.
mùgùnta *n.f.* Wickedness, evil deed. **mùguntą̀** *v.i.* Become wicked, evil.
mųgurji *n.m.* (*pl.* **mùgùrzai**) Stone on which cotton is hand-ginned.
Mùhàmmą̀diyyà *n.f.* Used in *makarantar* ~ Koranic school; *karatun* ~ Islamic studies.
Mùhar̃r̃àm *n.m.* First month of the Muslim calendar.
mùhibbà *n.f.* Respect, popularity.
mùhimmì *n. and adj.* (*f.* **mùhimmįya,** *pl.* **mùhimmai**) Important.
mùjaddą̀di *n.m.* Religious reformer (esp. ref. to Shehu Usman dan Fodio).
mùjazà *n.f.* Cause, means whereby sth. good has happened: *shi ne* ~*r samun aikin nan nawa* he was the reason for my getting this job.
mujįya *n.f.* (*pl.* **mujįyoyi**) Owl.
mųką̀ *pro.pl.* (rel. past tense subj.) We.
mųkàn *pro.pl.* (hab. tense subj) We.
mųkè *pro.pl.* (rel. cont. tense subj.) We.
mųkù *pro.pl.* (i.o.) You, to you, for you.
muƙà *v.t.* Hit with sth. heavy.
mùƙaddàs *n.m.* (*pl.* **mùƙàddą̀sai**) Deputy.
mųƙàmųƙi *n.m.* (*pl.* **mùƙàmùƙai**) Lower jaw.
mùƙù-mųƙu *n.m.* Being secretive, surreptitious.
mulkì *n.m.* Rule, government, control: ~*n soja* military regime; ~*n kai* self-government, independence; *shirin* ~ constitution.
mulmùla *v.t.* Knead into balls.
mųlukįyà *n.f.* Monarchy.
mumbą̀r̃i *n.m.* Inner pulpit of large mosque.
mumįni *n.m.* (*f.* **mumįna,** *pl.* **mùmįnai**) True believer in Islam.
mùmmuna *adj.* (*pl.* **munàna**) Bad, ugly, evil: *yana da* ~*r ɗabi'a* he has bad habits.
mun *pro.pl.* (past tense subj.) We.
mųnà *pro.pl.* (cont. tense subj.) We.
mųnafùki *n.m.* (*f.* **mųnafùka,** *pl.* **mùnàfùkai**) Hypocrite, backbiter.
mųnafuncì *n.m.* Being hypocritical, maligning s.o. behind his back.
munàna *pl.* of **mùmmuna.**
mundųwa *n.f.* (*pl.* **mundàye**) Heavy brass bracelet or anklet.
munì *n.m.* Ugliness, evil.
mûr̃ *n.m.* Myrrh.
mųr̃à *n.f.* Cold, any disease of nose and throat.
mùr̃abbą̀'i *n.m.* Approximation: *ya yi* ~*n mil biyar* it is approximately five miles away.
mùr̃abùs *n.m.* Resignation, abdication, retirement from office.
mùr̃adì *n.m.* Desire, wish.
mur̃ɗè *v.t. and v.i.* Wring out, twist.
murfì *n.m.* (*pl.* **mùrfai**) Cover, lid, stopper.
murfù, murhù *n.m.* (*pl.* **mųràfu**) Stove, fireplace.
mùr̃jani *see* **mùr̃zani.**

murjì *n.m.* Two-ply thread.
murƙùshe *v.t.* Knock down forcefully: *garin faɗa kishiyarta ta ~ ta* in the course of arguing, her co-wife knocked her down.
mùr̃mùshi *n.m.* Smile, smiling.
mur̃nà *n.f.* 1. Pleasure, gladness: *na yi ~ da ganinka* I am pleased to see you. 2. Congratulations: *na yi masa ~* I congratulated him.
murtsùke *v.t. and v.i.* Crumple, crush, trample.
mur̃tùke *v.t.* 1. Stir up dust, smoke: *dawakai sun ~ wuri* the horses stirred up dust all over the place. 2. Frown: *ya ~ fuska* he scowled. *v.i.* Become filled with dust or noisy confusion: *faɗa ya ~* the fight developed into a brawl.
mùruci *n.m.* Young shoot of deleb-palm.
muryà *n.f.* (*pl.* **muryoyi**) 1. Voice. 2. Melody, rhythm.
murzà *v.t.* 1. Roll strands of thread between palms of hand. 2. Rub with palms: *ya ~ mini baya* he massaged my back. **mùrza** *n.f.* Massage.
mùr̃zani *n.m.* Red coral.
mụsà *v.t.* Contradict, deny: *ya ~ zancen ƙagen da aka yi masa* he denied the allegation made against him.
mùsafạhà *n.f.* Shaking hands in greeting.
mùsammàn *adv.* 1. Especially, expressly: *na zo ~ don in gan ka* I came especially to see you. 2. Being independent, sovereign: *shi sarki ne ~* he is a paramount chief.
mùsanyà *see* **mùsayà.**
mùsayà (**i/e**) *v.t.* Exchange. **mùsaya** *n.f.* Exchange, barter: *sun yi ~r hula* they exchanged caps.
mushè *n.m.* 1. Carrion. 2. Meat which is prohibited as food according to Islamic law.
mụshịr̃ịki *n.m.* (*f.* **mụshịr̃ịka**, *pl.* **mùshịr̃ịkai**) Fetish-worshipper.
mụshịyi *n.m.* Small bone implement used for applying antimony to eyes.
mussà *n.f.* Cat.
mụsù *pro.pl.* (i.o.) Them, to them, for them.
mụsù *n.m.* Contradiction, denial: *ya cika ~* he is too argumentative.
mùsùlmi *n.m.* (*f.* **mùsùlma**, *pl.* **mùsùlmai**) Muslim.
Mụsụlunci *n.m.* Islam.
mùsùluntạ̀ *v.i.* Become a Muslim.
mụtạ̀gadi *n.m.* Mudguard, fenders.
mụtàne *pl.* of **mùtûm.**
mụtù *v.i.* (*vn.f.* **mụtụwà**) 1. Die. 2. Become useless, worn out, broken: *rigarsa ta ~* his gown is worn out.
mùtûm *n.m.* (*pl.* **mụtàne**) 1. Person, human being. 2. Man, male. 3. (*f.* **mùtunịya**) Native of a town or area: *shi mutumin Kano ne* he is a Kano man.
mùtum-mùtụmi *n.m.* Effigy, scarecrow, doll.
mụtunci *n.m.* 1. Decency, dignity: *yana da ~* he is a decent person. 2. Humaneness, respect for others: *ya yi mini ~* he was very considerate to me. *ci ~* humiliate s.o.
mùtùntạkà *n.f.* Human nature with its frailties and shortcomings.
mụtụwà *n.f.* 1. Death. 2. *vn.* of **mụtù.**
mù'ùjịzà *n.f.* (*pl.* **mụ'ụjịzoji**) Miraculous power (of a religious person).
mùwafạkà *n.f.* Good luck: *Allah ya yi mana ~* may we have good luck.
mùzakkạ̀r̃i *n.m.* (*f.* **mùzakkạ̀r̃a**, *pl.* **mùzàkkạ̀r̃ai**) Energetic, tireless person.
muzànta *v.t.* Make s.o. look foolish.
muzi *n.m.* Simpleton.
mùzu *see* **ƙịri.**
mùzùrai *n.m.* Silent contemptuous stare: *yana yi mini ~* he is staring at me with disdain.
mùzuru *n.m.* (*pl.* **mùzùrai**) Male cat.
mwa *see* **²ma.**

N

nạ *gen. link* (*f.* **tạ**, *pl.* **nạ**) 1. (**nạ** and **tạ** are usu. shortened to **-n** and **-r̃**, respectively, and suffixed to the noun. Note: fem. nouns ending in vowels other than **-a** use the suffix **-n** instead of **-r̃**.) Of, possessed by, belonging to, part of: *littafi* ~ *Musa* = *littafin Musa* Musa's book; *mota ta likita* = *motar likita* the doctor's car; *dawakin nan* ~ *wane ne?* whose horses are these? ~ *sarki ne* they belong to the chief. 2. Used to form ordinal numbers: *gida* ~ *biyu* the second house; *rana ta farko* the first day.

nà Cont. tense marker (*see* Appendix 1): *manomi* ~ *girbe gero* the farmer is harvesting millet.

na *pro.* (vl. and tone vary acc. to tense, *see* Appendix 1) I.

nạ̀'am *excl.* Yes (reply when called). **nạ'àm** *excl.* Quite so, I see (used in conversation).

nạ̀damà *n.f.* Regret, remorse, being concerned about sth.

nạɗà *v.t.* 1. Wrap around, roll up: *ya* ~ *rawani* he wound a turban round his head. 2. Appoint s.o. to office: *an* ~ *shi galadima* he was installed as *galadima*.

nạɗè *v.t.* 1. Wind around, roll up. 2. Turn (steering wheel). 3. (with i.o.) Do much of sth.: *an* ~ *wa jaki kaya* the donkey has been overloaded with goods.

nạɗèwa *n.f.* Conclusion, summary.

nạɗi *n.m.* (*pl.* **nạ̀ɗẹ-nạ̀ɗẹ**) 1. Winding, rolling sth. around. 2. Turban. 3. Turbanning, installation of a traditional official.

nafịlà *n.f.* (*pl.* **nafịloli, nafilfịli**) Prayers in addition to the five obligatory prayers of Islam.

nạgạ̀rị *n. and adj.* (*f.* **tạgạ̀rị**, *pl.* **nạgàrgạ̀ru**) Good, of good quality or character. ~ ***na kowa*** everybody likes something that's good.

nạ̀gàr̃ta *n.f.* Goodness, uprightness.

nạhạwù *n.m.* Grammar.

nai *n.m.* Ninepence in old Nigerian currency, equivalent to seven and a half kobo.

na'ịbi *n.m.* (*pl.* **nà'ịbai**) Deputy.

nair̃à *n.f.* (*pl.* **nair̃or̃i**) Naira.

nạ̀jạsà *n.f.* Human excrement.

nakạ̀ *pro.m.* (poss.) Yours (ref. to masc. or pl. noun).

nạkàn *pro.* (hab. tense subj.) I.

nạkè *pro.* (rel. cont. tense subj.) I.

nakị *pro.f.* (poss.) Yours (ref. to masc. or pl. noun).

[1]**nàkịyà** *n.f.* Food made of rice or guinea-corn flour and honey.

[2]**nàkịyà** *n.f.* Explosives.

nakụ̀ *pro.pl.* (poss.) Yours (ref. to masc. or pl. noun).

nạƙạ̀sa *v.t.* Injure, deform. **nạ̀ƙạsạ̀** *v.i.* Be injured, deformed.

naƙụdà *n.f.* Labour pains of pregnant woman.

namà *n.m.* (*pl.* **namu, namomi**) 1. Meat. 2. Wild animal.

nạmịjị *n.m. and adj.* (*pl.* **mạza, mạzàje**) 1. Male. 2. Masculine gender (in grammar). 3. Courageous man.

namụ̀ *pro.pl.* (poss.) Ours (ref. to masc. or pl. noun).

nân *adv.* Here. *dem.* (becomes **nàn** if preceded by word with final high tone) This, these: *dokin* ~ this horse; *ɗakunan* ~ these rooms.

nan *adv.* Over there (nearby). *dem.* 1. That, those (nearby). 2. This, these, that, those (the one(s) referred to). ~ ***da*** ~ at once.

nanàta *v.t.* Repeat, reiterate.

nanè *v.t.* Seal up, stop up. *v.i.* Stick to, adhere.

narkè *v.t. and v.i.* Melt, dissolve.

nâs *n.m. or f.* (*pl.* **nâs-nâs**) Nurse.

nasą̀ *pro.m.* (poss.) His (ref. to masc. or pl. noun).
nąsąbà *n.f.* Relationship by blood or marriage: *mun hada* ~ *da shi* we are related.
ną̀sar̃ą, ną̀sàr̃u *n.pl.* Christians.
nąsąr̃à *n.f.* (*pl.* **nąsąr̃or̃i**) Victory, success.
ną̀sihà *n.f.* (*pl.* **nąsihohi**) Good advice.
nàso *n.m.* Exuding of dampness, moisture, or perspiration.
nasų̀ *pro.pl.* (poss.) Theirs (ref. to masc. or pl. noun).
natą̀ *pro.f.* (poss.) Hers (ref. to masc. or pl. noun).
nątsà *v.i.* Settle, become calm: *ƙura ta* ~ the dust settled.
ną̀tsųwa *n.f.* Calmness, reflection.
nau'ì *n.m.* (*pl.* **nau'o'i**) Type, class.
nà'ur̃à *n.f.* (*pl.* **na'ur̃or̃i**) Machine.
nàusa (shį/she) *v.t.* (*vn.* **naushì**) Punch: *ya naushi Audu da ƙulli* he gave Audu a hard punch.
nausà *v.i.* Flee, go (in a certain direction): *ya* ~ *gabas* he went eastward.
naushì *n.m.* 1. Punch, blow (of fist). 2. *vn.* of **nàusa.**
nauyi *n.m.* 1. Heaviness. 2. Burden, responsibility: *ya ɗauki* ~*n ciyar da matan ubansa* he has taken on the responsibility of looking after his father's wives.
ną̀wa *n.f.* Slowness, slackness.
nąwą̀ *inter. adj.* How much, how many?: *shekara* ~ *ka yi a can?* how many years did you spend there? **nąwą̀ nąwą̀** how much each?: *lemon nan kuɗinsu* ~ *ne?* these oranges are how much each?
nàwą *pro.* (poss.) Mine (ref. to masc. or pl. noun).
nązą̀r̃i *n.m.* Investigation, study, research.
ne (*f.* **ce**, *pl.* **ne**) (tone is opposite to the final tone of the preceding word) 1. Used in non-verbal sentences to indicate *is, am, are, was, were*: *maciji* ~ it is a snake; *yarinyar nan ƙawata ce* this girl is my friend; *ba sababbi ba* ~ they are not new. 2. Used to indicate mild emphasis: *shi* ~ *muke nema* he is the one we are looking for; *ya faɗi gaskiya* ~ he really told the truth. 3. Used to form questions: *ya zo* ~*?* did he come?
nèma (į/e) *v.t.* (*vn.* **nema**) Look for, seek.
nesą̀ *adv.* Far away, far from, at a distance: *yana* ~ *da Kano* it is far from Kano.
ni *pro.* (vl. and tone vary acc. to use, *see* Appendix 1) I, me.
nį'įmà *n.f.* (*pl.* **nį'įmomi, nį'įmu**) Prosperity, fertility.
nįƙà *v.t.* Grind.
nîm *n.m.* Neem tree.
ninkà *v.t.* 1. Fold several times: *na* ~ *shi huɗu* I folded it into fourths. 2. Go somewhere frequently: *ina* ~ *kasuwa sau uku a rana* I go to market three times a day. 3. Exceed in number: *kuɗinka ya* ~ *nawa biyu* you have twice as much money as I do.
nìnƙaya *n.f.* Swimming.
nisà *v.i.* Heave a sigh.
nisa *n.m.* Distance: ~*nsa bai kai mil goma ba* it is less than ten miles away; *Katsina tana da* ~ *daga Kano* Katsina is a long way from Kano.
nįshaɗì *n.m.* Enjoyment, pleasure.
nishì *n.m.* Breathing heavily or with difficulty due to illness.
niso *v.i.* Approach from afar.
nįtsè *v.i.* Sink, vanish into, drown.
nįtsò *n.m.* Swimming under water.
niyyà *n.f.* Intention, goal.
noƙè *v.t. and v.i.* Withdraw, retreat: *kunkuru ya* ~ *kansa* the tortoise retracted his head.
noma *n.m.* Farming.
nomè *v.t.* Hoe, till, weed: *yana* ~ *kofar gidansa* he is clearing away the weeds from the front of his house.
nonò *n.m.* 1. Milk. 2. Female breast.
notì *n.m.* (*pl.* **notoci**) Nut (used with bolt).
notìs *n.m.* Notice.
nų̀fa (į/e) *v.t.* (*vn.* **nųfì**) 1. Intend. 2. Head towards a place: *ya nufi gida* he headed towards home.
nųkà *v.t.* Ripen fruit by storing. **nų̀ką** *v.i.* Become ripe by storing.

nukịlịyà *n.m.* Nuclear power: *makaman* ~ nuclear weapons.
nụkụr̃à *n.f.* Hostility.
nụ̀kùs *id.* Indicates dampness: *daki ya yi* ~ the room is damp.
numfashi *n.m.* Breath, breathing.
nùnạ *v.i.* Ripen, mature, be cooked.
nunà *v.t.* (*vn.* **nuni**) Show, point out, indicate.
nuni *n.m.* 1. Demonstration, show: ~*n sana'o'i* trade fair. 2. *vn.* of **nunà**.
nụtsè *see* **nịtsè**.
Nụ̀wambà *n.m.* November.

O

ọ *excl.* Indicates surprise.
obà *n.f.* Used in *yi* ~ be in excess of correct amount (esp. money or goods in business).
odà *n.f.* (*pl.* **odoji**) 1. Order, command: *an kafa* ~ *kowa ya sa yaransa makaranta* an order has been issued that everyone should put his children in school. 2. Prohibition against: *ya kafa* ~ *shan giya* he issued an order against drinking. 3. Prison sentence: *an yi masa* ~ *wata biyu* he has been sentenced to prison for two months.
odạ̀lẹ̀ *n.m.* (*pl.* **odạloli**) Orderly (military).
odịtạ̀ *n.m.* (*pl.* **odịtoci**) Auditor.
ofìs *n.m.* (*pl.* **ofịsoshi**) Office.
ọgạ̀nezà *n.m. or f.* (*pl.* **ọgạnezoji**) Organizer.
òhọ, òhọ'ọ'ọ *excl.* I don't know, I don't care.
òhô *excl.* I see!
Òktobà *n.m.* October.
o'ộ *n.pl.* So-and-so: *su* ~ *an yi miji sai gwadare* Whats-her-name has got a husband, which is why she's being so smug.
ozà *n.m.* (*pl.* **ozoji**) Ounce.

R

r̃ạ'ạ̀yi *n.m.* (*pl.* **r̃ạ'ạyoyi**) Opinion, point of view.
rạbà *v.t.* 1. Divide, separate. 2. Distribute, share: *ya* ~ *musu goron daurin aure* he distributed kolanuts to them in honour of the marriage. 3. Settle (a quarrel): *na* ~ *rigimar da suke yi* I settled the quarrel between them.
rạ̀bạ̀jà *id.* Describes sth. very spread out, voluminous: *bishiyar nan ta yi* ~ this tree has spreading branches.
rạ̀bantạ̀ *v.i.* Be lucky, be fortunate.
rạbè *see* **rarrạ̀be**.
rạbì *n.m.* Half, portion: *uku* ~*n shida ce* three is half of six. ~ **da** ~ half done: *abinci ya dafu* ~ *da* ~ the food is half cooked.
Rạ̀bi'ụ̀ Lahìr̃ *n.m.* Fourth month of the Muslim calendar.
Rạ̀bi'ụ̀ Lawwàl *n.m.* Third month of the Muslim calendar.
rạ̀bo *n.m.* (*pl.* **rạ̀bẹ-rạ̀bẹ**) 1. Division, share. 2. Separation: ~*nmu da ganinka an dade* it has been a long time since I've seen you. 3. Luck, fortune, success.
rạ̀bụ *v.i.* Part, be separated: *aurensu ya* ~ they are divorced.
ràɓa (ị/e) *v.t.* Go near, approach: *na gaya masa kar ya raɓe ni* I told him not to come close to me.

raɓa *n.f.* Dew.
raɓè *v.i.* Keep out of the way, make oneself inconspicuous: *na* ~ *jikin bango* I remained inconspicuously by the wall.
rąɗà *v.t.* Whisper: *ya* ~ *masa magana* he whispered to him.
r̃aɗà *v.t.* (with i.o.) Beat s.o. with sth.
r̃ąɗąɗą *id.* Crackling sound of fire: *wuta ta kama* ~ the fire is crackling.
r̃ąɗąɗi *n.m.* Severe pain, agony.
rąɗè-rąɗi *n.m.* Rumours, whisperings: *ana* ~*nsa* rumours are going around about him.
r̃af *id.* Describes quick movement used in snatching sth.: *kyanwa ta yi* ~ *ta kama ɓera* the cat sprang quickly to catch the rat.
r̃ąfąli *n.m.* Referee.
r̃afàni *n.m.* (*pl.* **r̃àfànai**) Maternal uncle.
ràfi *n.m.* (*pl.* **rafųkà, rafuffųkà**) 1. Stream. 2. Irrigated plot.
r̃afkà *v.t.* (with i.o.) Hit. ***ta*** ~ ***ado*** she got dressed up. ***ya*** ~ ***ihu*** he yelled. ***ya*** ~ ***ƙarya*** he told a whopping lie.
r̃àfkąną *v.i.* 1. Make a mistake. 2. Forget. **r̃àfkąnà** *n.f.* Mistake.
r̃afkè *v.i.* Become deteriorated, old, rotten, withered.
r̃àf-r̃àf *id.* Describes sound of applauding.
r̃afta *n.f.* Anything damaged or imperfect (esp. kolanut).
rąga (i/e) *v.t.* Reduce, decrease.
raga *n.f.* 1. Net, netting. 2. Wire screening (on windows).
ragąɗa *v.t.* Poke into hole, poke at.
rągąma *n.f.* Halter (for horse). ~***r mulki*** reins of government.
r̃ągą-r̃ągą *id.* Describes demolished state of sth.: *sun fasa masa mota* ~ they demolished his car.
r̃ągar̃gąje *v.i.* Be shattered, smashed up.
r̃ągar̃gąza *v.t.* Spoil, shatter. **r̃ągàr̃gązà (ji/je)** *v.t.* Eat too much of sth.
ràgąyà *n.f.* (*pl.* **ràgąyu, ragąyoyi**) Raffia hanger used to suspend a calabash or bowl from ceiling.
r̃ągayyà *n.f.* Respect, friendship.
rągè *v.t.* Reduce, decrease: *ya* ~ *gudun mota* he decreased the speed of the car. *v.i.* Remain: *abincina kaɗan ya* ~ I have a little food left.
rągi *n.m.* (*pl.* **rągę-rągę**) 1. Reduction, discount. 2. Decrease.
rągo *n.m.* (*f.* **rągųwa**, *pl.* **rągwàye**) Weak, lazy, idle person.
ràgo *n.m.* (*pl.* **ragųnà**) Ram.
rągowà *n.f.* Remainder.
r̃ąhà *n.f.* Pleasant chatting.
r̃ąhąmà *n.f.* Mercy.
r̃ąhamshe *v.t.* Used in *Allah ya* ~ *shi* may God have mercy on his soul!
r̃ąhotò *n.m.* Report, information. *ɗan* ~ spy, informer.
r̃ąhusa *n.f.* Cheapness.
râi *n.m.* (*pl.* **rayųkà**, *gen.* **rân**) 1. Life, spirit, mind. ***ranka ya daɗe*** may your life be long! (polite form of address to one's superior). 2. Salvation, hope: *ka yi mini* ~ help me! *ya fid da* ~ he lost hope. 3. Prosperity: *garin nan ya yi* ~ this town is flourishing. 4. Good condition, serviceable: *ga batir mai* ~ here is a good battery.
r̃a'i *n.m.* Willingness: *ba ni da* ~*n zuwa* I don't feel like coming.
ràina (i/e) *v.t.* (*vn.* **ràino**) Care for, nurse small child or animal.
rainà *v.t.* Despise, have contempt for.
raini *n.m.* Contempt, disdain.
ràino *vn.* of **ràina.**
rainųwa *n.f.* Being discontent with smallness of a gift.
rairąye *v.t.* 1. Sift (grain, sand). 2. Screen out: *an* ~ *dakikan aji an sa su maimaita* the dull students have been selected out and asked to repeat.
ràirąyi, ràirai *n.m.* Fine sand.
Rąjàb *n.m.* Seventh month of the Muslim calendar.
rajè *v.t. and v.i.* Erode.
r̃ąjimantį *n.m.* Regiment.
r̃ąjistą *n.f.* Register.
r̃ak *id.* Exactly.
rąkà *v.t.* Accompany, escort. *v.i.* Last, wait a while: *wandona ya dan* ~ my trousers have lasted quite a while.

r̃a̧ka̧'à *n.f.* (*pl.* **r̃a̧ka̧'o'i**) Complete set of genuflections in Islamic prayers.

r̃akaɗi *n.m.* Talking loudly, raising voice.

ra̧ke *n.m.* Sugar cane.

rakì *n.m.* Fear, cowardice.

ra̧kịyà *n.f.* Accompanying, escorting, seeing s.o. off.

r̃a̧kodà *n.f.* Tape-recorder.

r̃a̧kwa̧càm *id.* Disorderly state: *ya zuba kayansa* ~ *a ɗaki* he threw his clothes all over the room.

r̃a̧ƙas *id.* Describes a snapping, cracking sound: *ya karya yatsunsa* ~ he cracked his knuckles.

ràƙụmi *n.m.* (*f.* **ràƙụma**, *pl.* **raƙụmà**) Camel. **~n ruwa** wave (in ocean, river). **~n dawa** giraffe.

r̃am *id.* Describes closeness or tightness of relationship: *abotarsu ta ƙullu* ~ their friendship is firmly established.

ra̧mà *n.m.* Indian hemp.

ramà *v.t.* Retaliate, take revenge: *ya* ~ *duka* he struck back (met force with force).

Ra̧ma̧lân *n.m.* Ninth month of the Muslim calendar, during which the fast occurs.

r̃a̧mas *id.* Completely dry.

r̃amba̧ɗa *v.t.* Raise voice.

r̃àmba̧tsàu *id.* Disorderly, in a variety of odd colours.

ramè *v.i.* Become thin, emaciated.

ramì *n.m.* (*pl.* **ramụkà**) Hole, pit.

ramụwa *n.f.* 1. Retaliation, revenge. 2. Paying back, making up for: *yau Tanko yana* ~*r azumi* today Tanko is fasting to make up for the time that he broke it.

rân *gen.* of **râi.**

ran Alt. *gen.* form of **rana**: ~ *kasuwa* = *ranar kasuwa* market day; ~ *da suka tashi* = *ranar da suka tashi* the day that they left.

rana *n.f.* (*pl.* **rànàiku,** *gen.* **ranar̃, ran**) 1. Sun. ***fitowar*** ~ sunrise. ***faɗuwar*** ~ sunset. 2. Heat of the sun: *yau akwai* ~ it is hot today. 3. Day: ~*r kasuwa* market day. **rana̧** *adv.* (with **da̧**) In the daytime, mid-day. **rana-rana** *adv.* Occasionally, from time to time.

rànda *n.f.* (*pl.* **randụnà**) Large water pot.

r̃ângadì *n.m.* Touring (of an officer, administrator): *Sarki ya fita* ~*n ƙasarsa* the Emir is touring his domain.

ràngwa̧ɗà *n.f.* Swaying: *amarya tana* ~ *a kan dokinta* the bride is swaying on her horse.

rangwa̧mè *n.m.* 1. Reduction (price, sentence, pain). 2. Cheapness. 3. Favour.

rani *n.m.* Dry season. ***sa*** ~ sharing with others food which is only enough for one.

r̃anka̧ya *v.i.* Depart.

[1]**r̃ankì** *n.m.* Rank (of officer).

[2]**r̃ankì** *n.m.* Chain wheel of bicycle.

r̃ànƙwa̧sà (shị/she) *v.t.* (*vn.* **r̃anƙwa̧shi**) Rap s.o. on the head with knuckles.

rànta (cị/ce) *v.t.* Borrow sth. (esp. money), the same amount of which is to be returned. **rânta** *v.t.* (with i.o.) Lend.

rantsar̃ (da̧) *v.t.* Put under oath, swear into office.

rantsè *v.i.* Swear, take an oath: *ya* ~ *da Alkur'ani* he swore by the Holy Koran.

rantsụ̀wa *n.f.* Oath, affidavit.

rara *n.f.* Surplus.

ràra̧kà (ị/e) *v.t.* 1. Cadge, beg in indirect manner: *ya raraki kobo hamsin a wurina* he cadged fifty kobo from me. 2. Chase out, rout.

rara̧ke *v.t.* Strip or hollow out completely: *ɓera ya* ~ *mini ɗaki* the rat has made holes all over the room.

rarịya *n.f.* (*pl.* **rarịyoyi**) 1. Sieve for sifting. 2. Hole in wall for drainage.

rarra̧be *v.t.* 1. Differentiate, distinguish: *ka iya* ~ *tsakanin fari da baƙi?* can you distinguish black from white? 2. (with **da̧**) Recognize: *ban* ~ *da shi ba* I don't recognize him.

rarra̧fa *v.i.* Crawl.

ràrra̧fe *n.m.* Crawling.

ràrrasà *see* **làllasà.**

ràrụmà (ị/e) *v.t.* Grab, snatch: *ɓarayi sun rarumi dokina* the thieves snatched my horse.

r̃as *id.* Describes completeness of action: *nama ya gasu* ~ the meat is roasted just right; *itace ya karye* ~ the tree broke completely.
rasà *v.t.* (*vn.* **rashì**) 1. Lack: *na* ~ *kuɗin tafiya Ikko* I lack sufficient money to go to Lagos. 2. Fail to do sth.
r̃asha-r̃ashà *id.* Sprawled out: *ya zauna* ~ he sat all sprawled out.
r̃ashawa *n.f.* Bribe: *ya ci* ~ he accepted a bribe.
r̃ashè *v.i.* Loiter, linger: *sun* ~ *a gindin bishiya a lokacin tafiya gida* they lingered under a tree on their way home.
rashì *n.m.* 1. Lack, shortage. 2. Bereavement, loss. 3. *vn.* of **rasà**.
r̃àsìt *n.m.* Receipt.
r̃askwanà *n.f.* Ready reckoner.
râssa *pl.* of **reshè**.
ràsu *v.i.* Die (of person).
rata *n.f.* Head start, handicap (in a race or competition).
r̃atata *id.* Describes lots of things scattered about: *ya zuba kaya a ɗaki* ~ he has scattered his things all around the room.
r̃atattàke *v.i.* Deteriorate from age.
ratàya *v.t.* Hang, suspend. **ràtayà** *v.i.* Depend on: *aikin ya* ~ *a wuyanmu* the work depends on us. **ràtayà** *n.f.* Anything which is hanging.
ratàye *v.t.* Hang (criminal).
ratsà *v.i.* Pass through: *ya* ~ *gonar Audu* he passed through Audu's farm; *ya* ~ *kogi* he forded the river.
ratsè *v.i.* 1. Diverge, turn aside, swerve. 2. Deviate, stray (from one's aims, goals).
ratsì *n.m.* Stripe.
r̃attàba *v.t.* Arrange symmetrically, in the right order: *ya* ~ *mini labari* he told me the story step by step.
r̃au *id.* Emphasizes clarity of perception: *ina jin* ~ I hear it very clearly.
rau dà *v.t.* (= **raushe** before pro. d.o.) Alt. form of **rawar̃ dà**.
raunàna *v.t.* Weaken. **ràunanà** *v.i.* Become weak.
ràuni *n.m.* (*pl.* **raunukà**) Injury, wound, sore.
rauni *n.m.* Weakness.
raushe *see* **rau dà**.
rawa *n.f.* (*pl.* **ràye-ràye**) 1. Dancing, dance. 2. Trembling, quivering, shaking. **~r daji** army manœuvres. **~r soja** army drill.
rawàni *n.m.* (*pl.* **rawunà**) 1. Turban. 2. Parapet wall, protective wall.
rawar̃ (dà) *v.t.* (= **rau dà** before d.o.) 1. Shake, sway: *iska ta* ~ *da bishiya* the wind made the tree sway. 2. Bounce, dandle (e.g. child) on knee.
ràwayà *n.f.* Shrub from which yellow dye is made. *n. and adj.* (*pl.* **ràwàyu**) Yellow.
r̃awùl *n.m.* Roundabout.
rayà *v.t.* 1. Give life: *Allah ya* ~ *shi* may God give him long life. 2. Restore, revive: *an* ~ *Kano da masana'antu* Kano has been given new vitality by its factories.
r̃ayau *id.* Emphasizes dryness: *wakensa ya bushe* ~ his beans are completely dry.
ràye-ràye *pl.* of **rawa**.
rayukà *pl.* of **râi**.
ràyuwa *n.f.* Existence, life.
razàna *v.t.* Terrify, frighten. **ràzanà** *v.i.* Be terrified, frightened.
r̃ediyò *n.f.* (*pl.* **r̃ediyoyi**) Radio. **~ mai canja** broad-band radio. **~ mai canji** radio combined with record-player. **~ mai hoto** television.
reɗè *v.t.* Slice off in thin strips.
regè *v.t.* (*vn.f.* **rigà**) Shake (rice, corn, etc.) back and forth with water to rid it of sand.
r̃ehùl *n.m.* Raffle.
r̃elùwè, r̃elùwài *n.f.* Railway corporation.
renà *see* **rainà**.
renì *see* **rainì**.
rerà *v.t.* Usu. used in ~ *waka* sing a song.
r̃èr̃as *id.* Well arranged: *an jera kwanuka* ~ the pans have been well displayed.
reshè *n.m.* (*pl.* **râssa**) 1. Branch, offshoot (of tree). 2. Branch, section, division (of company or organization).

retò *n.m.* Dangling, hanging down heavily: *na ga laya a kofar ɗakinsa tana* ~ I saw a charm dangling from the door of his hut.

řezà *n.f.* (*pl.* **řezoji**) Razor-blade.

řì *id.* Describes sound of people or animals moving together as a group.

řibà *n.f.* Profit, gain, benefit.

řịbâs *n.m.* Reverse drive (of a vehicle): *ya yi* ~ he backed up the car.

řìbạtà (cị/ce) *v.t.* Get the better of s.o.

rịbịbi *n.m.* Clamouring, crowding: *suna* ~*n sayen dawa* they are clamouring to buy guinea-corn.

rịɓà *v.t.* 1. Multiply: *ya* ~ *kuɗinsa sau uku* he tripled his money. 2. Exceed (by a certain amount), outnumber: *kuɗina ya* ~ *naka sau biyar* I have five times as much money as you; *yawansu ya* ~ *yawanmu* they outnumbered us.

řidda *n.f.* Apostasy, turning away from one's beliefs.

riɗi *n.m.* Beniseed, sesame seed.

řif *id.* Describes sth. well-closed: *kwano ya rufu* ~ the bowl is closed tight.

rịga *v.t.* Precede: *mun* ~ *shi zuwa* we came before he did. *v.i.* Do previously or already: *ya* ~ *ya zo* he has already come.

riga *n.f.* (*pl.* **rigụnà**) 1. Man's loose-fitting gown, robe. (The *riga*, worn over a shirt and trousers, is the standard attire in much of West Africa.) 2. Woman's dress or blouse. 3. Membrane enclosing foetus.

rigà *vn.* of **regè**.

rịgàkạfị *n.m.* Prevention, precautionary measure, prophylactic: ~ *ya fi magani* prevention is better than cure.

rịgayà *see* **rịga**.

rịgẹ *n.m.* Being in competition or race: *muna* ~ *mu kawo aikin* we are having a race to finish the work.

řịgịf *id.* Describes completed state of action: *ya dafu* ~ it is fully cooked.

rịgịjà *id.* Describes fullness of sth.: *bishiya ta yi* ~ the tree is full-leaved and shady; *ya sa tufafi* ~ he put on lots of clothes.

rịgịmà *n.f.* (*pl.* **rịgịngịmu, rịgịmomi**) 1. Uproar, tumult. 2. Quarreling, dispute. 3. Meddlesomeness.

rịgịzà *n.f.* Huge sack for storing groundnuts and cotton.

rijịya *n.f.* (*pl.* **rijịyoyi**) Well.

rịkịce *v.i.* 1. Become tangled (e.g. rope). 2. Become confused (usu. of old people).

rịkịci *n.m.* 1. Causing trouble. 2. Disagreeableness. 3. Intrigue.

rịkịɗa *v.t.* Confuse s.o. **rịkịɗạ̀** *v.i.* Change oneself into a different form: *Gizo ya* ~ *ya zama kuturu* *Gizo* transformed himself into a leper.

rịkịto *v.i.* Fall down unexpectedly from a height: *magini ya* ~ *daga sama* the builder fell down from the roof.

rịƙa (ị/e) *v.t.* Devote one's attention to, look after sth. well: *ya riƙi gidansa* he was attentive to the needs of his household. **rịƙạ** *v.i.* Be fully developed, ripe.

rịƙà *v.t.* Keep on doing: *kada ka* ~ *yin haka* stop doing that!

rịƙè *v.t.* (*vn.* **rịƙò**) Hold, keep: ~ *tunkiyar kada ta kubce* hold the sheep so it won't get away. ~ ***a ka*** memorize. ~ ***a zuciya*** hold a grudge.

rịƙò *n.m.* 1. Used in *ɗan* ~ adopted child. 2. *vn.* of **rịƙè**.

řìm *id.* Describes sound of s.o. or sth. heavy falling.

rimi *n.m.* (*pl.* **rimàye**) 1. Silk cotton tree. 2. Kapok from the tree.

řịmis-řịmis *id.* Describes sound of eating crunchy food.

rịnà *v.t.* (*vn.* **rịni**) Dye.

rịna *n.f.* Wasp, hornet.

rincàɓe *v.i.* Become too much, too numerous: *aiki ya* ~ *musu* the work has become too much for them; *hanyar ta* ~ *da motoci* the road has become overcrowded with cars.

řingi *n.m.* Piston ring.

rìnjayà (ị/e) *v.t.* Overcome, overpower, predominate. **rìnjayạ̀** *v.i.* Tilt or tip over to one side.

rinjayè *n.m.* Victory, success: *ya sami ~ a kansu* he was victorious over them.
rintò *n.m.* Dishonesty, cheating.
rintsà *v.i.* Take a nap: *nakan ɗan ~ da yamma* I usually take a little nap in the afternoon.
rịris *id.* Describes intensity of crying, weeping: *suna kuka ~* they are weeping bitterly.
rìska (ị/e) *v.t.* Find, come upon, meet up with: *na riske shi a Kano* I caught up with him in Kano.
r̃ịtayà *n.f.* Retirement.
rịtsà *v.t.* Hem in, surround.
r̃ịyạ *n.f.* Being ostentatious for the sake of creating a false impression.
robà *n.f.* (*pl.* **robobi**) 1. Rubber. 2. Hard plastic material. 3. Eraser.
r̃oɗị-r̃oɗị *n.m.* Describes a pattern of cloth with many splotches or speckles of colour.
rogò *n.m.* Cassava.
r̃okà *n.m.* (*pl.* **r̃okoki**) Rocket.
ròƙa (ị/e) *v.t.* (*vn.* **ròƙo**) Beg, ask, request.
romo *n.m.* Broth, soup stock.
ròra (ị/e) *v.t.* (*vn.* **rorò**) Gather, harvest (esp. beans and groundnuts).
rotsà *v.t.* 1. Injure s.o. in the head. 2. Break, crack sth. brittle.
rowà *n.f.* Stinginess, miserliness.
r̃ubà *n.f.* Boasting, arrogance: *wane, da ~ kake* what a braggart you are!
r̃ùb-dạ̀-cịkị *adv.* Facing downwards: *ya kwanta ~* he lay face down.
r̃ụbụ̀'i *n.m.* One-fourth.
r̃ụbùta *v.t.* Write.
r̃ụ̀bùtu *n.m.* (*pl.* **r̃ụ̀bùcẹ-r̃ụ̀bùcẹ**) Writing.
rụɓà *v.t.* Cause to ferment. **rụ̀ɓạ** *v.i.* Be fermented.
rụɓè *v.i.* Be rotten, putrefied.
rùɗa (ị/e) *v.t.* (*vn.* **ruɗì**) Deceive, confuse. **ruɗà** *v.t.* (*vn.* **rùɗe**) 1. Perplex, bewilder s.o. 2. Stir sth. (e.g. *tuwo*) while cooking.
rùɗạ̀-kụ̀yàngị *n.m.* Redness of sun just before setting.
ruɗè *v.i.* Be confused, deceived.
ruɗu *n.m.* Deception, trickery.
r̃ụɗu-r̃ụ̀ɗù *id.* Swollen from insect bites, boils, beatings, etc.
rụ̀fa (ị/e) *v.t.* 1. Cover. 2. Deceive s.o. by concealment. **rụfà** *v.t.* Cover: *na ~ mata zane* I covered her with a cloth. *~ **ganga*** make a drum. **rụ̀fạ** *v.i.* Wrap oneself with sth., cover up.
rụfè *v.t. and v.i.* (*vn.* **rụfì**) 1. Close, shut. 2. Conceal (e.g. truth).
rụfì *n.m.* 1. Roof. 2. *vn.* of **rụfè**.
rụga *n.f.* (*pl.* **rụgogi, rụgàge**) Fulani cattle encampment, settlement.
rugà *v.i.* Rush, move abruptly: *ya ~ cikin ɗaki* he rushed into the room.
rụ̀gụ̀gi *n.m.* Rumbling (e.g. of stomach or thunder).
r̃ụ̀gùm *id.* Describes sound of sth. falling with a boom, bang, thud.
rụgungùnta *v.i.* Rush, hurry: *sun ~ sun gama aiki* they rushed to finish the work.
rụguntsụ̀ma *v.i.* Go as a group.
r̃ụgụ-r̃ụgụ *id.* Describes sth. shattered: *gilas ya fashe ~* the glass broke into splinters.
r̃ụgu-r̃ụ̀gù *id.* Describes sth. large and round: *goro ~* huge kolanuts.
r̃uhù *n.m.* Spirit, soul.
r̃ụkụ̀ni *n.m.* Group (of people, animals, things).
r̃ulà *n.f.* (*pl.* **r̃uloli**) Ruler.
rùmbu *n.m.* (*pl.* **rumbụnà**) Grain storage bin.
rùmfa *n.f.* (*pl.* **rumfụnà**) Shed, temporary shelter, market stall.
r̃ụmur̃mụ̀sa *v.t.* Crunch, chew loudly.
rùndụna *n.f.* Crowd, multitude, army.
rungụ̀me *v.t.* Embrace, clasp.
[1]**r̃untụ̀ma** *v.t.* (with i.o.) Thrash: *ta ~ mata taɓarya* she thrashed her with the pestle.
[2]**r̃untụ̀ma** *v.i.* Leave or depart in a group.
rurì *n.m.* Roaring (e.g. of lion or fire).
r̃ur̃ùma *n.f.* Clamour, loud confusion: *ban same shi a cikin ~r kasuwa ba* I didn't find him in all the confusion of the market.
r̃ụ̀r̃ụ̀mi *n.m.* Short pre-dawn nap.
rushè *v.t. and v.i.* 1. Destroy, collapse, demolish: *ya ~ maganar*

da muka yi he overruled our plans. 2. Dissolve (a body): *an ~ majalisa* the assembly was dissolved.

rụsụ̀na *v.i.* Bow down in obeisance: *mun ~ a gaban sarki* we bowed down before the chief.

r̃ụtụtụ *id.* Describes abundance of things.

r̃ụ'ụ̀ya *n.f.* Vision, revelation, dream.

rụwa *n.m.* (*pl.* **rụwàye**) 1. Water. 2. Rain. 3. Juice, liquid: *~n lemo* orange juice. 4. Interest on borrowed money. 5. Any blade without its handle. 6. Colour: *~n toka* grey colour. *~ **biyu*** child from an intertribal marriage. 7. Used in *ina ~nka?* what concern is it of yours? *ba ~na* it's none of my business. ***'yan ba ~nmu*** unaligned, neutral (e.g. nations). **rụwạ** *adv.* In the water: *ya fada ~* it fell into the water. **rụwạ-rụwạ** *adv.* Watery.

r̃ụwàita *v.t.* Spread or relate news.

rụwan ịdò *n.m.* Inability to decide on choice of one thing out of several.

S

sạ̀ *pro.m.* (for uses, *see* Appendix 1) His, him.

[1]sâ *v.t.* 1. Put, place: *~ shi a can* put it there. *~ **baki*** take an interest in a matter, interfere. *~ **hannu*** sign one's name, signature; lend a helping hand. ***aikin ~ kai*** voluntary work. *~ **rana*** fix, appoint a day or time. *~ **suna*** name a price (in bargaining). 2. Wear, put on: *ya ~ riga* he wore a gown. 3. Appoint: *an ~ shi sarki* he was made chief. 4. Cause, bring about: *me ya ~ ka yi fushi?* what made you angry? *Allah ya ~ ku dawo lafiya* may God bring you back safely.

[2]sâ *n.m.* (*pl.* **shanu**) Ox, bull. ***fuskar shanu*** frown.

sa *pro.pl.* (tone varies acc. to tense, *see* Appendix 1) They.

sạ'à *n.m. or f.* (*pl.* **sạ'o'i**) One's age-mate, peer.

sa'à *n.f.* (*pl.* **sa'o'i**) 1. Hour, time: *sun yi tafiyar ~daya* they travelled for one hour. 2. Propitious time, lucky moment, good luck: *yau na taki ~* I was lucky today.

sa'àd dạ̀, sa'àn dạ̀ *rel. adv.* When: *~ suka zo, mun yi musu magana* when they came, we spoke to them.

sa'àn nan *conj.* 1. Then, afterwards: *mun je kasuwa mun sayi yadi ~ muka wuce gida* we went to the market and bought some cloth and then went home. 2. At that time: *lokacin da ya zo ~ sun farka* when he came they were already awake. 3. In addition, moreover: *ga halin kirki ~ kuma ga wayo* he has good character as well as cleverness.

sabà *v.t.* 1. Be used to doing sth.: *na ~ ganinsa a nan* I'm used to seeing him here. 2. (with **dạ̀**) Be familiar with, be accustomed to: *mun ~ da juna* we are accustomed to each other.

sạbạ̀bi *n.m.* 1. Reason, cause. 2. Quarrel: *ya zo har gidana ya yi mini ~* he even came to my house to argue with me.

sạ̀bạ̀'in *n.f. and adj.* Seventy.

sabbịnạni *excl.* Long life to you!

sabgà *n.f.* (*pl.* **sabgogi**) Business, personal affairs: *bar shi ka shiga ~rka* leave him alone and go on with your own affairs.

sạ̀bili dạ̀ *prep. and conj.* On account of, because of: *~ zuwanka nake yin wannan* it is because of your arrival that I'm doing this.

sàbo *n.m.* Familiarity: *~n da kuka yi shi ya sa ya raina ki* it was because you were so used to each other that he took you for granted.
sabo *n. and adj.* (*f.* **sabųwa,** *pl.* **sàbàbbi**) New.
sąbòdą̀ *prep. and conj.* On account of, because of: *ya tashi ~ rashin lafiya* he left because he wasn't feeling well.
sàbųlù *n.m.* (*pl.* **sàbų̀lai**) Soap.
sąɓà *v.t.* Carry or fling over shoulder (e.g. sword or sleeve of gown). *~ **laya*** swear on the Koran. *v.i.* Make a move in draughts or similar games.
sàɓa *n.f.* Shedding or peeling of old skin.
saɓà *v.t.* 1. (with i.o.) Disagree with, deviate from: *Musa ya ~ mini kan kuɗi* Musa and I quarrelled over money; *wannan ya ~ wa al'ada* this deviates from custom. 2. Break promise: *ya ~ alkawari* he broke his promise. *v.i.* Miss person on road.
sàɓani *n.m.* 1. Missing a person just as one is on the way to seeing him. 2. Disagreement of opinion.
saɓè *v.t. and v.i.* Abrade, scrape skin.
sàɓo *n.m.* Grievous sin.
saɓų̀le *v.t.* Slip off, strip off: *ya ~ takalminsa* he slipped off his shoes.
sàce *n.f.* Type of large *riga* with dagger-like embroidery design.
sacè *v.t.* Steal.
sadà *v.t.* Cause to meet, introduce: *na ~ Musa da Audu* I introduced Musa to Audu.
sądąkà *n.f.* (*pl.* **sądąkoki**) Alms, charity.
są̀dâki *n.m.* Money given by bridegroom to bride through her *wali* to legally bind the marriage.
sądaukar̃ (dą̀) *v.t.* 1. Volunteer (time). 2. Sacrifice (life).
sądauki *n.m.* (*pl.* **są̀dàukai**) Brave warrior.
saddą̀ contr. of **sa'àd dą̀.**
są̀didàn *n.m.* Sure remedy: *ya sha magani na ~* he took the right medicine.
sàdų *v.i.* 1. Meet. 2. (with **dą̀**) Receive (message): *na ~ da sakonka* I have received your message.
są̀dudą̀ *v.i.* Give up, give in: *ya sha wuya ya ~* he suffered and finally gave up.
sąɗàɗa *v.i.* Go stealthily.
są̀ɗąr̃à *n.f.* (*pl.* **są̀ɗą̀r̃u**) Line of writing.
są̀fâ *n.f.* Bus.
sàfa *n.f.* (*pl.* **safofi**) Socks. *~r **hannu*** glove.
Sąfàr̃ *n.m.* Second month of the Muslim calendar.
sąfąr̃à *n.f.* Itinerant trading.
są̀fąyà *n.f.* Spare part(s).
safę *adv.* (usu. with **dą̀** or **ną**) In the morning.
safįya *n.f.* Morning.
są̀fįyò *n.m.* Surveying.
sągè *v.i.* Become stiff or paralysed.
sągo *n.m.* Snake.
są̀hanì *n.m.* (*pl.* **są̀hànai**) Kettle.
sahįbi *n.m.* (*f.* **sahįba,** *pl.* **sàhįbai**) Close friend.
są̀hihi *n. and adj.* (*f.* **są̀hihįya,** *pl.* **są̀hihai**) Real, authentic.
są̀horąmi *n.m.* (*f.* **są̀horąma,** *pl.* **są̀hòrą̀mai**) Weak, lazy person.
sąhu *n.m.* (*pl.* **sąhu-sąhu**) Row, line (of people).
są̀hûr̃ *n.m.* Pre-dawn meal during Ramadan fast.
sai 1. Except, other than: *ba wanda ya iya wannan ~ Garba* there is no one who can do this except Garba. 2. Only, nothing but: *daga bakin gari ~ daji* beyond the edge of town there is nothing but bush. 3. Until: *ba zan zo ba ~ gobe* I won't come until tomorrow. 4. Unless: *ba zan iya hawan wannan gini ba ~ an saka tsani* I won't be able to climb this wall unless a ladder is put up. 5. Nevertheless: *kome yawan aikin nan ~ na gama shi yau* regardless of how much work there is, nevertheless I'll finish it today. 6. When, only when, not until: *~ da muka ci mil goma sannan muka tuna ba mu sayi fetur ba* only when we had gone ten miles did we remember we hadn't bought petrol. 7. Then (indicates one action directly

following another): *da muka gan su ~ muka gaishe su* we greeted them when we saw them. 8. (with subjun.) Should: *~ mu tashi yanzu* we should leave now. 9. (with past) Have to, must: *~ kun biya kuɗin ƙafin ku debo kayan* you must pay before collecting the goods.

sa'ì *n.m.* 1. Time: *sai wani ~* until some other time. ***wani ~*** sometimes. 2. Predestined time of one's death: *Idi ya zo ~* Idi has died. **sa'ì-sa'ì** *adv.* Occasionally, sometimes.

sai dą̀ *v.t.* (= **saishe** before pro. d.o.) Alt. form of **sa̧yar̃ dą̀**.

są̀'idà *n.f.* 1. Luck, success. 2. Comfort, ease.

saifà *n.f.* (*pl.* **saifofi**) Spleen. ***ciwon ~*** anthrax (sheep and cattle disease).

saimo *n.m.* Infertile barren ground.

saisą̀ya *v.t.* Shear hair.

saishe *see* **sai dą̀.**

sâiwa *n.f.* (*pl.* **saiwoyi**) Root.

sajà *n.m.* Sergeant.

sàje *n.m.* Side whiskers, long sideburns.

sajè *v.i.* Resemble, look like: *hawainiya ta sauya launi ta ~ da ƙasa* the chameleon has changed its colour to match the ground.

sak *id.* Straight, erect: *bi yamma ~* go straight westward; *ya tsaya ~* he stood erect.

sa̧kà *v.t.* 1. Place, put. 2. Put on, cover. 3. Lay (egg).

sakà *v.t.* Retaliate: *zan ~ wa Musa muguntar da aka yi masa* I am going to retaliate for the wrong that was done to Musa.

sàką̀ce *n.m.* Picking one's teeth. ***tsinin ~*** toothpick.

sa̧ka̧ci *n.m.* Slackness, carelessness.

są̀kaina *n.f.* (*pl.* **są̀kàinu**) Broken piece of calabash.

są̀kali̧ya *see* **lą̀'a̧sàr̃.**

sàką̀ma̧ko *n.m.* 1. Returning good for good or evil for evil. 2. Result: *~n ƙidaya mai ban mamaki ne* the results of the census were surprising.

sa̧kàn *n.m.* Second (of time).

sa̧kandą̀r̃è *n.f.* Secondary school.

sa̧kankànce *v.i.* Know for certain, be confident.

saka̧r̃ai *n.m. or f.* (*pl.* **sakàr̃ka̧r̃i**) Useless fellow.

są̀ka̧tà *n.f.* (*pl.* **są̀ką̀tu**) Crossbeam on door for securing it.

sa̧ka̧ta̧r̃è *n.m.* (*f.* **sa̧ka̧ta̧r̃i̧ya,** *pl.* **sa̧ka̧ta̧r̃or̃i**) Secretary.

są̀ką̀ter̃i̧yà *n.f.* Secretariat.

saką̀ya *v.t.* 1. Hide fact by talking around it. 2. Partially close doorway (to shield oneself from view).

sa̧ka̧yau *id.* Light in weight.

są̀ke *n.m.* Slackness.

sakè *v.t.* 1. Change, alter: *ya ~ halinsa* he's changed his manners; *ya ~ gida* he moved to another house. 2. Repeat, do again: *kada ka ~ yin haka!* don't ever do that again!

sa̧kì (są̀ki̧/są̀ke) *v.t.* (*vn.* **sa̧ki, shi̧kà**) 1. Release, set free, let loose. 2. Divorce. 3. Fire or release (weapon). ***~ jiki*** feel at ease, be carefree or indolent. *v.i.* Become loose, frayed, rickety: *tuwo ya ~* the *tuwo* is mushy.

sa̧ki̧yà *n.f.* Releasing pus from an abscess.

sa̧ko̧-sa̧ko̧ *id.* Loosely.

są̀kwą̀ra *n.f.* Pounded yam.

są̀kwą̀tǫ̀ *n.m.* Woman's wraparound underskirt.

saƙà *v.t.* Weave (e.g. cloth or mat). *n.f.* (*pl.* **sàƙȩ-sàƙȩ**) 1. Act of weaving. 2. Thing which is woven. ***~r gizo-gizo*** spider's web. ***~r zuci*** pondering, planning.

saƙì *n.m.* Native material woven from black and blue strands.

sàƙo *n.m.* Message.

saƙò *n.m.* Nook, niche, crevice.

sal *id.* Emphasizes whiteness: *fari ~* snow-white.

salà *n.f.* Thin slice of meat.

sa̧lab *id.* Insipid, tasteless.

są̀lâk *n.m.* Salad, lettuce.

są̀lamà *n.f.* Relief from any difficulty.

są̀lamų̀ ą̀laikùm *excl.* General greeting on arriving at or leaving a place, response to which is *alaikum salam.*

sàlansà *n.f.* (*pl.* **sàlànsu**) Silencer, muffler.

są̀lati *n.m.* Invoking God by means

of certain fixed expressions such as '*la ilaha illallahu*'.

salè *v.t. and v.i.* Peel or scrape off skin.

salfà *n.m.* Used in *takin* ~ chemical fertilizer.

salga *n.f.* Pit latrine.

sali̧hi *n. and adj.* (*f.* **sali̧ha,** *pl.* **sàli̧hai**) Upright and patient.

salin-alin *adv.* On good terms, without any trouble, peacefully: *mun rabu da shi* ~ we parted with him on good terms.

sàlka *n.f.* (*pl.* **sa̧lèka̧ni, salkyunà**) Goatskin water container.

sallà *n.f.* 1. Each of the five daily prayers of Islam. ~***r Jumma'a*** the Friday prayer. 2. Religious holiday: *babbar* ~ Id-el-Kabir; *karamar* ~ Id-el-Fitr.

sàlla̧hù *n.m.* Verbal message: *ya bar* ~ *cewa in ka zo ka je wurinsa* he left a message saying that if you come you should go to see him.

sàlla̧mà (i̧/e) *v.t.* Dismiss from work.

sallà̧ma *v.t.* 1. Agree to sell sth. at price offered. 2. Give in, become convinced: *ya* ~ *maka* he has given in to your point of view.

salla̧mà *n.f.* 1. Asking permission to enter: *ana* ~ someone is at the door. 2. Taking one's leave to depart: *ya tafi ko bai yi* ~ *ba* he left without even saying good-bye.

sàllatà (ci̧/ce) *v.t.* 1. Perform one of the five prayers: *ya sallaci magariba* he performed the *magariba* prayer. 2. Perform a funeral service over a corpse.

sa̧lo *n.m.* 1. Style, fashion, pattern. 2. Affected manner of doing sth: ~*n tafiyarsa abin dariya ne* he has taken to walking in a funny way. ~***n magana*** wittiness, cleverness with words.

salùɓe *v.t. and v.i.* Peel or scrape off skin.

sà̧lûn *n.f.* Saloon car, sedan.

salwànce *v.i.* Be lost.

[1]**sam** *v.t.* (with i.o.) Give: ~ *mini 'yar gyada* give me a few groundnuts.

[2]**sam** *id.* Not at all: *ban san shi ba* ~ I don't know him at all.

sa̧mà̧ *n.m.* (*pl.* **sàmmai**) 1. Sky, heavens. 2. Top: ~*nsa yana da kyau* the top of it is fine. *adv.* Up, above, on top: *yana* ~ *da shi* it is on top of it, he is senior to him; *ka yi* ~ *da shi!* raise it!

sà̧mà̧mà̧ *id.* Shuffling, rustling movement.

sà̧màme *n.m.* Surprise attack.

sà̧mani̧yà *n.f.* Sky. ***sararin*** ~ outer space.

sàmanjà *n.m.* (*pl.* **samanjoji**) Sergeant-major.

sà̧màri *pl.* of **saurà̧yi.**

sa̧mà̧-sa̧mà̧ *adv.* Slightly, superficially: *na san shi* ~ I know him slightly.

sàmbàtu *n.m.* Idle talk.

sàmfefà *n.f.* Sandpaper.

samfùȓ *n.m.* (*pl.* **samfyuȓoȓi**) Sample.

sammà̧ce *v.t.* Bewitch or charm s.o.

sammaci *n.m.* Court summons.

sàmma̧ko *n.m.* Starting work or journey very early.

sàmmatsi *n.m.* Being more unlucky than others.

sammorè *n.m.* Trypanosomiasis (cattle disease caused by the tsetse fly).

sammù *n.m.* Bewitching s.o. with native medicine.

samù (sàmi̧/sàme) *v.t.* (*vn.* **samù**) 1. Obtain, get: *ya sami magani* he got some medicine. 2. Find: *na same shi a hanya* I found it on the road. 3. Befall, happen: *wani mugun abu ya sami Audu* something unfortunate happened to Audu. *n.m.* Wealth, possessions: *yana da* ~ he is wealthy.

[1]**san** *see* **sa̧ni.**

[2]**san** *gen.* of **sau.**

sà̧na'à *n.f.* (*pl.* **sa̧na'o'i**) 1. Trade, occupation, profession: ~*rsa gini* he is a builder. 2. Habit, way: ~*r yaron nan kuka* this boy has developed a habit of crying.

sa̧nà̧di *n.m.* (*pl.* **sà̧nà̧dai**) Cause: *mene ne* ~*n mutuwarsa?* what was the cause of his death?

sa̧naȓ (dà̧) *v.t.* Inform s.o.

sąnâr̃wa *n.f.* Announcement.

sànayyà *n.f.* Mutual acquaintance.

sànda *n.m. or f.* (*pl.* **sandųnà**) 1. Stick, club, baton, staff: *~n girma* sceptre. *ɗan ~* policeman. 2. Long bar of soap. 3. Unit for measuring length of cloth (about one metre). 4. Any kind of manufactured cotton cloth. 5. Two kerosene tins of water suspended from a stick.

sandą̀ contr. of **sa'àn dą̀.**

[1]**sandàl** *n.m.* Sandalwood or its perfume.

[2]**sandàl** *n.m.* Sandals.

sandą̀re *v.i.* Become rigid, stiff.

sanɗa *n.f.* Stalking, going along stealthily: *muzuru ya taho yana ~* the cat came in stealthily.

są̀nę (with **dą̀**) Being aware of, knowledgeable about: *gwamnati tana ~ da wahalolin mahajjata* the government is aware of the difficulties suffered by the pilgrims.

sàne *n.m.* Pilfering, picking pockets.

sangąli *n.m.* (*pl.* **sàngą̀lai**) Calf, shinbone.

sangàr̃ta *v.t.* Indulge or spoil: *hawan keke ya ~ shi har ba ya son yawo a ƙas* riding a bicycle has spoiled him so that he no longer enjoys walking.

sanhò *n.m.* (*pl.* **sanhųnà**) Two-handled bag woven from palm fronds.

sąnì *v.t.* (becomes **san** before d.o.) 1. Know sth. 2. Be acquainted with, know s.o. 3. Be intimate with person of opposite sex. *n.m.* Knowledge.

sanįya *n.f.* (*pl.* **shanu**) Cow.

sankącè *n.m.* (*pl.* **sànką̀tu, sànką̀tai**) Row of reaped corn laid down so heads can be cut off.

sanƙą̀me *v.i.* Become stiff (of corpse).

sànƙą̀rau *n.m.* Meningitis.

sanƙè *v.t.* Tuck cloth or loincloth into waistband.

sanƙo *n.m.* Baldness.

sânnan contr. of **sa'àn nan.**

sànnų *excl.* 1. Hello! (to which reply is *~ kadai*): *~ da aiki* how are you doing! *~ da zuwa* welcome! 2. Expression of sympathy. *n.f.* Carefulness, slowness: *yi ~ dai* be careful! **sànnų-sànnų** *adv.* Slowly.

sansàn *n.m.* Census.

sansą̀na *v.t.* Smell or sniff.

sànsąni *n.m.* (*pl.* **sansąnoni**) 1. War camp. 2. Corona (of sun or moon).

sànti *n.m.* Making complimentary remarks about food while eating it (considered to be ill-mannered or humorous).

santįlità *n.f.* Centilitre.

santįmità *n.f.* Centimetre.

santsi *n.m.* Slipperiness, smoothness, glossiness: *~ ya kwashe ni* I slipped.

sanwà *n.f.* Putting water on the fire in preparation for cooking.

sânya *v.t.* 1. Put, place. 2. Cause, bring about. 3. Wear, put on.

sanyi *n.m.* 1. Coldness (usu. damp), chill: *~ ya kama ni* I've caught a cold; *zan sha ruwan ~* I'll drink some cold water. 2. Cold, chilly weather: *yau ana ~* it is cold today. 3. Slackness, slowness: *~ gare shi* he is lethargic; *jikina ya yi ~* my heart sank (on hearing the bad news); *~n gwiwa* losing hope; *~n jiki* being lazy; *~n zuciya* being easy-going.

[1]**sàra (į/e)** *v.t.* (*vn.* **sara**) 1. Chop up (wood). 2. Speak maliciously about s.o.: *ya sare ni a gaban sarki* he spoke against me in front of the chief. 3. Bite (by snake). **sarà** *v.t.* 1. Cut an opening through a place: *ya ~ kofa* he made a door in the wall. 2. (with i.o.) Salute: *soja ya ~ mana* the soldier saluted us.

[2]**sàra** *n.f.* 1. Habit, practice, way. 2. Words or phrases having special meaning when used within a particular group of friends: *suna da wata ~* they have their own special jargon.

sąr̃ai *id.* Completely: *ya gane ~* he understood clearly.

sąràki *n.m.* Any member of royalty or person attached to royal household.

sąrakųnà *pl.* of **sarki.**

sąràkųwa *n.f.* (*pl.* **sųrų̀kai**) Mother-in-law or elder sister-in-law.

sạ̀rạ̀rạ̀ *id.* Walking aimlessly.

sạrạri *n.m.* 1. Open space. **~n sama** stratosphere. 2. Clear sky: *gari ya yi* ~ the storm has cleared up. 3. Chance, opportunity: *ba ni da ~n zuwa yau* I have no time to come today.

sạraunịya *n.f.* Queen.

sạ̀rautà *n.f.* (*pl.* **sạ̀ràutu**) 1. Kingship, chieftainship. 2. Any official position to which a person is appointed.

sar̃bụ̀ *excl.* Excuse me for trying to do sth. you are already an expert at. ~ **war haka** at this same time in the past (which you'll forgive me if I mention).

sàr̃daunạ *n.m.* A traditional title (in Sokoto).

sarè *v.t.* Slash, hack, cut down. *v.i.* 1. Be used up, give out, collapse. 2. Lose heart, give up.

sạrewà *n.f.* Bamboo or corn-stalk flute.

sàrị-kạ̀-noƙẹ̀ *n.m.* Type of snake which strikes and retreats. **'yan ~** guerrilla fighters.

sàrị-kụtuf *n.m.* Large gecko.

sarki *n.m.* (*f.* **sạraunịya**, *pl.* **sạrakụnà, sạ̀ràkai**) 1. Emir, chief, king. 2. Head, boss, leader of professional craft or guild: ~*n kiɗa* chief drummer; ~*n fawa* head butcher; ~*n tasha* lorry park boss. 3. Used in *Allah maɗaukakin* ~ God the Most Exalted.

[1]**sarƙà** *n.f.* (*pl.* **sarƙoƙi**) 1. Chain. 2. Chain necklace.

[2]**sarƙà** *v.t.* Lace sth. around, intertwine. ~ **magana** twist, distort meaning of words. *v.i.* Become bitter enemies.

sarƙạ̀fa *v.t.* Hook sth. around or onto sth.

sarƙạ̀fe *v.i.* Become caught up, hooked on.

sàrƙaƙƙịya *n.f.* Thicket.

sarƙè *v.i.* 1. Become intertwined, entangled, stuck. 2. Be momentarily at a loss for words.

sàrƙụ *v.i.* Become close friends.

sàro *n.m.* Woman's head-tie made of stiff woven cloth.

sar̃r̃ạ̀fa *v.t.* Manage, control, rule over.

sartsè *n.m.* Splinter.

sasànta *v.t.* Reconcile: *har za su yi faɗa sai na ~ su* they were about to quarrel but I reconciled them.

sashì, sashè *n.m.* (*pl.* **sâssa**) 1. District, region. 2. Portion, section. 3. Department (in a university).

sassạ̀be *v.t.* (*vn.* **sàssạ̀be**) Clear land for farming.

sassạ̀ƙa *v.t.* Do carpentry.

sassàuce *v.i.* Become slack or untied.

sassàuta *v.t.* Loosen, slacken.

sàta (cị/ce) *v.t.* Steal. **satà** *n.f.* Theft: *kayan ~* stolen goods.

sati *n.m.* 1. Week: *bayan ~ biyu* after two weeks. 2. Saturday: *zai zo ran ~* he'll come on Saturday.

sàtịfịkèt *n.m.* Certificate.

Sạ̀tumbà *n.m.* September.

sàu *n.m.* 1. Times (in multiplication): *na gan shi ~ biyu* I saw him two times, twice; *biyu ~ uku shida ne* two times three equals six. 2. Multiplication table: *~ na biyu* the multiplication table of times two.

sau *n.m.* (*pl.* **sawàye**, *gen.* **san**) 1. Foot. 2. Footprint. 3. Trip: *motar nan ta yi ~ biyu yau* this car has made two trips today.

sàuka (ị/e) *v.t.* 1. Help unload sth. from s.o. 2. Lodge s.o. *n.f.* 1. Completing recitation of the Koran. 2. Graduation (from school). **sàukạ** *v.i.* 1. Descend, come down. 2. Be lodged: *na ~ a gidan wane* I'm staying at so-and-so's house. 3. Arrive: *ku ~ lafiya* may you arrive safely. 4. Deliver, give birth.

saukè *v.t.* 1. Bring down, unload. 2. Complete one's studies: *ya ~ karatu* he has finished his schooling.

sauƙạ̀ƙa *v.t.* 1. Reduce, lessen, relieve. 2. Show leniency. **sàuƙạƙạ̀** *v.i.* Become easy, lessened, diminished.

sauƙi *n.m.* 1. Easiness, cheapness. 2. Relief (from pain or illness). 3. Scarcity, lack.

saunà *n.m.* or *f.* (*pl.* **saunoni**) Fool.

sàura *n.f.* Fallow, disused farm.

saura *n.m.* 1. Remainder, rest: *da ~?* is there any left? *ka ajiye wadannan ~n littattafai* keep the rest of these books; *~ wata uku a fara ruwa* the rains will begin in three months' time. ***~ kaɗan*** almost, nearly: *~ kaɗan mu yi karo* we very nearly had a collision. 2. Less (in telling time): *ƙarfe tara ~ minti biyar* five minutes to nine o'clock. **saurạ** *v.i.* Remain, be left over.

sàurarà (i/e) *v.t.* (*vn.* **sàuràre**) Listen attentively to, wait quietly for.

saurạ̀yi *n.m.* (*pl.* **sạ̀màri**) Young man, youth.

saurì *n.m.* Quickness, haste, speed.

sauro *n.m.* Mosquito. ***gidan ~*** mosquito net.

sautì *n.m.* Voice, sound.

sautụ̀ *n.m.* (*pl.* **saututtụkà**) Giving money to s.o. going on a journey to buy and bring back sth.

sauyà *v.t.* 1. Switch, change: *ya ~ baki* he switched languages (in middle of conversation). 2. Alter: *ya ~ magana* he contradicted himself, altered what he had said previously.

sạ̀wabà *n.f.* 1. Cheapness. 2. Relief.

sạ̀warwạ̀r̃i *n.m.* Misfortune.

sawàye *pl.* of **sau.**

sawu *see* **sau.**

sawwạ̀ƙe *v.i.* Used in *Allah ya ~* may God bring you relief! (said on hearing of any illness or misfortune).

sạ̀ya (i/e) *v.t.* (*vn.* **sạ̀ye**) Buy.

sạ̀yaki *see* **sịyaki.**

sạyar̃ (dạ̀) *v.t.* (= **sai dạ̀** before d.o.) Sell.

sạyau *id.* Emphasizes lightness of weight: *ya kawo wani dami ~ da shi* he brought a very light bundle of corn. ***ji ~*** feel relieved, feel better.

sạ̀yayyà *n.f.* Purchases.

sạ̀ye *n.m.* (*pl.* **sạ̀yẹ-sạ̀yẹ**) 1. Any purchase. 2. *vn.* of **sạ̀ya.**

sayè *v.t.* Cover (with garment): *ta ~ kanta da mayafi* she covered her head with a large cloth.

sêf *n.m.* Safe (for money).

shâ *conj.* Used to form the numbers from eleven to nineteen: *goma ~ ɗaya* eleven; *goma ~ shida* sixteen.

sha *v.t.* 1. Drink. 2. Eat (juicy fruits or sweets). 3. Smoke (cigarette or pipe). 4. Undergo (difficulty or loss): *mun ~ wahala a hannunsa* we suffered at his hands. 5. Do a lot of sth., do sth. often: *mun ~ kallo* we saw a lot of things; *ya ~ gari* he has been in the town a long time. ***~ azumi*** stop fasting for a short period. ***~ iska*** go for a walk, relax.

Shạ̀'ạ̀bân *n.m.* Eighth month of the Muslim calendar.

shạ̀'ạfạ̀ *v.i.* Forget momentarily.

shạ'ạ̀ni *n.m.* (*pl.* **shạ'ạnoni**) 1. Business, affair. 2. Disposition, nature.

shạ̀'ạwà *n.f.* 1. Liking, wanting, being interested in: *ina ~r zama likita* I want to become a doctor; *abin ban ~* sth. interesting. 2. Desire for women: *Audu ya cika ~* Audu is a woman-chaser. 3. Admiration: *ina ~r yadda yakan sa hula* I admire the way he wears hats.

shàɓụ̀ne *n.m.* Wiping one's nose on back of hand.

shacì *n.m.* 1. Marked out site for building. 2. *vn.* of **shatà.**

sha dạ̀ *v.t.* (= **shashe** before pro. d.o.) 1. Alt. form of **shạyar̃ dạ̀.** 2. Overcome, get the better of s.o.

shâdda *n.f.* (*pl.* **shaddodi**) Pit latrine.

shàddạdạ̀ *v.i.* Become severe: *zafin nan ya ~* this heat is unbearable.

shaɗì *see* **shạr̃ọ̀.**

shaf *id.* Used in *manta ~, sha'afa ~* forget completely.

shàfa (i/e) *v.t.* 1. Stroke, wipe: *ta shafi kan yaro* she stroked the boy's head. 2. Affect, concern: *kada laifin wani ya shafe ka* do not let another's faults affect you. **shafà** *v.t.* Rub, wipe, smear on: *ta ~ mai a jikinta* she rubbed some oil on her body.

shàfe *n.m.* Plaster (of wall): *an yi*

wa gidansa ~ his house has been plastered.

shafì *n.m.* (*pl.* **shafuffųkà**) 1. Lining (of garment). 2. Page of a book. 3. Coat (of paint). 4. Dim-witted person.

shą̀galą̀ *v.i.* 1. Be preoccupied with: *kowa ya* ~ *da abin kansa* everyone should look after his own affairs. 2. Be absent-minded.

shągą̀li *n.m.* (*pl.* **shągulgųlà**) Festivity, merrymaking.

shagįɗe *v.t.* Be askew.

shàgįri *n.m.* (*pl.* **shàgįrai**) Person with no facial hair.

shàgų̀ɓe *n.m.* Innuendo.

shągwą̀ɓa *v.t.* Spoil or pamper s.o. (esp. a child).

shą̀hadà *n.f.* (*pl.* **shąhadodì**) 1. Death in a holy war. 2. Certificate. ***kalmar*** ~ formulaic phrases uttered while performing certain Islamic rites.

shą̀hąr̃ą̀ *v.i.* Be famous, have a reputation.

shahò *n.m.* (*pl.* **shahųnà**) Hawk, falcon.

shai'àn Used in *bai ce mini* ~ *ba* he didn't say a word to me.

shâida *v.t.* 1. Give witness to, testify. 2. (with i.o.) Inform.

[1]**shaidà** *n.f.* Black-headed weaver-bird.

[2]**shaidà** *n.m. or f.* (*pl.* **shàidu**) 1. Witness. 2. Court evidence, testimony. **~r zur** perjury. 3. Mark, sign.

shàiɗân *n.m.* (*f.* **shàiɗanįya**, *pl.* **shàiɗànu**) 1. Satan, the Devil. 2. Bad-tempered person.

shaihù *see* **shehù.**

shąką̀sobà *n.f.* Shock absorber.

shakkà *n.f.* Doubt: *ba na* ~*rsa ga wannan aiki* I have no doubt about his being able to do this work.

shąkwąra *n.f.* (*pl.* **shąkwąrori**) Type of three-quarter-length *riga* with embroidery only at neck.

shàƙa (į/e) *v.t.* Smell, sniff at sth.

shaƙą̀ta *v.i.* Take a short rest.

shaƙè *v.t.* 1. Throttle, choke. 2. Fill sth. to the brim.

shą̀ƙiƙì *n.m.* (*f.* **shą̀ƙiƙįya**, *pl.* **shą̀ƙiƙai**) Full brother or sister.

shą̀ƙiyyì *n.m.* (*f.* **shą̀ƙiyyįya**, *pl.* **shą̀ƙiyyai**) Shameless rogue, rascal.

shàƙų *v.i.* Be fond of s.o., be good friends.

shąƙųwà *n.f.* Hiccough.

shàmąkì *n.m.* Stable, tethering place.

shàmmatà (cį/ce) *v.t.* Play a trick on s.o. by surprise.

shàmųwa *n.f.* White-billed stork.

shànshàni *n.m.* A centipede with painful sting.

shanshèra *n.f.* Unshelled or unhusked produce (groundnuts, beans, rice, etc.).

shantą̀ke *v.i.* Dawdle, loll about.

shàntu *n.m.* Long narrow gourd, open at both ends, used as musical instrument by women.

shanu *pl.* of **sâ** and **sanįya.**

shânya *v.t.* (*vn.f.* **shanyà**) Spread out to dry (e.g. clothes or peppers).

shânye *v.t.* Drink up.

shàra *n.f.* 1. Refuse, sweepings: *kwandon* ~ waste-basket. 2. *vn.* of **sharè.**

sharà *v.t.* Do much of sth.: *mun* ~ *barci* we slept a lot.

shar̃à *n.f.* Used in *kudin* ~ money paid to a joking partner in the month of *Muharram.*

shąr̃ą̀ɗì *n.m.* (*pl.* **shąr̃ųɗà**) 1. Condition, agreement, arrangement. 2. Reason.

shąr̃af *id.* Soaking wet.

sharè *v.t.* (*vn.f.* **shàra**) Sweep.

shą̀r̃į'à *n.f.* (*pl.* **shąr̃į'o'ì**) Law, justice.

shar̃hì *n.m.* Written commentary, critique.

shàr̃holįya *n.f.* Living for the moment with no thought about the future.

shą̀r̃ifì, shą̀r̃îf *n.m.* (*f.* **shą̀r̃ifįya**, *pl.* **shą̀r̃ifai**) Person who claims descent from the Prophet Muhammad and who, it is believed, cannot be harmed by fire.

shąr̃ǫ̀ *n.m.* Ritual test of manhood among Fulani youths in which they must endure flogging without showing pain.

shar̃r̃ì *n.m.* Evil act, wickedness, slander.

shashancì *n.m.* Stupidity.

shashàsha *n.m. or f.* (*pl.* **shàshà-shai**) Useless, unreliable person.
shashè *v.t.* Lessen after-effects of sth. unpleasant by introducing sth. more pleasant: *ta ~ turmi da dusa* she pounded bran in the mortar (to get rid of the bitterness left by the previous pounding).
shashe *see* **sha dą.**
shashì *see* **sashì.**
shâsshawà *n.f.* Tribal or decorative markings on face or body.
shàsshèka *n.f.* Gasping, panting.
shatà *v.t.* (*vn.* **shaci**) Indicate or outline plan or pattern.
shata *n.m.* Open-work style of weaving.
shàwaġì *n.m.* Hovering or waiting about.
[1]**shawąr̃à** *n.f.* (*pl.* **shawàr̃wąr̃i**) 1. Advice, opinion. 2. Decision, thinking sth. over: *mun yi ~ a kan wannan* we've come to a decision about this.
[2]**shawąr̃à** *n.f.* Jaundice.
shàwar̃tà (cį/ce) *v.t.* 1. Consult s.o. 2. Give advice.
Shàwwâl *n.m.* Tenth month of the Muslim calendar.
shąyar̃ (dą) *v.t.* (= **sha dą** before d.o.) 1. Give water to person or animal: *ya ~ da dokinsa* he watered his horse. 2. Irrigate. 3. Suckle.
shàyę-shàyę *n.m.* 1. Drinks served at a social event. 2. Drinking a lot of different drinks.
shàyi *n.m.* Used in *dan ~* circumcised boy.
shayį *n.m.* Tea.
shà-zųmamį *n.m.* Sugar ant.
shebùr̃ *see* [2]**tebùr̃.**
shedì *n.m.* Railway shed for goods.
shèɗân *see* **shàiɗân.**
shèġàntąkà *n.f.* Impudence, mischieviousness, rudeness.
sheġè *n.m.* (*f.* **sheġįya**, *pl.* **shèġu**) 1. Bastard. 2. Rascal, impudent person.
shehù *n.m.* (*pl.* **shèhùnnai**) 1. Learned pious person (esp. ref. to Usman dan Fodio). 2. (*f.* **shehų̀wa**) Professor. **shehų̀** Traditional title of the Emir of Borno.
shèkąrà *n.f.*(*pl.* **shèkąru**) 1. Year. 2. Age: *~rsa biyar da haihuwa* he is five years old.
shekąranjįyą̀ *n.f. and adv.* Day before yesterday.
[1]**shèƙa (į/e)** *v.t.* Sniff, inhale sth. powdery (e.g. snuff).
[2]**shèƙa** *n.f.* Bird's nest.
[1]**sheƙà** *v.t.* (*vn.f.* **shiƙà**) Winnow.
[2]**sheƙà** *v.t.* Do sth. well: *ta ~ ado* she was very well dressed. *v.i.* Take off suddenly: *ya ~ da gudu* he ran off suddenly.
shèƙèƙè *id.* Contemptuous look.
shèlą̀ *n.f.* Proclamation. ***mai ~*** town crier, narrator (in a play).
shewà *n.f.* Loud laughter of women.
shi *pro.m.* (vl. and tone vary acc. to use, *see* Appendix 1) He, him.
shibtà *n.f.* Dictation.
shįdą̀ *n.f. and adj.* Six.
shiɗè *v.i.* Draw in and hold a long breath.
shiftąma *n.f.* Ill-considered nonsensical speech.
shįgą *v.i.* Enter. ***~ soja*** join the army. ***~ uku*** be in a dilemma.
shįgè *v.i.* Pass by, go beyond.
shįgegè *n.m.* Intrusion.
shįgį dą fįcį *n.m.* Going in and out, back and forth, being restless.
shįkà *v.t.* Alt. form of **sąki.** *v.i.* Become loose, frayed, rickety.
shi kè nan That's all, O.K.
shiƙà *vn.* of **sheƙà.**
shįlà *n.m.* Used in *dan ~* young pigeon.
shillò *n.m.* Swinging, dangling, hanging down.
shimfįɗa *v.t.* 1. Spread sth. out, lay sth. down. 2. Establish, start: *ya ~ mulki* he established rule. **shìmfįɗà** *n.f.* 1. Anything which is spread out (e.g. mat or blanket). 2. Introduction (of book or article).
shįmî *n.m.* Woman's inner garment, slip.
shin Used to introduce questions of doubt: *~ ko ka san an ƙara mana albashi watan nan?* did you happen to know that they raised our wages this month?
shįnà *v.t.* Alt. form of **sąni.**
shinge *n.m.* (*pl.* **shingàye**) Fence.
shingì *n.m.* Remainder.

shìnkafa *n.f.* Rice.
shịr̃àyi *n.m.* Rectangular thatched mud house.
shir̃ɓụ̀na *v.t.* Apply a lot of oil to body.
shirgà *v.t.* (with i.o.) Do much of sth. bad, inflict: *ya ~ mini ƙarya* he told me a whopping lie.
shirgì *n.m.* Large disorderly pile.
shịrì *n.m.* 1. Preparation, plan. 2. Being about to do sth.: *yana ~n kuka* he is about to cry. 3. *vn.* of **shiryà.**
shịrịrìta *n.f.* Procrastination caused by laziness.
shịrịyà *n.f.* Guidance.
shir̃kà *n.f.* 1. Partnership, joint possession. 2. Belief in many religions.
shìrme *n.m.* Folly, foolish act or speech, nonsense.
shịru *n.m.* Silence.
shịrụ-shịrụ *n.m.* Taciturn disposition.
shirwà *n.f.* (*pl.* **shirwoyi**) Black kite (bird).
shiryà *v.t.* (*vn.* **shịrì**) 1. Prepare, arrange sth. 2. Reconcile s.o.: *an ~ mu da 'yan sanda* we have been put on good terms with the police.
shisshịgi *n.m.* Meddlesomeness, inquisitiveness.
shịwaka *n.f.* Shrub whose bitter leaves are used in cooking.
shiyyà *n.f.* Direction.
shòlịshò *n.m.* Rubber solution for patching inner tubes.
shôt *n.m.* Used in *yi ~* fall short of correct amount (esp. money or goods in business).
shucì *n.m.* Dry grass for thatching.
shuɗì *n. and adj.* (*f.* **shuɗịya,** *pl.* **shûɗɗa**) Blue.
shùgạ̀ba *n.m.* (*pl.* **shùgạ̀bànni**) Leader, head, chairman, president.
shukà *v.t.* Sow. *n.f.* (*pl.* **shùkẹ-shùkẹ**) 1. Crop, plant. 2. Act of sowing.
shuni *n.m.* Prepared indigo.
shurà *v.t.* (*vn.* **shurì**) Kick foot outward.
shurì 1. *vn.* of **shurà.** 2. *See* **surì.**
shụ'ụ̀mi *n.m.* (*f.* **shụ'ụ̀ma,** *pl.* **shụ̀'ụ̀mai**) 1. Person, place or thing inhabited by spirits. 2. Highly skilled person.
sìddạbạr̃ụ̀ *n.m.* Conjuring tricks.
sịɗik *id.* Emphasizes blackness: *baƙi ~* jet black.
siffà, sịfà *n.f.* (*pl.* **siffofi**) 1. Likeness, image, shape, form. 2. Description: *ya ba ni ~rsa* he described it to me. 3. Adjective (in grammar).
sịfilì *n.m.* Gears (of bicycle).
[1]**sịfịr̃i** *n.m.* Zero, nought.
[2]**sịfịr̃i** *n.m.* Renting or hiring any beast of burden.
sịfịr̃în *n.m.* Spring (metal).
sịgar̃ì *n.m.* Cigarette.
sịgịnạ̀ *n.f.* Signal, sign.
sịhir̃ce *v.t.* Bewitch.
sịhịr̃ì *n.m.* Magic, sorcery.
sịkawùt *n.m.* Boy Scout.
sịkelì *n.m.* (*pl.* **sịkeloli**) Scales (for weighing).
sịkinkịlạ̀ *n.m.* Second class accommodation (usu. on train).
sịƙè *v.i.* Become temporarily speechless or silent.
sìli *n.m.* Two-ply thread.
sịlịkì *n.m.* Silk material or thread.
sịlịmân *n.m.* Cinema.
silìn *n.m.* Ceiling.
sìlle *n.m.* Being dressed or covered up but without trousers.
sillè *v.t.* Wash one's body well.
sille *n.m.* Top part of corn stalk.
sịmintì *n.m.* Cement.
sịnadạ̀r̃i *n.m.* Solder.
singịletì *n.f.* (*pl.* **singịletoci**) Singlet.
sintạ̀lị *n.m.* A traditional title.
sir̃dì *n.m.* (*pl.* **sịr̃àda**) 1. Saddle. 2. Bicycle seat.
sịr̃inji *n.m.* Syringe.
sịr̃ir̃ì *n. and adj.* (*f.* **sịr̃ir̃ịya,** *pl.* **sịr̃àr̃a**) Thin, slender.
sir̃r̃i *see* **ạsir̃i.**
sisì *n.m.* Sixpence in old Nigerian currency, equivalent to five kobo. **~n kwabo** half-pence.
sistà *n.f.* (*pl.* **sistoci**) Nursing sister.
sịtatà *n.f.* Starter (of motor vehicle).
sịtatì *n.m.* 1. Starch. 2. Neatness of dress and appearance.
sịtịr̃à *n.f.* (*pl.* **sịtịr̃u**) 1. Clothing. 2. Shroud.

sitiyarì *n.m.* Steering wheel.
sitô *n.m.* Store, storeroom.
sitsirà *see* **sàdarà.**
sittà *n.f. and adj.* Six thousand.
sìttin *n.f. and adj.* Sixty.
siyaki *n.m.* (*pl.* **siyàkai**) Striped hyena.
siyasà *n.f.* 1. Politics. ***ɗan*** ~ politician. ***gwamnatin 'yan*** ~ civilian government. 2. Being accommodating in dealing with others. 3. Making a concession, giving a reduction in trading.
so *v.t.* Like, want, desire, love. **~n *kai*** selfishness.
soci *n.f.* Jersey, tee-shirt.
[1]**sodà** *n.f.* Solder.
[2]**sodà** *n.f.* 1. Washing soda. 2. Soda water.
sofanè *n.m.* Multi-coloured patches of animal's coat.
sojà *n.m.* 1. (*pl.* **sojoji**) Soldier. 2. Army.
sòka (i/e) *v.t.* (*vn.* **sukà**) Pierce, stab. **sokà** *v.t.* (with i.o.) Plunge, thrust weapon into s.o.
sòke *n.m.* Securing cloth round body by twisting corners together and tucking in.
sokè *v.t.* (*vn.* **sukà**) 1. Pierce, prick. 2. Slaughter (camel). 3. Cancel, delete, negate: *mu* ~ *sunansa daga cikin lissafi* let's take his name off the list. 4. Contradict, go against s.o.'s opinion or testimony.
sòki *n.m.* Insect pest which attacks groundnuts.
sokò *n.m.* (*f.* **sokùwa,** *pl.* **sokwàye**) Dim-witted person.
somà *v.t.* Begin, start.
somì *n.m.* Beginning, start.
sorō *n.m.* (*pl.* **soràye**) 1. Rectangular mud house with flat or domed roof. 2. Entrance room of compound.
sosà *v.t.* (*vn.f.* **susà**) Scratch to relieve itch.
sòsai *adv.* Well, correctly, perfectly.
soshiya *n.f.* Heads of guinea-corn or millet from which grains have been stripped.
sòso *n.m.* 1. Loofah sponge. 2. Any sponge.
sowà *n.m.* Yelling, shouting.
soyà *v.t.* (*vn.f.* **suyà**) 1. Fry. 2. Roast (e.g. groundnuts) usu. in hot sand.
sòyayyà *n.f.* Mutual affection, love.
sòye *n.m.* Pieces of roasted meat.
su 1. Used before noun to indicate a series of such nouns or persons: *na ga* ~ *Audu a tashar mota* I saw Audu and the others at the lorry park; *akwai naman daji a gidan zu kamar* ~ *zaki* ~ *kura* ~ *biri* there are wild animals at the zoo such as lions, hyenas and monkeys. 2. Used to pluralize *wa, wane ne, me,* and *mene ne*: ~ *wa suka zo?* who (pl.) came?
sû *n.m.* Fishing.
sû *id.* Slithering, sliding sound.
su *pro.pl.* (vl. and tone vary acc. to use, *see* Appendix 1) They, them, their.
sùbhanàllahì *excl.* Good heavens!
suɓùce *v.i.* Slip out, slip away, escape.
sùda *n.f.* Senegalese bush shrike (bird).
suɗè *v.t.* Wipe out remains of food inside pot with finger. *v.i.* Be rubbed smooth: *tayar motarsa ta* ~ his car tyre is completely smooth.
suɗì *n.m.* Food left over to be given away.
sufà *n.m.* 1. Premium grade (super) petrol. 2. Used in *takin* ~ chemical fertilizer.
sùfanà *n.f.* (*pl.* **sufanoni**) Spanner.
sùfetò *n.m.* (*pl.* **sufetoci**) Inspector of police.
sufùri *n.m.* Transport, transport cost, hiring, renting.
sùjjadà *n.f.* Prostration in worship.
sukà *pro.pl.* (rel. past tense subj.) They.
sukà *vn.* of **sòka** and **sokè.**
sukàn *pro.pl.* (hab. tense subj.) They.
sukàri *n.m.* Sugar.
sukè *pro.pl.* (rel. cont. tense subj.) They.
sùkolàshìf *n.m.* Scholarship.
sùkùndirebà *n.f.* Screwdriver.
sùkunì *n.m.* 1. Chance, leisure 2. Means of living.
sùkùtum *id.* As a whole, entirely

sụkụ̀wa *n.f.* Horse-racing, galloping.
sụkwàne *v.t.* Plunder, loot.
sụlai *id.* Smooth, slippery.
sụlàla *v.t.* Warm up (gruel).
sụlè, sụlài *n.m.* (*pl.* **sụlàlla, sụlullụkà**) Shilling in old Nigerian currency, equivalent to ten kobo.
sulhù *n.m.* 1. Reconciliation. 2. Arbitration. 3. Peace treaty.
sullụ̀ɓe *v.i.* Slip away, escape.
sùlmịyạ̀ *v.i.* Fall into, slip into.
sụ̀lụ̀lụ̀ *id.* Moving noiselessly, stealthily.
sụ̀lụ̀sani *n.pl.* Two-thirds.
sụlụ̀si *n.m.* One-third.
sùm *id.* Bad smelling.
sùma *n.f.* New hair on man's head.
sumạ *v.i.* Faint.
sumba *n.f.* Kiss.
sumbạ̀ce *v.t.* Kiss.
sụmul *id.* Smooth, shiny, clean: *kwanon nan ya wanku* ~ this pan has been washed spanking clean.
sụ̀mụ̀mụ̀ *id.* Silently and stealthily.
sụmụ̀ni *n.m.* One-eighth.
sụ̀munti *see* **sịminti.**
sun *pro.pl.* (past tense subj.) They.
sụnà *pro.pl.* (cont. tense subj.) They.
suna *n.m.* (*pl.* **sunàye, sunànnạki**) 1. Name. 2. Naming ceremony. 3. First price quoted at the start of bargaining: *ka sa* ~ name your price! 4. Fame, reputation: *ya yi* ~ *wajen ƙira* he is famous for smithing.
sùnduƙi *n.m.* (*pl.* **sùndùƙai**) Box.
sundụ̀me *v.i.* Be swollen.
sùngụmà (ị/e) *v.t.* Lift (heavy or large load).
sùngụmi *n.m.* Long-handled hoe for sowing.
sùnkụtà (cị/ce) *v.t.* Lift sth. up in a hurry.
sunkụ̀ya *v.i.* Bend over, stoop down.
sùnƙurù *n.m.* Thick bush, uncleared land.
[1]**sunnà** *v.t.* (with i.o.) Give sth. secretly to s.o.: *ya* ~ *mata kuɗi* he gave her money on the sly.
[2]**sunnà** *n.f.* (*pl.* **sunnoni**) The sayings and practices of the Prophet Muhammad.
sùnta (cị/ce) *v.t.* Catch fish.
sùntum *id.* Be puffed up, fat.
sur̃ *id.* Be full to the brim.
sùr̃a (ị/e) *v.t.* Swoop down to snatch sth.
sur̃à *n.f.* (*pl.* **sur̃or̃i**) 1. A chapter of the Koran. 2. Image, picture, appearance.
surfà *v.t.* Pound corn to remove bran.
sùr̃fani *n.m.* Open-stitched embroidery.
suri *n.m.* Large mound made by termites.
surkà *v.t.* Add cold water to hot.
sùr̃kulle *n.m.* A Fulani incantation composed of Arabic and meaningless words.
sur̃ƙụƙi *n.m.* Thicket.
sụ̀rụki *n.m.* (*pl.* **sụ̀rụ̀kai**) Father-in-law or elder brother-in-law.
sùr̃utù *n.m.* (*pl.* **sùr̃ùtai**) Talkativeness, chattering.
susà *vn.* of **sosà.**
susanci *n.m.* Foolishness, folly.
sussụ̀ka *v.t.* Thresh.
susùce *v.i.* Fail, come to nought: *shirinmu ya* ~ our plans have fallen through.
susùsu *n.m. or f.* Witless fool.
sutu *n.m.* Teasing of cotton before spinning.
sụ̀waità *n.f.* (*pl.* **sụwaitoci**) Sweater.
suyà *n.f.* 1. Pieces of fried or roasted meat. 2. *vn.* of **soyà.**
swa *see* **sa.**

T

[1]**tạ** *see* **nạ.**
[2]**tạ** *prep.* 1. Via, by means of, by way of: *ya dawo* ~ *hanyar Zariya* he returned by the Zaria road. 2. (in cont.) Keep on doing: *yau ana* ~ *ruwa* it has kept on raining today. 3. (with **yị**) Proceed to: *ya yi* ~ *dariya* he started to laugh.
ta *pro.f.* (vl. and tone vary acc. to use, *see* Appendix 1) She, her.
tạ̀'adà *see* **ạ̀l'adà.**
tạ'àdda *n.f.* Inciting trouble.
tạ̀'ạdi *n.m.* Serious damage.
tạ̀'ala Used in *Allah* ~ God the Most High.
tạ̀'ammạ̀li *n.m.* Trading, business dealings.
tạ̀'annạ̀ti *n.m.* 1. Asking questions which put s.o. on the spot, esp. student questioning teacher. 2. Damaging or spoiling.
tạ̀'ạ̀ziyyà *n.f.* Condolence given upon bereavement.
tạ̀'àzzạr̃ạ̀ *v.i.* Become serious or difficult: *rayuwa ta* ~ living has become difficult.
tàba *n.f.* Fraud, dishonesty.
tabà *n.f.* 1. Tobacco, tobacco plant, cigarette. *sha* ~ to smoke. 2. News: *zan busa maka* ~ I'll tell you the news.
tababà *n.f.* Doubt.
tạ̀bàrau *n.m.* Eye-glasses.
tàbarma *n.f.* (*pl.* **tàbàrmi**) Mat.
tabbạ̀ci *n.m.* Assurance, confirmation.
tabbàs *adv.* Undoubtedly.
tabbạ̀ta *v.t.* Make sure of, confirm. **tàbbạtạ̀** *v.i.* Be certain, be confirmed, be permanent: *aikinka ya* ~ your appointment has been confirmed.
tàbbạ̀tacce *adj.* (*f.* **tàbbạ̀taccịya,** *pl.* **tàbbạ̀tàttu**) Outstanding in quality, genuine.
tabɗị *excl.* Fancy that! Imagine! Marvellous!
tabkà *v.t.* Do a lot of, put a lot of sth. on: *ta* ~ *hoda* she put on a lot of powder; *an* ~ *ciniki jiya* there was a lot of trading yesterday.
tạbò *n.m.* (*pl.* **tâbba, tabbụnà**) Scar, blemish, stain.
tạɓà *v.t.* 1. Touch, feel. 2. Taste. 3. Concern, affect: *wannan labari ya* ~ *ni* this news concerns me. 4. Do a little of, take a little of: *ka* ~ *aiki kafin ka tashi* work a little before you go. 5. Have ever (never) done sth.: *ka* ~ *zuwa Kaduna?* have you ever been to Kaduna?
tạ̀ɓaɓɓe *n. and adj.* (*f.* **tạ̀ɓaɓɓịya,** *pl.* **tạ̀ɓàɓɓu**) Slightly mad or deranged: *asibitin masu* ~*n hankali* asylum for the mentally ill.
tạ̀ɓạ̀-kunnẹ *see* **tàttạ̀ɓạ̀-kunnẹ.**
tạɓarya *n.f.* (*pl.* **tạɓàre**) Pestle.
taɓè *v.t.* Rip open (cloth), open up with force (e.g. drawing back a bow or forcing a ring apart). *v.i.* Be disappointed, fail in achieving desires.
tạ̀ɓẹ-tạ̀ɓẹ *n.m.* Repeated touching, pilfering, or stealing.
tạ̀ɓo *n.m.* Mud.
tạ̀ɓu *v.i.* Be mentally ill, mad.
tacè *v.t.* (*vn.f.* **tàta**) Strain, filter.
ta dạ̀ *v.t.* Alt. form of **tayar̃ dạ̀.**
tadà *n.f.* (*pl.* **tadodi**) Custom, tradition.
tạ̀dạwà *see* **tạ̀wạdà.**
tad dạ̀ *v.t.* Alt. form of **tạrar̃ dạ̀.**
taɗà *v.i.* Chat, converse: *zo mu ɗan* ~ come and let's chat a little.
taɗè *v.t.* Trip s.o. by putting foot in front of him.
taɗi *n.m.* Conversation, chatting.
taf *id.* Completely full or filled up: *na cika tanki* ~ *da fetur* I filled the tank up with petrol.
tafà *v.t.* 1. Clap hands, applaud. 2. Slap one another's hands as sign of friendship or in enjoyment of joke. 3. (with i.o.) Give handful of sth. to s.o.: *na* ~ *mata gishiri* I gave her a handful of salt.
tạfarkì *n.m.* (*pl.* **tạ̀fàrku**) 1. Road.

2. Path, way, fate: *yana bin ~n gaskiya* he is following the true path of salvation.

tą̀farnųwa *n.f.* Garlic.

tą̀fą̀sa *n.f.* Type of senna plant whose leaves are used in making *miya* and *kwado*.

tąfą̀sa *v.t.* 1. Boil, bring to boil. 2. Make angry: *abin ya ~ mini zuciya* that made me angry. **tą̀fąsą̀** *v.i.* 1. Boil. 2. Become enraged.

tàfa-tàfa *n.f.* Game played by young girls in which they hit or clap each other's palms.

tą̀fį *v.i.* (*vn.f.* **tą̀fįyà**) Go, travel, be off, walk.

tàfi *n.m.* (*pl.* **tafųkà**) 1. Palm of hand, sole of foot. 2. Handful. 3. Applause. 4. Slap.

tąfidą̀ *n.m.* A traditional title (usu. held by younger brother or son of an emir).

tąfi dą̀ *v.t.* Alt. form of **tąfįyar̃ dą̀.**

tafintą̀ *n.m.* (*pl.* **tafintoci**) 1. Interpreter, translator. 2. Translating.

tàfįr̃età *n.f.* (*pl.* **tafįr̃etoci**) Typewriter.

tą̀fįyà *n.f.* (*pl.* **tą̀fįyę-tą̀fįyę**) 1. Journey. 2. *vn.* of **tą̀fį.**

tąfįyar̃ (dą̀) *v.t.* (= **tąfi dą̀** before d.o.) 1. Push or move sth. along. 2. Administer, manage: *ana shiryeshiryen ~ da shagalin a filin wasa* arrangements are being made to hold the celebration at the playgrounds.

tafkì *n.m.* (*pl.* **tafkųnà, tąfukkà**) Lake, pond.

tàfsir̃i *n.m.* (*pl.* **tàfsir̃ai**) Commentary on a Koranic text.

tagà *n.f.* (*pl.* **tagogi**) Window, window hole in wall.

tągą̀rį *f.* of **nągą̀rį.**

tą̀gàyyąr̃ą̀ *v.i.* Suffer hardship and deprivation.

tàgįyà *n.f.* (*pl.* **tàgįyu, tagįyoyi**) Cap, hat.

tągomą̀shi *n.m.* Popularity.

tągùlla *n.f.* Copper or bronze.

tàgųmi *n.m.* Resting head on hand or knee in thought.

tągųwà *n.f.* (*pl.* **tągųwoyi**) Any kind of man's fitted gown, knee-length or longer, with long sleeves and round neck.

tàgųwà *n.f.* (*pl.* **tàgų̀wai**) Female camel.

tągwàye *n.pl.* 1. Twins. 2. Pair of sth.

tąho *v.i.* Come.

tàibą̀ *n.f.* Cooked cassava flour.

tàiɓa *n.f.* Roll of fat around belly.

taikì *n.m.* (*pl.* **taikųnà**) Large hide bag used on pack animal.

tàimąkà (į/e) *v.t.* (*vn.* **tàimąko**) Help.

tàimąko *n.m.* 1. Help, aid. 2. Charm for medicinal purposes. 3. *vn.* of **tàimąkà.**

tàimąmą̀ *v.i.* Be compelled to use sand for ablution in the absence of water.

tàitąyà (į/e) *v.t.* Help along tired or sick person or animal.

tajè *v.t.* 1. Separate out cotton strands in preparation for weaving. 2. Comb hair.

tą-jįką̀ *n.f.* Jaundice.

tàjìn-tàjìn *id.* Feeling agitated, distressed (of a group).

tajį̀r̃i *see* **àttajįr̃i.**

tajir̃ta *v.t.* Enrich. **tàjir̃tą̀** *v.i.* Become wealthy.

[1]**tak** *id.* (with **ɗąyą** expressed or understood) Only: *ya ba ni ɗaya ~* he gave me only one; *babu ko ~* there's not even one.

[2]**tak** *id.* Sound of dripping: *~ da na ji ruwa ne yake zuba a kwano* the sound that I heard was water dripping into the pan.

taką̀ *pro.m.* (poss.) Yours (ref. to fem. noun).

takà *v.t.* 1. Step on, tread on. 2. Measure distance by pacing. 3. (with i.o.) Walk along with, escort s.o. **tàka (į/e)** *v.t.* Stand upon, rely upon: *me ka ~?* what are your grounds (for making such a claim)? *na taki ƙarfina* I am relying upon my own ability. ***taki sa'a*** happen to be lucky.

tąkąbà *n.f.* Period of mourning done by a widow.

tàką̀-bąɗǫ̀ *n.m.* Lilly-trotter (bird with long legs and claws).

tą̀kâici *n.m.* Indignation.

tàkąlà (į/e) *v.t.* Provoke, incite.

tàkàlmi *n.m.* (*pl.* **takalmà**) Shoe, sandal.

tą̀ką̀maimai *n.m.* Real nature or origin of sth.: *ban san ~n aikinsa ba* I don't know the real nature of his work.

tąkàn *pro.f.* (hab. tense subj.) She.

tą̀ką̀nas *adv.* Especially, purposely, mainly.

[1]**tą̀kàndа** *n.f.* Type of guinea-corn whose sweet stalk is eaten like sugar-cane.

[2]**tą̀kàndа** *n.f.* Fillet steak, the tender strip of meat along backbone of an animal.

tą̀ką̀r̃a *n.f.* Group reading where individuals read aloud simultaneously different sections of the Koran.

takąr̃a *n.f.* Rivalry, competition: *'yan ~r zaɓe* candidates in an election.

tąkàr̃da *n.f.* (*pl.* **tą̀kàr̃du**) 1. Paper. **~r *shaida*** certificate. **~r *izni*** permit. 2. Letter.

tą̀ką̀r̃imi *n.m.* Showing respect, honour.

tą̀karką̀ri *n.m.* (*pl.* **tą̀kàrką̀rai**) Pack ox.

tąkè *pro.f.* (rel. cont. tense subj.) She.

tàkę *adv.* On the spot, right then and there: *nan ~ suka mutu* they died on the spot.

take *n.m.* Musical theme or rhythm associated with an individual or official position. **~n *Nijeriya*** Nigerian national anthem.

tàkę-tàkę *n.m.* Showing one's intentions indirectly.

taki̧ *pro.f.* (poss.) Yours (ref. to fem. noun).

[1]**taki** *n.m.* 1. Step, pace. 2. Measurement of distance by placing one foot right after the other.

[2]**taki** *n.m.* Manure, fertilizer.

tàko *n.m.* Hoof.

tąkòbi *n.m.* (*pl.* **tąkubbà**) Sword.

tàksî *n.m.* Taxi.

takų̀ *pro.pl.* (poss.) Yours (ref. to fem. noun).

tàkunkų̀mi *n.m.* 1. Muzzle for animal. 2. Economic embargo or blockade.

takų̀ra *v.t.* Cause to huddle up: *sanyi ya ~ su* the cold made them huddle up. **tàkų̀rą̀** *v.i.* Sit huddled or crouched up from fear or cold.

tąkwakkwą̀ɓe *v.i.* Become worn-out.

tąkwąla *n.f.* Fine thread used in sewing machines.

tą̀kwą̀r̃a *n.f.* 1. Namesake, person bearing the same name as another. 2. Counterpart in rank or occupation.

tąkwàs *n.f. and adj.* Eight.

tą̀ƙa *n.m.* Pace, stride.

tą̀ƙą̀dir̃i *adv.* Approximately, at least.

tąƙài *n.m.* Dance done by young men, characterized by striking sticks together and stamping with rattles on ankles.

tą̀ƙàicę *adv.* (with **ą̀**) In short, briefly, to make a long story short.

tąƙàita *v.t.* Shorten, summarize.

tą̀ƙaitą̀ *v.i.* Become shortened, abridged.

tàƙąma *n.f.* 1. Swaggering, boasting, putting on airs, conceit. 2. Prancing gait taught to horse. 3. Relying on s.o. or sth.: *yana ~ da kuɗinsa ne* he's relying on his money.

tąƙarƙą̀re *v.i.* Strive hard, exert oneself.

tąƙi *n.m.* Short distance: *yana da ɗan ~ daga nan* it is only a short distance from here.

tąlą̀ką̀ *n.m. or f.* (*pl.* **tąląkawa**) Commoner, 'man-in-the-street'.

talala *n.f.* Long tethering rope.

[1]**Tą̀latà** *n.f.* Tuesday.

[2]**tą̀latà** *n.f. and adj.* Three thousand.

tą̀làtin *n.f. and adj.* Thirty.

tąlàuce *v.i.* Become poor.

tąlauci *n.m.* Poverty, destitution.

tąlàuta *v.t.* Cause to become poor: *yawan aure-aure ne duk ya ~ shi* his marrying so many times has made him poor.

tâlbodi *n.f.* Tailboard lorry.

talè *v.t.* Spread apart, open wide (e.g. arms, legs, or mouth).

tàlge *n.m.* Thin gruel which is the first stage of *tuwo* before it thickens.

tàli̧bambam *n.m.* Tadpole.

talifi *n.m.* 1. (*pl.* **tàlifai, talifofi**)

Any literary composition. 2. Act of writing, composing an original work.

talįki *n.m.* (*f.* **talįka**, *pl.* **tàlįkai**) Creature, being.

tàlįyà *n.f.* Macaroni.

tàllą̀ *n.m.* (*pl.* **tàllą̀cę-tàllą̀cę**) 1. Hawking, displaying goods for sale. 2. Advertisement.

tàlląfà (į/e) *v.t.* Support, provide for, give relief to: *gwamnati ta tallafi 'yan gudun hijira* the government provided for the refugees. **tallą̀fa** *v.t.* Support, carry sth. in palm of hand.

tallą̀fi *n.m.* Adopting a child.

tallą̀ta *v.t.* Expose wares for sale.

talle *n.m.* (*pl.* **tallàye**) 1. Small soup pot. 2. Hunting drum.

tą̀lǫtą̀lǫ *n.m.* Turkey.

tam *id.* Firmly tied.

tąma *n.f.* Iron ore.

tą̀mammą̀na *n.f.* Thick excretion which collects inside boy's foreskin or girl's genitals.

tąmą̀ni *n.m.* High price, value.

tą̀mànin *n.f. and adj.* Eighty.

tą̀mat *n.f.* Formula meaning 'The End', used with song, poem, or letter.

tąmą̀tą *n.f. and adj.* (*pl.* **mata**) 1. Female. 2. Feminine gender (in grammar).

tambą̀ri *n.m.* (*pl.* **tambųrà**) 1. Large bowl-shaped drum, played by official musicians of an Emir. 2. Official government seal. 3. Name of a circular embroidery pattern.

tàmbąyà (į/e) *v.t.* Ask, inquire, ask about. *n.f.* (*pl.* **tambąyoyi**) Question.

tàmfâl *n.m.* Tarpaulin.

tàmka *n.f.* Fruit-bearing branch of a date-palm or banana tree.

tàmkar̃ *conj.* As: *yana takama ~ shi sarki ne* he is swaggering as if he were the chief.

tàmmanì *see* **tsàmmanì**.

tamoji *n.pl.* Wrinkles resulting from old age or thinness: *fuskarsa ta yi ~* his face is full of wrinkles.

tąmolą *n.f.* Children's game of pelting each other with ragballs.

tamų̀ *pro.pl.* (poss.) Ours (ref. to fem. noun).

tąnà *pro.f.* (cont. tense subj.) She.

tana *n.f.* Earthworm.

tànądà (į/e) *v.t.* (*vn.* **taną̀di**) Prepare sth. in advance, get sth. ready.

taną̀di *n.m.* 1. Thrift, economizing, planning for future needs. 2. *vn.* of **tànądà**.

tànakà *n.f.* (*pl.* **tànàku**) Metal container for perfume.

taną̀na *v.t.* Fry meat slightly to prevent it from spoiling.

[1]**tandà** *n.f.* Earthenware tray with indentations in which *waina* is fried.

[2]**tandà** *n.f.* Tender made by contractor or supplier.

tandą̀ra *v.t.* Throw down forcefully.

tandąrà *n.f.* A small harmless snake.

tàndèr̃u *n.m.* Earthenware oven for baking *gurasa*.

tandu *n.m.* (*pl.* **tandàye**) 1. Gourd-shaped hide container for storing oil or honey. 2. Gourd-shaped hide drum.

tànɗa (į/e) *v.t.* Lick.

tàngąɗi *n.m.* 1. Staggering, reeling. 2. Rolling, rocking movement: *kwalekwale yana ~ a ruwa* the boat is rocking back and forth in the water.

tangą̀r̃ahò Used in *wayar ~* telegram.

[1]**tangąr̃an** *n.m.* Chinaware, dishes.

[2]**tangąr̃an** *id.* Seeing clearly, being bright and clear: *yana nan da idonsa ~* he sees very clearly.

tangar̃ɗà *n.f.* Difficulty, hitch: *aikin nan yana tafiya sosai babu ~* this work is going along well without a hitch.

tąnìs *n.m.* Tennis.

tankà *v.i.* Reply back: *kada ka ~ masa* don't say anything back to him.

tanka *n.f.* Grass or cornstalk rows lashed to inside of thatch or fence for reinforcement.

tanką̀ɗe *v.t.* Winnow flour by shaking it sideways on a *faifai* or through a sieve.

tankè *v.t.* Reinforce thatch or fence by lashing rows of grass or cornstalk across it.

tankì *n.m.* (*pl.* **tankųnà**) 1. Tank (petrol, water, etc.). 2. Tanker lorry. 3. Military tank.
tankifą̀ *n.m.* (*pl.* **tankifofi**) Time-keeper.
tankįya *n.f.* Quarrelling, arguing.
tanƙwą̀ra *v.t.* Bend, make sth. bowed (e.g. stick or bamboo).
tanƙwą̀re *v.i.* Become bent.
tanƙwą̀she *v.t.* Tuck one's legs under while sitting.
tàntąbą̀r̃a *n.f.* (*pl.* **tàntąbą̀r̃ai**) Pigeon.
tàntąkwą̀shi *n.m.* Soft part of inside of bone near marrow (used for making broth or soup).
tantą̀la *v.i.* Used in *ya ~ da gudu* he took to his heels.
tantąma *n.f.* Doubt: *na ga kana ~ da abin da nake faɗa* I see that you doubt what I am saying.
tantànce *v.i.* 1. Deteriorate, become useless. 2. Be spent (of money).
tantani *n.m.* Membrane from abdominal wall of cow used for covering children's drums.
tàntàr̃wai *id.* Seeing clearly, being glossy or bright.
tantebùr̃ *see* [3]**tebùr̃**.
tantì *n.m.* Tent.
tàntir̃ì *n. and adj.* (*f.* **tàntir̃įya**, *pl.* **tàntìr̃ai**) Poor, penniless.
tą̀ra (į/e) *v.t.* 1. Go to meet or welcome s.o.: *mun tari sarki a kofar Wambai* we went to meet the Emir at Wambai gate. 2. Intercept and buy up goods to be resold later for profit: *mata sun tafi su tari ƙwai a hanya* the women have gone out to the road to buy up the eggs being brought in.
tąr̃ą̀ *n.f. and adj.* Nine.
[1]**tàra** *n.f.* Fine (of money): *an ci shi ~r naira biyu* he was fined two Naira.
[2]**tàra** *n.f.* Being mindful of: *ba ya ~r shiga rijiya da baya* he couldn't care less about going backwards into a well.
tarà *v.t.* 1. Collect, gather, assemble. **~ hankali** concentrate. 2. Add up, total.
tąr̃ąfìs *n.m.* Traffic policeman.
tą̀r̃ągù *n.m.* (*pl.* **tą̀r̃ą̀gwai**) Railway truck, coach.
tą̀r̃aktà *n.f.*(*pl.* **tąr̃aktoci**) Tractor.
tą̀rarą̀ *v.i.* Drip.
tąrar̃ (dą̀) *v.t.* (= **tad dą̀** before d.o.) 1. Happen to find, come upon. 2. Overtake, go to meet.
tàrayyà *n.f.* 1. Partnership, amalgamation. 2. Federation: *Jamhuriyar ~r Nijeriya* Federal Republic of Nigeria.
tàrba (į/e) *v.t.* Go out to meet or welcome s.o. (esp. an important person).
tàr̃biyyà *n.f.* Training, education (regarding character).
tar̃dè *n.m.* (*pl.* **tar̃dųnà**) Ring woven of hemp used by Fulani women to carry load on head.
tąrè *v.t.* Block, ward off: *'yan sanda sun ~ mana hanya* the police prevented us from passing.
tàrę *adv.* Together, gathered, collected: *sun zo ~ da 'yan makaranta* they came together with the students.
tarè *v.i.* Move into new dwelling or house: *amarya ta ~ gidan ango* the bride has moved to her husband's house.
tarfà *v.t.* Pour out small quantity, pour out drop by drop.
tarfì *n.m.* Small amount of anything.
targąɗè *n.m.* Sprain, dislocation: *ya yi ~ a ƙafa* he sprained his foot.
tàr̃hô *n.m.* Telephone.
tàri *n.m.* 1. Cough, coughing. 2. General term for lung disease.
tarì *n.m.* Pile, heap, collection. *adv.* In abundance, in great quantity: *akwai kaya a kasuwa ~* there's an abundance of goods in the market; *sau ~* countless times.
tar̃ihì *n.m.* History, biography. **~n kai** autobiography.
tarįya *n.f.* Putting spun thread from small spools onto big spool.
tàrką̀ce *n.pl.* 1. Odds and ends. 2. Belongings, personal property.
tarką̀ta *v.t.* Collect one's scattered articles, luggage, debts. *v.i.* Do one's normal activity, go about one's business: *ya zo ya ~ ya tafi abinsa* he came, did his business and went away.

tarkò *n.m.* (*pl.* **tarkųnà**) Trap.

tarko *v.t.* Bring trouble upon oneself: *ya ~ wa kansa wahala* he invited trouble upon himself.

tar̃nąƙe *v.t.* 1. Hobble horse or donkey by tying a front and back foot together. 2. Incapacitate s.o. (usu. through illness): *ciwon ciki ya ~ shi* he came down with a bad stomach ache.

tàr̃nąƙi *n.m.* Hobbling horse or donkey by tying a front and back foot together.

tar̃nątsa *n.f.* Thunder. *excl.* I swear! By thunder!

tąr̃o *n.m.* (*pl.* **tąr̃àr̃e**) Threepence in old Nigerian currency, equivalent to two and a half kobo.

tàro *n.m.* Meeting, gathering, crowd of people.

tàr̃sąshi *n.m.* Whole group, totality of: *~n ma'aikata sun shiga yajin aiki* all the workers went on strike.

tàr̃tsątsi *n.m.* Sparks (from fire, electrical source, etc.).

taru *n.m.* (*pl.* **tarųnà**) Large fishing-net.

tar̃wąɗa *n.f.* (*pl.* **tąr̃èwąɗi**) African catfish. ***wankan ~*** person of medium dark skin colour.

tar̃wątsa *v.t.* Scatter out, disperse: *'yan sanda sun ~ masu zanga-zanga* the police dispersed the demonstrators.

tàrya *see* **tąra.**

tàr̃zòma *n.f.* Struggle, dispute.

tàsa (shį/she) *v.t.* (*vn.* **tashì**) 1. Raise up, awaken s.o. 2. Start up an engine. 3. Move location of one's place of business: *wasu suna fata za a tashi hedkwatar Nijeriya ta koma Kaduna* certain people are hoping that the capital of Nigeria will be moved to Kaduna. 4. Correct s.o.'s recitation: *na tashe su karatu* I corrected their reading. **tasà** *v.i.* Rise up, grow up: *yarinya ta ɗan ~* the girl has grown up a little.

tasą *pro.m.* (poss.) His (ref. to fem. noun).

tasà *n.f.* (*pl.* **tasoshi**) Metal bowl, basin, or plate.

tasam *v.t.* (with i.o.) 1. Attack: *mun ~ ma ƙasar nan* we attacked that country. 2. Set out for a place: *ya ~ ma gida* he set out for home.

tąshà *n.f.* (*pl.* **tąshoshi**) Station (e.g. railway station, lorry park, harbour).

tàshe *n.m.* 1. Holiday, esp. in Koranic school. 2. Children going from house to house during Ramadan singing and dancing.

tashe *n.m.* Being popular, enjoying sth. ***~n balaga*** proud feelings in young people upon reaching puberty.

tashį *v.i.* 1. Stand up, get up. 2. Awaken, arise. 3. Fly up, fly. 4. Leave, go away. 5. Set out, proceed to: *sun ~ tafiya* they set out on a trip. 6. Rise, rise to, reach: *buhun dawa ya ~ naira goma* the price of a bag of guinea corn has gone up to ten Naira. 7. Become aroused, flare up, break out: *hankalinsa ya ~* he has become angry; *yaƙi ya ~* war has broken out. 8. Become invalid: *magana ta ~* what was said no longer holds.

tasir̃ì *n.m.* 1. Influence, power. 2. Benefit, usefulness.

taskà *n.f.* (*pl.* **taskoki**) 1. Private room of head of household. 2. A safe.

taskįlą *n.m.* Third-class accommodation (usu. on train).

taskù *n.m.* Tyranny, oppression.

tąsono *n.m.* Dried mucus from nose.

tasų *pro.pl.* (poss.) Theirs (ref. to fem. noun).

tàswir̃à *n.f.* (*pl.* **taswir̃or̃i**) 1. Map. 2. Floorplan.

tàta *vn.* of **tacè.**

tatą *pro.f.* (poss.) Hers (ref. to fem. noun).

tàtacce *adj.* (*f.* **tàtaccįya,** *pl.* **tàtàttu**) 1. Filtered. 2. Officially authorized (of news, etc.).

tatàta *n.f.* Baby's first efforts at walking.

tatįke *v.t.* Reduce to poverty (usu. from gambling).

tàtil *id.* Being full after eating or drinking a lot.

tàtsa (į/e) *v.t.* Milk a cow, goat, etc.

tàtsunịya *n.f.* (*pl.* **tatsunịyoyi**) 1. Fable, folktale. 2. Riddle.
tàttą̀ɓą̀-kunnẹ *n.m. or f.* Great-grandchild.
tàttąbą̀ra *see* **tàntąbą̀ra.**
tàttągà (ị/e) *v.t.* Attempt sth. beyond one's ability.
tattą̀ke *v.i.* Become worn out.
tàttąlà (ị/e) *v.t.* Look after, care for.
tattąli *n.m.* Planning for future, thrift: *~n arziki* economics, economy.
tàttàsai *n.m.* Large red peppers.
tattashịya *n.f.* Learning to read in syllables.
tattàuna *v.t.* Discuss, talk over.
tàuhidi *n.m.* Belief in the oneness of God.
tàula *n.f.* Stick with ropes on either end used to carry water buckets.
taunà *v.t.* Chew.
¹**taura** *n.f.* (*pl.* **tauràye**) Woman's plaited hair at temples.
²**taura** *n.f.* Small tree with white flowers and edible fruit.
tàuraro *n.m.* (*f.* **tàurarų̀wa,** *pl.* **tàuràri**) 1. Star. ***~ mai wutsiya*** comet. 2. Star (of entertainment or sports). 3. Winner (of contest).
taurè *n.m.* (*pl.* **tąmàre**) Castrated goat.
tauri *n.m.* 1. Hardness, toughness. ***~n kai*** stubbornness, obstinacy. 2. Charm for making skin resistant to cuts. ***ɗan ~*** person who can draw a knife across his skin without getting cut.
tausà *v.t.* Press down gently: *na ~ tufa a ruwa* I pressed the clothes down into the water. **tàusa (shị/she)** *v.t.* Calm s.o. down by talking gently. *n.f.* Massage.
tàusą̀yi *n.m.* Pity, mercy, sympathy.
tàushe *n.m.* Type of *miya* made with sorrel.
taushè *v.t.* Damage (usu. done by termites).
¹**taushi** *n.m.* Softness.
²**taushi** *n.m.* Bowl-shaped drum, beaten with the fingers.
tautàu *n.m.* 1. Long-legged spider. 2. Skin disease thought to be caused by contact with a spider.
tauyè *v.t.* Hinder, retard: *rashin zuwansu da wuri ya ~ mana aiki* their failure to come on time has slowed down our work.
tauyi *n.m.* Beams laid across walls to support main beams that are shorter than required length.
tàwą *pro.* (poss.) Mine (ref. to fem. noun).
tą̀wąda *n.f.* (*pl.* **tą̀wą̀du**) Ink. ***~r Allah*** mole or small dark part of human skin.
tą̀wakką̀li *n.m.* Leaving oneself in God's hands.
tawayè *n.m.* Rebellion, revolt. ***ɗan ~*** rebel.
tawùl *n.m.* Towel, towelling.
tąyà *v.t.* 1. Make an offer (in bargaining). 2. Assist, help: *na ~ shi aiki* I helped him in his work. 3. Flirt with.
tàya (ị/e) *v.t.* Strip off outer covering (e.g. bark, skin).
tayà *n.f.* (*pl.* **tayoyi**) Tyre.
tayar̃ (dą̀) *v.t.* (= **ta dą̀** before d.o.) 1. Lift, raise. 2. Wake up. 3. Set in motion, start: *ya ~ babur ɗinsa* he started his motorcycle.
tàyi *n.m.* Foetus.
tąząra *n.f.* Some distance away: *ya yi mini 'yar ~ ba na ganinsa* he has moved out of my sight.
tązar̃gą̀dẹ̀ *n.m.* A fragrant, medicinal herb.
¹**tebùr̃** *n.m.* (*pl.* **tebų̀r̃à**) Table.
²**tebùr̃** *n.m.* (*pl.* **tebų̀r̃à**) Shovel.
³**tebùr̃** *n.m.* Long, heavy lorry trailer made completely of iron.
têf *n.m.* 1. Measuring tape. 2. Recording tape. 3. Cinema film.
teki *see* **taiki.**
tèkų *n.f.* Sea, ocean.
telą̀ *n.m.* (*pl.* **teloli**) 1. Tailor. 2 Sewing machine.
tẹlịbịjin *n.f.* Television.
tète *n.m.* First efforts of a child at walking while being held up by the hands.
tî *n.m.* Tea.
tîb *n.m.* Inner tube.
tibi *n.m.* Tuberculosis (T.B.).
tifà *n.f.* (*pl.* **tifofi**) Tipper lorry, dump truck.
¹**tịjar̃à** *n.f.* Trading.
²**tịjar̃à** *n.f.* Public humiliation. ***mai ~*** quick-tempered person.

tik *id.* Sound of heavy thing falling: *dutse ya faɗi* ~ the stone fell down with a thud.

tik *id.* In naked state: *na yi* ~ *sai ta shigo* I was stark naked when she entered.

tịkis *id.* Emphasizes great tiredness.

tịkis-tịkis *id.* Walking in a tired, dragging manner: *mun gan shi yana tafe* ~ we saw him dragging along the road.

tịkịtị *n.m.* (*pl.* **tịkịtoci**) Ticket.

tịƙa *n.f.* Chewing the cud.

tìƙa (ị/e) *v.t.* Give s.o. a thorough beating. **tiƙà** *v.t.* (with i.o.) Thump s.o. on the back.

tilàs *n.f.* Necessity: ~ *ce ta kawo ni nan* it was necessity that brought me here. *adv.* By force, necessarily: ~ *ka zo ka yi wannan aiki* you must come to do this work.

tilàsta *v.t.* (with i.o.) Force s.o. to do sth.

tìlo *n.m.* Just a single one: *ɗan* ~ one and only son.

tìma *n.f.* A sound beating.

tindirmi *n.m.* Elephantiasis of the foot or hand.

tìnjim *id.* In large numbers, in great abundance: *mutane sun taru cikin ɗaki* ~ people have packed the room.

tìnkarà (ị/e) *v.t.* Go towards.

tinkịya *see* **tunkịya.**

tìnƙahò *n.m.* Showing off, putting on airs.

tir̃ *excl.* Expression of annoyance: *ya yi* ~ *da su* he was annoyed with them.

tịrà *v.t.* 1. Dye with material other than indigo, often a pale dye. 2. Re-dye, renew colour. 3. Cause formerly mad person to become mad again.

tịr̃ê *n.m.* Tray.

tịrè *v.t. and v.i.* Provoke, incite.

tịr̃edà *n.m.* Trading in any kind of goods. *ɗan* ~ trader.

tịr̃edì *n.m.* Thread of a screw: *kusa mai* ~ screw.

tịr̃elà *n.f.* (*pl.* **tịr̃eloli**) 1. Trailer of lorry. 2. Child carried on back.

tịrịri *n.m.* Steam.

tirjè *v.t.* 1. Come to a sudden stop. 2. Balk. 3. Disagree.

tìr̃mis *id.* In abundance: *yana da kuɗi* ~ he has loads of money.

tịsà *v.t.* Re-do, repeat an action: *ta nika gero kuma ta* ~ she ground the millet and then reground it.

tis'in *see* **cạsạ'in.**

tìtì *n.m.* (*pl.* **titụnà**) Street.

titisị *n.f.* Teacher Training College.

titse *n.m.* Unexpected intrusion causing embarrassment.

tịtsịye *v.t.* Badger s.o. until he gives in.

tittir̃na *n.m. or f.* Short, squat person or animal.

tịyatà *n.f.* Operating theatre of hospital.

tịyatì *n.m.* Public humiliation.

[1]**tịyà** *n.f.* Bowl of a standard size for measuring out grain.

[2]**tịyà** *n.f.* A score of 'twenty-one' in a card game.

tìzga (ị/e) *v.t.* Pull or pluck out with force (e.g. hair).

tô *excl.* 1. All right, O.K., fine. 2. Then, well then . . .

tocịlàn *n.m.* Torchlight.

tofà *v.t.* Spit.

tofa *n.f.* Elephant grass.

tòfi *n.m.* Lightly spitting on s.o. as a kind of medical treatment performed by a *malam.*

togè *v.t.* Deny, take back one's word: *ya* ~ *maganar da ya yi jiya* he denied what he had said yesterday. *v.i.* Hold back, withdraw: *jaki ya* ~ *ya ƙi tafiya* the donkey held back and refused to budge.

togịya *n.f.* Excuse: *ya ci mushen saniya amma ya kawo* ~ *da cewa yunwa yake ji* he ate the carrion of a cow but excused himself saying that it was because he was hungry.

tògo *see* **togịya.**

toho *v.i.* Sprout, bud (of leaves, hair). **tòho** *n.m.* Buds, newly sprouted leaves, new-grown hair.

tòka *n.f.* Ashes.

tokạra *v.t.* Prop against: *na* ~ *sanda ga tufaniya* I propped a stick against the door.

tokạre *v.t.* 1. Prop sth. up: *na* ~ *tufaniya da sanda* I propped up the door with a stick. 2. Block a doorway.

tòkạ-tòkạ *adj.* Grey.

toljya *n.f.* Tuft of hair or grass, crest of cock.
tôn *n.m.* Ton.
tòna (j/e) *v.t.* (*vn.* **tòno**) Provoke, tease.
tonà *v.t.* (*vn.* **tòno**) Dig up, unearth. ~ ***asiri*** reveal a secret.
tòr̃o *n.m.* Male duck. ~***n giwa*** bull elephant.
toshè *v.t. and v.i.* Stop up (hole, drain, etc.).
toshì *n.m.* Presents given by man to woman to gain favour.
toshįya *n.f.* 1. Bribe. 2. Present given to younger sister or mother of one's sweetheart to gain favour.
totùr̃ *n.m.* Accelerator, throttle.
totų̀wa *n.f.* Pulp of gourds, sugar-cane, maize, etc.
toyà *v.t.* (*vn.f.* **tuyà**) 1. Fry cakes made from a batter (e.g. *waina* or *ƙosai*). 2. Heat up oil or butter. 3. Fire (a pot).
tòyę-tòyę *n.m.* Various kinds of fried cakes.
tòyi *n.m.* Purposely burning sth. such as trash, grass, etc.
tozą̀li *n.m.* Antimony.
tozàr̃ta *v.t.* Treat contemptuously.
tòzar̃tą̀ *v.i.* Be despised.
tozo *n.m.* Hump (e.g. of camel, ox). ~***n kabari*** mound of grave.
tsabà *n.f.* Seed kernels of corn, groundnuts, etc. ~***r kuɗi*** coins.
tsabagè *n.m.* Plentiful quantity: ~*n kuɗi* plenty of cash.
tsabgà *n.f.* (*pl.* **tsabgogi**) Cane used for beating donkeys.
tsą̀bi'à *see* **ɗą̀bi'à.**
tsabtà *n.f.* Cleanliness.
tsabtą̀ce *v.t.* Clean.
tsàbųrà (j/e) *v.t.* Tickle by poking s.o. in the side.
tsàdą *n.f.* Senegal fire-finch (bird).
tsàda *n.f.* Costliness, expensiveness.
tsadà *n.f.* Tree with yellow plum-like fruit.
tsadànce *v.i.* Agree mutually on amount to be paid for doing work.
tsadą̀rakì *n.m.* Type of cobra.
tsą̀dąri *n.m.* Very hard soil that is difficult to farm.
tsaf *id.* Completely and neatly: ~ *da shi* he's neatly dressed.
tsafà *v.t.* Squeeze into a place, squeeze oneself between other people.
tsafì *n.m.* Magic, object containing supernatural spirits.
tsagà *v.t.* 1. Split, crack, rip. 2. Make cut or incision in sth.
tsaga *n.f.* 1. Crack, slit. 2. Marks on face or body which identify person by tribe or profession.
tsągągi *n.m.* Hadada or wood ibis (bird).
tsągàita *v.t. and v.i.* Lessen, decrease.
tsąge *n.m.* Tiger-fish.
tsàge *n.m.* Facial markings.
tsagè *v.i.* Become split, cracked.
tsągèra *n.m. or f.* (*pl.* **tsą̀gèru**) Bad-tempered, quarrelsome person.
tsagì *n.m.* 1. Bits of cloth discarded by tailor. 2. A quarter of a kolanut.
tsągįya *n.f.* Bilharzia (esp. with reference to young boys).
tsai *id.* Still, pensive: *ya tsaya* ~ *yana kallona* he stood still looking at me.
tsàida *see* **tsìdau.**
tsai dą̀ *v.t.* Alt. form of **tsąyar̃ dą̀.**
tsaikò *n.m.* Roof frame for thatched roof.
tsâiwa *n.f.* Plaited string curtain for doorway.
tsaiwa *vn.* of **tsąyà.**
tsąką̀ *adv.* In the middle: *ya zo da rana* ~ he came in the middle of the day; *yana* ~ *da buge-buge* he is right in the midst of the fighting. ***ɗan*** ~ clitoris.
tsąka *n.f.* (*pl.* **tsąkàke**) 1. Small gecko lizard. 2. Unpopular person.
tsą̀kani *n.m.* 1. Interval between two points: *da kogi biyu* ~ there are two rivers in between. 2. Mutual relationship: *ya ɓata* ~*nmu* he spoiled our relationship; *na yi musu* ~ I reconciled them.
tsą̀kanin *prep.* Between: *Kura tana* ~ *Kano da Zariya* Kura lies somewhere between Kano and Zaria; *ya shiga* ~ *ɗa da mahaifi* he came between the father and his son.
tsąkar̃ Alt. *gen.* form of **tsąkįyà:** ~ *rana* = *tsakiyar rana* midday; *ina* ~ *aiki ya shigo* = *ina tsakiyar aiki ya shigo* I was in the midst of

work when he entered. **~ *gida*** *n.f.* Central open area of compound where women work and relax.

tsą̀kà-tsąki *adv.* 1. In the middle of, half-way through. 2. (with **ną/tą**) Of medium size.

tsą̀ki *n.m.* The coarse part of ground flour.

tsàki *n.m.* Sucking noise made with pursed lips to indicate disgust or contempt.

tsąkįyà *n.f.* (*gen.* **tsąkįyàr̃, tsąkar̃**) 1. Middle, centre. 2. Prime, height: *yana ~r kuruciyarsa mota ta take shi* he was in the prime of his youth when he was killed in a car accident.

tsàkįyà *n.f.* Beads of cornelian stone strung into necklaces.

tsàko *n.m.* (*f.* **tsàkųwa**, *pl.* **tsàki**) Usu. used in *ɗan ~* baby chick.

tsàkųrà (į/e) *v.t.* Take a little.

tsąkųwà *n.f.* (*pl.* **tsąkųwoyi**) 1. Small stone. 2. Gravel.

[1]tsąlà *n.m.* *kindirmo* which is thinned with water.

[2]tsąlà *n.m.* Fulani-style trousers with narrow legs and wide, loose top.

tsalà *v.t.* Do much of: *an ~ ruwa jiya* it rained heavily yesterday.

tsallą̀ka *v.t.* Cross, go from one side to the other.

tsallą̀ke *v.t.* 1. Jump over. 2. Omit, skip: *ka ~ sunana* you have skipped my name.

tsalle *n.m.* (*pl.* **tsàllę-tsàllę**) Jumping.

tsam *id.* Sudden movement upward: *ya tashi ~* he got up suddenly.

tsamà *n.m.* Indirectly preventing s.o. from getting what he wants from s.o. else.

tsamari *n.m.* Increase of intensity, quantity: *matsalar wasa ta yi ~* the game turned into a very serious affair.

tsàmbam *id.* In abundance, full up (usu. of money): *na cika jakata da kuɗi ~* I stuffed my bag full of money.

tsàmbą̀re *see* **tsùmbų̀re.**

tsamè *v.t.* Pick from, withdraw from: *ya ~ Audu daga halaka* he saved Audu from danger. *v.i.* Withdraw, keep aloof.

tsami *n.m.* 1. Sourness, acid taste. 2. Soreness of body from hard work or being beaten. 3. Tingling sensation in limbs. **~n *baki*** mispronouncing certain sounds (by children or characters in folktales).

[1]tsamįya *n.f.* (*pl.* **tsamįyoyi**) Tamarind tree or fruit.

[2]tsamįya *n.f.* Brown and white striped cloth.

tsą̀mmanì *n.m.* 1. Thought, thinking: *ina ~ na san shi* I think I know him. 2. Expectation: *ina ~n zuwansa* I'm expecting him to come.

tsąmo-tsą̀mò *id.* Dripping wet, soaked through and through.

tsą̀na (į/e) *v.t.* Dislike, hate.

tsą̀nàkę *adv.* (with **ą̀**) Slowly but surely.

tsąnąni *n.m.* 1. Extreme, severe condition: *an yi yaki mai ~* they waged a terrible war; *ana cikin ~n yunwa* there is great famine around. 2. Sternness, strictness.

tsąnànta *v.t.* 1. Recommend, urge: *an ~ mu zo aiki a kan kari* we were strongly urged to come on time. 2. (with i.o.) Harass, aggravate. **tsą̀nantą̀** *v.i.* Become severe, serious.

tsandauri *n.m.* Barren place where soil is very hard.

tsando *n.m.* Usu. used in *ƙudan ~* tsetse fly.

tsąnè *v.i.* Become partially dry.

tsàngąyà *n.f.* Large congregation of malams and students gathered in area away from town for study of the Koran.

tsanì *n.m.* (*pl.* **tsanųkà**) Ladder.

tsantsa *n.f.* Pure state, all and only: *zinariya ~* pure gold; *'yammata ~* only girls.

tsan tsan *id.* Firmly, securely, cautiously.

tsàntsànì *n.m.* Aversion to filth.

tsanwa *n.f.* Green colour.

tsànwakà *n.f.* Senegal roller (bird).

tsanyà *n.f.* (*pl.* **tsanyoyi**) Small cricket.

tsarà *v.t.* (*vn.* **tsarì**) 1. Arrange,

line up, organize. 2. Compose, arrange (of song or poem). 3. Edit.

tsara *n.m. or f.* (*pl.* **tsaràrrąki**) Age-mate, contemporary, one's equal.

tsąràbà *n.f.* (*pl.* **tsąrąbobi**) Souvenir or small present given by s.o. returning from a journey.

tsàràṅce *n.m.* Fondling between boys and girls.

tsąrè *v.t.* 1. Guard, protect. 2. Imprison, confine. 3. Block, obstruct: *mota ta ~ hanya* the car is blocking the road.

tsàr̃ga (į/e) *v.t.* Ostracize, discriminate against s.o.

tsar̃gè *v.t.* Slit.

tsąrì *n.m.* 1. Putting women in purdah: *matan ~ ba sa fita* women in purdah do not go out. 2. Confinement, imprisonment.

tsàri *n.m.* Water in which corn with bran removed has been soaked (often given to animals to drink).

tsari *n.m.* (*pl.* **tsàrę-tsàrę**) Arrangement, composition, plan, organization.

tsarkàka *v.t.* Purify, cleanse.

tsarki *n.m.* Cleanliness, purity. ***Littafi Mai*** ~ the Holy Bible.

tsàr̃nu *n.pl.* Poles (e.g. for making fence posts).

tsàro *n.m.* Defence, protection: *~n kasa* military defenses.

tsar̃tà *v.t.* Spit out (saliva or water) in a thin stream.

tsatsà *n.f.* Rust.

tsątsò *n.m.* Waist.

tsatsò *n.m.* Earwig.

tsattsąfa *n.f.* Fried sweet cake made of millet, rice, or wheat flour.

tsattsąfi *n.m.* Light rain, drizzle.

tsàttsągà (į/e) *v.t.* Peck continuously (by chickens).

tsattsàga *v.t.* Tap down, shake down (contents of a filled sack).

tsâttsewà *n.f.* Swallow, swift (bird).

tsaunì *n.m.* (*pl.* **tsaunųkà**) Hill.

tsauràra *v.t.* Pull taut (e.g. bowstring or rope). **tsàurąrą̀** *v.i.* Be pulled taut.

tsaure *n.m.* A tall, coarse grass used for making *zana* mats.

tsauri *n.m.* 1. Dry hardness of ground. 2. Hardness of a subject. 3. Stinginess. 4. Tautness, tightness (e.g. of thread or rope). ***yi*** ~. be stunted. ***~n ido*** insolence.

tsàutsàyi *n.m.* Accident involving physical injury or financial loss.

tsawa *n.f.* 1. Thunderclap. 2. Shouting at or scolding in a loud voice.

tsąwàita *v.t.* Lengthen, drag. **tsàwaitą̀** *v.i.* Become lengthened.

tsawàta *v.t.* (with i.o.) Give scolding or warning.

tsąwo *n.m.* Length, height.

tsąyà *v.i.* (*vn.f.* **tsaiwa**) 1. Stop, stand in place, wait. 2. Be limited to, come to an end: *ilminsa ya ~ a firamare kawai* his education stopped at primary school. 3. Persist, persevere: *ya ~ kan karatu* he kept at his studies. 4. (with i.o.) Give guarantee for, stand behind. ***wata ya*** ~ the new moon has appeared.

tsąyar̃ (dą̀) *v.t.* (= **tsai dą̀** before d.o.) 1. Bring to a stop. 2. Cause to wait, stay in one place. 3. Establish, set up: *an ~ da doka a kan shan kwaya* a law has been passed with regard to drug-taking.

tsàyayyà *n.f.* Perseverance, steadfastness.

tsàyę *adv.* In a standing position, stationary. ***ya ta da zaune*** ~ he caused an uproar; ***tashi*** ~ be persistent, persevere: ***mun tashi*** ~ *kan aikinmu* we persevered in our work; ***yi*** ~ stand fast, insist: *ya yi ~ sai mu yi* he insisted that we do it; ***kai*** ~ at once, without delay.

tsąyì *see* **tsąwo.**

tsefè *v.t.* (*vn.f.* **tsifà**) Comb out hair in preparation for plaiting.

tsegùmi *n.m.* Gossip, talking about s.o. behind his back.

tserar̃ (dą̀) *v.t.* Rescue, save.

tserę *n.m.* Race, contest.

tserè *v.i.* 1. Escape, flee. 2. (with i.o.) Outstrip, surpass.

tsįbà *v.t.* (*vn.* **tsįbì**) Pile up.

tsįbì *n.m.* 1. Pile, heap. 2. *vn.* of **tsįbà.**

tsįbìrce *v.i.* Sit by oneself.

tsįbįri *n.m.* (*pl.* **tsįbįrai**) Island

tsidau *n.m.* Thorny weed.

tsịdik *id.* Happening suddenly, unexpectedly: *ya faɗo* ~ *a cikin ɗaki* he suddenly came into the room.
tsifà *vn.* of **tsefè.**
tsiga (ị/e) *v.t.* Pull out (e.g. hair, burrs).
tsigè *v.t.* (with i.o.) Abuse s.o.
tsigi *n.m.* Warbler, lark (bird).
tsigigi *id.* Very small and thin.
tsikà *n.f.* Prickly spike on grasses. ***~r jikina ta tashi*** my hair stood on end.
tsikąrà (ị/e) *v.t.* Tickle s.o.'s sides.
tsilą *n.f.* Tapeworm.
tsịlum *id.* Sound of small object falling into water.
tsịmà *v.t.* (*vn.* **tsịmì**) Soak, steep, infuse. **tsịmą** *v.i.* Become soaked infused.
tsima *n.f.* Trembling, shivering.
tsịme *n.m.* Ink made by soaking *bagaruwa* pods.
tsịmì *n.m.* 1. Medicinal concoction of soaked herbs. 2. *vn.* of **tsịmà.**
tsịmi *n.m.* Thrift, economizing, placing in reserve: *ina ~n hatsi don baɗi* I'm keeping a reserve of corn for next year.
tsìna (ị/e) *v.t.* Select or pick out separately, one by one.
tsìndùm *id.* Sound of medium-size object falling into water.
tsìngarò *n.m.* (*pl.* **tsìngàru**) Small piece of broken pottery.
tsìni *n.m.* (*pl.* **tsininnụkà**) Sharp point.
tsìnka (ị/e) *v.t.* Pick, pluck off (fruit, leaves, etc.). **tsinkà** *v.t.* Break, snap in two (of rope, thread, wire).
tsìnkayà (ị/e) *v.t.* See s.o. vaguely in the distance. 2. Foresee (through experience rather than by magic).
tsinkè *v.t.* 1. Pluck (fruit), break off, snap off. *v.i.* 1. Break or snap loose. 2. Escape (of tied-up animal).
tsinke *n.m.* (*pl.* **tsinkàye**) 1. Piece of dry grass. 2. Thin stick: *~n ashana* matchstick. 3. Skewer. 4. A goad: *an yi masa* ~ s.o. poked him.
tsìnta (cị/ce) *v.t.* Pick up sth. by chance, chance upon sth.
tsinta *n.f.* Inferior kolanuts set aside.
tsintsịya *n.f.* (*pl.* **tsintsịyoyi**) Broom.
tsintụwa *n.f.* A lucky find.
tsịrą *v.i.* Sprout, germinate.
tsịra (ị/e) *v.t.* Be first to introduce or initiate sth.: *wa ya tsiri rubutun Hausa da boko?* who was the first to write Hausa in Roman script?
tsirą *v.i.* Escape, get away safely.
tsira *n.f.* Salvation, escape. ***gidan*** ~ the Next World.
tsirà *v.t.* Pile up.
tsịràita *v.t.* Strip clothes off. **tsịraitą̀** *v.i.* Be naked.
tsịrarà *n.f.* Nakedness: *na ga wani mahaukaci ~ da shi* I saw a stark-naked madman.
tsịràri *n.m.* Small amount or number of sth.
tsirè *v.t.* Impale, pierce (e.g. with spear or skewer). **tsìre** *n.m.* Pieces of skewered meat stuck into ash mound and cooked close to the fire.
tsịrę-tsịrę *pl.* of **tsịrò.**
tsirgagịya *n.f.* Hard part of a stalk surrounding the pulp.
tsirì *n.m.* Large pile, heap.
tsiri *n.m.* Rising high (e.g. of water or fire).
tsir̃ir̃i *id.* Describes protuberant belly of s.o. suffering from malnutrition.
tsịr̃it *id.* Tiny: *ɗan yaro ne* ~ he's a tiny little boy.
tsirkịya *n.f.* 1. Bowstring. 2. String of musical instrument.
tsịrò *n.m.* (*pl.* **tsịrę-tsịrę**) 1. Sprout, shoot. 2. (in *pl.* only) Plants.
tsit *id.* In complete silence.
tsittsịgè *n.m.* (*pl.* **tsịgàtsịgai**) Small stump of tree.
tsiwà *n.f.* (*pl.* **tsiwącę-tsiwącę**) Insolence, arrogance, lack of humility
tsịya *n.f.* 1. Destitution, poverty. 2. Quarrelsomeness.
tsịyàta *v.t.* Impoverish **tsịyatą̀** *v.i.* Become poor.
tsịya-tsịyà *n.f.* Mutual disagreement, argument: *sai mun yi ~ da*

shi kafin ya biya mu we'll have to fight with him before he'll pay us. *id.* In destitute condition.

tsi̧yàya *v.t.* Pour out liquid in thin stream. **tsi̧yayà̧** *v.i.* Come out in thin stream.

tsoho *n. and adj.* (*f.* **tsohu̧wa,** *pl.* **tsòfàffi**) 1. Old (person or thing). 2. Father, mother: *~na* my father; *tsohuwata* my mother.

tsokà *n.f.* (*pl.* **tsokoki**) 1. Muscle. ***mai*** **~** substantial, abundant. 2. Piece of meat other than entrails. 3. Flesh or edible part of fruit around the seed.

tsòkà̧nà (i̧/e) *v.t.* Tease, provoke s.o. **tsokà̧na** *v.t.* (with i.o.) Poke s.o. with sth.: *na ~ masa tsinke a ido* I poked him in the eye with a piece of dried grass.

tsokà̧ne *v.t.* Poke, prod s.o.

tsòlolò *n.m.* (*f.* **tsòlolù̧wa**) Tall, thin person. **tsòlòlò** *id.* Very tall and thin.

tsomà *v.t.* Dip into liquid, soak. **~ *baki*, ~ *hannu*** interfere, poke one's nose into s.o.'s affairs.

tsomì *n.m.* Dipping thin layer of meat into crushed groundnuts or *kulikuli* to make *kilishi*.

tsonè *v.t.* Poke, prod s.o.

tsòr̨atà (ci̧/ce) *v.t.* Fear sth.: *ya tsoraci ɓacin ran ubansa* he feared his father's wrath. **tsòr̨atà̧** *v.i.* Be afraid, get scared. **tsorà̧ta** *v.t.* Frighten s.o.

tsòro *n.m.* (*pl.* **tsòrà̧cę-tsòrà̧cę**) Fear, apprehension.

tsor̃o *n.m.* 1. Bun or plait of hair. 2. Bird's crest. 3. Cock's comb.

tsor̃or̃u̧wa *n.f.* Summit, apex, top.

tsòtsa (i̧/e) *v.t.* Suck.

tsotsè *v.i.* Become thin, emaciated.

tsubbù̧ *n.m.* Magic, sorcery.

tsududu *id.* Emphasizes narrowness (e.g. of doorway or neck of pot).

tsufa̧ *v.i.* Become old, aged.

tsugà *v.t.* Pour out in great quantity: *ana ~ ruwa kamar da bakin ƙwarya* the rain is coming down in buckets.

tsu̧gul *id.* Very short.

tsu̧gù̧na *v.i.* 1. Squat on heels. 2. Relieve oneself.

tsu̧gu̧nar̃ (dà̧) *v.t.* 1. Make s.o. squat down. 2. Impoverish s.o. by taking away his means of livelihood.

tsù̧gù̧no *n.m.* Squatting position.

tsukè *v.t. and v.i.* Draw together, tighten with drawstrings. **~ *baki*** purse one's lips.

tsu̧kù *n.m.* 1. Crunching sound. 2. Pangs.

[1]**tsulà** *v.t.* Pour out great quantity of liquid.

[2]**tsulà** *n.f.* A small yellowish monkey.

[3]**tsulà** *n.f.* A one-seater motorbike.

tsuli̧ya *n.f.* (*pl.* **tsuli̧yoyi**) Anus.

tsu̧lu̧lu̧ *id.* Overly diluted with water: *nono ya yi ~* the milk is too watery.

tsu̧magi̧ya, tsu̧mangi̧ya *n.f.* (*pl.* **tsu̧magi̧yoyi**) Stick, cane, switch.

tsù̧mammi̧ya *n.f.* 1. Thing which has been soaked. 2. Rankling dislike.

tsù̧mayà (i̧/e) *v.t.* Wait for.

tsumbù̧re *v.i.* Be incompletely developed, stunted. **tsùmbù̧re** *n.m.* Work done carelessly, incompletely.

tsûmma *n.m.* (*pl.* **tsummok̨arà, tsummoki**) 1. Rag. 2. Prostitute.

tsu̧mulmu̧la *n.f.* Stinginess.

tsuntsu *n.m.* (*f.* **tsuntsu̧wa,** *pl.* **tsuntsàye**) Bird.

tsur̃a *n.m.* 1. Handleless knife. 2. Being alone and empty-handed: *ya zo ~nsa* he came without bag or baggage.

tsu̧ru-tsù̧rù *id.* Acting in uneasy manner from shame or fear.

[1]**tsutsà** *n.f.* (*pl.* **tsutsotsi**) Worm, maggot, caterpillar.

[2]**tsutsà** *n.f.* Putting perfume on cotton to apply to children.

tsuwwà *n.f.* Squeaking of small rodents.

tuba̧ *v.i.* Be sorry, repentent.

tubà̧li *n.m.* (*pl.* **tuba̧là**) Brick.

tù̧bani *n.m.* A food made from bean flour.

tù̧bar̃kallà *excl.* God be praised! Bravo!

tu̧bù̧ra *n.f.* Inner stomach of animal.

tu̧bu̧r̃àn *id.* Complete state of

madness: *mahaukaci ne* ~ he's a raving madman.

tuɓè *v.t.* 1. Take off clothes. 2. Depose.

tụɓuȓ-tụ̀ɓùȓ *id.* Shaking of large buttocks.

tụdù *n.m.* (*pl.* **tùddai**) 1. High ground, hill. 2. Dry land, river bank.

tụfà *n.f.* (*pl.* **tụfafì**) Garment, article of clothing.

tụfanịya *n.f.* *Zana*-like mat used for covering doorway.

tufkà *v.t.* Braid, twist into rope. **tùfka** *n.f.* 1. Braiding (of rope). 2. Strand, ply: *igiya mai* ~ *biyu* two-ply rope.

tuǥè *v.t.* Uproot, pull out by roots.

tụ̀hụmà *n.f.* (*pl.* **tụ̀hùmcẹ-tụ̀hùmcẹ**) 1. Suspicion. 2. Interrogation (of suspect).

tụ̀humtà (cị/ce) *v.t.* 1. Suspect. 2. Interrogate a suspect.

[1]**tujè** *v.t.* Scrape from surface (hair from hide, weeds from ground, etc.).

[2]**tujè** *n.m.* Bustard.

tuji *n.m.* A wild grass.

tukku *n.m.* (*pl.* **tukkàye**) 1. Braid or bun (of hair). 2. Cock's comb, bird's crest. 3. Tassle, plume of hat or helmet.

tụkụ̀ba *n.f.* (*pl.* **tụkụbobi**) Mound where *tsire* is roasted.

tụ̀kụɗi *n.m.* Drink made for a marriage celebration from millet, spices, and honey or milk.

tụkuf-tụkuf *id.* Very old (of person).

tụ̀kụ̀nạ, tụ̀kùn *adv.* 1. Not yet: *ba su zo ba* ~ they haven't come yet; *ya tafi?* ~ has he gone? Not yet. 2. (with **sai** at beginning of clause) Only after, not until: *sai da suka tashi* ~ *muka huta* it was only after they left that we rested; *ba zan je ba sai na gama* ~ I won't go until I've finished. 3. First, before (with following clause understood): *bari mu duba* ~ let's look first.

tụkunya *n.f.* (*pl.* **tụkwàne**) Cooking pot.

tụkụ̀ȓi *n.m.* Group recitation from memory of whole sections of the Koran.

tụkurwa *n.f.* (*pl.* **tụkurwoyi**) Raffia palm tree whose branches are used in roofing and making biers.

tụkwicì *n.m.* Small gift, esp. of money, given to person bringing a present from s.o. else.

tuƙà *v.t.* (*vn.* **tuƙì**) 1. Stir sth. thick (e.g. *tuwo* or indigo). 2. Propel or drive (e.g. boat, bicycle, car). *v.i.* Have sharp pain in the stomach. **tùƙa** *n.f.* Abdominal pains.

tụƙụ̀rụ *id.* Great amount: *suna karatu* ~ they are doing a lot of reading.

tụlà *v.t.* Pile up (earth, goods, etc.). ~ ***ƙasa*** behave obsequiously.

tụlì *n.m.* 1. Heap, crowd. 2. In abundance: *ga su can* ~ there they are in a large crowd.

tullụwa *n.f.* Summit (of mountain, building).

tùlu *n.m.* (*pl.* **tulụnà**) Earthenware water jar with narrow mouth.

tum *id.* Completely: *ya kawo mini kuɗina* ~ he brought me all my money.

tụ̀mạ *v.i.* Jump.

[1]**tụmà** *v.t.* Prepare young millet for eating by roasting and picking off grains.

[2]**tụmà** *n.m.* Country bumpkin.

tụmaki *pl.* of **tunkịya.**

tụmàƙạsà *n.f.* Crotcheted cover used to keep dishes of food warm.

tụmamì *n.m.* Jumping, bouncing up and down.

tụ̀matiȓ *n.m.* Tomato.

tumbạ̀tse *v.i.* Overflow.

tùmbi *n.m.* (*pl.* **tumbụnà**) 1. Stomach. 2. Pot-belly (of stout person).

tumbi *n.m.* (*pl.* **tumbàye**) Partially filled container (bag, pot, bottle, etc.).

tumɓụ̀ke *v.t.* 1. Uproot. 2. Depose.

tùmfafịya *n.f.* Shrub with white sap, broad leaves, and round hollow fruit.

tùntùm *n.m.* Hassock, pouf. *id.* Stuffed full.

tụmù *n.m.* Heads of newly ripened millet.

tụmuȓ *id.* Firm, filled out: *tuwo ya yi* ~ the *tuwo* is firm.

tun *conj. and prep.* 1. Since, ever since, beginning from: ~ *da safe ya fita* he has been out since morning; ~ *da suka tafi ba su dawo ba har yanzu* they haven't come back since they left; ~ *yanzu* since just recently. 2. Ago: *ya dawo* ~ *kwana biyu* he returned two days ago. 3. While, during: ~ *tana ƙarama aka yi mata aure* she was married while she was still very young; *na ɗauki hotonsa* ~ *wancan taron* I took his picture during that meeting. 4. Used in ~ *da yake* since, in view of the fact that: ~ *da yake ba ka riga ka gaya masa ba, sai ka fasa* since you haven't told him yet, you might as well leave the matter alone. 5. (with neg. past or **kàfin**) Before: *na gama aiki* ~ *ba ka zo ba* = *na gama aiki* ~ *kafin ka zo* I finished the work before you came; ~ *kafin su dawo na cinye shi* I had eaten it up before they returned. 6. (with neg.) Especially: *yana son su,* ~ *ba Kande ba* he likes them, especially Kande.

tụnà *v.t.* 1. (usu. with **dạ̀**) Remember. 2. (with i.o.) Remind.

tụ̀nàni *n.m.* 1. Thinking, reflecting. 2. Apprehension: *abin da nake* ~ *kada a kama ni* what I fear is that they might catch me.

tunga *n.f.* Stubbornness.

tungụ̀me *v.t.* Tie securely (e.g. of criminal under arrest, cow in preparation for slaughter).

tụ̀nị *adv.* Long ago: ~ *ya tafi ai* he's been gone for a long time. *tun* ~ long, long ago.

tụni *n.m.* Reminder.

tùnjere *n.m.* Syphilis.

tunkịya *n.f.* (*pl.* **tụmaki**) Sheep, ewe.

tùnku *n.m.* (*pl.* **tunkụnà**) Mongoose.

tunkụ̀ɗa *v.t.* Push aside.

tùnkụyà (ị/e) *v.t.* Butt, gore (by horned animal).

tùnkụ̀yau *n.m.* Flea(s).

tùnkuzà *n.f.* Residue after oil has been extracted from groundnuts, used for *kulikuli*.

tùnƙas-tùnƙas *id.* Very slow movement of walking.

tuntsụ̀ra *v.t.* Tip over, cause to topple over.

tuntu *n.m.* (*pl.* **tuntàye**) Tassel or knob on top of cap or crown.

tùntụɓà (ị/e) *v.t.* Inquire into, seek opinion.

tuntụɓè *n.m.* Stumbling. ~*n alƙalami* skipping a letter or word in writing. ~*n harshe* slip of the tongue.

tuntụmi *n.m.* Hadada ibis (bird).

tùntụzù *n.m.* Thick cluster or bunch: *gonarsa ta yi* ~ *da ciyawa* his farm is thick with grass.

tùnzụrạ̀ *v.i.* 1. Become angry. 2. Be alarmed, frightened. **tunzụ̀ra** *v.t.* Incite: *an* ~ *ma'aikata su yi yajin aiki* the workers were incited to strike.

tùra *n.f.* Being pushed to the extreme: ~ *ta kai bango* the limit has been reached.

turà *v.t.* 1. Push. ~ *wuta* push unburned part of wood into fire. 2. Send s.o. *v.i.* Be well-advanced, in progress: *aikinmu ya* ~ our work is well-advanced.

tụ̀raka *n.f.* Householder's room.

tur̃anci *n.m.* English language.

tụ̀ràre *n.m.* Perfume, scent. ~*n wuta* incense.

tụ̀rarre *n. and adj.* (*f.* **tụ̀rarrịya**, *pl.* **tụ̀ràrru**) Mad, stubborn, difficult.

tùr̃àwa *pl.* of **bạ̀tur̃è.**

turbà *n.f.* Road, track, path, lane.

turbụ̀ɗa *v.t.* Put or thrust sth. into a powdery substance (e.g. ashes, flour, or sand).

tùr̃ɓaya *n.f.* Fine, sandy soil.

tùre *n.m.* Fodder left by animals, usu. mixed with manure and carried off for fertilizer.

turè *v.t.* 1. Knock or push over, knock down. 2. Depose.

turka *n.f.* Keeping and fattening an animal for slaughter.

turkè *v.t.* 1. Tether an animal or person. 2. Curtail s.o.'s movements, tie s.o. down: *aiki ya* ~ *shi a ofis* he's tied down with work at the office. 3. Expose s.o. as having lied about sth. *n.m.* 1. (*pl.* **tụràka**) Tethering post, stake. 2. A children's game.

[1]turmi *n.m.*(*pl.* **tụràme**) 1. Mortar. 2. Molar tooth.

[2]turmi *n.m.* (*pl.* **tụràme**) Six-yard bolt of printed cloth.

turmụ̀sa *v.t.* 1. Make clothing dirty by sitting on ground, kicking dirt on it, etc. 2. Throw to the ground.

tur̃nịƙe *v.i.* Become thick (of smoke, dust, haze, etc.). 2. Quarrel violently.

tụ̀r̃ozà *n.m.* Western-style trousers.

turù *n.m.* Wooden stocks for restraining mad person.

[1]turu *n.m.* (*pl.* **turàye**) 1. Drum similar to *kalangu* but played between the legs. 2. Small drum made by children from gourd or neck of old water jug.

[2]turu *n.m.* Rebellion against authority. **~n bashi** refusal to pay debts.

tụ̀rumbà *n.f.* (*pl.* **tụrumbobi**) Small oil can (for sewing-machine oil).

tụ̀rụ̀ri *see* **tịrịri.**

tụ̀rurụwa *n.f.* A large black ant.

turzà *v.i.* Exert one's utmost efforts: *ya ~ yi ci jarrabawa* he exerted every effort to pass the examination.

tusạ̀ *n.f.* Fart, breaking wind.

tushè *n.m.* 1. Shoot of young plant. 2. Base, trunk (of tree). 3. Foundation, basis: *noma shi ne tushen arzikinmu* farming is the basis of our wealth. 4. Origin, source: *yana binciken ~n wannan jita-jita* he is looking into the source of this rumour.

tushịya *n.f.* (*pl.* **tushịyoyi**) Stump of millet or guinea-corn.

tutà *n.f.* (*pl.* **tutoci**) Flag, banner.

tutịyà *n.f.* Showing off, esp. with sth. which doesn't belong to one.

tutsu *n.m.* Bucking by donkey, horse, etc.

tutù *n.m.* Human excrement.

tụ̀tur̃ *adv.* Forever, always.

tụwo *n.m.* Staple food made from rice or flour of millet, guinea-corn etc. which is cooked in boiling water and stirred until thick.

tuyà *vn.* of **toyà.**

tụ̀zuru *n.m.* (*pl.* **tụ̀zùrai**) Bachelor, person who has never married.

U

ụ̀ba *n.m.* (*pl.* **ụ̀bànni**) 1. Father. 2. Head, leader, patron: *~n ɗaki* master, patron of praise-singer; *~n gida* head of household.

ụ̀bakạ̀ *excl.* Damn you!

Ụ̀bangịjì *n.m.* The Lord God.

udạ̀ *n.m.* Black and white sheep.

ufè *v.i.* Run away quickly, disappear.

uffàn Used in *bai ce ~ ba* he didn't utter a single word.

ụjịla *n.f.* Itinerant trading usu. done on donkeys.

ụkụ̀ *n.f. and adj.* Three. ***shiga ~*** be in a dilemma.

ụ̀ƙubà *n.f.* Misery, anguish.

ulụ̀ *n.m.* Wool, woollen thread.

ụ̀màr̃ni *see* **ụ̀mùr̃ni.**

ụ̀mar̃tà (cị/ce) *v.t.* Order, command.

umr̃a *n.f.* The Lesser Hajj.

ụ̀mùr̃ni *n.m.* Command, order, instructions.

ùngọ *excl.* Here you are! Here it is! Take it!

ùngozòmạ̀ *n.f.* Midwife.

ùngụ̀lụ *n.f.* (*pl.* **ùngụ̀làye**) Vulture. ***jirgi mai saukar ~*** helicopter.

ùngụwa *n.f.* (*pl.* **ungụwoyi**) Quarter of a town, town ward. ***za ni ~*** I'm going out visiting.

ụshịr̃a *n.f.* One-tenth of settlement paid as fee to court in property cases.

ụshịr̃i *n.m.* One-tenth.

ɣsùr̃ *n.m.* Metal whistle.
ɣwa *n.f.* (*pl.* **ịyàye**) 1. Mother. 2. (in compounds) Largest part or most important member of sth.: **~r** *makera* anvil; **~r** *riga* body of gown; **~r** *soro* senior concubine of chief; **~r** *tukunya* body of pot; **~r** *yaki* commander-in-chief.
ɣwaką̀ *excl.* Damn you!
ɣwar̃gịda *n.f.* 1. Senior wife. 2. Respectful form of address to any woman.
ɣzɣ̀r̃i *n.m.* Excuse.

W

wą̀ To, for (independent form of i.o. marker): *shi ne na gaya* ~ he is the one I told it to; *ta dafa* ~ *'ya'yanta abinci* she cooked food for her children.
wâ *n.m.* (*pl.* **yayye, yayu**) 1. Elder brother. 2. Any male of the same age or status as one's elder brother.
wà *inter. pro.* (*pl.* **sų wà**) Who? Whom?: ~ *ya kawo bauca?* who brought the voucher? ~ *suka biya?* whom did they pay?
wą'ą̀di *n.m.* Promise.
wą'ą̀zi *n.m.* 1. Preaching, sermon. 2. Warning, admonition.
wabì *n.m.* Frequent death in infancy of a woman's children. ***ɗan*** ~ child whose elder brothers and sisters died young.
waccàn *f.* of **wancàn.**
wàcce *f.* of **wànne.**
waccę̀ *f.* of **wandą̀.**
wą̀cę̀ *f.* of **wą̀nę̀.**
wàce cè *f.* of **wàne nè.**
wą̀da *n.f.* Wealth. **~r** ***zuci*** contentment.
wàda *n.m. or f.* Dwarf.
waddą̀ *f.* of **wandą̀.**
wądai *excl.* Used in *Allah* ~ damn it!
wą̀datà (cị/ce) *v.t.* Suffice s.o. *n.f.* Wealth. **wą̀datą̀** *v.i.* 1. Become rich. 2. Suffice, be enough, have enough. **wądàta** *v.t.* Enrich.
wąɗàncân *pl.* of **wancàn.**
wąɗàndą̀ *pl.* of **wandą̀.**
wąɗànnân *pl.* of **wannàn.**
wą̀ɗànnę̀ *pl.* of **wą̀nę̀.**
wą̀ɗànne *pl.* of **wànne.**
wąɗansų *pl.* of **wąnị.**
wąɗą̀ri *n.m.* Arranging thread in required lengths for weaving.
waga *n.m.* (*pl.* **wagàge**) 1. Pair of (hide) bags for carrying goods on pack animal, motorcycle, etc. 2. Grass bag for packing kolanuts.
wagɣ̀nɣ̀ *n.m.* (*pl.* **wagɣnoni**) Railway wagon, coach.
wąhà *n.f.* Playing in water. ***wurin*** ~ swimming pool.
wą̀hąlà *n.f.* Trouble, suffering, inconvenience.
wâi *excl.* 1. (always repeated) Expression on feeling slight pain (from burn, sting, etc.). 2. Oh, I mean . . ., what I meant to say was . . .
[1]**wai** *excl.* Fancy that! My word!
[2]**wai** 1. They say, it is said that: ~ *mutanen Amirka sun tafi duniyar wata* they say that the Americans have gone to the moon. ***ba*** ~ there's no doubt about it! 2. Known as, called: *akwai wani* ~ *shi Audu* there is someone named Audu. 3. (after verbs of saying, hearing, etc.) That: *an ce* ~ *su zo* they are asked to come. 4. In order to: *ya zo* ~ *yana son ganinka* he came in order to see you.
waigà *v.t.* Turn head around to look.
waigì, waijì *n.m.* Wedge, piece of wood used to block sth. from moving.
wàina *n.f.* Fried cake made from rice, millet, or guinea-corn flour. ***juyin*** ~ coup, overthrow of government.

waiwai *n.m.* Gossip, rumour.
wàiwạyà (ị/e) *v.t.* Turn to, refer to s.o. about sth.: *na waiwaye shi da zancen tafiya* I turned to ask him about the trip. **waiwạ̀ya** *v.i.* Turn head to look.
wàiwạ̀ye *n.m.* 1. Turning head around to look. 2. Allusion (literary).
wạ̀jạbạ̀ *v.i.* Be necessary, compulsory.
wạjàbta *v.t.* Make compulsory, essential: *an ~ wa kowa neman ilmi* everyone is duty-bound to be educated.
wạje *n.m.* (*pl.* **wạjèje**) Side, place, direction, vicinity: *sun koma ~ ɗaya* they went off to one side; *ya tafi ~n Bala* he went to Bala's place; *na gan shi ~n kasuwa* I saw him in the vicinity of the market.
wạ̀jẹ *adv.* Outside: *sun fita ~* they went outside.
wạjen *prep.* 1. To, towards: *ya yi ~ Zariya* he went towards Zaria. 2. About, approximately: *~ ƙarfe biyu* about two o'clock. 3. With, at: *yana ~ Bala* it is with Bala.
wajịbi *n.m.* (*pl.* **wàjịbai**) Sth. necessary, compulsory: *~ne mutum ya ci da iyalinsa* a man must look after the needs of his family.
wạ̀jịya *n.f.* Meat which has layers of fat.
wake *n.m.* Beans. ***~n turawa*** peas.
wạ̀kili *n.m.* (*pl.* **wạ̀kilai**) 1. Representative, agent. 2. Member of legislature.
wạkilta *v.t.* Appoint s.o. as one's representative.
wạ̀kịyà *n.f.* (*pl.* **wạkịyoyi**) Small perfume bottle.
waƙà *n.f.* (*pl.* **waƙoƙi, wàƙẹ-wàƙẹ**) Song, poem.
wạƙạ̀fi *n.m.* 1. Detention on remand. 2. Pause, comma (in speech or writing).
wàƙe *n.m.* (*pl.* **waƙoƙi**) Religious song, poem.
walà *v.i.* Be at ease, relax.
wạlạ̀'allạ̀ *adv.* Perhaps.
wạ̀lạ̀ha *n.f.* Time of day from about 8 a.m. to 9 a.m.
wạ̀la-wạ̀la *n.f.* 1. A card trick involving gambling. 2. Playing a trick on s.o.
wạ̀lî *see* **wạ̀lịyi.**
wali *n.m.* A traditional title.
wạ̀limà *n.f.* (*pl.* **wạlimomi**) Marriage or birth feast.
wạ̀lịyi *n.m.* (*pl.* **wạ̀lịyai**) 1. Saint, holy man. 2. One who represents the bride or bridegroom in contracting a marriage.
wàlƙịya *n.f.* 1. Lightning. 2. Glossiness, sheen.
wàllạfà (ị/e) *v.t.* Compose, write (book, poem, etc.).
wàllahị *excl.* By God! ***~ tallahi*** I swear by God!
walle *n.m.* Being exposed, vulnerable.
wàlwạ̀la *n.f.* Happiness.
wàlwàlwàl *id.* Glossy, glistening appearance: *rawaninsa yana walkiya ~* his turban is very shiny.
wanà *v.t.* (*vn.* **wani**) Wind, crank (clock, watch, engine, etc.).
wancàn *pro. and dem.* (*f.* **waccàn,** *pl.* **wạɗàncân**) That, that one (distant but visible). **wàncan** *pro. and dem.* (*f.* **wàccan,** *pl.* **wạ̀ɗàncan**) 1. That, that one (not visible). 2. That, that one (the one referred to).
wancẹ̀ *f.* of **wanẹ̀.**
wandạ̀ *rel. pro.* (*f.* **waddạ̀, waccẹ̀,** *pl.* **wạɗàndạ̀**) 1. Who, which: *yaro ~ ya faɗi* the boy who fell. 2. That which, the one who: *~ ya zo ƙanensa ne* the one who came is his younger brother.
wandạ̀ra *v.t.* Bend sth.
wàndàr̃-wandar̃ *id.* Zigzagging, swaying from side to side.
wàndo *n.m.* (*pl.* **wandụnà**) Trousers.
wạ̀nẹ̀ *inter. dem.* (*f.* **wạ̀cẹ̀,** *pl.* **wạ̀ɗànnẹ̀**) Which?: *~ doki ya ci ƙwallo?* which horse won the race?
wàne *inter. pro.* Used in *~ ni?* what makes you think I could do that? *~ kai?* who do you think you are?
wanẹ̀ *pro.m.* (*f.* **wancẹ̀,** *pl.* **sụ wanẹ̀, sụ wancẹ̀**) So-and-so.
wàne nè *inter. pro.* (*f.* **wàce cè,** *pl.* **sụ wàne nè**) Who is it? Who? Whom?: *shi ~?* who is he? *~ ya*

kawo bauca? who brought the voucher? ~ *suka biya?* whom did they pay?

wạnị *indef. pro.* (*f.* **wạtạ**, *pl.* **wạsụ, wạɗansụ**) 1. Some, someone: ~ *ya zo* someone has come. 2. Another, another person: *kawo* ~ bring another one! 3. One . . ., the other: ~ *ya bi nan,* ~ *ya bi can* one went this way, the other went that way. *dem.* A, some: ~ *mutum ya zo* a man came; *sai* ~ *lokaci* until some other time.

wanì *vn.* of **wanà.**

wanka *n.m.* Bathing, taking a bath, washing oneself. *~n **janaba*** ritual purification.

wànke *n.m.* Ink made from soot on cooking pot.

wankè *v.t.* 1. (*vn.* **wankì**) Wash sth. 2. Wash off, away. ~ ***laifi*** exonerate s.o. ~ ***kai*** absolve oneself of blame. **wànkẹ-wànkẹ** *n.m.* Washing up of dishes, pots, etc.

wankì *n.m.* 1. Laundering, laundry. 2. Menstruation. 3. *vn.* of **wankè.**

wankìn ịdò *n.m.* Charm enabling person to see what others cannot see.

wannàn *pro. and dem.* (*pl.* **wạɗànnân**) This, this one. **wànnan** *pro. and dem.* (*pl.* **wạ̀ɗànnan**) 1. That, that one (nearby). 2. That, that one (the one referred to).

wànne *inter. pro.* (*f.* **wàcce,** *pl.* **wạ̀ɗànne**) Which one?

wân shekạrè *n.f. and adv.* The following day.

wantsạ̀la *v.i.* Fall headlong, roll into, topple into.

wàn-wâi *n.f.* One-way street.

wânye *v.t.* Finish, complete sth.

wànzamì *n.m.* (*pl.* **wànzàmai**) Barber.

wànzụ *v.i.* 1. Happen, occur. 2. Be eternal.

wạr̃antị *n.m.* Warrant.

wạrạ-wạrạ *id.* Spaced apart: *ya jera su* ~ he arranged them apart from each other.

wàr̃dị *n.m.* Rosewater perfume.

warè *v.t.* Separate, set aside.

wargạ̀je *v.i.* 1. Become scattered, disarranged, disorderly. 2. Fail (plan): *shirin da muka yi ya* ~ the plans we made came to nothing.

wargạ̀za *v.t.* 1. Scatter, make disorderly. 2. Cause plan to fail.

wargì *n.m.* 1. Game, sport. 2. Playing, joking.

wàr̃ hạkạ̀ *adv.* At the same time on another day: *gobe* ~ at this time tomorrow; *bara* ~ at this time last year.

warì *n.m.* 1. One of a pair, one of two halves: *~n takalmi* one shoe. 2. Part or share of sth.

wari *n.m.* Stench, bad smell.

warkè *v.i.* Be cured, recover from illness.

wàr̃ki *n.m.* (*pl.* **war̃kụnà**) Leather loincloth.

war̃ƙà *n.f.* (*pl.* **war̃ƙoƙi**) 1. Sheet of paper. 2. Leaf of tree or plant. 3. Currency note.

wartsạ̀ke *v.i.* 1. Become fully awake, alert. 2. Become clear, bright: *gari ya* ~ the weather has cleared up. 3. Be cured. 4. Cease being shy.

war̃wạ̀ɗa *v.t.* Write hastily.

warwạ̀re *v.t.* 1. Unwind, unravel, disentangle. 2. Cancel, revoke. 3. Exercise (body). *v.i.* 1. Become unravelled. 2. Become well.

wàsa *n.m.* (*pl.* **wàsànni**) 1. Game, sport. 2. Playing, joking.

wasà *v.t.* (*vn.* **washì**) 1. Sharpen (e.g. knife). 2. Sharpen one's wits. ~***ƙwaƙwalwa*** quiz. 3. Praise s.o. lavishly. ~ ***baki*** put sth. hard or sweet in mouth to chew on.

wạsàlce *v.t.* Insert vowel signs into Arabic script.

wạsạ̀li *n.m.* (*pl.* **wạsụlà**) Vowel.

wạ̀sà-wạsà *n.m.* Small, cooked bean-flour balls.

wàsạ-wàsạ *adv.* Gradually: ~ *har ya sami digiri* little by little, he finally got his degree.

wâsh *excl.* Expression of grief or worry over pain, bad news, etc.

washà *n.f.* (*pl.* **washoshi**) Washer (metal or rubber ring).

washè *v.t.* Raid, confiscate property. *v.i.* Improve (e.g. appearance or condition): *gari ya* ~ the weather has cleared up.

wàshègạ̀ri *n.f. and adv.* The following day, on the following day: *in an yi salla ran Lahadi sai mu tafi* ~ if *salla* takes place on Sunday, we will leave the following day.

washì *n.m.* 1. Sharpening. 2. Lavish praise. 3. *vn.* of **wasà**.

wàsiƙà *n.f.* (*pl.* **wàsiƙu**) Letter.

wàsiyyà *n.f.* (*pl.* **wasiyyoyi**) Legacy, will.

wàsosò *n.m.* Scrambling to grab a share of sth. for oneself.

wassàlam *see* **haza wassàlam.**

wasu *pl.* of **wani.**

wàswasì *n.m.* Reflection, pondering, deep thought.

wata *f.* of **wani.**

watà *n.m.* (*pl.* **wàtànni**) 1. Moon. 2. Month.

wataƙilà *adv.* Perhaps, maybe.

wàtò, wàtàu That is to say, so: *na ba shi fam daya* ~ *naira biyu* I gave him one pound, that is, two Naira; ~ *ba ka yarda ba ke nan* so you don't agree after all.

watsà *v.t.* (*vn.* **watsì**) Scatter, disperse, squander. ~ ***labari*** broadcast news.

wàtsàl-watsal *id.* Wriggling, squirming movement (of fish, snake, boiling water, etc.).

watsè *v.i.* Be scattered, dispersed, squandered.

wâuta *n.f.* Foolishness, senselessness.

wawà *n.f.* Scrambling to grab a share of sth. for oneself.

wawa *n.m. or f.* (*pl.* **wawàye**) Fool, clown. ~***n sarki*** court jester. ~***n barci*** deep sleep. ~***n bugu*** thorough beating. ~***n ci*** greedy appetite.

wawilo *n.m. or f.* Toothless person.

wàwurà (i/e) *v.t.* Snatch, grab.

[1]**wayà** *n.f.* 1. Wire, telegram, telephone call. ***gidan*** ~ post-office. 2. Any type of wire. ~***r keke*** spoke(s).

[2]**wayà** *n.f.* 1. Pound (weight). 2. Weighing scales.

wayam *id.* Complete emptiness: *na tarar da ajin* ~ I found the classroom deserted.

wàyê *inter. pro.* Who is it?

wayè *v.i.* 1. Dawn, become light: *gari ya* ~ the day dawned. 2. Become enlightened, broad-minded: *kansa ya* ~ he became enlightened. *v.t.* (with i.o. and **kâi**) Explain, clarify: *na* ~ *masa kai* I explained it to him.

wàyo *n.m.* Cleverness, cunning. ***yi*** ~ grow up, reach maturity.

wâyyo *excl.* Expression of deep regret, sorrow, pain.

wazanà *n.f.* Calling to prayers by *ladan.*

wàzifà *n.f.* One of the set of group prayers of the Tijjaniya sect of Islam.

wàziri *n.m.* (*pl.* **wàzìrai**) 1. A traditional title. 2. Chief political minister, vizier.

wo *see* **yiwo.**

wòfi *n.m. or f.* (*pl.* **wofàye**) 1. Silly, useless person. 2. Emptiness: *na zo hannuna* ~ I came empty-handed.

wokàci *see* **lokàci.**

wû *excl.* Expression of surprise on feeling slight pain.

wucè *v.t.* Go beyond, exceed: *shaye-shayensa ya* ~ *ka'ida* his continual drinking has gone beyond the limit. *v.i.* 1. Pass, pass by, pass beyond. 2. Pass (of period of time): *na gan shi ran Litinin da ta* ~ I saw him last Monday; *mun fara wannan aiki tun shekara biyu da suka* ~ we began this work two years ago. 3. Die, pass on.

wucin gadì *n.m.* Spare, reserve, spare part: *sojojin* ~ reserve army.

wuf *id.* Sudden, quick movement: *ina tafiya sai wani ya yi* ~ *ya rike ni.* I was going along when someone suddenly grabbed me.

wujiga-wùjìgà *id.* Describes action done with great effort and seriousness: *suna aiki* ~ they are working with all their might.

wujijjiga *v.t.* Twirl, swing, shake sth. or s.o.

wuƙa *n.f.* (*pl.* **wuƙàƙe**) Knife. ~***r siminti*** trowel.

wuƙi-wùƙì *id.* Feeling ashamed.

wùl *id.* Passing by very quickly.

wul *id.* Emphasizes blackness: *baki* ~ jet black.

wùlàƙài *adv.* Contemptuously,

harshly: *ya yi mata wani duba* ~ he looked at her contemptuously.

wųlaƙànta *v.t.* Treat s.o. harshly, belittle s.o.

wùlga (į/e) *v.t.* Eat much of sth.

wulgà *v.i.* Pass quickly by.

wundì *n.m.* (*pl.* **wundàye**) Large circular mat.

wųnį *v.i.* Spend a day: *na ~ ina aiki* I spent the whole day working.

wųnì *n.m.* Period of daylight, day: *ina ~?* how was your day?

wų̀ni-wųni *n.m.* Behaving or speaking in a suspicious, shifty manner: *~n me kake yi?* why are you behaving in such a shifty way?

wur̃ *id.* Emphasizes redness: *ja ~* bright red.

wur̃gà *v.t.* 1. Throw. 2. Swing, jerk (arms).

wur̃gì *excl.* How fast!

wųrį *adv.* (with **dą̀**) Early, in good time: *sun zo da ~* they came early.

wųrì *n.m.* Cowrie.

wųri *n.m.* (*pl.* **wųràre**) Place, area, side: *na gan shi a wani ~* I saw it somewhere.

wųrin *prep.* With, at: *yana ~ malamin* it is with the teacher; *suna ~ aiki* they are at work.

wųr̃ìdi *n.m.* Islamic prayers recited privately after obligatory prayers.

wur̃jànjàn *id.* Doing sth. relentlessly: *tana kuka ~* she is crying bitterly.

wus *excl.* Expression of disapproval, disgust.

wųshirya *n.f.* Wide space between front teeth.

wųta *n.f.* 1. Fire. 2. Electricity. *sa ~* accelerate, speed up. *rage ~* decelerate, slow down.

wųtsįyà *n.f.* (*pl.* **wųtsįyoyi**) 1. Tail. ***taurarųwa mai*** ~ comet. 2. Penis (impolite term).

wų̀ya *n.f.* Difficulty, suffering, trouble.

wųyà *n.m.* (*pl.* **wųyoyi**) 1. Neck. 2. Narrow part of sth. (neck of bottle, wrist, etc.).

wų̀yątą̀ *v.i.* 1. Become difficult. 2. Become scarce: *shinkafa ta ~ a kasuwa* rice is scarce in the market.

Y

yą̀ *prep.* 1. Just like, equivalent to: *ka ɗinka mini riga ~ wannan* make me a gown just like this one; *rana ~ ta yau* a week from today; *ya fassara shi kalma ~ kalma* he translated it word for word. 2. (between identical pronouns) Among one's own kind: *mun yi taro mu ~ mu* we had a meeting just among ourselves.

yâ *n.f.* (*pl.* **yayye, yayu**) 1. Elder sister. 2. Any female of the same age or status as one's elder sister.

ya *pro.m.* (vl. and tone vary acc. to tense, *see* Appendix 1) He.

yą̀ba (į/e) *v.t.* (*vn.* **yą̀bo**) Praise, approve of.

yąbanyà *n.f.* Young crops.

yàbirbįra *n.f.* Fruit bat.

yą̀bo *n.m.* 1. Praise. 2. *vn.* of **yą̀ba.**

yàɓa (į/e) *v.t.* (*vn.* **yàɓe**) 1. Plaster (wall). 2. Smear.

yacè *v.t.* 1. Wipe off perspiration. 2. Spurn, snub.

ya dą̀ *v.t.* (= **yashe** before pro. d.o.) Alt. form of **yar̃ dą̀.**

yaddą̀ *rel. adv.* How, the way in which: *nuna mini ~ ake yinsa* show me how it is done.

[1]yadì *n.m.* Yard (three feet).

[2]yadì *n.m.* Manufactured cloth.

[3]yadì *n.m.* Public works yard.

yàɗa (į/e) *v.t.* Skim off.

yaɗà *v.t.* Spread, disseminate.

yaɗì *n.m.* Thin white membrane on meat.

yàfa (į/e) *v.t.* Forgive.

yafà *v.t.* 1. Wear or throw sth. over one's shoulders. 2. Scatter (seeds, grain), sprinkle (water).

yàfątà (cį/ce) *v.t.* Beckon: *ta yaface shi da idonta* she beckoned him with her eyes.
yafè *v.t.* (with i.o.) Forgive. *v.i.* Renounce (claim, share, etc.).
yągalgąla *v.t.* Tear sth. in pieces or strips.
yagè *v.t. and v.i.* Rip, tear.
yajì *n.m.* 1. Any sharp-tasting spice (e.g. pepper, ginger). 2. Going off in a huff, leaving home (of wife). 3. Strike, boycott.
yąkàn *pro.m.* (hab. tense subj.) He.
yąkè *pro.m.* (rel. cont. tense subj.) He.
yàkųsà (shį/she) *v.t.* Scratch with claws or fingernails.
yakų̀wa *n.f.* Red sorrel.
yàƙa (į/e) *v.t.* Make war on.
yàƙądò *n.m. or f.* Quick-tempered person.
yàƙayyà *n.f.* Mutual hostility, warfare.
yàƙe *n.m.* Smiling expression while hiding pain or anger.
yaƙè *v.t.* 1. Bare teeth. 2. Open mouth wide.
yaƙì *n.m.* (*pl.* **yàƙę-yàƙę**) War, hostility.
yą̀ƙinì *n.m.* Certainty: *ya yi ~ zai sami kuɗi* he was certain he would get the money.
yallàɓai *excl.* Respectful form of address used for one's superior.
yalo *n.m.* Light yellow tomato-like fruit.
yàlòlò *id.* Describes long, fine hair.
yàlwa *n.f.* Abundance: *akwai ~r abinci bara* there was an abundance of food last year.
yàlwątà (cį/ce) *v.t.* Suffice amply. **yàlwątą̀** *v.i.* Be ample, abundant, have plenty to spare. **yalwą̀ta** *v.t.* 1. Increase size of sth. 2. (usu. with i.o.) Provide liberally for s.o.
yambą̀la *n.m.* Boy dressed as woman during *tashe*.
yami *n.m.* Sour smell or taste.
yâmmą *n.f.* West.
yâmma *n.f.* Afternoon. **yâmmą** *adv.* (usu. with **dą̀** or **ną**) In the afternoon.
yammącin *prep.* West of.
yamsùr̃ *n.m.* Black rosary decorated with silver.
yamų̀tsa *v.t.* 1. Mix, stir up. 2. Confuse, muddle. 3. Crumple up, wrinkle. *v.i.* Quarrel, have a misunderstanding.
yamų̀tse *v.i.* 1. Be mixed up. 2. Be in muddled or confused state. 3. Be crumpled up.
yàmųtsi *n.m.* 1. Confusion. 2. Quarrelling.
yàm-yam *n.m.* Cannibal.
yąnà *pro.m.* (cont. tense subj.) He.
yana *n.f.* 1. Film (on milk, gruel, etc.), froth, scum. 2. Film over eyes. 3. Spider's web.
yąną̀yi *n.m.* 1. Climate, weather. 2. Disposition, temperament. 3. Atmosphere (of book or play).
yandą̀ *see* **yaddą̀**.
yànga *n.f.* Boastfulness, showing off (esp. by women).
yànka (į/e) *v.t.* (*vn.* **yanka**) 1. Cut off a piece of sth. 2. Make a cut in or through sth. 3. Cut across a place. **yankà** *v.t.* (*vn.* **yanka**) 1. Cut up. 2. Slaughter animal by cutting throat. ***sunan yanka*** name given to a person on his naming-day.
yànke *n.m.* Short-cut in travelling.
yankę *n.m.* Lie.
yankè *v.i.* Become reduced, in short supply: *ruwa ya ~* water is scarce.
yankì *n.m.* (*pl.* **yankųnà**) 1. Piece, part, section. 2. District.
yànƙwąną̀ *v.i.* Become withered, emaciated.
yantà *v.t.* Prepare grass for thatching.
yantsą̀r̃a *v.t.* Produce in abundance: *bishiya ta ~ 'ya'ya* the tree produced a lot of fruit.
yanyą̀na *v.t.* Cut (meat or leather) into long strips.
yânyawà *n.f.* (*pl.* **yànyàyi**) Fennec (African fox).
yànzų *adv.* Now, at present: *har ~* up till now.
yar̃ (dą̀) *v.t.* (= **ya dą̀** before d.o.) 1. Throw away, discard one thing. 2. Leave, abandon s.o. 3. Overcome (e.g. pride, shame, shyness).
yâra *pl.* of **yarò**.
yàràntąkà *n.f.* Boyishness, childishness.
yar̃ɓà *v.t.* (with i.o.) Splash s.o.

with sth. sticky: *ya ~ mını taɓo a fuska* he flung some mud in my face.
yaȓɓaȓ (dą̀) *v.t.* 1. Fling s.o. down. 2. Ignore, snub s.o.
yàȓdą *v.i.* Agree, consent, approve.
yàȓe *n.m.* 1. Mother tongue, native language. 2. Dialect. 3. Any language unknown to one.
yą̀ri *n.m.* Earring(s).
yarì *n.m.* Chief warder of prison. *gidan ~* prison.
yą̀ȓimą̀ *n.m.* A traditional title (usu. held by younger brother or son of an emir).
yarinyà *n.f.* (*pl.* **'yammata**) Girl, young woman.
yaȓjè *v.t.* (with i.o.) Agree, allow: *na ~ masa ya shiga gidana* I allowed him to enter my house.
yàȓjejenįya *n.f.* 1. Coming to terms, settling one's differences. 2. Mutual agreement, treaty.
yarò *n.m.* (*pl.* **yâra**) 1. Boy, child. 2. Follower or retainer of an important person. 3. Servant.
yąȓo-yą̀ȓò *id.* Ragged or thoroughly soaked appearance.
yaȓyàɗi *n.m.* A climbing vine whose leaves are used for fodder.
yasà *v.t.* Clean out well or latrine.
yashe *see* **ya dą̀**.
yàshi *n.m.* Sand.
yatsà *n.f.* (*pl.* **yatsu**) Finger. *~r ƙafa* toe.
yàtsįnà *n.f.* Grimace.
yatsįne *v.i.* Contort face due to pain.
yâu *n.f. and adv.* Today. *~ da gobe* sooner or later, gradually. *'yan ~* the younger generation.
yau *n.m.* (*gen.* **yan**) Saliva.
yauci *n.m.* Lateness.
yàudąȓà (į/e) *v.t.* Deceive, trick.
yauƙi *n.m.* Sliminess (e.g. of cooked okra).
yausą̀sa *v.t.* Cause to wither, dry up. **yàusąsą̀** *v.i.* 1. Wither. 2. Feel weak.
yàushę̀ *inter. adv.* When?: *~ suka tashi?* when did they leave?
yaushi *n.m.* Withering up, weakening.
yautai *n.m.* Nightjar (bird).
yąwà *n.m.* Abundance, large quantity: *da ~, mai ~* much, many, a lot of.
yąwàita *v.t.* Increase sth., produce much of.
yąwanci *n.m.* Majority, greater part, most of.
yawò *n.m.* (*pl.* **yàwą̀cę-yàwą̀cę**) Walk, stroll.
yawu *see* **yau**.
yâwwa *excl.* 1. Response to standard greetings: *barka da asuba! ~ barka kadai!* good morning! good morning to you also! 2. That's right! 3. Bravo! Well done!
yàyà *inter. adv.* How?: *~ ciniki yau?* how is business today? *~ sunansa?* what is his name?
[1]**yàya (į/e)** *v.t.* Gather grass for fodder.
[2]**yàya** *see* **wâ** and **yâ**.
yayè *v.t.* 1. Wean. 2. Separate out, clear away, remove. *v.i.* 1. Cease. 2. Disappear, vanish.
yàyi *n.m.* 1. Time: *a wane ~ zai zo?* at what time will he come? 2. Current fashion: *ba ya ~n wannan riga* this gown is not fashionable nowadays. **yàyîn dą̀** *rel. adv.* When: *na gan shi ~ na je Kano* I saw him when I went to Kano.
yayì *n.m.* Sparse grass.
yayu *pl.* of **wâ** and **yâ**.
yayyą̀fa *v.t.* Sprinkle.
yayyąfi *n.m.* Drizzle, light rain, sprinkling.
yayye *pl.* of **wâ** and **yâ**.
yàyyo *n.m.* Leak, leaking, dripping.
yazġa *see* **izġa**.
yekų̀wa *n.f.* Proclamation.
yį *see* **yą̀**.
yį *v.t.* 1. Make, do: *ki ~ kunu da yawa* make a lot of gruel; *me suka ~?* what did they do? *~ ta* keep on doing sth.: *na ~ ta kiransa bai amsa ba* I kept on calling him but he didn't answer. *na ~ na ~* I did my best, I tried and tried. *an ~* there once was : *wata rana an ~ shahararrun mawaƙan Hausa* once upon a time there were some famous Hausa poets. 2. Used with action nouns to form verbal phrases: *ya ~ tsalle* he jumped; *mun ~ magana da su* we spoke with them; *ba ta ~ barci ba* she didn't sleep. 3. (with quality

nouns) Be, become, be too much: *kunun nan ya ~ tsami* this gruel has become sour; *~ sauri* be quick! *ya ~ mini nauyi* it is too heavy for me. 4. (with time nouns) Spend: *za mu ~ shekara biyu a Kano* we will stay for two years in Kano. 5. (with location words) Go in direction of: *ayari ya ~ arewa* the caravan headed north. *v.i.* Be ready, done, accomplished: *abinci ya ~* the food is ready; *dabara ta ~* the plan worked out; *lokaci ya ~* the time has come; *dare ya ~* it is night-time.
yịfà *v.t.* Cover sth. temporarily.
yịnị *see* **wụnị.**
yịwo *v.t.* Do sth. (in this direction): *ya ~ ciyawa* he went to cut some grass and bring it back.
yịwụ *v.i.* Be possible.
yô *excl.* Oh, I see! So that's it!
yòyo *see* **yàyyo.**
Yulị *n.m.* July.
yumɓu *n.m.* Clay for making pottery.
Yunị *n.m.* June.
yunƙụ̀ra *v.i.* Make an effort, strain.
yunwà *n.f.* 1. Hunger. 2. Famine.
yùnwạtạ̀ *v.i.* Be or go hungry.

'Y

'ya *n.f.* (*pl.* **'ya'ya**) Daughter.
'yammata *n.pl.* Girls, young women.
'yan *pl.* of **ɗan.**
'yancì *n.m.* 1. Freedom. 2. Independence.
'yankamancì *n.m.* 1. Comical performance, usu. characterized by reference to food and often consisting of imitations and parodies of famous singers. 2. Shamelessness. **ɗankama** comedian who performs *'yankamanci*, shameless person.
'yânta *v.t.* Free s.o. from slavery.
'yar̃ *f.* of **ɗan.**
'yar̃ cịki *n.f.* Any type of shirt, but esp. that worn under a *riga.*
'yar̃ Jòs *n.f.* A three-quarter-length *taguwa* made of lightweight material.
'ya'ya *pl.* of **ɗa** and **'ya.**

Z

zâ *v.i.* (followed by pro.) Go to: *~ mu kasuwa* we are going to market.
za Fut. tense marker (*see* Appendix 1): *gobe ma'aikata ~ su tashi wajen ƙarfe biyu* tomorrow the workers will leave around two o'clock.
zàbga (ị/e) *v.t.* Do sth. excessively: *mun zabgi karatu yau* we read a lot today.
zabgè *v.t. and v.i.* Take away a lot: *ruwa ya ~ garuna* the rain has eroded my wall; *ka ~ mini ɗorawa* pick all the fruit of the locust bean tree for me; *tunkiya ta ~* the sheep has become thin.
zạ̀bir̃à *n.f.* (*pl.* **zạ̀bir̃u**) Leather pouch with two or more compartments, esp. used by barbers.
zạ̀bịya *n.m. or f.* Albino.
zabịya *n.f.* Woman lead-singer.
zàbo *n.m.* (*f.* **zàbụwa,** *pl.* **zàbi**) Guinea-fowl.
zàbụr̃ạ̀ *v.i.* Spring or leap up,

move quickly away: *ya* ~ *da gudu* he took off running.

zą̀buřa *n.f.* Psalms.

zàɓa (į/e) *v.t.* (*vn.* **zàɓe**) 1. Choose, select. 2. Elect.

zą̀ɓaką̀ *v.i.* Be boiled, cooked.

zàɓe *n.m.* 1. Choice. 2. Election. 3. *vn.* of **zàɓa.**

zaɓì *n.m.* Option to choose: *zan ba ka* ~ I'll give you a choice.

zafą̀fa *v.t.* 1. Heat, warm up. 2. (with i.o.) Annoy, anger s.o. **zàfąfą̀** *v.i.* 1. Be warmed up. 2. Become heated (argument, discussion).

zafi *n.m.* 1. Heat: *ruwan* ~ hot water. 2. Intensity (esp. of illness, pain): *ciwonsa ya yi* ~ his illness has become serious; *harbin kunama yana da* ~ the scorpion's sting is painful. 3. (in compounds) Quickness: *~n nama* being energetic, agile; *~n rai*, *~n zuciya* being quick-tempered.

zàga (į/e) *v.t.* (*vn.* **zagì**) Abuse, insult.

zagà, zagą̀ya *v.t.* Go around a place: *ya* ~ *gari cikin mota* he went around the town by car.

zą̀gè *v.i.* 1. Undress. 2. Be busy doing sth.: *ya* ~ *cikin aikin nan* he was busily working.

zagè *v.t.* Erode. *v.i.* 1. Become eroded. 2. Crumble (e.g. of *ɗan wake* cooked in water).

zągi *n.m.* (*pl.* **zągàge**) Escort who leads the horse of an important person.

zagì *n.m.* (*pl.* **zàgę-zàgę**) 1. Insult, abuse: *mun dura masa* ~ we insulted him. 2. *vn.* of **zàga.**

zągo *n.m.* Large termite.

zągo-zą̀gò *id.* Long bushy (of hair), long protruding (of teeth).

zahįři *n.m.* Clearness, obviousness of fact or statement: *ya fadi ~n gaskiya* he spoke the obvious truth. *a~* in fact, actually.

zâi (contr. of fut. tense marker **za** and pro. **yą̀**) He will.

zaibà *n.f.* Quicksilver, mercury.

za'įdà *n.f.* Exaggeration.

zaitì *n.m.* Eucalyptus oil.

zaizą̀ye *v.i.* Erode, be worn down (of earth).

zą̀kąrà *n.m.* (*pl.* **zą̀ką̀ru**) 1. Cock. 2. Outstanding person, hero. 3. One who leads responses during prayers.

zakì *n.m.* (*f.* **zakanyà**, *pl.* **zakoki**) Lion.

zàkka *n.f.* Religious tithe paid in form of farm produce, livestock, or money.

zakų̀ɗa *v.i.* Move away a little.

zą̀ƙa (į/e) *v.t.* Eat too much, overeat.

zàƙàƙà *id.* Appearance of sth. very long (snake, stick, etc.).

ząƙalƙą̀le *v.t.* Dominate conversation.

zaƙi *n.m.* Sweetness, pleasantness. ***~n magana*** sweet-talk.

zą̀laƙà *n.f.* Eloquence.

zalɓè *n.m.* Grey heron.

zalla *adv.* Solely, purely, only: *ina son shinkafa* ~ I only want rice (nothing else); *wannan magana ƙarya ce* ~ this statement is utterly false.

zallò *n.m.* Sudden reaction to being tickled.

zaluncì *n.m.* Oppression, cruelty, tyranny.

zàluntà (cį/ce) *v.t.* 1. Oppress, bully, mistreat. 2. Cheat.

zalząlo *v.i.* Hang out tongue from panting.

ząmą *v.i.* 1. Be: *maganarsa ta* ~ *gaskiya* what he said is true; *ya* ~ *haka* the matter is thus. 2. Become: *ya* ~ *sarki* he became chief. **ząma** *n.m.* Condition, sitting, dwelling: *~n duniya iyawa ne* getting along in life requires good planning; *ya ci* ~ he stayed a long time; *a cikin ~n da muke yanzu* in the present state of affairs; *abokin* ~ companion.

zamą̀ni, zàmanì *n.m.* Period, epoch: *a ~n nan* in modern times; *a ~n da* in former times; *dan* ~ modern person; *Allah ya ja ~nka* may God prolong your life.

zàmbą *n.f.* (*pl.* **zàmbą̀cę-zàmbą̀cę**) Fraud, swindling.

zambą̀ɗa *v.t.* Put a lot of sth. into sth. (esp. seasoning in food).

zambàř *n.m.* One thousand (used only in multiples): ~ *takwas* eight thousand; ~ *dubu* one million.

zàmbạtà (cị/ce) *v.t.* 1. Swindle, embezzle, deceive. 2. Mock, ridicule.
zàmbo *n.m.* Satire, ridicule.
zamè *v.t.* 1. Rein in a horse sharply so that it slides along ground. 2. Deduct money owed to one from a payment. *v.i.* Slip, slide (of foot). 2. Slip out of position, become displaced, slip away.
zân (contr. of fut. tense marker **za** and pro. **in**) I shall.
zanà *v.t.* 1. Draw a design or picture. 2. Etch or carve out ornamental design (e.g. on gourd). 3. (with i.o.) Cut decorative markings in skin. 4. Count up, account for.
zana *n.f.* (*pl.* **zànạ̀ku**) Large rectangular grass mat used for fencing and roofing.
zànce *n.m.* 1. (*pl.* **zantụkà**) Conversation, talk. 2. Subject, matter: *mun yi magana a kan ~n kudi* we talked about the matter of money. 3. Courting: *Audu ya tafi ~ da Kande* Audu went to court Kande; *kayan ~* obligatory gifts given to prospective bride. 4. (*pl.* **zantuttụkà**) Mere talk, unreliable statement.
zàne *n.m.* (*pl.* **zànẹ-zànẹ**) 1. Line, marking, stripe, drawing. 2. Decorative markings on body.
zạnè *n.m.* (*pl.* **zannụwà**) Woman's body cloth.
zangar̃nịya (*pl.* **zàngàr̃nu**) Head of any corn.
zàngạ̀-zangà *n.f.* Protest demonstration.
zangò *n.m.* (*pl.* **zangụnà**) 1. Camping ground, lodging place. 2. Distance of day's march between two camping sites. 3. Cessation of day's activities: *za mu ya da ~ da ƙarfe biyu* we're going to stop work at two p.m.
zanko *n.m.* 1. Cock's comb, bird's crest. 2. Pointed top of mud-walled house.
zânta *v.i.* Speak, converse.
zanzạna *n.f.* Smallpox, smallpox marks.
zànzạro *n.m.* Mason wasp. ***yi*** **~** act of tucking shirt inside trousers.
[1]**zạ̀ra (ị/e)** *v.t.* Snatch, grab.
[2]**zạ̀ra** *n.f.* Vacillation.
[1]**zàr̃ạ** *n.f.* Planet, big star.
[2]**zàr̃ạ** *n.f.* Starling (bird).
zạr̃ạ̀fi *n.m.* 1. Opportunity, leisure time: *ya cinye mini ~* he wasted my time. ***iyakar*** **~** one's best, one's might. 2. Wealth.
zarar̃ *conj.* (with **dạ̀**) As soon as: *da ~ kun gama, ku tafi* as soon as you finish, you may go.
zạrạ-zạrạ *id.* Describes sth. thin, frayed or near breaking point: *igiya ta yi ~* the rope is about to break.
zar̃cè *v.t.* 1. Exceed, surpass: *kuɗinsa ya ~ naira goma* he has more than ten Naira. 2. Pass on to a place: *Audu ya ~ cikin gari* Audu has gone into town.
zạ̀re *n.m.* (*pl.* **zạrurrụkà, zạrurụwà**) Thread, string.
zàre *n.m.* Goods rejected due to poor quality. 2. Outcast (person).
zarè *v.t.* Pull out, unsheath, disengage. 2. Withdraw from, be unconcerned with: *ya ~ hannunsa daga cikin maganar* he has washed his hands of the matter. ***ya*** **~** ***mini ido*** he glared at me.
zàrga (ị/e) *v.t.* Accuse, blame.
zargà *v.t.* Fasten noose to s.o.
zàrge *n.m.* Noose, slip-knot.
zargè *v.t.* Ensnare, trap by entanglement.
zàrgi *n.m.* Accusation, blame.
zàr̃ginà *n.f.* Washing blue, blueing.
zàri *n.m.* Gluttony, greed.
zarịya *n.f.* Trouser string.
zar̃ni *n.m.* Pungent smell of urine.
zar̃tar̃ (dạ̀) *v.t.* Finalize, carry out, execute (instructions, law, verdict, etc.).
zar̃tò *n.m.* (*pl.* **zar̃tụnà, zạr̃àta**) 1. Saw, file. 2. Energetic person.
zar̃tsi *n.m.* Slightly salty, unpleasant tasting water: *ruwan rijiyata na ~ ne* the water in my well is brackish.
zar̃ụ̀mi *see* **jar̃ụ̀mi.**
zar̃yà *n.f.* Hurrying to and fro.
zạ̀ta (cị/ce) *v.t.* (*vn.* **zạ̀to**) Think, imagine, expect, suppose: *na zaci zai zo* I thought he would come.
zạ̀to *n.m.* 1. Thinking, imagining,

supposing. **ba~ ba tsammani** unexpectedly. 2. *vn.* of **zàta.**

zaunà *v.i.* 1. Sit. 2. Settle down, live, remain in a place.

zàurànce *n.m.* Talking in a secret language.

zaurè *n.m.* (*pl.* **zaurụkà**) Entrance room to a compound.

zạwạrawa *pl.* of **bạzạwạri.**

zawạye *v.t.* Soil sth. with excrement.

zawạyi, zawò *n.m.* Diarrhoea.

zàwwatì *n.m.* Soft shirting material.

zayyạna *v.t.* Describe sth. in detail, give a full account of sth. **zàyyạnà** *n.f.* Illuminated designs on copies of the Koran and other religious books.

zàzzạɓi *n.m.* Fever, high temperature: *~n cizon sauro* malaria. **~n wata** eclipse of the moon.

zazzạga *v.t.* Sprinkle or shake out (powder, grain, liquid, etc.): *ya ~ taba* he shook out a cigarette (from packet).

zî *n.m.* Diamonds (suit in playing cards).

zîk *n.m.* Zipper, zip-fastener.

zịna *n.f.* (*pl.* **zịnàcẹ-zịnàcẹ**) Fornication, adultery.

zinaȓi *n.m.* (*f.* **zinaȓịya**) Gold.

zìndiƙi *n.m.* (*f.* **zìndiƙịya,** *pl.* **zìndìƙai**) 1. Heretic. 2. Destitute person.

zìndiȓ *id.* Stark naked.

ziȓgà-ziȓga *n.f.* Constantly going to and fro.

ziȓnàƙo *n.m.* Black hornet.

zịyaȓà *n.f.* (*pl.* **zịyàȓcẹ-zịyàȓcẹ**) 1. Visit, visiting. 2. Courtesy call, homage.

zịyaȓtà (cị/ce) *v.t.* 1. Visit. 2. Pay homage to.

zizà *id.* 1. Exceedingly good, fine: *abin wuyanki ya yi miki kyau ~* your necklace looks beautiful on you. 2. Zig-zag stitching.

zo *v.i.* (*vn.* **zụwà**) 1. Come. 2. Become: *abin ya ~ da sauki* the matter became simple.

[1]**zobè** *n.m.* (*f.* **zobanyà,** *pl.* **zôbba**) 1. Ring. 2. Encirclement: *sojoji sun yi musu ~* the soldiers surrounded them.

[2]**zobè** *v.t.* Withdraw or take back sth. given: *ya ~ kyautar da ya yi mana* he took back the gift that he gave us.

zoɓà *v.t.* 1. Be a little bigger than. 2. Overlap.

zogạlạgandị, zogạlẹ *n.m.* Horseradish tree.

zògi *n.m.* Throbbing pain.

zòlạyà (ị/e) *v.t.* 1. Cross-examine: *an ~ shi sai da ya faɗi gaskiya* they cross-examined him until he confessed. 2. Tease, pick on s.o.

zòlolò *n.m.* (*f.* **zòlolụwa**) Very tall person or animal.

ẓomo *n.m.* (*pl.* **zomàye**) Hare. **barcin ~** sleeping with one eye open.

zòȓòȓò *id.* Very long or tall: *garu ya yi tsawo ~* the wall is very high.

zozạye *v.i.* Become worn or eroded.

zû *n.m.* Used in *gidan ~* zoo.

zụbà *v.t.* 1. Pour into. 2. Put several things into: *na ~ batura a tocilan* I put some batteries in the torch. 3. Do a lot of sth.: *ya ~ karatu* he read a lot. **~ ido** wait patiently. **zụbạ** *v.i.* 1. Leak. 2. Erode (of wall). 3. Fall out (e.g. hair). 4. Fade (of colour).

zụbaȓ (dạ) *v.t.* (= **zub dạ** before d.o.) 1. Pour out or away. 2. Throw away quantity of sth. **~ da ciki** abort.

zub dạ *v.t.* (= **zubshe** before pro. d.o.) Alt. form of **zụbaȓ dạ.**

zụbè *v.i.* 1. Pour away, leak or flow out completely. 2. Collapse (of wall). 3. Become emaciated.

zụbe-ban-ƙwaryata *n.m.* Heart-to-heart talk.

zụbi *n.m.* 1. Paying one's contribution to a pool. 2. Casting in metal. 3. Preparing indigo infusion in dye-pit. **wani ~** sometimes.

zụbò *n.m.* Pile (grass, cornstalks, etc.).

zubshe *see* **zub dạ.**

zucị *adv.* (with **ạ**) In the heart, mind: *karatu a ~* reading silently; *rike a ~* hold a grudge.

zucịya *n.f.* (*pl.* **zụkàta**) 1. Heart. 2. Mind, soul, spirit. 3. Will-power, courage. **ɓacin ~** vexation, annoyance. ***saurin*** ~ quick-temperedness.

zucį-zucį *n.m.* Intention or anxiety to say sth.: *yana ~n ya fada mini sai ya manta* he was intending to tell me but he forgot.

zųfà, zuffà *n.f.* 1. Hot weather. 2. Perspiration.

zųgà *v.t.* 1. Blow up a fire with bellows. 2. Incite, cause an uprising: *ya ~ dalibai su yi tawaye* he incited the students to rebel.

zųgàzųgi *n.m.* (*pl.* **zų̀gàzų̀gai**) Bellows.

zugè *v.t.* Tighten drawstring of trousers, zip up trousers.

zùgugù *n.m.* Exaggeration: *Audu ya faye ~ a zancensa* Audu always exaggerates.

zùƙa (į/e) *v.t.* 1. Draw into mouth, suck, inhale. 2. Do sth. thoroughly.

zuƙè *v.i.* 1. Suck or inhale. 2. Dodge, avoid s.o.

zùƙę-zùƙę *n.m.* Hesitation, looking for excuse to get out of doing sth.

zų̀ƙùt *id.* Loud sound of swallowing sth. whole: *ya hadiye abinci ~* he gulped his food down.

zų̀laikà *n.f.* An ankle-length *taguwa*.

Zulhajjį *n.m.* Twelfth month of the Muslim calendar.

Zùlƙidà *n.m.* Eleventh month of the Muslim calendar.

zųlų̀mi *n.m.* Thoughtfulness, reflection, pondering.

zųmà *n.m.* 1. Honey. 2. (often *ƙudan* ~) Bee.

zumbų̀ɗa *v.t.* Do a lot of sth.: *ta ~ gishiri a miya* she put a lot of salt in the *miya*.

zùmɓutù *n.m.* Tail end of chicken, 'parson's nose'.

zųmù *n.m.* Close friend, confidant.

zų̀muɗi *n.m.* Anxiety, eagerness.

zųmuncì *n.m.* 1. Blood relationship. 2. Friendship, fellowship, friendly relations: *yana da ~* he is very considerate of his relatives and friends.

zų̀mùnta *see* **zųmuncì**.

zùndùm *id.* Sound of heavy object falling into water.

zùndum *id.* Describes sth. very full of liquid.

zùnɗa (į/e) *v.t.* (*vn.* **zùnɗe**) Point out, indicate (with lips or eyes): *ya zunɗe shi da baki* he pointed him out with his lips.

zùnɗe *n.m.* 1. Speaking ill of s.o. in his absence. 2. *vn.* of **zùnɗa.**

zungų̀ra *v.t.* (*vn.* **zungų̀ri**) Poke or prod with rod, stick, etc.

zùngų̀r̃u *n.m.* 1. Long, tubular gourd worn by women for applying henna to the hands. 2. Gourd of same shape, fitted with metal rings and used as a musical instrument.

zunkų̀ɗa *v.t.* Shift or hitch up (e.g. child on back or load on donkey).

zunkų̀ɗe *v.i.* Slip off to one side (of load).

zų̀nųbì *n.m.* (*pl.* **zų̀nų̀bai**) Sin.

zûr̃ Used in *shaidar* ~ false evidence, perjury.

zųrà *v.t.* Lower or insert sth. into place (bucket into well, thread into needle, etc.). ~ ***ido*** wait eagerly.

zurà *v.t.* (with i.o.) Inflict a lot: *na ~ masa mari* I slapped him very hard. *v.i.* Rush away: *ya ~ da gudu* he took to his heels.

zų̀rarą̀ *v.i.* Trickle or slide down (of water).

zurfą̀fa *v.t.* Deepen, make sth. deep. *v.i.* Go deeply into.

zurfi *n.m.* Depth. ***~n ciki*** secretiveness, reticence.

zų̀r̃įyà *n.f.* (*pl.* **zųr̃įyoyi**) Offspring, descendant.

zurmà *v.t.* Put hand or foot into pocket, hole, etc. *v.i.* Collapse (well, wall, roof, etc.).

zų̀r̃ututù *n.m.* Meddlesomeness, idle chatter.

zųru-zų̀rù *id.* Wide-eyed staring (from surprise, fear, hunger, etc.).

zųwà *n.m.* 1. Arrival. ***mai*** ~ next, coming: *wata mai ~* next month. 2. *vn.* of **zo.** *prep.* 1. To, towards: *ya kama hanya ~ Kano* he took the road to Kano. ~ ***ga*** form of address at beginning of a letter: *~ ga Edita* Dear Editor. 2. As far as, up to, until: *daga safiya ~ dare* from morning till night. **zųwà-zųwà** *adv.* From time to time.

APPENDIX 1

Tables of Hausa Pronouns

1. Independent Pronouns

ni	I
kai	you (m.)
ke	you (f.)
shi	he
įtą	she
mu	we
ku	you (pl.)
su	they

Notes: Some uses of these pronouns are:

(*a*) As subject of non-verbal sentences, e.g.:

shi sarki ne	he is the chief

(*b*) As object of **dą̀** and **babų̀**, e.g.:

sun zo da ita	they came with her
babu su a nan	there aren't any of them here

(*c*) As direct object when it is separated from the verb, e.g.:

kawo mini shi	bring it to me

(*d*) For emphasis, e.g.:

ke ce muka gani	you were the one we saw
shi ne ya tafi	he is the one who went

2a. Subject Pronouns: Past Tenses

Past		*Relative Past*		*Negative Past*	
na yị	I did it	**ạbîn dạ̀ nạ yị**	what I did	**bàn yị bạ**	I didn't do it
ka yị	you (m.) . . .	**ạbîn dạ̀ kạ yị**	what you (m.) . . .	**bạ̀ kạ̀ yị bạ**	you (m.) . . .
kin yị	you (f.) . . .	**ạbîn dạ̀ kịkạ̀ yị**	what you (f.) . . .	**bạ̀ kị yị bạ**	you (f.) . . .
ya yị	he . . .	**ạbîn dạ̀ yạ yị**	what he . . .	**bài yị bạ**	he . . .
ta yị	she . . .	**ạbîn dạ̀ tạ yị**	what she . . .	**bạ̀ tạ̀ yị bạ**	she . . .
mun yị	we . . .	**ạbîn dạ̀ mụkạ̀ yị**	what we . . .	**bạ̀ mụ̀ yị bạ**	we . . .
kun yị	you (pl.) . . .	**ạbîn dạ̀ kụkạ̀ yị**	what you (pl.) . . .	**bạ̀ kụ̀ yị bạ**	you (pl.) . . .
sun yị	they . . .	**ạbîn dạ̀ sụkạ̀ yị**	what they . . .	**bạ̀ sụ̀ yị bạ**	they . . .
an yị	someone . . ., it was done	**ạbîn dạ̀ ạkạ̀ yị**	what someone . . ., what was done	**bạ̀ ạ̀ yị bạ**	no one . . ., it wasn't done

2b. Subject Pronouns: Continuous Tenses

Continuous		*Relative Continuous*		*Negative Continuous*	
įnà yî	I am doing it	**ąbîn dą nąkè yî**	what I am doing	**ba nà yî**	I am not doing it
kąnà yî	you (m.) are . . .	**ąbîn dą kąkè yî**	what you (m.) are . . .	**ba kà yî**	you (m.) are . . .
kįnà yî	you (f.) are . . .	**ąbîn dą kįkè yî**	what you (f.) are . . .	**ba kyà yî**	you (f.) are . . .
yąnà yî	he is . . .	**ąbîn dą yąkè yî**	what he is . . .	**ba yà yî**	he is . . .
tąnà yî	she is . . .	**ąbîn dą tąkè yî**	what she is . . .	**ba tà yî**	she is . . .
mųnà yî	we are . . .	**ąbîn dą mųkè yî**	what we are . . .	**ba mà yî**	we are . . .
kųnà yî	you (pl.) are . . .	**ąbîn dą kųkè yî**	what you (pl.) are . . .	**ba kwà yî**	you (pl.) are . . .
sųnà yî	they are . . .	**ąbîn dą sųkè yî**	what they are . . .	**ba sà yî**	they are . . .
ąnà yî	someone is . . ., it is being done	**ąbîn dą ąkè yî**	what someone is . . ., what is done	**ba à yî**	no one is . . ., it isn't done

Note: The continuous tense pronouns are also used in non-verbal sentences indicating possession, location, or state. When the relative continuous pronouns are used in such sentences, the **-kę̀** has a short vowel.

yana da kwallo	he has a ball	*wa yake da kwallo?*	who has a ball?
akuya tana can	the goat is there	*na san inda akuya take*	I know where the goat is
suna zaune	they are seated	*a zaune suke*	they are seated!

2c. Subject Pronouns: Subjunctive Tense

Subjunctive		*Negative Subjunctive*	
ya cê ìn yị	he said I should do it	**ya cê kạdạ̀ ìn yị**	he said I shouldn't do it
ya cê kạ̀ yị	he said you (m.) . . .	**ya cê kạdạ̀ kạ̀ yị**	he said you (m.) . . .
ya cê kị̀ yị	he said you (f.) . . .	**ya cê kạdạ̀ kị̀ yị**	he said you (f.) . . .
ya cê yạ̀ yị	he said he . . .	**ya cê kạdạ̀ yạ̀ yị**	he said he . . .
ya cê tạ̀ yị	he said she . . .	**ya cê kạdạ̀ tạ̀ yị**	he said she . . .
ya cê mụ̀ yị	he said we . . .	**ya cê kạdạ̀ mụ̀ yị**	he said we . . .
ya cê kụ̀ yị	he said you (pl.) . . .	**ya cê kạdạ̀ kụ̀ yị**	he said you (pl.) . . .
ya cê sụ̀ yị	he said they . . .	**ya cê kạdạ̀ sụ̀ yị**	he said they . . .
ya cê ạ̀ yị	he said it should be done	**ya cê kạdạ̀ ạ̀ yị**	he said it shouldn't be done

2d. Subject Pronouns: Future Tenses

Future		*Indefinite Future*	
zân zo	I shall come	**nâ zo**	I may come
za ką zo	you (m.) will . . .	**kâ zo**	you (m.) may . . .
za kį zo	you (f.) will . . .	**kyâ zo**	you (f.) may . . .
zâi zo	he will . . .	**yâ zo**	he may . . .
za tą zo	she will . . .	**tâ zo**	she may . . .
za mų zo	we shall . . .	**mâ zo**	we may . . .
za kų zo	you (pl.) will . . .	**kwâ zo**	you (pl.) may . . .
za sų zo	they will . . .	**sâ zo**	they may . . .
za ą zo	someone will . . .	**â zo**	someone may . . .

2e. Subject Pronouns: Habitual Tense

Habitual	
nąkàn samù ą kàsųwa	I usually get it at the market
kąkàn samù ą kàsųwa	you (m.) . . .
kįkàn samù ą kàsųwa	you (f.) . . .
yąkàn samù ą kàsųwa	he . . .
tąkàn samù ą kàsųwa	she . . .
mųkàn samù ą kàsųwa	we . . .
kųkàn samù ą kàsųwa	you (pl.) . . .
sųkàn samù ą kàsųwa	they . . .
ąkàn samù ą kàsųwa	it is usually found at the market

3. Object Pronouns

Direct Object		*Indirect Object*	
nį	me	**mįnį̀**	to me, for me
ką	you (m.)	**mąką̀**	to you (m.), for you (m.)
kį	you (f.)	**mįkį̀**	to you (f.), for you (f.)
shį	him	**mąsą̀**	to him, for him
tą	her	**mątą̀**	to her, for her
mų	us	**mąną̀**	to us, for us
kų	you (pl.)	**mųkų̀**	to you (pl.), for you (pl.)
sų	them	**mųsų̀**	to them, for them

Notes:

(*a*) The tone of a direct object pronoun usually changes to low if the preceding tone is high; however, if the pronoun is preceded by a verb with high-low-high tone, the tone remains high.

(*b*) The direct object pronouns are also used after the following words:

(i)	**ą̀kwai**, e.g.:	*akwai su da yawa*	there are many of them
(ii)	**bâ** (neg. marker), e.g.:	*ba mu da kome*	we don't have anything
(iii)	**gà**, e.g.:	*ga ta can a zaune*	there she is seated
(iv)	**gą̀re**, e.g.:	*suna gare ni*	they are with me
(v)	**zâ**, e.g.:	*za shi gida*	he's going home

4. Possessive Pronouns

Suffixed Possessive Pronouns				*Independent Possessive Pronouns*			
with masc. or pl. nouns		*with fem. nouns*		*ref. to masc. or pl. nouns*		*ref. to fem. nouns*	
aikìna	my work	**motàta**	my car	**nàwą**	mine	**tàwą**	mine
aikìnką̀	your (m.) . . .	**motàřką̀**	your (m.) . . .	**naką̀**	yours (m.)	**taką̀**	yours (m.)
aikìnkį̀	your (f.) . . .	**motàřkį̀**	your (f.) . . .	**nakį̀**	yours (f.)	**takį̀**	yours (f.)
aikìnsą̀	his . . .	**motàřsą̀**	his . . .	**nasą̀**	his	**tasą̀**	his
aikìntą̀	her . . .	**motàřtą̀**	her . . .	**natą̀**	hers	**tatą̀**	hers
aikìnmų̀	our . . .	**motàřmų̀**	our . . .	**namų̀**	ours	**tamų̀**	ours
aikìnkų̀	your (pl.) . . .	**motàřkų̀**	your (pl.) . . .	**nakų̀**	yours (pl.)	**takų̀**	yours (pl.)
aikìnsų̀	their . . .	**motą̀řsų̀**	their . . .	**nasų̀**	theirs	**tasų̀**	theirs

Notes:

(*a*) The first person suffixed pronoun is pronounced short when it comes at the end of a phrase.

(*b*) The suffixed possessive pronouns are also used as direct object pronouns following verbal nouns, e.g.:

tana taimakonsa	she is helping him
suna zaginmu	they are insulting us

APPENDIX 2

Forms of the Negative Marker **ba**

1. bà . . . bą

Used to form the negative of non-verbal sentences, nouns, noun phrases, etc.:

ba haka ba ne	it is not so
shi ba mawaƙi ba ne	he is not a poet
hular nan ba tawa ba ce	this cap is not mine

2. bą̀ . . . bą

Used to form the negative of sentences in the past, future, indefinite future, and habitual tenses:

ba ta je ko'ina ba	she didn't go anywhere
yaran ba za su bari ba	the children won't leave it alone
ba kya ci jarrabawa ba	you won't pass the examination
ba sukan fita da dare ba	they do not go out at night

3. ba

Used to form the negative of sentences in the continuous tense:

ba ma jin tsoro	we are not afraid
ba ya nan	he isn't here

4. bâ

Used to form the negative of "have" sentences:

ba shi da aiki	he doesn't have any work

APPENDIX 3

Nouns Formed with the Prefix mą-

(*) Agential Nouns

Nouns indicating persons who perform an action habitually or by profession are formed from verb (or occasionally noun) roots by use of the prefix **mą-**. These nouns are indicated in the dictionary by the symbol *. Agential nouns normally have three forms: masculine, feminine, and plural. The masculine forms end in **-i**, the feminine in **-įya**, and the plural in **-a**. For example, the noun **mąhàifi** 'parent' is composed of the prefix **mą-**, the root **haif-** (from **hàifa** 'to give birth'), and the suffix **-i**. In masculine and plural forms the root has low tone; in the feminine forms it has high tone. The formation of agential nouns is illustrated below.

	Masculine	*Feminine*	*Plural*	*Related Verb*
parent	**mąhàifi**	**mąhaifįya**	**mąhàifa**	**hàifa** give birth
weaver	**mąsàƙi**	**mąsaƙįya**	**mąsàƙa**	**saƙà** weave
worker	**mą'àikąci**	**mą'aikącįya**	**mą'àikąta**	**aikąta** do, perform
heir	**mąɠàji**	**mąɠajįya**	**mąɠàda**	**ɠàda** inherit
lover	**mąsòyi**	**mąsoyįya**	**mąsòya**	**so** want, love

(†) Locative Nouns

Nouns indicating a place or location are formed from verb roots by use of the prefix **mą-**. These nouns are indicated in the dictionary by the symbol †. Most locative nouns end in **-a** and are feminine; some end in **-i** and are masculine. The tones of these nouns are all high. Locative nouns do not normally have plural forms; where they exist, they are indicated in the dictionary. The formation of locative nouns is illustrated below.

	Singular	*Related Verb*	
kitchen	**mądąfa**	**dąfà**	cook
birth-place, womb	**mąhaifa**	**hàifa**	give birth
tannery	**mąjema**	**jemà**	tan leather
place where grain is sold	**mą'auna**	**aunà**	measure, weigh
store-room	**mą'ąjįyi**	**ąjįye**	put aside, store
lodging place	**mąsauki**	**sàuką**	be lodged

(‡) Instrumental Nouns

Nouns indicating a tool or implement are formed from verb roots by use of the prefix **mą-**. These nouns are indicated in the dictionary by the symbol ‡. Singular instrumental nouns end in **-i** and are masculine; plurals end in **-ai.** The tones of the singular forms are all high; the tones of the plurals are all low except for the final tone which is high. The formation of instrumental nouns is illustrated below.

	Singular	*Plural*	*Related Verb*	
measuring device, scales	**mą'auni**	**mą̀'àunai**	**aunà**	measure, weigh
key	**mąbuɗi**	**mą̀bùɗai**	**buɗè**	open
glass, mirror	**mądubi**	**mą̀dùbai**	**dubà**	look at
brush, eraser	**mągogi**	**mą̀gògai**	**gogè**	rub
pin for scratching	**mąsoshi**	**mą̀sòsai**	**sosà**	scratch
prop, support	**mądogąri**	**mą̀dògą̀rai**	**dogą̀ra**	lean on

APPENDIX 4

Geographical Names

The following is a selected list of countries, cities, and other geographical names which have their own Hausa spelling and pronunciation. Many other geographical names tend to use English spelling, even though they may have Hausa pronunciation; these are not included.

Ą̀fir̃ką̀	Africa
Àlƙahį̀r̃ą	Cairo
Ą̀mìr̃ką̀	America
Ą̀ną̀cą̀	Onitsha
Anką̀r̃ą̀	Accra, Ghana
Asį̀yą̀	Asia
Bą̀gą̀dazą̀	Baghdad
Bą̀hàr̃ Malį̀yą̀	Red Sea
Cadį̀	Chad
Fą̀r̃ansą̀	France
Fą̀takwàl	Port Harcourt
Hąbąshą̀	Ethiopia
Ìkkǫ	Lagos
Ingį̀lą̀	England
Ìsƙandą̀r̃į̀yą̀	Alexandria
Ìsr̃a'ilą̀	Israel
Indį̀yą̀	India
Į̀talį̀yą̀	Italy
Jamùs	Germany
Ką̀mą̀r̃ų	Cameroon
Kwarą̀	River Niger
K'ąsar̃ Makką̀	Saudi Arabia
Lų̀bayyą̀	El Obeid
Mą̀diną̀	Medina
Makką̀	Mecca
Mąsàr̃	Egypt
Nìjer̃į̀yą̀	Nigeria
Pą̀làsɗinų̀	Palestine
Par̃į̀są̀	Iran
Rashą̀	Russia
Sàlį̀yô	Sierra Leone
Sàntàmbûl	Istanbul
Shâm	Syria
Sin	China
Tambutų̀	Timbuktu
Tąr̃abųlùs	Tripoli
Tur̃ai	Europe
Yąmàl	Yemen

APPENDIX 5

DAYS OF THE WEEK

Jummą'à	Friday
Ą̀sąbàr̃	Saturday
Ląhą̀dį̀	Sunday
Lìtįnîn	Monday
Tą̀latà	Tuesday
Làr̃ą̀ba	Wednesday
Àlhą̀mîs	Thursday

MONTHS OF THE YEAR

Ją̀nair̃ų̀	January	**Yulį̀**	July
Fą̀br̃air̃ų̀	February	**Ą̀gustà**	August
Mar̃ìs	March	**Są̀tumbà**	September
Ą̀fr̃ilų̀	April	**Òktobà**	October
Mayù	May	**Nų̀wambà**	November
Yunį̀	June	**Dįsambà**	December

MUSLIM MONTHS OF THE YEAR

Mų̀har̃r̃àm	first month	**Rąjàb**	seventh month
Sąfàr̃	second month	**Shą̀'ą̀bân**	eighth month
Rą̀bi'ų̀ Lawwàl	third month	**Rą̀mą̀lân**	ninth month
Rą̀bi'ų̀ Lahìr̃	fourth month	**Shàwwâl**	tenth month
Jįmada Lawwàl	fifth month	**Zùlƙidà**	eleventh month
Jįmada Lahìr̃	sixth month	**Zulhajjį̀**	twelfth month